# SUPPORTING TEACHING & LEARNING IN SCHOOLS

Louise Burnham

Brenda Baker

Heinemann
Part of Pearson

Heinemann is an imprint of Pearson Education Limited, Edinburgh Gate, Harlow, Essex, CM20 2JE.

www.pearsonschoolsandfecolleges.co.uk
Heinemann is a registered trademark of Pearson Education Limited.
Text © Louise Burnham, Brenda Baker 2011

Edited by Juliet Mozley
Designed by AM design
Typeset by Phoenix Photosetting
Original illustrations © Pearson Education 2011
Illustrated by Phoenix Photosetting/Gemma Correll
Cover design by Woodenark
Picture research by Susie Prescott
Cover photo © ImageSource

The rights of Louise Burnham and Brenda Baker to be identified as authors of this work have been asserted by them in accordance with the Copyright, Designs and Patents Act 1988.

Pearson Education Ltd would like to thank Claire Dickinson for providing all information and features relating to Functional Skills in this book.

First published 2011

**British Library Cataloguing in Publication Data**
A catalogue record for this book is available from the British Library.

ISBN 978-0-435032-05-0

**Websites**
The websites used in this book were correct and up to date at the time of publication. Pearson Education Limited is not responsible for the content of any external Internet sites. It is essential for tutors to preview each website before using it in class so as to ensure that the URL is still accurate, relevant and appropriate. We suggest that tutors bookmark useful websites and consider enabling students to access them through the school/college intranet.

# Contents

# Acknowledgements

The authors would like to thank the following individuals for their help and advice during the writing of this book:

Sue Robertson and Unicorn Primary School in Beckenham for allowing us to reproduce excerpts from school policies; Val Hughes and Sandhurst Junior School in Catford for a copy of their feedback form; Graham Jameson and Edmund Waller School in New Cross for their example of a staffing structure; Lewisham Local Authority for a copy of a teaching assistant's job description; Richard Rieser and Disability Equality in Education for their medical and social model of disability; Linda Mellor and Elizabeth Evans for their thorough proofreading; and Virginia Carter, Juliet Mozley and Céline Clavel for all of their support during this project. Louise Burnham would like to thank Tom, Lucy and Richard and Brenda Baker would like to thank John for his support and encouragement.

The publisher would like to thank the following organisations for permission to reproduce material: retributive and restorative justice table, Transforming Conflict, an organisation which supports schools wanting to develop a whole-school approach based on the principles of restorative justice, p.82; BSI, Kitemark logo, p.133; the British Toy & Hobby Association, Lion Mark logo, p.133.

The publisher would like to thank the following for their kind permission to reproduce photographs (Key: b-bottom; c-centre; r-right; t-top):

Alamy Images: Angela Hampton Picture Library 299, John Powell 67, Roger Bamber 327; Getty Images: Bachrach / Archive Photos 153, Image Source 325; iStockphoto: Monkey Business Images 136; Pearson Education Ltd: Ian Wedgewood 1, 2, 7, 17, 50, 68, 91, 108, 117, 118, 177, 215, 289, 333, 340, Jules Selmes 14, 34, 42, 72, 92, 103, 128, 147, 257, Rick Chapman 131, Studio 8 15, 35, 73, 81, 87, 101, 129, 145, 165, 199, 207, 212, 222, 233, 243, 248, 268, 273, 280, 307, 317, 331, 345, 348, Clark Wiseman 148; PhotoDisc: Kevin Peterson 100; Shutterstock.com: Arrow Studio LLC 192, AVAVA 144, Dean Mitchell 183, Dmitriy Shironosov 112, 182, Monkey Business Images 344, Stephen Coburn 164, Yuri Arcurs 113; www.imagesource.com: Nigel Riches 56, 86

All other images © Pearson Education

Every effort has been made to trace the copyright holders and we apologise in advance for any unintentional omissions. We would be pleased to insert the appropriate acknowledgement in any subsequent edition of this publication.

# Introduction

Welcome to this handbook for the Level 3 Diploma for Supporting Teaching and Learning in Schools (Secondary edition). If you are using this book you will be setting out to be or already working in school as a teaching assistant. This handbook has been written specifically for assistants in secondary schools, although if you are working in a primary school you may find that many ideas and principles will apply to you as well.

You may find yourself referred to under the general title of 'teaching assistant' within your school, but you may also be called a classroom assistant, school assistant, individual support assistant, special needs assistant, or learning support assistant. These different job titles have come into effect due to the different types of work which assistants are required to do within the classroom. In recent years the role of the teaching assistant has developed and become professionalised so that qualifications now exist at different levels. These reflect the diverse job roles which are now present in schools for learning support staff.

This book contains everything you need to complete your Level 3 in Specialist Support for Teaching and Learning in Schools. It also contains the mandatory units you need if you are studying for the Level 3 Certificate in Cover Supervision.

As you work towards this qualification, you will be developing your skills and expertise in a number of areas and you will need to think about how the theory fits in with your experiences in the classroom. As you gain experience and expertise in your work with children and young people, you may also find it a useful reference, particularly for specific issues such as working with bilingual children.

Level 3 is made up of a number of different units of assessment which sit within the QCF (Qualifications and Credit Framework). When you complete a unit successfully you will gain a certain number of credits.

The credit value of each unit indicates the size of the unit and approximately how long it will take to achieve. Credit is based on how long an average learner would take to complete a unit, and 1 credit is roughly equal to 10 hours of learning, including time spent in the following ways:

- classes or group sessions
- tutorials
- practical work
- assessments.

It also includes any time you spend that is not supervised, for example doing homework, independent research or work experience.

## Units of assessment

The units that make up these qualifications have been developed by the Sector Skills Councils responsible for setting and monitoring standards for specific occupational groups. In the case of Supporting Teaching and Learning, this is the Training and Development Agency, known as TDA. You will see that the unit reference numbers (see table page vii) carry the prefix TDA, which shows that TDA is the Sector Skills Council who developed or owns the units. There are other Sector Skills Councils or awarding organisations that work closely with TDA, and you may come across these acronyms linked to other units that you study:

● SfCD – Skills for Care and Development

● CWDC – Children's Workforce Development Council

● ASDAN – Award Scheme Development and Accreditation Network.

## Level 3 overview

Although the units in the new qualification are not exactly the same as the National Occupational Standards that made up NVQs, the areas they cover are similar. Each unit has several learning outcomes and each of these is broken down into a number of assessment criteria. All the learning outcomes of the unit have to be assessed in order for you to complete the unit.

The Level 3 Diploma in Specialist Support for Teaching and Learning in Schools is made up of three groups of units:

● Mandatory units

● Optional Group A units

● Optional Group B units.

Everyone taking this qualification needs to complete all 11 units in the mandatory group (32 credits), and then choose additional units from the optional groups to make the full credit total of 44. There are certain rules of combination that apply to the optional units, so check with your tutor or assessor to see which ones you can choose.

For the Level 3 Certificate in Cover Supervision, you need to complete 11 mandatory units giving a total credit value of 30. The table opposite indicates with an asterisk the units which are mandatory for this qualification.

# List of units in this book

| Unit reference No. | Unit title | Credit value |
|---|---|---|
| **Mandatory units** | | |
| TDA 3.1* | Communication and professional relationships with children, young people and adults | 2 |
| TDA 3.2* | Schools as organisations | 3 |
| TDA 3.3 | Support learning activities | 4 |
| TDA 3.4* | Promote children and young people's positive behaviour | 3 |
| TDA 3.5* | Develop professional relationships with children, young people and adults | 2 |
| TDA 3.6* | Promote equality, diversity and inclusion in work with children and young people | 2 |
| TDA 3.7 | Support assessment for learning | 4 |
| SfCD SHC 32* | Engage in personal development | 3 |
| CYP 3.4* | Support children and young people's health and safety | 2 |
| CYP 3.1* | Understand child and young person development | 4 |
| CYP 3.3* | Understand how to safeguard the well-being of children and young people | 3 |
| **Optional units** | | |
| TDA 3.10 | Plan and deliver learning activities under the direction of a teacher | 4 |
| TDA 3.13 | Support teaching and learning in a curriculum area | 3 |
| TDA 3.14 | Support delivery of the 14–19 curriculum | 3 |
| TDA 3.17 | Support bilingual learners | 4 |
| TDA 3.18 | Provide bilingual support for teaching and learning | 6 |
| TDA 3.19 | Support disabled children and young people and those with special educational needs | 5 |
| TDA 3.20 | Support children and young people with behaviour, emotional and social development needs | 4 |
| CYPOP 44 | Facilitate the learning and development of children and young people through mentoring | 4 |
| CYPOP 9 | Provide information and advice to children and young people | 3 |
| TDA 3.9 | Invigilate tests and examinations | 3 |
| ASDAN TW3* | Team working | 3 |
| TDA 3.8* | Supervise whole-class learning activities | 3 |

Units marked with an * = units that are mandatory for the Level 3 Certificate in Cover Supervision

## Assessing your skills and knowledge

Your awarding organisation, such as Edexcel, CACHE or City & Guilds, will allow you to be assessed using a range of different methods, based on the learning outcomes and assessment criteria in the unit. Your assessor or tutor will provide you with help and support throughout the assessment process. Some common assessment methods are described below but others may be used as well:

● knowledge, understanding and skills competence that you demonstrate through your practice in a work setting and that are observed directly by your assessor

● evidence from an expert witness who may be an experienced practitioner who has worked alongside you, or others with suitable backgrounds who can vouch for your practice

● questions (oral and written) and professional discussion, usually with your assessor, which allows you to talk about what you know

● assignments and projects of different types

● assessment of your work products such as plans, displays, observations, materials you have made to support children

● recognised prior learning.

Sometimes your awarding organisation will insist on a specific method such as a test or an assignment. Again your tutor or assessor will provide you with help and support to decide the best approach.

## Units that must be assessed in the workplace

In this qualification, TDA require that the following assessment criteria MUST be assessed in an appropriate setting, for example a primary school or secondary school:

| | |
|---|---|
| **TDA 3.3** | Assessment criteria 1.3, 1.4, 1.5, 2.1, 2.2, 2.3, 3.1, 3.3, 3.4, 3.5, 4.1, 4.2, 4.3, 5.2 |
| **TDA 3.4** | Assessment criteria 2.2, 2.3, 2.4, 2.5, 3.1, 3.2, 3.3, 3.4, 4.1, 4.2, 4.3, 4.4, 4.5, 5.1, 5.2, 5.3, 5.4 |
| **TDA 3.6** | Assessment criteria 1.4, 1.5, 3.3 |
| **TDA 3.7** | Assessment criteria 2.1, 2.2, 2.3, 2.4, 2.5, 3.1, 3.2, 3.3, 3.4, 4.1, 4.2 |
| **TDA 3.10** | Assessment criteria 1.3, 1.4, 2.1, 2.2, 2.3, 2.4, 3.1, 3.2, 3.3, 3.4, 3.5 |
| **TDA 3.13** | Assessment criteria 1.4, 2.4, 3.3, 3.4 |
| **TDA 3.14** | Assessment criteria 2.2, 2.3, 2.4, 3.3, 3.4 |
| **TDA 3.17** | Assessment criteria 1.1, 1.2, 2.3, 2.4, 3.1, 3.2, 3.3, 3.4, 3.5 |
| **TDA 3.18** | Assessment criteria 1.1, 1.2, 1.4, 1.5, 2.1, 2.2, 2.3, 2.4, 2.5, 2.6, 3.1, 3.2, 3.3, 3.4, 4.1, 4.2, 4.3, 4.4 |
| **TDA 3.19** | Assessment criteria 3.1, 3.3, 3.4, 3.5, 4.1, 4.2, 4.3, 5.1, 5.2, 5.3 |
| **TDA 3.20** | Assessment criteria 3.1, 3.3, 3.4, 3.5, 3.6, 4.1, 4.2, 4.3, 4.4, 4.5, 4.6, 5.1, 5.2, 5.3, 5.4 |
| **CYPOP 44** | Assessment criteria 2.1, 2.2, 2.3, 3.1, 3.2, 4.1, 4.2 |
| **CYPOP 9** | Assessment criteria 2.1, 2.2, 2.3, 3.1, 3.2, 3.3, 3.4 |
| **TDA 3.9** | Assessment criteria 2.1, 2.2, 2.3, 2.4, 2.5, 3.2, 3.3, 4.2, 4.3, 4.4, 5.1, 5.2 |
| **TDA 3.8** | Assessment criteria 1.2, 1.3, 1.4, 2.1, 2.2, 2.3, 2.4, 2.5, 3.1, 3.2, 3.3, 3.4, 4.1 |

## How to use this book

All the units in this book are matched closely to the specifications of each unit in the syllabus and follow the unit learning outcomes and assessment criteria — making it easy for you to work through the criteria and be sure you are covering everything you need to know.

## Key features of the book

An activity that brings learning to life and suggests how to introduce new ideas, activities or practice into your school or setting

A real-life scenario exploring major issues to broaden your understanding of key topics; demonstrates how theory relates to everyday practice and poses reflective questions

An activity that helps you to create or gather evidence for your portfolio

An activity that encourages you to reflect on your own performance

A short task to enhance your understanding of a piece of information (for example Internet research or a practical idea you could introduce in your school)

A short activity linked thematically to the unit, specifically designed to develop your professional skills

Highlights where content in the unit enables you to apply Functional Skills in the broad areas of English, ICT and Maths (matched to the FS Standards at Level 2). The tips and explanations given show how Functional Skills can be contextualised to work in early years and will be of particular benefit to learners on Apprenticeship programmes

Simple definitions of some of the more complex terms or pieces of jargon used in the book

Link  Highlights where text gives evidence for Assessment Criteria or where related information can be found in other units

Getting ready for assessment An activity to help you generate evidence for assessment of the unit

Check your knowledge At the end of each unit, questions to help you consolidate your understanding and ensure you are ready to move on to the next unit

BEST PRACTICE CHECKLIST A checklist of key points to help you remember the main underpinning knowledge in a unit

**School Life** – Some units end with a full-page magazine-inspired feature covering a key issue or topic, with expert guidance relating to problems that may be encountered in your working life. It contains the following 'mini-features':

- **My Story** – a teaching assistant's personal account; sometimes inspirational or uplifting, other times sharing a problem

- **Ask the expert** – questions and answers relating to working practice

- **Viewpoint** – topical issues discussed around the wider issues of supporting teaching and learning.

# TDA 3.1 Communication & professional relationships with children, young people & adults

Building trusting and effective relationships with children, young people and adults is an essential part of your role. In this unit, you will explore the ways to communicate in different situations and contexts and the importance of following procedures for confidentiality and information sharing.

## By the end of this unit you will:

1. understand the principles of developing positive relationships with children, young people and adults

2. understand how to communicate with children, young people and adults

3. understand legislation, policies and procedures for confidentiality and sharing information, including data protection.

# Understand the principles of developing positive relationships with children, young people and adults

## Why effective communication is important

In order to contribute to **positive relationships**, you will need to demonstrate and model effective communication skills in your dealings with others. This means that you should consider both how you approach other people and how you respond to them. We are more likely to communicate information to one another if we have positive relationships. Parents and other adults who come into the school are more likely to give beneficial support if communication is strong and effective — this, in turn, benefits pupils. It is also important for pupils that we model effective communication skills. This means checking what we are saying sometimes in moments of stress or excitement, so that they can understand what our expectations are in school. If we ask pupils to behave in a particular way when communicating and then forget to do so ourselves, they will find it harder to understand the boundaries of what is acceptable.

Effective communication and positive relationships do not happen by chance. You should think about the way you relate to others and the messages that this sends out. In situations where communication breaks down, misunderstandings can lead to bad feeling.

### Key term

**Positive relationships** — relationships that benefit children and young people, and their ability to participate in and benefit from the setting

*How good are your relationships with other adults in your work environment?*

## CASE STUDY: The importance of effective communication

Tricia works as a teaching assistant in a large secondary school. She supports pupils who have special educational needs during their English lessons. Tricia is also a first aider at the school. During break time, she was called to an incident outside. A pupil had fallen during a game of football and had a suspected broken arm. By the time she had ensured that the pupil was comfortable, and an ambulance been summoned, the class had almost finished. The English teacher had not been informed that Tricia was dealing with an accident. As Tricia entered the classroom, the teacher asked where she had been for the last 30 minutes. Tricia was upset at the way she was spoken to and told the teacher that she had been called to administer first aid. However, the teacher misunderstood, thinking she had been dealing with a minor injury. Both the teacher and Tricia were unhappy and hardly spoke to one another until lunchtime.

- Who was in the wrong?
- Do you think that pupils in the class would have noticed?
- How might this have been handled better by both the teacher and Tricia?

### Functional skills

**English: Speaking, listening and communication**
You could role-play this scenario and then experiment with different ways of dealing with the situation. This would provide you with a good opportunity to develop your speaking and listening skills.

## The principles of relationship building

The principles of relationship building with children and adults in any context are that if others are comfortable in our company, they will be more likely to communicate effectively. Where people do not get along or are suspicious of one another, they are likely to avoid one another wherever possible. Positive relationships are not something which should be left to chance and it is important to consider the ways in which we can develop them.

We build relationships with others in school on a daily basis in a number of different ways. Although you may do some of these without necessarily thinking about it, it is worth taking time to consider whether you do all of the following.

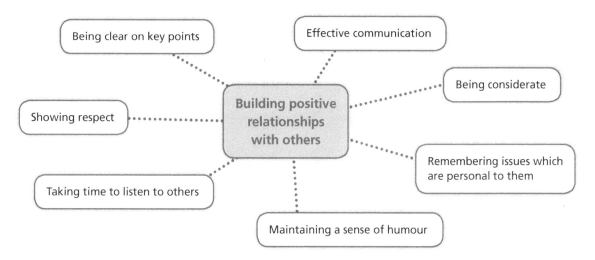

- Being clear on key points
- Effective communication
- Being considerate
- Showing respect
- Building positive relationships with others
- Remembering issues which are personal to them
- Taking time to listen to others
- Maintaining a sense of humour

*Do you use all of these when building relationships with others?*

## Functional skills

### English: Writing
You could recall a time when you have communicated with another adult in school and write a brief account of what happened. Using the points on the spidergram reflect on how you could have approached this situation differently. When you write your account, consider the layout and structure of the text.

- **Effective communication** — this is the key area for developing relationships with others and also covers many different forms of communication (see below).

- **Showing respect** — in order to develop positive relationships with others, it is very important to be courteous and respectful, and to listen to their points of view. Adults and pupils with whom you work may also be from different cultures and have different beliefs or values from your own. You should ensure that you acknowledge and respect the views of others at all times and take time to remember names and preferred forms of address.

- **Being considerate** — take the time to consider the positions of others. You may be working with a child, young person or adult who is under particular pressure at a given time and need to understand why they may have behaved or reacted in a certain way or out of character.

- **Remembering issues which are personal to them** — it will always help to build positive relationships if you enquire after particular aspects of another person's life — for example, if you know that a colleague is concerned about their child getting into a particular secondary school, or if you are aware that it is a child's birthday.

- **Taking time to listen to others** — make sure that you take time to listen to other people, in particular if they are asking for advice or help, or if they need to confide in you. You should always show that you are interested in what they have to say and respond appropriately.

- **Being clear on key points** — when you have conversations with others in which you are giving them information, you should always ensure that they understand what you have said at the end of the discussion. This is because it can be easy to be distracted from the main point of the conversation. When talking to children, always ask them to repeat back to you what they need to do.

- **Maintaining a sense of humour** — although the nature of our work in school is important, we should also sometimes take time to see the funny side of different situations. Laughter can be a good icebreaker and is also a great way of relaxing and relieving stress.

## Social, professional and cultural contexts

When communicating with others, you will need to consider the context in which you are working. You will need to adapt the way you communicate in different situations. It is likely that you will do this automatically — for example, you should use more formal language and behaviour in a meeting. Your school will have a range of types of planned communication with other adults — when dealing with other professionals, there will be meetings and discussions as well as more informal communication at different times. However, the spoken word is not the only way in which we communicate — it happens through the way we respond to others, for example, how quickly we respond to an email or phone message, how attentive we are when speaking to someone, how we dress. You may find that the non-spoken forms of communication can be an issue if they are misread by others. You should also remember that different cultures will have their own norms of behaviour which will extend to gestures, body language and eye contact. In some cultures, for example, it is not polite to look another person in the eye when speaking to them.

## Reflect

Think about the ways in which your school passes information to adults outside school. They may be parents, carers or outside agencies. You may want to list the methods of communication under 'Formal' and 'Informal' headings.

# Understand how to communicate with children, young people and adults

## Skills needed to communicate with children and young people

You will need to demonstrate a number of skills in order to communicate effectively with children and young people. Although it is likely that you will do this every day without thinking, it is worth reflecting on the ways in which you do this – effective communication is a vital part of your role. Children learn to communicate through the responses of others: if they do not feel that their contribution is valued, they are less likely to initiate communication themselves. You will need to do the following.

- **Find opportunities to speak.** Make sure that pupils are given sufficient opportunities to talk. Some children have very little chance to put their own thoughts forward and express themselves with adults. They may lack confidence and need to be given a chance to 'warm up' first so that they feel able to do so.

- **Make eye contact and actively listen.** If you say that you are listening, but are looking away and are busy doing something else, this gives the child the message that you are not really interested in what they are saying. Make sure that if a pupil is talking, you are giving them your attention.

- **Use body language and facial expressions,** and be approachable. Make sure that you show your

interest by the way in which you act when speaking to pupils. For example, if a young person is sitting down, sit next to them so that you are at their level. It can be very intimidating to have someone towering over them. Also make sure that you smile and react in a positive way to what they are saying.

- **React and comment on what they are saying.** You may need to repeat back to pupils to check on your understanding, particularly if they have used incorrect language: for example, 'I ain't gonna do PE today.' 'You're not going to do PE today, why is that?'

- **Be interested, responding and questioning to maintain conversation.** It is important to model and invite the 'norms' of conversation with children so that they build up an understanding about how it works. They will do this through experience, so show that you are interested and respond to their questions.

For children to be able to communicate effectively, you should encourage them to ask questions and put their ideas forward. Pupils should feel relaxed and confident enough in school to be able to do this, as it is by questioning and finding out that they learn. They should also be able to offer their own suggestions and ideas so that there is a two-way dialogue between adults and pupils rather than a one-way flow of instructions. This also encourages the formation of positive relationships.

# How to adapt communication with children and young people

In order to build relationships with children, you will need to adapt your behaviour and communication accordingly. Children and young people of all ages, cultures and abilities need to feel secure and valued, and your interactions with them should demonstrate this. Through positively communicating with and being involved with children and young people, you will show them that they are part of the school community. However, this is not the same as giving all pupils attention whenever they demand it!

- **The age of the child or young person** — children of different ages will require varying levels of attention. Children and young people may need more reassurance, particularly when they first transfer to secondary school. They may also need to have more physical contact as a result. As children mature, and particularly during puberty, they may need more help with talking through issues and reflecting on their thoughts. You will need to adapt your vocabulary as older children are often more self-conscious and may be more emotional.

- **Context** — you will be dealing with children and young people in a variety of different situations. You will always need to be mindful of this and adapt your verbal communication accordingly. If you are working on a learning activity, it is important that the pupils are focused and that you deal with any distractions before they interrupt what you are doing. However, if talking to pupils in more social situations such as in the dining hall, you should use this as an opportunity to develop positive relationships with pupils, although you should always speak to them in the context of a professional to a young person. Pupils may question you about your private life. It is sometimes best to answer these kinds of questions with humour, for example, 'I don't think that you would find it very interesting.' Pupils may even ask for your contact details, such as a mobile phone number or if they can list your name on their social networking page. You should never give these details or become involved in personal communication.

- **Communication differences** — you should ensure care and sensitivity with children and young people who have communication differences, as they will need to take their time and feel unpressured when they are speaking. Some pupils may not have many opportunities to speak, or may be anxious or nervous. You should adapt the way in which you communicate according to their individual needs. If they have a speech disorder, such as a stammer, or conditions which make communication difficult for them, they should be allowed to take their time. Try not to fill in words for them or guess what they are going to say, as this may add to their distress.

You may need additional training — for example, in sign language — to be able to communicate effectively or know the most effective strategies to use. In some cases where pupils have special educational needs, you may need to have additional equipment in order to communicate with one another.

## Functional skills

**ICT: Finding and selecting information**
**Maths: Representing**
There is now a wide range of electronic equipment available to support children and staff who may experience barriers to communication, such as sensory impairment or dyslexia. Use the Internet to research what is available. You could then speak to whoever is in charge of purchasing equipment and ask for a rough guide of their budget for such equipment. Calculate the most effective way of spending the budget.

# Main differences between communicating with adults and with children and young people

There are many similarities between communicating with adults and with children — always maintaining eye contact and interest, responding to what they are saying, and treating them with courtesy and respect. However, when communicating with children, we also need to think about how we maintain the relationship of support worker to the child or young person and what this means in a school context. However well you get on with pupils, remember that they need to see you as a carer and that your relationships with them will always need to be formal when in school.

When communicating with children and young people, we also need to be very clear and unambiguous in what we say. They need us to communicate what is expected of them so that they can learn to communicate well themselves. Sometimes we forget the importance of making sure that children understand what we mean and might ask them, 'What did I just ask you to do?' when they cannot answer the question! Make sure that the vocabulary and verbal expressions you use are at the right level for the children.

You also need to be aware that physical contact with children and young people should not be encouraged when communicating with them. It can sometimes be hard to avoid this, but you should not offer physical contact with pupils or be overly physical with them at any time.

## How to adapt communication to meet different communication needs of adults

It is important that we are sensitive to the needs of other adults, particularly if they have communication difficulties. It is possible that you will adapt the way you communicate with them without realising that you are doing it. We often change the way we react to others, depending on the way in which they react to us. For example, if you are speaking to a parent or carer who is hearing-impaired, you might make sure that you are facing them and making eye contact so that they can lip-read. However, if you have contact with adults who have other communication difficulties, you may need to reflect and make sure you adapt your means of communication.

### Link

See TDA 3.5, pages 75–77, for more on communication needs.

Often, schools will send out or gather information in a particular way, for example, through letters or emails. Depending on their individual needs, the recipients may not be able to access this method of communication easily, and this will not always be clear. You may need to observe sensitivity, for example, if you need to ask a parent or carer why they have not responded to a note that was sent home.

*In what ways can you show interest in what someone is saying?*

If you need to communicate with other adults who speak English as an additional language, you may need to have a translator and meet together if the information you are communicating is complex or difficult to convey.

---

**CASE STUDY:** Adapting communication to deal with the needs of adults

Pritpal's mother has requested a meeting with his form teacher because she is unhappy about the way in which an incident was dealt with. English is not her first language. You have been told that she is very angry that you spoke to Pritpal and reported his behaviour, which resulted in him being given detention (which is your school's policy for managing this type of negative behaviour). You are upset as Pritpal's behaviour was unacceptable and you acted according to school policy. The form teacher has invited you to the meeting with her, but you are reluctant to do so.

- Should you go and speak to Pritpal's mother even if you do not want to?
- How might you reflect on the incident before going to meet with the parent?
- How might communication difficulties have influenced her reaction?
- What strategies can you think of to prevent this from happening again?

---

## How to manage disagreements

It is likely that at some point in your work you will have disagreements with others. In many cases, disagreements are down to lack of communication or miscommunication with others. However, they should be managed very carefully so that bad feeling does not persist afterwards. As adults we can sometimes misread or perceive information wrongly and may think that someone has communicated something to us when they have not. We will sometimes blame others for saying things that could be ambiguous or for having a different point of view from ourselves.

Where there are areas of conflict with other adults, you will need to show sensitivity and try to resolve the situation as soon as possible. The longer a problem is allowed to go on, the more difficult it will be to resolve it. You should not be drawn into a disagreement with a child or young person and you will need to manage this sort of situation carefully and seek advice if necessary. (See also TDA 3.4 on promoting positive behaviour.)

### Poor communication

Often areas of conflict occur when communication has not been effective. This may be because:

- letters have not been passed on by parents or children
- there is a lack of time
- there has been a misunderstanding.

The best way to resolve areas of poor communication is to discuss them to establish a cause, and then find a way forward together. The important thing is not to ignore the problem or talk to anyone else about it except the individual concerned.

### Opposing expectations

Sometimes adults may not have the same ideas about the purpose of an activity or meeting, or come with a different idea in mind. You should always clarify exactly the aims of what you are there to do and why.

### Different values and ideas

Parents and schools may sometimes have different methods of dealing with situations. Whereas the school may request that children do things in a particular way, parental views may be very different. You may need to work alongside others to explain or clarify why things need to happen in a different way in school.

### External factors

You may be working with an individual who has considerable home pressures or other issues, which are affecting how they communicate. External professionals or parents are likely to have time pressures and other pressures of which you are not aware. As we get to know people, we will be able to identify if they are behaving in an uncharacteristic way and be able to ask if there is anything wrong or if we can help.

### Lack of confidence

Sometimes adults can act in an aggressive way if they are not sure about what they are doing or if they lack confidence. This may come across in a personal way to others, but is more to do with how they perceive themselves and their own abilities. You may need to be sensitive to this and offer them encouragement and support.

---

**BEST PRACTICE CHECKLIST:**
Communicating with others

- Make sure you are friendly and approachable – smile!
- Speak clearly and make eye contact with the person with whom you are speaking.
- Ensure you use the correct form of address when speaking to others.
- Use an appropriate method of communication for the other person.
- Use positive body language and gestures.
- Be sympathetic to the needs of others.
- Acknowledge the help and support of others as much as you can.
- Do not interrupt or anticipate what others are going to say.

---

**Functional skills**

**ICT: Developing, presenting and communicating information**
The checklist above provides you with an excellent opportunity to use and develop your ICT skills. You could transfer this information into a poster to display in your staff room.

# Understand legislation, policies and procedures for confidentiality and sharing information, including data protection

## Legislation and procedures covering confidentiality, data protection and the disclosure of information

Adults who work with children in any setting need to have some idea about current legislation, as this will affect their practice. There is an increased awareness of how important it is to recognise the uniqueness of

each child and have respect for their human rights. Legislation is an area which is constantly under review and you will need to keep up to date through reading relevant publications.

### Every Child Matters (England 2003)
This Green Paper stresses the importance of more integrated services and sharing of information between professionals. It came into being after the tragic case of Victoria Climbié, when there was no communication between health and social workers.

### Data Protection Act 1998
In schools we ask parents and carers for a variety of information so that we are able to care for children as effectively as we can while they are with us. However, we can only ask for information which is directly relevant – for example:

- health or medical information
- records from previous schools
- records for children who have special educational needs.

This is **confidential information** and must be used only for the purpose for which it was gathered. If the information needs to be passed on to others for any reason, parental consent will need to be given. This usually involves parents signing a consent form.

---

**Key term**

**Confidential information** – information that should only be shared with people with a right to have it, for example, your teacher, your line manager or an external agency

---

Under the Data Protection Act 1998, any organisation which holds information on individuals needs to be registered with the Information Commissioner's Office. This is designed to ensure that confidential information cannot be passed on to others without the individual's consent. There are eight principles of practice which govern the use of personal information. Information must be:

- processed fairly and lawfully
- used only for the purpose for which it was gathered

- adequate, relevant and not excessive

- accurate and kept up to date where necessary

- kept for no longer than necessary

- processed in line with the individual's rights

- kept secure

- not transferred outside the European Union without adequate protection.

You will need to be aware of a range of information in your role as a teaching assistant, from issues around the school to the individual needs of the children and young people with whom you work. You should know how and when to share any information you have access to. If you are at all concerned or unclear about whom you can speak to, your first point of contact should be your line manager, or in the case of pupils with special educational needs (SEN), the SENCO. Many teaching assistants working in schools are also parents of pupils at the same school, and other parents may sometimes put pressure on them to disclose information. You should not pass on any information about the school or the pupils before being certain that this is the correct thing to do. If you pass on information without following the correct channels, you will be abusing your position of professional trust and this can be very damaging.

You should also be very careful if taking photographs for displays or if filming children and young people for any purpose; again, parental permission will need to be given for this. You should not take pictures of pupils for your portfolio!

You should not pass on information to:

- other pupils in the school

- other parents

- other professionals unless parents have been consulted

- visitors.

*What damage do you think idle gossip about a child or parent could do?*

## CASE STUDY: Keeping information confidential

You are working as a teaching assistant supporting pupils in Key Stage 3. You have a new child in Year 7 who is on the **autistic spectrum**. He is being monitored by all staff during his settling in. You have been asked to support him as much as you can and have been given information on his background and access to reports from other professionals. At present, his behaviour can be unpredictable. A parent who used to help out at the child's primary school last year has witnessed his behaviour. She is now speaking about it to other parents. One day, as you are leaving the school with your own daughter, a parent asks you about the child. She wants to know where he has come from and why he is in a mainstream school. She says it is 'not the right place for him'.

- What would you say to her?
- What would you do if other parents continued to ask you about the child and voice their opinions?

### Key term

**Autistic spectrum** — a spectrum of psychological conditions characterised by widespread abnormalities of social interactions and communication, as well as severely restricted interests and highly repetitive behaviour

## Reassuring children, young people and adults of the confidentiality of shared information

When you are party to gathering information, whatever this is, you may sometimes be in a position where you need to reassure others about the fact that it is confidential. If you attend meetings or need to be told about confidential items, you should make sure that you let others know your obligations. In most cases, parental consent would need to be given before any information about children can be shared with other professionals. However, if there are any issues to indicate that the child is at risk from harm or abuse, or if there is a legal obligation placed on the school to disclose information, this can be done (see the following case study). There may also be cases where information on pupils needs to be accessible to all staff, for example, where pupils have specific medical conditions such as asthma or epilepsy. In this case there should be an agreed system within the school for making sure that all staff are aware of these pupils.

## Situations when confidentiality protocols must be breached

If you find yourself in a position where another individual confides in you, it is important to remember that there are some situations in which you will need to tell others. This is particularly true in cases of suspected child abuse or when a child or young person is at risk. You should at all times tell the individual that you will not be able to keep confidentiality if they disclose something to you which you cannot keep to yourself for these reasons.

## CASE STUDY: Procedures for sharing information

Chris works in a secondary school where he supports children with special educational needs. He lives locally and one day when he was leaving school, he was stopped in the street by a parent who told him information about another pupil at the school. Chris has noticed that the child referred to has been missing school quite regularly, and when he is there, he appears withdrawn. The parent asks Chris not to tell anyone else, but says that she is very concerned and is asking for his advice.

- What should Chris say to the parent?
- Why should Chris act immediately in this instance?

## Getting ready for assessment

Your school has an open-door policy, and parents and other adults are always welcome. Recently there has been an incident where a parent has complained to you at hometime that the open-door policy is not a reality. She has said that teachers are always too busy to speak to her, and anyway it is so difficult to get into the school because of security measures that she does not feel the description of 'open door' to be particularly accurate. She says that she has already mentioned it to the Head Teacher some time ago, but nothing seems to have been done about it.

- What would be your first reaction in this situation?
- What else could you do or say in order to support the parent?
- Can you think of any other strategies which would help to deal with the complaint?
- Why is it important that you and the school act to resolve this matter?

In this unit you will need to show that you know what to do in sensitive situations such as the above, where there are communication issues or relationships between adults or children have broken down. You may or may not have had to deal with them.

- If you have not, you can use the portfolio activities and case studies in this unit so you can show that you know what procedures you would follow.
- If you have been involved in a situation where communication has broken down, and do not want to write a reflective account about it, you can tell your assessor about it during a professional discussion. They can then record that you have told them and whether you have acted appropriately. The actual incident and individuals involved will not need to be named. This will avoid recording any sensitive information in your portfolio.

## Functional skills

**English: Speaking, listening and communication**
When holding a professional discussion, it is important always to think about using appropriate language and to keep the discussion moving.

### Websites

**www.atl.org.uk** – Association of Teachers and Lecturers

**www.businesslink.gov.uk** – Business Link

**www.dcsf.gov.uk/everychildmatters** – Every Child Matters

**www.education.gov.uk** – Department for Education: you can obtain the SEN Code of Practice 2001 England and Wales from this site

**www.restorativejustice.org.uk** – Restorative Justice Consortium

**www.transformingconflict.org** – Transforming Conflict

**www.unicef.org** – UNICEF

**www.unison.org.uk** – UNISON

**www.voicetheunion.org.uk** – Voice: the union for education professionals

### Functional skills

#### ICT: Using ICT

You should keep a log in a Word® document of all the relevant websites that you find, so that you can refer back to them. Make sure that you save this file with an appropriate name so that you can retrieve it a later date in order to edit your list.

### Check your knowledge

1. What key things should you remember in order to communicate effectively with others?

2. How can you develop positive relationships with children as well as adults?

3. What kinds of contexts may affect relationships and how you communicate with others?

4. In which of these situations might you need to adapt the way in which you communicate with others?

   a) if the individual has communication difficulties

   b) if you do not have time to speak to them properly

   c) if the child is distressed

   d) if they have not understood what you are saying.

5. Give two differences you may need to consider between communicating with children and communicating with adults.

6. How can you make sure that you do not have disagreements with others? (For example, what kinds of strategies could you use?)

7. What should you do if you have concerns about a child who has confided in you, but the child has asked you not to tell anyone?

# School life

## My story: Paula

I have been working in my school for three years. For the last two terms, I have been supporting Ania, who has communication difficulties. Ania came to the UK with her family last year. As well as having a speech and language disorder, she speaks English as a second language. Within a few weeks we really noticed a change in her progress and she has made friends. She is now nearing the end of Year 8 and starting to think about options for Key Stage 4. Her parents will be moving shortly and have said that they want to move her to a school which is closer to their new house and easier to get to. However, we all feel at school that she would benefit enormously from staying at our school which has a speech and language unit attached. Ania can easily get to our school as it is a short bus ride away. The SENCO and I tried to speak to Ania's mum a couple of times about this, but as her English is quite poor, we did not think that she had really understood how important it is for Ania to continue to have the close support of speech and language professionals.

After trying to speak to Ania's mum after school one day, the SENCO and I decided it would be useful to set up a meeting between the school, Ania's speech and language therapist, Ania herself and her parents. We also invited a translator to help to explain to Ania's parents in more detail. We were able to discuss all the issues we wanted to and the parents also had the opportunity to ask questions about what was available to Ania. At the end of the meeting, we all felt that it had been useful for her parents to spend a morning at the school observing the support she receives.

## Ask the expert

**Q** Sometimes as a teaching assistant I don't feel able to make suggestions or say what I think to other adults in the school as I don't think it's part of my role – should I say what I think?

**A** You should always voice any concerns or take opportunities to put your ideas forward. As an individual support assistant in particular, you may have closer contact with the pupils than teachers do, so you have a clearer idea about what is needed. You may need to ask first if nobody seeks your opinion, but it should be a matter of course.

### VIEWPOINT

Do staff at your school have opportunities to say what they think? Support staff should have some opportunities to communicate and discuss their own ideas, whether this is through their own meetings or meetings with the whole-school staff. If this is not available to you, ask for some time to be set aside and emphasise the importance of whole-school communication.

# TDA 3.2 Schools as organisations

For this unit, you will need to know and understand the structure of schools and how they work. You should also be aware of your own school's mission, ethos and values and the implications of these. You will also need to understand how the school fits in at a local and national level. You should know about the roles and responsibilities of others within and outside the school who contribute to the education process. You will have to understand the wider context of legislation which affects schools and the principles and policies which are needed.

## By the end of this unit you will:

1. know the structure of education from early years to post-compulsory education

2. understand how schools are organised in terms of roles and responsibilities

3. understand school ethos, mission, aims and values

4. know about the legislation affecting schools

5. understand the purpose of school policies and procedures

6. understand the wider context in which schools operate.

# Know the structure of education from early years to post-compulsory education

## Entitlement and provision for early years education

As part of the Every Child Matters agenda and the Childcare Act 2006, it became an entitlement of all 3- and 4-year-olds in England to receive a free part-time **early years education** of up to 12.5 hours per week for 38 weeks of the year. The government funds local authorities to ensure that every child receives up to two years of free education before reaching school age. Parents do not need to contribute to this, but will be charged fees for any additional hours the child receives.

Early years provision in school is about supporting very young children. It is distinct from Key Stage 1 in each country within the UK and is based on the concept of learning through play rather than more formal education, as play has been shown to be an important vehicle for children's early learning. Although you may not work with this age group, you should have some understanding of the early years curriculum and the statutory requirements of the Early Years Foundation Stage or the requirements of your home country. As a member of support staff, you may be asked to work with pupils in school nurseries as well as Reception classes. If you have not worked at all with children of this age range, you may need to attend specific training if you are to be there for any length of time.

### Early Years Curriculum Frameworks in your home country

In English and Welsh schools, the Foundation Curriculum runs from the ages of 3 to 5 years and is therefore used in Reception classes and in school nurseries. The Early Years Foundation Stage (EYFS), which was introduced in England in September 2008, sets out one standard framework for learning, development and care for all children from birth to the end of the Reception year. Year 1 teachers should continue to work to the principles of the EYFS until the end of the autumn term in their class (for more information, see http://nationalstrategies.standards.dcsf.gov.uk/earlyyears).

In Scotland, the curriculum is focused around the document *Curriculum for Excellence*. This document concerns the curriculum for 3- to 18-year-olds. The curriculum for 3- to 4-year-olds and the early primary phase (Primary 1) are presented as one level. This means that, although in Scotland there is a distinction between the phases, children will only move on to Primary 1 when they are ready. There is also a strong emphasis on active learning and on deepening pupils' knowledge.

In Northern Ireland, pupils in Years 1 and 2 are in the Foundation Stage. Key Stage 1 consists of Years 3 and 4, and Key Stage 2 of Years 5, 6 and 7. Although the year groups are divided up differently from those in other countries, the Foundation Stage remains distinct from the Primary Curriculum and again only introduces children to formal learning when they are ready.

The way in which learning is usually managed in the early years is that adults work alongside children on focused activities that involve specific concepts, such as using numbers or carrying out writing or language activities. Children also work independently and self-select from a wide range of activities within and outside the classroom. This encourages them to develop their **autonomy**.

### Knowledge into action

Ask your local primary school if you can observe practice. Find out how the structure of the day there is different from a secondary school.

### Key terms

**Early years education** — education for children up to the age of 5 in Nursery and Reception classes

**Autonomy** — doing things in a self-governed way

*How does it help children's development for them to play independently?*

## The different types of schools in relation to educational stage(s) and school governance

There are four main types of mainstream state schools which will all be funded by local authorities and are known as maintained schools. They will all have to follow the National Curriculum, and include:

● **community schools** – these are run and owned by the local authority (or Education and Library Board in Northern Ireland). This will also support the school through looking to develop links with the local community, and by providing support services. They will also usually determine the admissions policy. They may develop the use of the school facilities by local groups such as adult education or childcare classes

● **foundation and Trust schools** – foundation schools are run by their own governing body, which determines the admissions policy in consultation with the local education authority. The school, land and buildings will also be owned by the governing body or a charitable foundation. A Trust school, although a type of foundation school, will form a charitable Trust with an outside partner, such as a business. The school will have to buy in any support services. The decision to become a

Trust school will be made by the governing body in consultation with parents

● **voluntary schools** – these come under two types:

  • voluntary-aided schools are mainly religious or 'faith' schools, although anyone can apply for a place. They are run by their own governing body in the same way as a foundation school, although the land and buildings are normally owned by a religious organisation or charity. They are funded partly by the governing body, partly by the charity and partly by the local education authority, which also provides support services

  • voluntary-controlled schools are similar types of schools to voluntary-aided schools, although they are run and funded by the local authority which also employs the staff and provides support services. The land and buildings are usually owned by a charity, which is often a religious organisation

● **specialist schools** – these are usually secondary schools which can apply for specialist status to develop one or two subject specialisms. They will receive additional government funding for doing this. Around 92 per cent of secondary schools in England have specialist status (source: Teachernet, April 2009). Special schools can also apply for specialist school status to be given for an SEN specialism under one of the four areas of the **SEN Code of Practice**.

There are also other types of schools which are not funded directly by the local education authority (Education and Library Board in Northern Ireland).

### Key term

**SEN Code of Practice** – document which sets out the requirements for the identification and monitoring of pupils with special educational needs

### Independent schools

Independent schools are set apart from the local education authority since they are funded by fees paid by parents and also income from investments, gifts and charitable endowments. Most therefore have charitable status, which means that they can claim tax exemption. They do not have to follow the National Curriculum, and the head teacher and governors decide on the admissions policy. There are approximately 2,300 independent schools in the UK, which are obliged to register with the Department for Education (DfE) so that they can be monitored on a regular basis, although this may not be by Ofsted but the ISI (Independent Schools Inspectorate).

## Academies

Historically these have been set up by sponsors from business although, in 2010, the government introduced more opportunities for communities to become involved in giving schools academy status. Academies have close links with the local education authority, but they are not maintained by it and have more freedoms than state schools. For more on academies, see the Specialist Schools and Academies website at the end of the unit.

### Over to you!

What type of school do you work in? How easy is it to find out this information and does everyone working in the school know about it?

### Functional skills

**English – Reading**
You could develop your reading skills by working in groups of three with people who come from different settings and carrying out a comparative study of admissions, prospectuses, policies and procedures, and general operation.

## Post-16 options for young people and adults

The opportunities for pupils aged 16 and over have traditionally been either to leave school and start employment, or to stay and continue with their studies. Although many pupils do still choose one of these options, it is likely that there will be more opportunities available as there has been an increased government focus on and funding of education for 14- to 19-year-olds, and in particular a focus on reducing the number of young people not in education, employment or training (NEET) post-16. At the time of writing, the government guarantees that by

the end of September of the year that each young person leaves compulsory education, they will have a place in further learning available. This 'September Guarantee' was implemented nationally in 2007 and was later extended so that 17-year-olds who have completed a short course or who have chosen to leave the activity they selected on completing school will have the opportunity to extend their learning.

### The September Guarantee

Under the last Labour government the guarantee was as follows:

- full or part-time education in school, sixth form college, independent learning provider or further education (FE) college
- an Apprenticeship or programme-led Apprenticeship, which must include both the training element and a job or work placement
- Entry to Employment (E2E)
- employment with training to NVQ level 2.

The reason behind these requirements is that by 2013, all pupils will be required to continue in education or training to at least 17 years of age. This does not mean that they will be required to remain in school, but they should be following one of the pathways above.

It is possible that under the new government these may change and you should check the DfE website for updates. Go to www.education.gov.uk and enter a search for 'Supporting young people'.

### Knowledge into action

Consider the wider educational environment of your school — for example, with regard to other primary and secondary schools, and further and higher education in your area. How do you think your school relates to other schools and colleges? Find out about any contact and projects which they may do together.

### Functional skills

**Maths: Representing**
Research the choices made by young people at the age of 16 in your own school. Find the percentage of those continuing in school, transferring to college or training etc. Produce a graph to illustrate your findings.

# Understand how schools are organised in terms of roles and responsibilities

## The strategic purposes of members of the school team

### School governors

School governors are usually a team of 10 to 12 people, although there can be up to 20, who have the responsibility of running the school. They will be made up of a variety of people who will have links with the school and local community. There should be at least one parent governor and at least one staff governor, in addition to the Head Teacher. There may also be a support staff governor. In addition there will be a local authority governor, appointed by the local authority (LA), and a local community governor who will usually work or live in the community served by the school. Governors will work closely with the Head Teacher and Senior Management Team, although you may not see them around the school often during the school day. Governors will be based on different committees which are responsible for various areas of school management — for example, the school site,

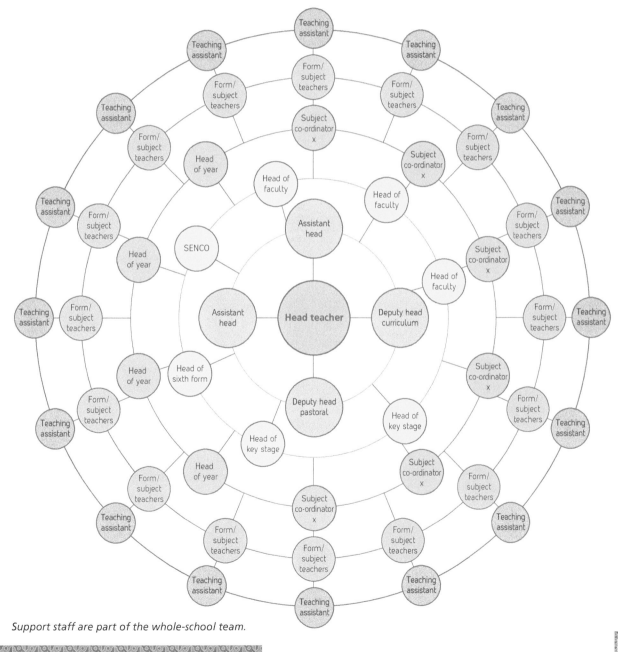

*Support staff are part of the whole-school team.*

personnel issues or **community cohesion**. They will meet in these committees and then report back to the full governing body. Their main duties are:

- to set aims and objectives for the school
- to adopt new policies for achieving the aims and objectives
- to set targets for achieving the aims and objectives.

You can find more information on school governorship and governor responsibilities at www.governornet.co.uk

## Senior management team

The school's Senior Management or Senior Leadership Team will work closely with the Head Teacher. The team will usually be made up of more experienced staff who have management positions – in a primary school this will probably be the deputy head teacher, year group leaders (if the school has more than one form entry), SENCO (Special Educational Needs Co-ordinator) and Foundation Stage leader. In a secondary school they may also be heads of faculty or departments, heads of year and SENCOs, but may also be subject area leaders. They will usually meet once a week or on a regular basis to discuss issues which have come up and to make decisions concerning the running of the school or around the implementation of the **school improvement plan**. They will then discuss how this information will be spread to teachers and support staff.

## Other statutory roles

There will be other staff roles in school which are legally required to be fulfilled in terms of staffing. Apart from the Head Teacher and deputy, the two main others are SENCOs and, in primary schools, the Foundation Stage manager.

The SENCO is responsible for managing and monitoring the provision for those with special educational needs within the school. This includes:

- 'ensuring liaison with parents and other professionals in respect of children with special educational needs
- advising and supporting other practitioners in the setting
- ensuring that appropriate **individual education plans** are in place
- ensuring that relevant background information about individual children with special educational needs is collected, recorded and updated.'

*SEN Code of Practice 2001: 4.15*

The SENCO will also need to monitor and review the provision for pupils with special educational needs and make sure that the paperwork is in place for those who are on Early Years or School Action and Action Plus.

The Foundation Stage Manager must ensure that the Early Years Foundation Stage (that is, Reception and any Nursery classes) is being run according to the statutory requirements of the Early Years Foundation Stage document. They will be responsible for making sure that observations, assessments and record keeping are up to date, as well as ensuring that all staff in the Foundation Stage are trained in its implementation.

### Key terms

**Community cohesion** – the togetherness and bonding shown by members of a community, the 'glue' that holds a community together

**School improvement plan** – document which sets out priorities for the school over a four- or five-year period

**Individual education plan (IEP)** – targets and plans implementation strategies for pupils with special educational needs (see also pages 260–61)

## Teachers

All teachers have the responsibility for the planning and preparation of the curriculum for pupils in their class. In a primary school, this will usually be for all subjects under the National Curriculum. As well as being responsible for their own class, teachers will generally also have another area of responsibility in school. This may be as a member of the senior management team, but in a primary school it could also be a subject area. In secondary schools, classroom teachers will be subject specialists. Some teachers will also act as form teachers and with a responsibility for pastoral care for a group of pupils. In all schools, each subject will need to be represented. In secondary schools and some primary schools there will be subject co-ordinators, but in smaller primary schools with fewer teachers, staff may each be responsible for two or three subjects. Co-ordinators will be expected to know about any curriculum developments in their area and to feed back to all staff through staff meetings. They should also be available to advise and support other teachers

| Role of teacher | Role of teaching assistant |
|---|---|
| • To be responsible for planning and preparing to the National or Early Years Curriculum<br>• To teach pupils according to their educational needs<br>• To assess, record and report on the development, progress and attainment of pupils<br>• To take responsibility for all other adults within the learning environment<br>• To communicate and consult with the parents of pupils<br>• To communicate and co-operate with persons or bodies outside the school<br>• To participate in meetings arranged for any of the above purposes<br>• Usually to be responsible for managing an area of the curriculum, such as geography, as included in the job description | • To plan and prepare work alongside the teacher<br>• To support learning activities effectively as directed by the teacher<br>• To assess/evaluate pupils' work as directed by the teacher<br>• To report any problems or queries to the teacher<br>• To give feedback to the teacher following planned activities |

Table 1: Some of the duties around planning and implementing learning activities of the teacher and teaching assistant.

in their subject, and monitor teaching. The local authority will also arrange subject leader forums which they will be expected to attend.

**Link**

See also TDA 3.3 on supporting learning activities.

## Support staff roles

The number of support staff in schools has risen dramatically in recent years. The DfE's Statistical First Release in May 2010 shows that the total number of teaching assistants across all LA maintained schools in England was 79,000 in 2000 and rose to 181,600 in 2009 (source: DfE: May 2010). This has been due to an increase in government funding which was based on the reduction of responsibilities on class teachers and a gradual increase in initiatives to raise pupil progress, many of which have been carried out by teaching assistants.

Types of support staff may be:

● breakfast, after-school or extended school staff

● midday supervisors and catering staff

● office or administrative staff

● caretakers or site managers

● teaching assistants

● individual support assistants for SEN children

● specialists or technicians (for example, in ICT)

● work placement officers

● learning mentors

The roles of each of these members of staff may be different and their job descriptions should reflect this.

**Skills builder**

Produce an organisational structure of the school. Speak to colleagues to discuss their role and specific responsibilities, so that you can understand how each person contributes to the effective working of the school. Complete your organisational structure by outlining each of the roles and responsibilities identified.

**Functional skills**

ICT: Developing, presenting and communicating information
You could produce a flow chart on a computer to show the roles and responsibilities of the staff in your school. This is something that you could display in the staff room for any new members or visitors to the school.

**Portfolio activity**

Consider and write about the different ways in which you contribute to pupils' well-being and achievement in your school. Use records of pupil achievement for the groups with whom you work as evidence to support your response.

## Roles of external professionals

There will be a huge range of external professionals who may work with a school on a regular basis. If you are working with an individual pupil and collaborate with your school's SENCO, you are more likely to come into contact with different agencies or individuals. Even if you do not, you still need to be aware of the variety of people who may come into school to work with the Head Teacher and other staff. These include the following.

● The school should have an educational psychologist allocated to them through the local Special Educational Needs department. They will support the SENCO in providing assessments and observations to pupils each year and plan the provision for pupils who have additional needs. They may also lead meetings with parents and make recommendations for work with individual pupils.

● Speech and language therapists (SLTs) will work with pupils on speech, language and communication problems, in both producing and understanding language. There should be a number of SLTs working in your local area who have links with the school and in some cases are based there. However, most will work from an alternative location and will come into school to work with children, parents and teachers.

● Specialist teachers may come into school to offer advice and support to pupils with a range of needs. These may be:

  • behaviour support needs

  • social and communication needs such as autism

  • English as an additional language needs.

● The Education Welfare Officer (EWO), sometimes known as Education Social Worker, will usually be based within local authorities. They will visit schools and work with the Head Teacher to monitor pupil attendance and to provide support with issues around absenteeism. They will also work alongside parents to support excluded pupils on their return to school.

● The School Improvement Partner (SIP) will come into school to advise and support the Head Teacher for three to five days each year. They will have previous experience of school leadership and/

or have worked in a senior advisory role in a local authority. They work alongside the local education authority and will support the Head Teacher in looking at ways of developing the school through both the **school self-evaluation** and pupil progress and attainment. This means focusing not only on academic factors but through looking at **extended school provision** and liaison with parents.

● Physiotherapists/occupational therapists may work with pupils outside school, but may also be asked to come in for meetings and discussions to support pupil progress.

### Key terms

**School self-evaluation** – document which looks at and evaluates the school's progress

**Extended school provision** – extra out-of-school activities, such as breakfast and after-school clubs

You will also find that other teachers may visit your school for various meetings such as 'cluster or network groups'. These provide opportunities for teachers to work collaboratively and share expertise. Staff may come together, focusing on a curriculum area or wider school issues such as behaviour management or gifted and talented pupils.

### Functional skills

**ICT: Developing, presenting and communicating information**
You could produce an information booklet of names and contact details of each of these outside agencies that are linked to your school. You could do this by using a table within a Word® document that you could save then update later, as and when needed.

## Understand school ethos, mission, aims and values

You will need to understand the following terms as you will see them regularly on school literature and may be asked to define them for your own school. It is likely that your school prospectus or mission statement will outline them with regard to your particular workplace.

● **Ethos** – the school's values and beliefs and how it 'feels'; it is usually based on the philosophy or atmosphere of the school. This may also be affected by the type of school, for example, a church school may have a more spiritual ethos. The ethos should have been developed through discussion with staff, parents, pupils, governors and outside agencies or those in the community who have dealings with the school. Studies have shown that a positive school ethos is a key factor in raising pupil achievement, developing effective behaviour management and anti-bullying and peer support strategies.

● **Mission** – the school's overall intention, as set out by the Head Teacher. The school's mission is sometimes seen as a modern equivalent to a motto, in that it should be short and easy to

remember. It will also overlap with the school's vision and aims.

● **Aims** – it is likely that the school's aims or vision will be in the prospectus and in other school literature. They will usually be set by the Head Teacher in collaboration with parents, staff and the community.

● **Values** – the values of the school are based on the moral code which will inform its development. Core values are at the heart of many communities and belief systems. Although there may be some differences in the way in which people view them, they will usually include respect for self and others and are related closely to Personal, Social, Health and Economic education (PSHE) and Citizenship education. They may also be tied in with the school rules.

# Aims and Objectives

- To provide a caring atmosphere in which our children can develop their skills and abilities in all curriculum areas and fulfil their potential.

- To ensure that staff and children will be able to participate in every aspect of school life, within the school community, whatever their needs or abilities.

- To foster an environment in which children and staff have high self-esteem and the confidence to achieve the highest standards.

- To harness our children's natural curiosity, encouraging a lifelong thirst for learning.

- To stimulate our children to develop enquiring minds and the confidence to pose questions and discuss ideas rationally.

- To help our children to understand that learning is an exciting challenge, part of which is taking risks and learning from mistakes.

- To encourage our children to take a pride in their achievements and appreciate the value of hard work.

- To promote an understanding of and care for the environment both within the school and the outside world.

- To encourage children and staff to have the confidence to grasp opportunities afforded by new technologies.

- To encourage parents to become partners in their child's education and support the school's focus on expected standards of behaviour.

- To enrich our children's knowledge and understanding of the diversity of the world we live in and develop a respect for other cultures, races and religions.

*(Source: Unicorn Primary School prospectus)*

*How do the aims of your school compare with those above?*

## How ethos, mission, aims and values may be reflected in working practices

A school's ethos should always be reflected in the working practices of the staff. The school's literature may set out a very clear ethos, but it should be apparent from walking around the school that pupils and staff carry it out in their day-to-day practice.

- **Children at the centre of everything** — children should be valued in the school and there should be a culture that their learning and development is celebrated in a variety of ways.

- **Working together** — it should be clear that pupils collaborate with one another effectively to achieve both as part of the learning process and in forming relationships with others.

- **Attitudes of pupils and staff** — there should be a positive atmosphere in the school, demonstrated through the way in which pupils and staff take pride in their surroundings and in the way in which learning takes place.

- **Community cohesion** — this is the way in which the school forms links with external members of the community and through partnerships with others to advance children's learning.

- **Inclusive environment** — a positive recognition of the importance of diversity and equal opportunities should be part of the school's commitment to a safe and secure learning environment for all pupils.

## Methods of communicating a school's ethos, mission, aims and values

The school's aims and values will need to be communicated as much as possible in school literature and on its website as well as in school. This is because these sources will be where parents and others gain their first impressions. You will need to make sure that you have considered how schools, and in particular your own, communicate their aims and values, and whether they do this successfully.

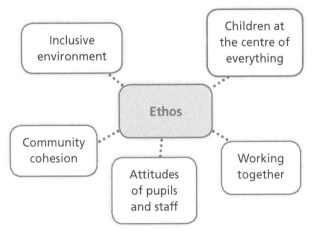

*It is good practice for everyone who works in the school to be aware of its ethos.*

# Know about the legislation affecting schools

## Laws and codes of practice and how schools are affected by legislation

Schools, as with any other organisation, are obliged to operate under current legislation. Although you may not need to know about these in depth, it is helpful to have some idea about why schools will need to work in a particular way, or why they have to draw up particular policies or documents. Some of the key pieces of legislation which you should know about are the:

- Data Protection Act 1998
- UN Convention on Rights of the Child 1989
- Education Act 2002
- Children Act 2004 and Childcare 2006
- Freedom of Information Act 2000
- Human Rights Act 1998
- Special Educational Needs (SEN) Code of Practice 2001 and Disability Discrimination Act 1995/2005.

### The Data Protection Act 1998

The Data Protection Act 1998 means that schools need to keep and use information only for the purpose for which it was intended. It also needs to be kept securely on site, either locked in filing cabinets or on password-protected computers. If you are asked to update any pupil information, you should do this while you are on school premises and not take any information off site. You should consider all information about pupils as **confidential** and ensure that you do not share it with others without parental consent. When discussing pupils with others – for example, if you are working as an individual support assistant – you should take care to ensure that you only share necessary information. Adults working with a particular pupil will need to receive information, while those who are merely curious do not.

### Key term

**Confidential** – when information is provided only to those who are authorised to have it

### The UN Convention on Rights of the Child 1989

The UN Convention on Rights of the Child 1989 (UNCRC) was drawn up in 1989 and ratified by the UK in 1991. There are 54 articles included; those which relate directly to schools are as follows.

- Article 2 – children have a right to protection from any form of discrimination.
- Article 3 – the best interests of the child are the primary consideration.
- Article 12 – children are entitled to express their views, which should be given consideration in keeping with the child's age and maturity.
- Article 13 – children have a right to receive and share information as long as that information is not damaging to others.
- Article 14 – children have a right to freedom of religion, although they should also be free to examine their beliefs.
- Article 28 – all children have an equal right to education.
- Article 29 – children's education should develop each child's personality, talents and abilities to the fullest. They should also learn to live peacefully and respect the environment and other people.

For more information, see www.unicef.org/crc

### Education Act 2002

There have been a number of educational acts and these will continue to be updated with the corresponding year. The 2002 Act brought in several changes to school regulations, staffing and governance, and was further amended in 2006 to include a duty of schools to promote community cohesion. This means that schools are required to work alongside other community-based organisations and to develop links and a 'shared sense of belonging' while valuing the contributions of 'different individuals and different communities'. For more information, see www.teachingcitizenship.org.uk/dnloads/comm_cohesion_doc.pdf

### Children Act 2004 and Childcare Act 2006

The Children Act 2004 came in alongside the Every Child Matters framework and had a huge impact on the way in which schools address issues of care, welfare and discipline. It took its root from the Victoria Climbié inquiry. Under the joint requirements, agencies such as Social Services and Education work together to take on more responsibility for pupil welfare. There are five basic outcomes for children and young people under Every Child Matters, as Table 2 shows.

The Childcare Act 2006 places more responsibility on local authorities to:

- improve well-being for young children, and reduce inequalities

- ensure that there is sufficient childcare to enable parents to work

- provide information to parents about childcare

- ensure that local childcare providers are trained

- introduce the Early Years Foundation Stage for the under-5s

- reform the regulation system for childcare, with two new registers of childcare providers, to be run by Ofsted.

Your work will have been affected directly by the Children and Childcare Acts and you should have had some training or guidance in their implementation. One of the main outcomes for schools is that there is more 'joined-up' work between schools and other agencies for the best interests of children. There have also been many more breakfast and after-school clubs through the introduction of extended schools (see www.teachernet.gov.uk/wholeschool/extendedschools for more about these).

## Freedom of Information Act 2000

This Act was introduced in January 2000 to promote transparency and accountability in the public sector. It is fully retrospective, which means that information can be sought from any time in the past. Any person may request information held by a school, although this must be done in writing. Schools have a duty to provide advice and assistance to anyone who requests information; however, there are some cases in which schools will need to protect information which may be confidential. At the time of writing, the DCSF (now the DfE) has produced guidance for schools and governing bodies to give advice when dealing with requests for information. For more information, visit www.teachernet.gov.uk and search for 'freedom of information for schools'.

## Human Rights Act 1998

There are a number of equalities laws which may affect schools. These are designed to ensure that inequalities do not exist and that all children will have the same entitlements to education. The Human Rights Act 1998 is linked to the 1950 European Convention on Human Rights. This came in after the

| Outcome | Description |
|---|---|
| Be healthy | Children should be physically, mentally, emotionally and sexually healthy. They should have healthy lifestyles and be able to choose not to take illegal drugs. |
| Stay safe | Children should be safe from neglect, violence, maltreatment, bullying and discrimination. They should be cared for and have security and stability. |
| Enjoy and achieve | Children should be ready for, attend and enjoy school. They should achieve national educational standards at both primary and secondary school. They should be able to achieve personal and social development, and enjoy recreation. |
| Make a positive contribution | Children should engage in decision making and support the local community. They should show positive behaviour in and out of school. Children should be encouraged to develop self-confidence and to deal with significant life changes and challenges. |
| Achieve economic well-being | Children should engage in further education, employment or training on leaving school. They should be able to live in decent homes with access to transport and material goods. They should be free from low income. |

*Every Child Matters: Change for Children – DfES-1109–2004*

*Table 2: The five outcomes under Every Child Matters.*

end of the Second World War, and although it was a binding international agreement, it was not law. Under the Human Rights Act, individuals in the UK have particular rights and freedoms, but these must be balanced against the rights and freedoms of others. A key provision of the Act is that 'it is unlawful for a public authority to act in a way which is incompatible [not in line] with a Convention right'.

Some of the articles which have a direct link to school provision are:

● Article 2 of Part II: The First Protocol – the right to education (although this does not mean the right to go to a particular school)

● Article 8 – the right to respect for private and family life

● Article 10 – the right to freedom of expression.

Restraint of pupils is permitted under the Act, to protect the rights of others or to prevent crime or injury. However, your school or local authority should have a policy on this and you should read it so that you are aware of guidelines for its use. There is a guidance leaflet for schools setting out their responsibilities under the Act: http://nihrc.org/dms/ data/NIHRC/attachments/dd/files/42/HRAguide_ schools.pdf

### The Special Educational Needs (SEN) Code of Practice 2001 and Disability Discrimination Act 1995/2005

Under the SEN Code of Practice, parents and SEN children have an increased right to a mainstream education. This has had an impact on the number of children who have special educational needs being included in mainstream schools and on the number of individual support assistants who support them. It has also had training implications, as in order to support inclusion, schools must now manage pupils with a more diverse range of needs. This has meant that more children are integrated into mainstream schools, which has had a positive effect.

The Disability Discrimination Act and subsequent legislation regarding access for all has meant that all schools built from this date have had to make provision

for pupils with disabilities – for example, they will need to have ramps, lifts and disabled toilets. Existing schools built before the Act was first introduced do not need to do this unless they have modifications to existing buildings, such as extensions or new blocks. The Act also means that pupils should not be excluded from any aspect of school life due to disabilities, for example, school trips or other outside provision.

Legislation will affect how schools work as they will need to comply fully with all legal requirements. They will also affect your work with children, although this may seem to happen indirectly. As laws and codes of practice affecting work in schools change regularly, it is not possible to list them all here. However, you should know that schools may need to seek advice and guidance if and when needed. This will often be through the governing body.

## Regulatory bodies relevant to the education sector which exist to monitor and enforce the legislative framework

### The Health and Safety Executive (HSE)

The Health and Safety Executive provides guidance and monitors the legislative framework for all organisations, whether these are industrial, business or education based. Schools are required to comply with the Health and Safety at Work Act (1974). This means that they will need to comply with health and safety law in a number of ways. The employer is responsible for health and safety and this will depend on the type of school, and is required to:

● carry out risk assessments and appropriate measures put in place in new situations or those which may pose an increased risk to adults or children such as on school trips

● complete and hold appropriate paperwork (such as accident recording) which may be requested for inspection under the Act

● have a school health and safety policy, and alert all staff to this.

## School-specific regulatory bodies

Ofsted (the Office for Standards in Education, Children's Services and Skills) was brought in to regulate and inspect the provision and education of children and young people, and to report their findings. They report directly to Parliament and details of all school inspections are obtainable through their website.

All registered teachers in England are required to be members of the General Teaching Council (GTC). Its functions are that of a regulatory role of the teaching profession. There is a Code of Conduct and Practice to which teachers are required to adhere.

The Independent Schools Council (representing independent schools in the UK) exists to provide information on independent schools, and also to inspect and regulate them. There is a separate Independent Schools Inspectorate (ISI) for each UK country.

# Understand the purpose of school policies and procedures

## Why schools have policies and procedures

All schools, as with other organisations, are required to have clear **school policies** and procedures. This is so that parents, staff, governors and others who are involved in the running of the school are able to work from a comprehensible set of guidelines. There are likely to be a large number of policies and you should know where to find them in your school so that you are able to refer to them when necessary. Although each school will have a slightly different list or they may have varying titles, each will need to outline its purpose and aims, and the responsibilities of staff.

### Key term

**School policy** – the agreed principles and procedures for the school

## Policies and procedures schools may have

Schools may have polices and procedures relating to:

- staff
- pupil welfare
- teaching and learning
- equality, diversity and inclusion
- parental engagement.

| Area | Policies |
|---|---|
| Staff | • Pay policy<br>• Performance management policy<br>• Grievance policy |
| Pupil welfare | • Safeguarding policy<br>• Health and safety policy<br>• Drugs awareness policy<br>• Behaviour management policy<br>• Personal, social, health and economic education policy<br>• Anti-bullying policy |
| Teaching and learning | • Curriculum policies (a policy for each subject, such as history, maths, art)<br>• Post-16 policy<br>• Teaching and learning policy<br>• Planning and assessment policy<br>• Marking policy |
| Equality, diversity and inclusion | • Equal opportunities policy<br>• Race equality and cultural diversity policy<br>• Special educational needs (or inclusion) policy<br>• Gifted and talented policy<br>• Disability and access policy |
| Parental engagement | • Homework policy<br>• Attendance policy<br>• Home-school agreement |

*Table 3: Policies and procedures relating to different aspects of a school's running.*

### Responsibilities

Final responsibility for health and safety within the school lies with the Head Teacher.

The Site Manager (or in her absence the Head Teacher) is responsible for the following areas:

- Admin. areas
- Boiler room
- Classrooms
- Corridors, foyers
- ICT suite
- Science labs
- Kitchen and servery

- Libraries
- Hall
- Senior managers' offices
- Shared learning areas
- Gym
- Playground, playing fields and garden areas
- Toilets

It is the duty of every member of staff, both teaching and non-teaching, to report any unsafe conditions to the Head Teacher, Site Manager or the Administrative Officer in their absence. In addition, an attempt should be made to eliminate the danger before reporting it, without causing undue risk to self.

All employees have the responsibility of co-operating with the Head Teacher to achieve a healthy and safe workplace, and to take reasonable care of themselves, pupils and others. Health and Safety issues will be raised as a regular agenda item at the staff briefing meetings, which are held each Friday afternoon.

### Review of Training Needs

The Head Teacher is responsible for keeping under constant review the safety training needs of staff within their jurisdiction. This includes induction and update training. As soon as possible after joining, the induction Co-ordinator ensures new staff are made aware of emergency procedures and fixtures relevant to their place of work, that they receive all necessary documents and are aware of Health and Safety procedures.

*Excerpt from a school's policy.*

**CASE STUDY:** When policies are needed

Gill is working as a learning support assistant. She supports a group of three Year 7 pupils to improve their reading. One day, when working with the children in a small meeting room, the fire alarm rings. Gill is not sure which way to exit the school building and where to meet once outside. She is responsible for the safety of the group, but has not received advice on evacuation during her induction.

- What should have happened in this instance?
- How could this situation have been averted?

**Functional skills**

English: Speaking, listening and communication
This case study could be completed in the form of a discussion to develop your speaking and listening skills. Remember to listen carefully to what others are saying, so that you can respond in an appropriate way.

## Portfolio activity

You will need to know about each of these policies and how they relate to you and your school. In your groups, allocate two or three policies so that each of you can find out about them to give a presentation to others. Make notes on each during the presentations, for your portfolio.

## Reflect

Following school policy helps you to remain professional in your approach at all times. How much are you and other support staff aware of policies in your school? To what extent do you think it is important that staff should be involved in drawing up new policies?

## Functional skills

**ICT: Developing, presenting and communicating information**
Completing this Portfolio activity in PowerPoint® will provide you with the opportunity to develop your ICT skills further.

## How school policies and procedures may be developed and communicated

Schools need to ensure not only that policies are in place, but also that they are revised and updated on a regular basis. It is likely that each policy will be dated and also have a date for its revision. There are a large number of 'model' policies available through local education authorities as well as through the Internet to assist schools in drawing them up, as this can be a time-consuming process. Depending on the policy, the school's Senior Management Team or person responsible for a curriculum area (for example, the science co-ordinator) may draft a policy and then have it checked by other staff during a staff meeting. It will then need to be agreed or ratified by the governing body before it takes effect. Although you will not be required to know the contents of every school policy, you should have read and know your responsibilities, in particular regarding the:

● safeguarding policy

● health and safety policy

● behaviour management policy.

You should also know the contents of any policies with which you work on a regular basis. For example, if you are a SENCO assistant, you should know the SEN policy, or if you work with mathematics groups, you should have read the mathematics policy.

## Understand the wider context in which schools operate

### Roles and responsibilities of national and local government

**National government**
The role of the DfE (Department for Education) is to 'lead the whole network of people who work with children and young people' (source: DfE website). This means that as well as being responsible for drawing up education policy – for example, in setting the National Curriculum and Early Years Foundation Stage from which schools and nurseries operate – it is also looking into new ways of developing the quality of services available to children under the five outcomes of Every Child Matters. It has also set up and administers the schools' league tables.

Other aspects of its role include:

● funding research into education-based projects and those which are concerned with children and young people

● developing workforce reform

● promoting integrated working for all those who work with children and young people

● developing the role of the third sector (those who are non-governmental – voluntary and community organisations, charities and others who work with children).

For more information, see the DfE website: www.education.gov.uk

Leon works as a teaching assistant in a large secondary school. He supports one particular Year 8 pupil who is physically disabled and a wheelchair user. Leon also supports the boy, Mark, with his personal care. As Mark's health and movement is deteriorating, Leon finds that he is now providing increasing support in care and for practical skills in class. The form tutor has requested a meeting with Mark, his parents, a health specialist, a physiotherapist and Leon, so that they can discuss Mark's physical needs and strategies for physical support.

- How might this be beneficial to all parties?
- Is there anything Leon could do in preparation for the meeting?

## Local government

Local government departments for education will provide services to schools in the area in the form of advice and support. The local education authority is responsible for providing accessible local services for:

- staff training and development
- special educational needs
- the curriculum, including early years
- promoting community cohesion
- school management issues
- behaviour management
- the development of school policies.

Local authorities will need to provide documentation which outlines their own vision and plans for the development of government-based initiatives. This will be through, for example, their local Children and Young People's Partnership (CYPP) plan, which will set out the way in which children's services are integrated and describe how and when improvements will be achieved in the local area. In a similar way to school policies, local authorities will also have policies which relate to wider issues, such as their

own guidelines for schools for the use of restraint or guidance on the use of medicines.

Most local education authorities will employ specialist advisors to deal with different curriculum areas such as maths or ICT, or to advise on areas such as special educational needs or support for pupils with English as a second language. They will also have specifically trained teachers who will provide support for pupils who, for example, have behaviour needs, or need to be assessed for a specific learning need such as dyslexia. They will sometimes provide these services free to schools, but in some cases schools may be expected to pay for them, in particular if specialist teachers need to come into school to advise teachers or work with specific children.

If there is a change in education policy which all schools need to know about, the local education authority will be expected to pass on this information to schools and offer training to key staff through their local education development centre. They may also come on site and deliver whole-school training or INSET (In-Service Education and Training) to all staff if needed.

### Over to you!

Investigate whether your local authority has developed a Children and Young People's Partnership plan. If so, what are their priorities according to the plan?

## The role of schools in national policies relating to children, young people and families

Schools are expected to know about and show that they are working from national policies which relate to children, young people and families. An example of this is the Every Child Matters framework, which has had a wide-ranging impact on provision for children and young people nationally. As part of this and community cohesion, schools have been developing their central role in local communities through projects such as the extended schools programme, and Ofsted will also inspect against this criterion. Schools need to develop their own policies in line with national requirements, such as child protection and safeguarding children, following guidelines from local education authorities.

## Knowledge into action

Show how your school has developed policies with regards to the following and what national policies they may be linked with:

- school trips
- safeguarding
- premises and security.

## Roles of other organisations working with children and young people

Since there is a wide range of organisations which work with children and young people, it makes sense that they should liaise with one another and share their knowledge and experience. As well as developing links with one another for pupil support and community cohesion, it is likely that meetings will also be held between different services. Although they will work with and alongside schools, they may work in a different way, and all parties will need to be aware of this. However, the impact of a closer working relationship between organisations can only be beneficial to all concerned and is in the best interests of the children.

| Organisation | Description |
|---|---|
| Social services | Social services will link with schools in cases where it is necessary for them to share information or prepare for court hearings. They may also liaise with your school's family worker or have meetings with teachers. |
| Children's services | These are linked to the five outcomes of Every Child Matters, but may be from a range of providers including education, health, social services, early years and childcare. |
| Youth services | These will have more impact on secondary schools but will be concerned with training and provision post-14, the Youth Matters programme and Targeted Youth Support. |
| National Health Service | Many professionals which come into and work with schools may be employed by the National Health Service and Primary Care Trust, including speech therapists, physiotherapists and occupational therapists. |

*Table 4: Organisations which come into contact with schools. Have you been involved with these or any others?*

## Getting ready for assessment

You will need to show that you understand the ethos, policies and working practices of your own school and how it fits into the wider community. You can present your evidence in different ways, such as:

- writing a short report about your school

- having a professional discussion with your mentor or an expert witness and keeping a record of this (this may be a written record or a recording) to use as evidence

- using witness testimonies from colleagues in school or professionals from outside agencies to show how you have liaised or communicated with them

- using any other evidence of meetings you have set up or been involved in, such as emails or letters.

## Functional skills

**English: Writing**
Producing these written documents provides a good opportunity to develop your writing skills. Take particular care with spellings, grammar and punctuation when creating these documents.

## Check your knowledge

1. Name the four different types of mainstream school.

2. What are all children in early years education entitled to?

3. What is a school's ethos?

4. What are the role and responsibilities of a school governor?

5. Why do some schools adopt specialist status?

6. Explain the term 'community cohesion'.

7. What is the role of the form tutor in a school?

8. Which of these organisations or professionals might come into schools to liaise with staff?
   a) speech and language therapist
   b) health and safety executive
   c) school improvement partner
   d) community cohesion officer.

### Websites

**www.governornet.co.uk** – this site gives useful information for school governors
**www.education.gov.uk** – the site for the Department for Education
**www.ssatrust.org.uk** – Specialist Schools and Academies Trust (SSAT)
**www.tda.gov.uk** – up-to-date advice on all areas of education and training
**www.teachernet.gov.uk/wholeschool/extendedschools** – advice and information about extended schools provision

# School life

## My story: Madie

I had been working as a teaching assistant for three years when a colleague suggested that I would make a good support staff governor and added that it would be useful experience for my own professional development. I didn't know at that stage what governors actually do. After I'd been voted for and approved by others, I had some initial training run by the local education authority. I started to attend governors' meetings and was surprised at the amount of things I learned about how schools are run even from the very earliest stages. Because of my interest and experience, I have now taken on the role of SEN governor. During meetings I raise awareness of SEN issues and provide information on what is happening in the school relating to SEN provision. I must ensure that SEN and inclusion policy are reviewed and updated regularly. Being a governor means I can contribute to the running of the school in a different way. I feel I have a better understanding of the whole process, and a real appreciation of the amount of work governors do, often behind the scenes.

## Ask the expert

**Q** What happens if I want to be a governor but don't think I know enough about it? How can I find out more?

**A** If you are interested in being a governor, you should talk either to your Head Teacher or to someone else who is on the governing body, as a first point of contact. They will be able to tell you more about what is involved and the expected level of commitment in terms of time, meetings and so on at your particular school. Your local authority will also be able to provide you with literature and information on the work of a school governor.

### VIEWPOINT

Governors play a crucial role in schools although their contact with school staff may be limited, as they are likely to mainly work in another job. How much are your governors visible in your school to staff and pupils? What do you think about this?

# TDA 3.3 Support learning activities

You should be taking part in planning meetings with the teacher regularly as well as discussing pupil progress and evaluating the work you have done with pupils. The activities you carry out may be in any learning environment, including educational visits and extended school provision. You should show how you contribute to meetings in order to discuss your contribution to the planning and evaluation process. You may also like to look at this unit alongside TDA 3.10 Plan and deliver learning activities under the direction of a teacher.

## By the end of this unit you will:

1. be able to contribute to planning learning activities

2. be able to prepare for learning activities

3. be able to support learning activities

4. be able to observe and report on learner participation and progress

5. be able to contribute to the evaluation of learning activities

6. be able to evaluate own practice in relation to supporting literacy, numeracy and ICT.

# Be able to contribute to planning learning activities

## The planning, delivery and review of learning activities

In your role as a teaching assistant, you may be asked to help with the planning of learning activities in the learning environment. **Planning**, teaching and **evaluating** follow a cycle which gives structure to the learning process, as the diagram opposite shows.

It could be that the teacher plans for the long and medium term, and that you are involved in short-term planning or individual lesson plans. You should know the learning objectives so that you are clear about what the children will be expected to have achieved by the end of the session.

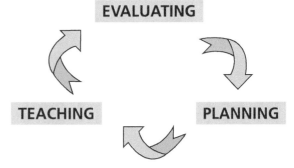

*The planning, teaching and evaluation cycle.*

Although the class teacher will have completed long-term plans for the class, you may be asked to work with them to discuss and plan activities for the week so that you are aware in advance of what you are required to do. You will need to work with the subject teacher to ensure that the work you are covering fits in with activities and topics which have been planned for the term.

### Key terms

**Planning** – deciding with the teacher what you will do, when, how and with which pupils, to ensure that planned teaching and learning activities are implemented effectively

**Evaluating** – assessing how well the teaching and learning activities achieved their objectives

### Link

See TDA 3.2, Schools as organisations pages 20–21 for the roles of the teacher and the teaching assistant.

Depending on your role, you may be invited to attend medium- or short-term departmental planning

| Stage of planning | Purpose | Content |
|---|---|---|
| Long term (curriculum framework) | Shows coverage of subject and provides breadth | Summary of subject content |
| Medium term (termly or half termly) | Provides a framework for each subject or curriculum area | Shows overview of subject content, teaching and learning activities, assessment opportunities, relevant links to national secondary strategy, functional skills (FS), personal, learning and thinking skills (PLTS) |
| Short term | Provides a plan for the week or for an individual lesson | Should include:<br>• learning intentions<br>• activities<br>• resources required<br>• organisation/differentiation<br>• provision for special educational needs (SEN)<br>• role of TA or LSA<br>• rough time allocations<br>• space for notes |

*Table 1: There are three different types of planning which you may be involved with.*

meetings so that you have some idea of the area of learning before the planning itself takes place. At this stage, you should have an opportunity to give suggestions, as well as informing the teacher of any difficulties you anticipate when considering the needs of the pupils. Your role and the role of the teacher should be in a partnership, where there are clear roles and responsibilities for working together to support the pupils. You may also be involved in planning a series of learning activities to be carried out over several sessions. This could be with the same group, if the pupils need to work on a particular concept or skill, or with different pupils on a similar, perhaps differentiated, task. As you become more experienced, or if you are working with a pupil who has special educational needs, you may add some of your own ideas during the sessions so that the pupil or pupils may build on their knowledge each time.

Medium-term Planning Sheet
Week 4

| Topic: Year 8 – Using historical sources | | Week beginning: | |
|---|---|---|---|
| Activities | Learning objectives | Learning outcomes | Comments |
| work in groups to identify and sort historical accounts from different sources, including primary and secondary evidence<br><br>evaluate information, for example type, validity, value, language | **NC History**<br>**2.2 Using evidence**<br>**a)** identify, select and use a range of historical sources, including textual, visual and oral sources, artefacts and the historic environment<br><br>**b)** evaluate the sources used in order to reach reasoned conclusions | **Pupils will be able to:**<br>• identify and describe different ways that the past has been interpreted<br><br>• use information to answer their original question<br><br>• use historical terminology | |
| assess the validity and significance of information<br><br>present conclusions about two sources of information to the class | **NC English**<br>**2.1 Speaking and listening**<br>**a)** present information and points of view clearly and appropriately<br>**b)** vary vocabulary, structures and grammar to convey meaning, including speaking standard English fluently<br>**c)** engage an audience, using a range of techniques to explore, enrich and explain their ideas | **Pupils will be able to**<br>• describe information and own opinions clearly<br><br>• use appropriate language, grammar, tone and pace to explain ideas | |
| select information from different sources to answer questions | **ICT Functional skills**<br>evaluate fitness for purpose of information | **Pupils will be able to**<br>• recognise the validity and value of the information selected | |
| review own contribution to group activity | **Personal learning and thinking skills**<br>**Team workers**<br>**a)** collaborate with others to work towards common goals<br>**b)** take responsibility, showing confidence in themselves and their contribution | **Pupils will be able to:**<br><br>• work effectively within a team<br>• contribute own ideas and opinions | |

*A medium-term planning sheet.*

Following the lesson, both you and the class teacher should reflect on the effectiveness of the teaching and learning activities, and their success in relation to the learning objectives.

When evaluating, you will need to look at whether the learners you were working with were able to meet the learning objective through their task. If the majority of learners achieved the objectives but one or two found certain aspects difficult, it would be appropriate to record by exception, for example, 'All in this group were able to calculate the perimeter of the shapes and could record their findings, but James and Abdul were not able to calculate the areas accurately and required support.' Similarly, if a pupil completes the task quickly and is more able than the rest of the group, this should be recorded (see also page 52 in this unit on feedback). You may be involved in meetings or discussions with others in the year group during which you talk about concepts or long-term plans for the year and strategies used to support children and young people.

## Knowledge into action

Using a medium- or short-term plan which you have devised with others, annotate and highlight this where relevant, to show the input of both yourself and others in your team. You should also show how you have evaluated the effectiveness of the plan.

## Your own strengths and weaknesses

In secondary schools, teachers are subject specialists but support staff may have to work in many different subjects and situations. You are not just teaching the subjects of the National Curriculum, but also social skills, contributing to school life and so on. You are likely to feel more confident in some areas than others and this will subsequently impact on learning activities. However, if you are asked to do something about which you are unsure or unclear how to approach, you should always speak to the teacher about it at the planning stage. You should be absolutely clear about what you are required to do and what the children are going to learn — if you are not sure, the outcome is unlikely to be satisfactory.

## Use knowledge of the learners and curriculum to contribute to the teacher's planning

When planning, we should always take account of pupils' experiences and interests. Learning needs to be relevant to pupils in order to engage them and keep them motivated: we need to be able to relate what we are doing to their experiences, in order to ensure that what they are learning makes sense to them.

## CASE STUDY: Identifying strengths and weaknesses

Marie works in the Special Educational Needs Department in a secondary school. She supports individual pupils in class as well as taking groups for intervention reading programmes. She is currently supporting a pupil who has severe learning needs within Year 7. Today the pupil is absent, so Marie has been asked to support pupils in Year 10 who are studying the Diploma in Information Technology. She was informed that their usual learning support assistant had gone home because he was feeling ill. When Marie arrived the class had just started. The IT teacher

asked her to support a group of pupils who were entering information on a spreadsheet. Marie was asked to help learners who were struggling with the task. Marie is not confident in the use of IT, so she was unsure how to approach the task, but she did try to advise individuals in the group.

- What is likely to happen?
- How could Marie have handled this situation differently?
- What are the implications for the group of Marie's chosen course of action?

---

**CASE STUDY:** Meeting pupils' interests

You have been asked to work with a group of pupils on a history project about the development of industry in the 19th century. This will take place over six weeks and the pupils will be required to produce a multimedia presentation based on the history of the local town and present it to their peers.

You are working with six pupils and this is what you know about them.

1. Matthew has average ability and enjoys working with others.

2. Claire lacks confidence and is reluctant to express her own opinions during group work. She is very creative. She also has average ability for her age.

3. Tariq appears to lose interest very quickly. You think that he is a **kinaesthetic learner** as you have noticed that he works best when he is moving around and engaged in 'active' learning.

4. Alana has excellent ICT skills, but has dyslexia, which means that her reading and writing skills are lower than average for her age.

5. Luda speaks English as an additional language, but her ability is above average. She has been in school for two terms and receives additional help with her understanding of language.

6. Paul is immature and small for his age. He has an unsettled home background and has recently been in trouble with the police for unsociable behaviour. You have noticed that when he engages with a particular subject, he can produce some high-quality work.

• Show how you could use this knowledge to plan and deliver a series of lessons which would incorporate what you know about the pupils.

---

### Key term

**Kinaesthetic learner** – someone who learns best through physical experience: touching, feeling and doing

### Functional skills

**English: Writing**
You could use the case study above to practise the planning skills you have learned about so far. Remember that when writing a plan, you need to present information clearly and concisely.

## Constructive suggestions for own role in supporting planned learning activities

Ideally, you should be given this opportunity to input some of your own ideas into the resources and strategies you can use to support pupils during the planning stage. This is because you may have your own areas of expertise, or ideas which may help the teacher to introduce new concepts. This is especially true for assistants who support individual pupils with special educational needs, as there will be some activities in which these pupils need more structured tasks. You should also be aware of your own areas of weakness: if you know that you will find it difficult to support a group of learners in a science or maths lesson because you have not used particular knowledge or skills for a long time, for example, then say so. You should feel comfortable with what you are doing, because it is important to be confident when supporting children and young people with particular learning activities. If you anticipate any other difficulties in carrying out the plan which the teacher has not foreseen, you should also point these out.

## CASE STUDY: Offer constructive suggestions

Megan works as a learning support assistant in Year 7. She usually works with a group of pupils but provides particular support for Paul, who has social and emotional needs. She regularly attends planning meetings with subject teachers and makes suggestions on ways to introduce or, where necessary, adapt work for Paul or others in the group. Next term, in geography, the class are studying earthquakes and volcanic activity. As Megan's husband is interested in this subject, he has some samples of volcanic rock. Megan suggests that she brings some of these in to start a discussion. She also suggests that the group could produce a display with information to show the rest of the class. The teacher asks Megan if her husband could possibly talk to the group and show photographs from his visit to Iceland where he observed volcanic activity.

- Why is it important to discuss plans beforehand as much as possible?
- How will Megan's involvement enhance the experience of the children?

## Information required to support learning activities

Information required to support learning activities includes:

- relevant school curriculum and age-related expectations of pupils
- the teaching and learning objectives
- the learning resources required
- own role in supporting learning activities
- any additional needs of the children involved.

Before carrying out learning activities, you will need to have an awareness of the curriculum and the stage at which pupils will be working. Depending on their age, pupils will be working at different stages within the National Curriculum (see also TDA 3.13, Support teaching and learning in a curriculum area, for a description of these stages). As you become more experienced with different age groups, you will develop your own knowledge and expectations about what pupils will be able to achieve.

You should have access to school records about pupils' learning, and be able to refer to paper or electronic-based records if required. This will give you details about pupils' educational background and will be particularly useful if you do not know the children well. Form and subject tutors will have a class file, which support and teaching assistants can refer to in preparation for supporting pupils in particular subjects.

You may also gather information more informally through your own observations or discussions with other staff. You will, without realising it, pick up information in different ways all the time that you are in the class with the children.

If your plan is adequate and you have thought about resources beforehand, you should know exactly what is needed when you prepare for the activity. You should think about individual pupils and how they learn best when you are deciding what resources might be useful.

The teacher should make learning objectives and your role in each activity very clear, so that you know exactly what you are required to do and what the children should have learned by the end of the session. This will also make evaluating the activities straightforward.

One advantage of planning is that you will be able to think about additional resources which you might have to buy or gather from outside school. It may be straightforward — for example, if you have been asked to use some artefacts to help you to discuss and find out about different religions, and you know that these are always kept in the RE resources cupboard. However, if you have to think about and make or find resources to use, more preparation may be required.

When working with pupils who have particular needs, you may seek advice from specialist teachers or be able to borrow equipment or resources which are helpful (for more on this, see below).

# Be able to prepare for learning activities

## Select and prepare the resources required

The school will have specialist classrooms, for example, science labs, drama studios or gyms. These departments will have storage areas or cupboards for specialist **resources**. Some subjects will be taught in general classrooms, so there will also be central resource areas where members of staff can access a range of resources and equipment, for example:

- maths equipment
- geography/history resources
- stationery
- CD-ROMs
- RE resources
- laptops
- digital cameras
- personal, social, health and economic education (PSHE) resources.

Some of these resources, such as PE equipment, may be immediately obvious. However, if there is a subject area which you are not often required to support, you may need to ask other members of staff. You should make sure that you are familiar with how different items of equipment work before you come to use them.

You will also be responsible for more general classroom preparation, for example, ensuring that there are sufficient resources for planned activities within the classroom. This should have been discussed and directed by the teacher if there is anything specific or unusual required, for example, something that is subject based. You will also be expected to maintain the learning environment during and in between lessons. This may include jobs such as making sure there are adequate pens, rulers or stocks of paper ready for use. It is important for you to be aware of items such as these, which are constantly in use and which may run out quickly. There will always be something to do in a classroom and when the class teacher is busy or unable to speak to you in between activities, you should always have the initiative to keep busy.

The types of **materials** and equipment which may be needed within the learning environment might include:

- written materials such as books or worksheets
- equipment for different curriculum areas
- general classroom items such as pencils, pens, paper, rulers or glue sticks
- specific items, for example, artefacts for RE topics
- outdoor equipment for maintaining the school garden.

## Develop and adapt resources

You will need to consider the needs of learners when planning learning activities, as some children will need specific resources to enable them to access the curriculum. The SENCO (Special Educational Needs Co-ordinator) may need to advise on how you achieve this if you have to support a child who has very specific needs. The school may already have some of the resources required, or they may be available through catalogues. However, in some cases it is likely that you will need to develop or adapt some of your own.

**CASE STUDY:** Adapt resources to meet the needs of learners

Consider the needs of the following pupils.

1. Jack is a visually impaired child who has just transferred to Year 7.
2. Paul is in Year 8 and has dyslexia.
3. Chloe has problems controlling her **fine motor skills**.

- How might you need to adapt learning resources for each of these pupils?
- Find out about any additional resources which you think could support them in their learning.

### Key terms

**Resources** — furniture and equipment needed to support the learning activity, including classroom furniture and curriculum-specific equipment, such as computers for IT or apparatus for science

**Materials** — written materials and consumables needed for the learning activity, including general classroom items, written materials and curriculum-specific materials

**Fine motor skills** — control of the smaller muscles, such as those in the fingers — for example, holding a pen

### Functional skills

**ICT: Finding and selecting information**
You could search the Internet for ideas on how you could support these children. Try using a range of search engines to broaden your results.

*Does your setting's learning environment cater for the needs of all pupils?*

## Health, safety, security and access requirements

**Link**

See CYP 3.4 for more on health and safety.

Whatever the needs of pupils, they are entitled to a safe and secure learning environment. You should always be aware of health and safety issues and younger pupils may need more reminding about hazards and the possible consequences. Schools will also have security measures in place and procedures for identifying any visitors who are in school, such as signing-in books and visitors' badges. If you encounter unfamiliar persons on school premises, you should always challenge them politely.

**Functional skills**

ICT: Using ICT
Using a video camera, you could carry out a short 'walk and talk' activity where you video the area in which you are about to carry out an activity with children and talk through the health and safety elements that you have considered. It is important that this activity is done prior to the children entering the area. Once you have recorded your footage, you could edit it and present it to your college group to show your understanding of health and safety.

Sufficient storage space can be an issue in schools, but it is important that storage areas are locked and kept tidy so that they do not present an additional hazard. Spaces such as cleaning cupboards or areas where resources are kept can sometimes be untidy due to lack of time or staff being unsure of where items should be stored.

Gavin has just started a new job in a secondary school. He has been given a copy of the school's health and safety policy, which emphasises the importance and necessity of vigilance among members of staff. He is surprised to notice that this policy does not appear to be observed, however. The signing-in procedure is often ignored by office staff and visitors to the school are not identified. He knows that many parents help in the school and that the attitude of staff is: 'It's OK — it's only a parent, we know who they are.'

- Should Gavin say something and if so, to whom?
- Why is it important for the children that health and safety policies are not only in print but adhered to by all staff?

# Be able to support learning activities

## Learning support strategies

When delivering teaching and learning sessions, you will need to ensure that the methods you have selected will support and motivate all pupils. There should be a variety of delivery methods according to the needs of individual pupils. Some learners will need to have more practical tasks in order to stimulate and motivate them, whereas others will find that they work well researching through books or the Internet. As a general rule, it is best to devise sessions which incorporate different methods of teaching and learning, so that you will be able to meet the needs of all pupils.

Learning support strategies include:

- creating a positive learning environment
- managing behaviour
- encouraging group cohesion and collaboration
- prompting shy or reticent pupils
- translating or explaining words and phrases

- reminding learners of teaching points made by the teacher
- modelling correct use of language and vocabulary
- ensuring learners understand the learning tasks
- helping learners to use resources relevant to the activity
- providing individual attention, reassurance and help with learning tasks as appropriate to learners' needs
- modifying or adapting activities.

### Creating a positive learning environment

In order to establish and maintain a purposeful learning environment, you will need to develop positive expectations of pupils and encourage them to take responsibilities for their environment. They should respect the classroom or other learning environments in the school and take ownership of them, for example, through picking up litter or looking out for lost property. All members of the school community should have high expectations of the learning environment. If it is tidy and well organised, pupils will learn to take pride in their school surroundings. Having a purposeful learning environment means that the school should be conducive to learning, with clear, well-labelled displays, a welcoming atmosphere and clear behaviour boundaries of which all learners are aware.

- Resources and facilities should be accessible for all pupils, including those with special educational needs (SEN).
- The environment should be welcoming and contain clearly defined areas.
- Storage areas should be tidy and clearly labelled.
- Items hazardous to children should be stored safely.
- Displays and information should be kept up to date and relevant for all children and young people.

## Managing behaviour

It is important to establish ground rules and high expectations of pupils from the start of your work with children, so that they have clear boundaries and are aware of consequences of their actions. It is important to praise good behaviour so that this is recognised, and you should ensure that any poor behaviour is challenged and dealt with straight away, so that learning can continue uninterrupted. If the behaviour persists, you should remove the child or children from the activity and refer to the teacher.

### Link

See TDA 3.4, Promote children and young people's positive behaviours, for more on boundaries.

## Encouraging group cohesion and collaboration

You will need to show that you encourage groups of pupils to work together where necessary in order to discuss different aspects of the task. If necessary, you may need to manage disruptions so that learning can continue.

### CASE STUDY: Managing disruptions within your group

Jean is working with a group of Year 7 pupils on a science activity. She is a very experienced assistant and regularly works with groups and individuals on activities set by the teacher. Today the group is quite lively and one pupil in particular is calling out and distracting the others. Jean uses all the strategies she knows to refocus the pupil, but he continues to disrupt the group.

- What would you do in this situation?
- Why is it important to refer incidents like this to the appropriate person?

## Prompting shy or reticent pupils

You will need to ensure that you include all pupils with whom you are working and in particular that you prompt those who are less keen to put forward their thoughts and ideas. You can do this by encouraging paired discussion to build their confidence and by direct questioning if this is appropriate.

## Translating or explaining words and phrases

In some cases, you may need to explain specific words or phrases where there is misunderstanding by pupils, particularly if they have communication difficulties or speak English as an additional language.

## Reminding learners of teaching points made by the teacher

As the task is progressing, you may need to 'bring pupils back' to remind them to keep on task and also make sure that they remember specific teaching points as they are working.

## Ensuring learners understand the learning tasks

Whenever starting a learning activity with pupils, you should clarify the learning objective and individual targets they may have been given. Some children, in particular those who are less confident, may start an activity even though they are not sure what they are required to do, because they are anxious about speaking out.

## Helping learners to use resources relevant to the activity

Always check that pupils know how to use specific resources which are part of the activity. Do not assume that they have all used them before, particularly if the equipment is subject specific.

## Providing individual attention, reassurance and help with learning tasks as appropriate to learners' needs

You will need to be aware of the needs of the pupils with whom you are working so that you can provide them with the right level of support. This may mean that they have specific learning needs, or that their personality is such that they are either more or less demanding of your attention than other pupils. You should try to reassure less confident pupils through praise and encouragement, and extend all pupils through questioning. Although you are with the children to give support, you must remember that your role is not to do the work for them.

## Modifying or adapting activities

For learning to take place, information needs to be presented in a way that is relevant to the learner. As you get to know pupils, you will be able to identify how they learn best. The way in which you support their learning should depend on the learning styles and needs that they have. Some pupils may not be able to remain on task for very long, or may find written work more challenging than others. You may need to spend time discussing activities with some pupils, or present information in a more visual way such as through photographs or artefacts in order to support their learning. It is also possible that the plan may not be appropriate for the needs of the children and that you need to change what they have been asked to do in order to help them achieve, perhaps at a different level than the one set. However, the most likely situation is that you will have a group of pupils with varying needs and you will need to maintain the interest of the group.

### CASE STUDY: Adapting strategies for pupils' differing needs

You have been asked to work with a group of Year 7 pupils on an activity to look through a poem and identify the way in which the poet has described different experiences using his senses. You have read the poem to the pupils and they now have to think of some descriptive phrases of their own.

1. Jamal has dyslexia and **dyspraxia**, and is full of original ideas.

2. George has some difficulty in remaining focused for long periods of time.

3. Charlotte and Harry are of average ability.

4. Michelle is of average ability and very musical.

5. Ryan is above average in maths, but finds language activities challenging.

- Looking at the best practice checklist at the end of this section, and bearing in mind the needs of the pupils, how could you adapt the strategies you used for the different pupils in the group?
- If planned carefully, how might this take some of the pressure off you as the adult?

## How social organisation and relationships may affect the learning process

Social organisation and relationships include, for example:

- learner grouping
- group development
- group dynamics
- the way adults interact and respond to learners.

Another way in which pupil learning may be affected is by the group they are working with. Depending on the age of the pupils and their stage of development, they may be easily distracted or influenced by the opinions of others. Some pupils may be concerned about what their peers think of them and reluctant to put their ideas forward in case they are wrong. Others may want to show off to their classmates in order to gain attention. If there has been a disagreement or particular problem during break times, pupils may be upset or agitated and therefore unable to concentrate on their learning. As the adult, you need to be aware of and manage these kinds of issues and their effects on pupils' learning.

### CASE STUDY: Managing circumstances that affect pupils' learning

You are working with a group of Year 8 pupils on a maths activity. They are recording data which they have collected on a frequency table. One of the pupils in your group is not at all engaged in the activity and as he appears agitated, he disturbs the others in the group.

- What steps could you take to involve the pupil in the task?
- Are there any other strategies that you could use to make sure that he completes the activity?

### Key term

**Dyspraxia** — a brain condition causing co-ordination problems, poor concentration and poor memory

# Give attention to learners balancing the needs of individuals and the group

When working with groups of pupils, you must make sure that you are able to give attention to all pupils, rather than to those who seek your support the most, or those who have particular needs. This can be difficult to manage, in particular if a child in your group is demanding or has behaviour issues, or if you are working with a larger group. However, there are a number of ways in which you can minimise queries and problems which may arise by speaking to the group before you start.

1. You will need to be very clear on ground rules and establish high expectations of behaviour at the start of your work with pupils.

2. You should ensure that you have clarified what children have been asked to do and that they understand and know the learning objective.

3. If pupils have been asked to work with any resources or artefacts, they should have some time to look at them before starting the activity.

You should then focus on any children who you think may need more support and then gradually move around the group, checking on each child's progress. If you are having discussions with the children, make sure all of the group are included and not just those who are more anxious to participate.

## Reflect

Using the information below, think about how you could tailor the rest of the lesson to the strengths of the four pupils in the group. You may also find that although you are primarily working with an individual pupil, you are regularly asked to take groups of pupils to support their learning. This is because when working with children who have additional needs, it is important that they are not isolated by continually working on their own with an adult. What benefits do you think pupils get from working with others on group activities and listening to their ideas?

| | |
|---|---|
| **Learning objective:** To be able to select and use visual information to develop their art work (Y8) | |
| **Teaching and learning methods** | |
| General intro | Escort pupils around the school garden and natural area to capture visual forms on a digital camera which they can use to develop their art and design work. |
| Alex | Enjoys games and practical activities. Lower ability. Possibly dyslexic but no diagnosis. |
| Ashley | Very creative, lively. |
| Katy | Good general ability and focus. |
| Sanjay | Difficult to engage in learning. Finds written work hard. |

*Do you make it clear to children what they have been asked to do and what the learning objective is?*

# Encourage learners to take responsibility for their own learning

## Link

See TDA 3.7 for more about assessment for learning.

It is important for pupils to understand what they are learning and its purpose. The now common practice of displaying learning objectives at the start of the lesson has supported the view that pupils are more likely to be engaged in their learning if they understand the aim of what they are doing. You can then encourage them at intervals during the learning process to think about how they are progressing.

Assessment for learning has become a regularly used motivational way of encouraging children to take responsibility for their own learning. It is a way of ensuring that learners are clear on the purpose of what they are doing, what they need to do and how close they are to achieving it. Research has shown that there is a clear relationship between being part of the process of assessment and pupil motivation. Those who are actively engaged with their progress will feel empowered to improve their performance, as they have more ownership of their learning.

## CASE STUDY: Encouraging learners

Ben has just transferred to Year 7. His report from primary school shows that he has found school work challenging. You provide support for him and several other pupils who have been identified as requiring intervention in maths and English. Ben is reluctant to participate, particularly in maths activities. When you talked to him about it and tried to encourage him to carry on with his work, his response was, 'I can't, I'm rubbish at maths.'

- Outline how you could help Ben to regain his confidence and present some ideas you could work on with the maths teacher.
- Why is it particularly important that you monitor Ben's progress in this case?

## Getting ready for assessment

1.  Ask permission to observe three different subject lessons. If possible, also visit and observe a local primary school. In your observations, reflect on:

    - how the classroom is organised, layout and groupings
    - how the lesson is introduced, how it develops and draws to a conclusion
    - how the pupils are encouraged to become independent learners
    - the resources being used
    - any hazards, and strategies used to minimise these
    - examples of where teaching and learning strategies or resources have been adapted for individual pupils or groups
    - the role of other adults, for example, teaching or learning support assistants.

2.  Think about your own experience when supporting learning activities.

    - How do you encourage independent learning in pupils while enabling them to achieve?
    - What strategies do you use to support children with special educational needs?
    - How do you minimise the risk of injury or harm when preparing the classroom and supporting children?

Find out who in your school has overall responsibility for health and safety. Show how your school's health and safety policy is publicised in school to ensure that all staff are aware of its contents. Does it include guidance for the use of learning materials and their preparation? What opportunities does your school have for recycling and disposal of waste materials? Children will also need to be made aware of health and safety issues. Think about different subject areas (for example, PE, art, science) and outline some of the health and safety issues which may occur in these environments and how they can be prevented.

# Support learners to develop literacy, numeracy, ICT and problem-solving skills

When supporting learning in any subject, you should also encourage learners to develop skills in the use of language, maths and ICT. If, for example, you recognise that there are opportunities to include ICT in a learning activity for another subject area, you could discuss ways of doing this with the teacher. When your assessor comes to see you working with pupils, you will need to think about how you show that you support these subjects in different ways, as well as through English and ICT sessions.

## Functional skills

### Maths, English and ICT
This information highlights the importance of including maths, English and ICT in all areas of your work. This is what makes functional skills so important.

## Link

See also TDA 3.14, Support delivery of the 14–19 curriculum.

## Personal, learning and thinking skills
This framework includes six skills which support learners to manage their own learning and personal development. The skills are:

- independent enquiry
- creative thinking
- reflective learning
- team working
- self-managing
- effective participation.

## Over to you!

Think about ways you can support the pupils you work with to develop each of the six skills included in the framework of personal, learning and thinking skills.

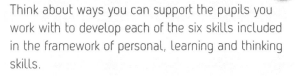

## Functional skills

### English: Writing
Reflect on one of the activities that you have undertaken. When writing an activity evaluation, it is important that you present the information clearly and concisely, using language that is fit for purpose.

# Problems when supporting learning activities

It is likely that when you are supporting individuals, groups or the whole class, at some stage you will encounter problems when supporting learning activities. These could take different forms, but could relate to:

- the learning activities
- the learning resources
- the learning environment
- the learners.

## The learning activity
Sometimes the teacher may set activities that are not suitable for the pupils involved or you may not have clear or complete information to support the activity. You may need to change the activity to make it more achievable for the pupils by going back and checking with the teacher. If this is not possible, you may need to modify it yourself so that they are able to carry out the task (see the case studies on page 45 regarding strategies for adapting work).

## Learning resources
The task usually requires certain resources such as calculators, paper, worksheets or textbooks, laptops, interactive whiteboards and so on. If you have been asked to set up for the lesson, make sure that you have enough equipment and that it is accessible to all the pupils. Also, where you have equipment that needs to be in working order, check that you know how to use it, that it is functioning and that pupils will be able to use it. If the teacher or another adult has set up for your task, it is still worth doing a check to ensure that you have everything you need. In this way you can avoid potential problems before they arise.

## The learning environment

This relates to the suitability of the area in which pupils are working. Problems may arise in the following circumstances.

- **Insufficient space to work:** If pupils are working on weighing, for example, and there is no room for them all to have access to the scales, they may quickly lose their focus on the task. There may not be space around the table or work area for the number of pupils that you have been asked to work with. Always ensure that you have sufficient space for people and equipment before you start.

- **Too much noise:** The pupils may be working with you in a corner of the classroom, but any other kind of noise will be a distraction, whether it is from other pupils in the room or from some kind of outside disturbance such as grass cutting or a nearby road. It may be possible in this situation for you to investigate another area within the school which is free from this kind of noise, or to inform the teacher that the noise level within the classroom is preventing the pupils from benefiting from the activity.

- **Disturbances from other children:** This can often be a problem if you are working in the classroom, because tasks with close adult supervision can often seem exciting to other pupils. They may be naturally curious to find out what the group or individual is doing, and if there is a continual problem, the teacher should be informed. A good diversion is often to say that they will all be having a turn as long as they allow others to have theirs.

### CASE STUDY: Managing disturbances outside your group

You have been asked to work in the classroom on a practical task of science investigation with a group of Year 7 pupils. Although you have sufficient space to carry out the activity, you quickly find that due to the interest generated, pupils from other groups are repeatedly disturbing your activities, because they are interested in finding out what is happening.

- How could you ensure that other pupils do not continue to disturb you?
- What could you say to the pupils with whom you are working?

## The learners

Here, again, there may be a variety of reasons why pupils are not able to achieve.

- **Pupils' behaviour:** If any pupils are not focused on the task due to poor behaviour, you need to intervene straight away. If they are able to continue interrupting, they will do so and you will be unable to continue with the task. Always praise the good behaviour of any pupils who are doing what is required of them, as this sometimes makes the others try to gain your attention by behaving well. If there is a particular child who is misbehaving and disturbing others, a last resort is to remove them from the group and work with them later.

- **Pupils' self-esteem:** Sometimes a child with low self-esteem may not think that they are able to complete the task that has been set. Some pupils are quite difficult to motivate and you need to offer reassurance and praise wherever you can to improve their self-esteem. However, it is very important to remember that your role is one of a facilitator and that you are not there to complete the task for the child. Some pupils may just need a little gentle reassurance and coaxing to have a go, while others may be more difficult to work with and require you to use your questioning skills.

- **Pupils' lack of concentration:** There may be a few reasons for pupils finding it hard to concentrate on the task that has been set. These could include an inability to complete the work (the teacher has made the task too difficult) or the pupil completes the task quickly and needs more stimulation. Some pupils have a very short concentration span and the task may be taking too long to complete. If this is the case, you need to break the task into smaller steps.

- **Pupils' range of ability:** You may find that you are working with a class or group of pupils whose wide range of ability means that some of them are finished before others. In this situation, you may need to have something else ready for them to move on to. For example, if a group of Year 8 pupils are working on an activity on the correct use of apostrophes, you could ask those who finish early to write a paragraph which requires the use of apostrophes to show possession and contractions.

**BEST PRACTICE CHECKLIST:** Supporting children during learning activities

- Ensure both you and the pupils understand what you are required to do.
- Use a range of questioning strategies.
- Remind the pupils of the main teaching points.
- Model the correct vocabulary.
- Make sure you carefully and actively listen to all the pupils.
- Encourage the pupils to work together in pairs.
- Help pupils to use the relevant resources and ensure there are enough.
- Reassure pupils who are less confident about their ideas.
- Give praise wherever possible.
- Have high expectations of pupils.
- Adapt work where necessary.
- Inform the teacher of any problems that have taken place that you have been unable to resolve.
- Provide a level of assistance that allows pupils to achieve without helping them too much.

# Be able to observe and report on learner participation and progress

When you are supporting learning, you will also be observing how children are working and coping with the activity so that you are able to feed back to the teacher. However, you should not confuse this with more formal observations which the teacher may ask you to carry out and which require you to sit away from the children and not interact with them. Observations are important, as through them we can assess and evaluate pupil participation and progress even more closely.

*What knowledge have you picked up through observation?*

## Monitor learners' response and assess their participation and progress

You will need to constantly monitor pupils' responses to learning activities and find new ways to engage them where necessary. Pupils will find some subjects more stimulating than others or need help to achieve learning objectives. It is important that you monitor their responses and check what they know, because you need to feed back to the teacher whether they have achieved the learning objective.

You might monitor and promote pupil participation in different ways.

| Method | Examples |
|---|---|
| Instructing pupils | • Talk through with pupils what they have to do.<br>• Give pupils a starting point so that they are able to focus. |
| Questioning pupils | • Use open-ended questions – what/when/why/how? – rather than questions that invite 'yes' or 'no' answers.<br>• Find out what the pupils already know or remember from last time.<br>• Involve all the pupils in a group.<br>• Probe, using questions, if pupils are unable to understand the task. |
| Explaining to pupils | • Explain any words or phrases that pupils are not clear about.<br>• Remind pupils of key teaching points.<br>• Model the correct use of vocabulary.<br>• Ensure all pupils understand the teacher's instructions. |

*Table 2: Methods of monitoring and promoting pupil participation.*

## Record observations and assessments of learner participation and progress

The teacher with whom you are working should give you information about the **format** of the observation you are carrying out and your method of recording. Observations may be presented in a number of ways depending on their purpose. Some different types of recording are listed below.

- **Free description** enables you to write everything down during the period of the observation (usually five to ten minutes). It means that the observation will be quite short, as it will be very focused on the pupil. Free descriptions need to include what the pupil says to others, how they express themselves non-verbally and the way in which the activity is carried out. These are used when a lot of detail is required and are usually written in the present tense.

- **Structured description** may require the observer to record what the pupil is doing against specific headings or in response to planned questions. Structured descriptions are used to guide the observer on what needs to be recorded, for example, a series of steps towards achieving a task.

- **Checklists** used to check and record whether pupils can carry out a particular activity quickly and in a straightforward way. They usually require the observer to make a judgement on whether a pupil is able to achieve a task; the focus is not on how they do it, but whether or not they can. Checklists may take different forms and schools can devise their own easily, depending on what is being observed.

- **Event samples** are used to record how often a pupil displays a particular type of behaviour or activity. Event samples need to be carried out without the observer participating in the activity to retain objectivity.

- **Informal observations** may arise if you are, for example, asked 'just to keep an eye' on a pupil or to watch them during breaktime, especially if there have been any specific concerns, and then feed back to teachers. In this case you can make your own notes, but should be careful about confidentiality if you are writing things down and remember not to leave notebooks lying around, particularly if you have recorded pupils' names.

### Key term

**Format** – the way in which results of observations are recorded and presented

# Be able to contribute to the evaluation of learning activities

## The importance of evaluating learning activities

Evaluation is important as it feeds into the planning cycle mentioned at the beginning of this unit and enables both children and teaching staff to think about the learning that has taken place. When evaluating teaching and learning activities and outcomes, it is important that you look back to the learning objectives involved. We cannot measure what children have learned without knowing what we are measuring against. If we do not think carefully about learning objectives at the planning stage, it will not always be possible to evaluate whether pupils have achieved them. Learning objectives need to be clear for this to be possible.

- Learners must understand what the outcomes mean.

- They must be achievable.

- We must be able to assess pupils against them.

### Skills builder

Look at the following lesson objectives. Which of the following learning objectives can you clearly measure against? Try using the following words in front of them – 'At the end of the lesson, we will be able to...'

- name different types of cloud
- multiply decimal numbers
- cut and paste from the Internet
- research coastal change
- spell polysyllabic words
- find features of a map
- identify features of different shapes.

You should also have an idea about the success criteria when evaluating pupils' learning. Pupils may not meet the learning objective, but they could have a real enthusiasm for the subject and have participated fully in all aspects of the lesson – you will need to

record this somewhere. You should also look at the resources you have used and whether these were successfully used.

## Use the outcomes of observations and assessments to provide feedback and improve practice

Through feedback, you can reflect on your practice and identify areas which you can improve.

### Provide feedback to learners on progress made

After most teaching and learning activities with pupils, we will ask them about their learning and discuss with them the next steps. We may do this at the end of the session, or plenary, depending on the structure of the lesson and time available. However, depending on the age and needs of the child, we may also use assessment for learning (see TDA 3.7) as a tool to support them in assessing their own work. It is important for pupils to have time to think about their learning and to understand any feedback given before moving on with their learning.

### Provide the teacher with constructive feedback on the learning activities and on learners' participation and progress

It is very important that you give teachers constructive feedback on the learning activities which you have carried out with children. Finding time to give feedback to teachers can be very difficult. There is often little time in school to sit down and discuss pupils' work with teachers. Some teachers and teaching assistants will discuss the day's activities on the phone on a daily basis. Another way in which feedback can be given, if there is not time for verbal discussion, is through the use of feedback forms. If these are planned and set out correctly, you will be able to show whether pupils have achieved learning objectives, how they responded to the activity and how much support they needed. Issues such as problems you have faced during the activity should also be noted.

If you have carried out more formal observations as detailed at the end of the previous section, you may not need to give the teacher as much verbal feedback, as the purpose of these observations is different and they will give all the detail required.

# Teacher/TA Feedback Sheet

**Class:** Year 7

To be filled in by teacher:
**Teacher's name:** Margot Dixon
**TA's name:** Fred Baxter

### Brief description of activity

Revision of Year 6 work on plotting different points and shapes using co-ordinates on x and y axes.
Follow up to revise reflecting shapes.

### How session is linked to medium-term plans

Departmental schemes of work — revision of work on shape carried out in Year 6.

### TA's role

To check understanding of how to plot co-ordinates.

### Important vocabulary

Axis, perimeter, shape, diagonal, co-ordinate, edge, corner names of shapes

### Key learning points

To be able to plot points using co-ordinates.
To identify and reflect shapes.

### For use during group work:

| Children | D | H | Feedback/Assessment |
|----------|---|---|---------------------|
|          |   |   |                     |
|          |   |   |                     |
|          |   |   |                     |
|          |   |   |                     |
|          |   |   |                     |
|          |   |   |                     |
|          |   |   |                     |

D = Can do task
H = Help required to complete task

*What do you think makes a feedback form most useful?*

You may need to be tactful when feeding back to teachers about learning activities. There may be a number of reasons why an activity has not gone well. However, if it is clearly due to planning, or the children have not found the task engaging, you may have to suggest this to the teacher. Depending on their personality and how well you get along with one another, this may or may not present problems. If you have a relationship which allows you both to give suggestions to one another and discuss any issues as they arise, you will find it easier. Sometimes, however, if you are more experienced than the teacher, or they are not used to working with other adults, it may be difficult.

Even if you believe you are right in your views about ways to support children, it is important that you are positive when you make suggestions or give feedback.

## Reflect ?

Which phrase would you use in each of these situations?

1. 'There is no way that group will only take half an hour to do that piece of work; it's just too hard for them.'
   'Would you mind if next time I did that activity I made the introductory activity longer and the focused activity shorter? I don't think the next group will be able to go straight into the main task.'

2. 'I knew that those two couldn't work together.'
   'What do you think about putting Charlie and Sam together, so that Charlie can guide Sam by reading the problems to him? Then I can swap some of the other pairs round too.'

3. 'Why don't we try it slightly differently with Kaleb so that he doesn't have to go straight into the abstract method?'
   'Kaleb just won't be able to understand it if we do it that way.'

## Reflect on and improve own practice in supporting learning activities

You should always reflect on what you have done with pupils, not only in order to evaluate what pupils have learned, but also to consider the way in which

you have managed different activities. You may find that sometimes you are not as satisfied as others with the outcome and this may be for a variety of reasons. It may be that there were unforeseen circumstances which meant that the session did not go as planned, as sometimes happens in school, or the task was inappropriate for the needs of the different children. You should not be disheartened about this — it happens to everyone — but you will need to consider why it did happen, so that you can learn from the experience. As well as looking at observations and assessments, a good way of doing this is to ask yourself the following questions at the end of an activity.

- How did it go?
- What was I pleased with?
- What didn't go as well as I had planned?
- What would I change if I had to do the activity again?

This will then help you to move on and evaluate what you have done with children, which will in turn benefit your own practice.

## Portfolio activity

Write a reflective account of a learning activity which you have planned and prepared alongside the teacher. Comment on the strategies you used to support the pupils and whether individuals in the group achieved the learning outcomes.

## BEST PRACTICE CHECKLIST: Evaluation

- Pupils should have met the learning objectives.
- They should have participated fully in the session.
- Pupils should have understood the vocabulary or terminology used.
- The resources you used should have been appropriate for the session.
- You should have retained control of the session and the pupils should have responded well to you.

### English: Writing

Answering the questions in the checklist above will allow you the opportunity to develop your report-writing skills. Be honest in your answers and share your evaluation report with others. You could even share your evaluation with your manager at your appraisal.

# Be able to evaluate own practice in relation to supporting literacy, numeracy and ICT

## How own knowledge, understanding and skills impact on practice

In order to support pupils effectively, you should have a good level of competence in literacy, numeracy and ICT. Increasingly, schools are requiring those who support teaching and learning to have at least a level 2 qualification (GCSE level) in these three areas. This is because pupils should be given the best possible support in their learning. It is also of benefit to you, as it will improve your own confidence when working with pupils.

## Develop a plan for improving own knowledge, understanding and skills

As part of your qualification in supporting teaching and learning, you will need to think about how you can improve your own knowledge, understanding and skills in literacy, numeracy and ICT, and develop a plan. You should be able to discuss this with your line manager or other member of the Senior Management Team in school so that you can develop a plan together. If this is not possible, you should have access to a college representative, such as your tutor or assessor, who will know about the opportunities in your local area. Some local authorities offer additional literacy, numeracy and ICT courses at convenient times for support staff, to encourage them to undertake the training.

## Check your knowledge

1. Give three ways in which you might contribute to planning an activity.
2. What information will you need to have about the children before starting a learning activity?
3. What kinds of issues do you need to be aware of in any learning environment?
4. When might you need to develop and adapt learning resources for learners?
5. When would you use the following methods of observation:
   a) checklist
   b) free description
   c) event sample?
6. Outline some of the benefits of evaluating learning activities for:
   a) you
   b) the teacher
   c) the pupils.
7. When might you use assessment for learning with pupils?

### Websites

**www.ccea.org.uk** – National Curriculum documents (Northern Ireland)

**www.dcsf.gov.uk/everychildmatters** – Every Child Matters (Green Paper)

**www.ltscotland.org.uk** – National Curriculum documents (Scotland)

**www.wales.gov.uk** – go to 'education and skills', then 'schools' for information on the Welsh curriculum

# School life

I work in a large inner-city secondary and have been at the school for about a year. I mainly work in Key Stage 3. Although I get on really well with the teachers, when I first came to the school I found it quite difficult, as I was never given any advance notice about the support I was going to be giving the children. I literally went into the lesson without knowing what was going to be taught or having any idea about the plans or the learning objective. I found this very hard, as I could not get myself ready and often thought afterwards, 'If only I had known before, I could have done that.' I have a good relationship with my line manager and it came up at my performance management review that I did not feel I was doing my job properly, as I couldn't support the children effectively without seeing the plans. I had a meeting with the English and maths teachers who I work with and I told them how I had the plans in advance at my last school, which really helped me. Now the teachers send me through the plans as soon as they complete them, and I can prepare better for the lessons. Both teachers say that they have noticed a difference too.

## Ask the expert

**Q** What if the teacher can't send the plans in advance?

**A** In some schools, the teacher will enter plans on computer planning software and print out plans at the beginning of the week for support staff. This may depend on when they do their planning, as some will wait until the weekend to get it done. In some schools there are planning meetings to which only teachers are invited – if this is the case in your school, you can ask if you can also be present so that you are more aware of plans of those lessons you support. You should always speak out if you are unable to share plans, as you should be working in partnership with teachers to ensure that pupils are getting full access to the curriculum.

## VIEWPOINT

If you have a difficult working relationship with any of the teachers you work with, it is likely that this will be based around personalities. However, you must remember that you will need to remain professional and that you are both there for the children. Could you speak to the teacher or set aside some time each week so that you can discuss plans? Remember that avoiding speaking will only make the problem worse.

# TDA 3.4 Promote children & young people's positive behaviour

You will need to demonstrate that you are able to promote positive pupil behaviour in a variety of contexts. You will need to show that you understand and implement agreed classroom management strategies and are part of a whole-school approach to encourage positive behaviour. You will also need to be able to encourage pupils to take responsibility for their own behaviour within the framework of a code of conduct. For more on behaviour management, see TDA 3.20 Support children and young people with behaviour, emotional and social development needs.

## By the end of this unit you will:

1.  understand policies and procedures for promoting children and young people's positive behaviour

2.  be able to promote positive behaviour

3.  be able to manage inappropriate behaviour

4.  be able to respond to challenging behaviour

5.  be able to contribute to reviews of behaviour and behaviour policies.

# Understand policies and procedures for promoting children and young people's positive behaviour

When managing pupils' behaviour, all staff will need to be aware of school policies. This means that you should know where they are and have read them, so that the pupils will understand when you apply **sanctions** and behaviour management strategies. Although the main policy dealing with behaviour will be the behaviour policy, other school policies will also have an impact on managing behaviour – for example, the health and safety, safeguarding, and anti-bullying policies.

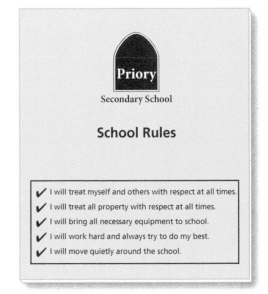

**School Rules**

✔ I will treat myself and others with respect at all times.
✔ I will treat all property with respect at all times.
✔ I will bring all necessary equipment to school.
✔ I will work hard and always try to do my best.
✔ I will move quietly around the school.

*A simply and attractively laid out code of conduct will appeal to pupils.*

## Policies and procedures of the setting

### Behaviour policy

The school's behaviour policy is important as it gives guidelines to all staff on how they should manage pupil behaviour. All staff need to be familiar with school policy so that they can apply it consistently in the school.

### Code of conduct

It is likely that your school will have a set of rules or **code of conduct**. It is imperative in any school for children to have guidelines so that they have a clear understanding of how to behave. Pupils need to be aware of the boundaries within which to manage their behaviour, so that they understand what is expected of them.

These rules should be written in such a way that the pupils are given positive targets, for example, 'I will walk quietly around the school' rather than the negative 'Do not run in school'. Staff should discuss the rules frequently with the children, both in class and during assembly times, so that they remember them.

As well as this list of school rules, staff should encourage pupils to behave in a positive way through watching the behaviour of adults. Children and young people will soon notice if an adult is not acting in a way that they would expect, or if there are inconsistent expectations between adults. When a pupil is behaving particularly well, you should remember to praise this behaviour so that it is recognised. Children and young people need to be praised for work, behaviour, effort and achievement

genuinely and frequently. This will reinforce good behaviour and build self-esteem.

### Rewards and sanctions

Your school should have a scale of sanctions for instances when behaviour is undesirable despite modelling and encouraging good behaviour. All staff should be able to apply these sanctions and pupils should be aware of this. There should be a clear, structured approach, which defines what is expected and the consequences of **inappropriate behaviour**.

Consequences could be:

- removal to another part of the classroom or room
- withdrawal of a privilege
- referral to senior teacher
- detention
- letter sent to the parents.

### Key terms

**Sanctions** – penalties for disobeying rules

**Code of conduct** – an agreed set of rules by which all children are expected to behave

**Inappropriate behaviour** – behaviour that conflicts with the accepted values and beliefs of the school and community

Your school's behaviour policy should give a clear indication of the procedures you can use when implementing rewards and sanctions. You should make sure that both you and the children are aware of what will happen if their behaviour is not acceptable.

All adults in the school should be able to give rewards and sanctions, although some will be specific to certain members of staff. An example of this might be certificates, which may only be handed out by the Head Teacher in Friday assembly. If, as a member of support staff, you are not sure about what you can pass on to pupils, you need to find this out so that you are ready at the appropriate moment.

### Dealing with conflict and inappropriate behaviour

It is likely that your school policy will give you guidance and information about how you should manage more difficult behaviour. It is important that children and young people see a clear structure to what will happen if they choose not to pay attention to the school rules that are in place. They will be much more likely to keep to the rules if they know exactly what will happen if they do not. In this situation, adults are prepared for the types of behaviour which may occur and are teaching pupils that they are responsible for their actions (see also page 61).

### Anti-bullying

This policy may be addressed as part of the behaviour policy, but should set out school procedures for dealing with any incidence of bullying within or outside the school. Bullying can take many forms, particularly through cyber-bullying with the increase in technologies such as mobile phones and the Internet, and the majority of children and young people have access to these.

### Attendance

The attendance policy will set out how the school manages issues around attendance. In all schools, attendance is monitored closely and recorded on computer systems so that patterns can be noted and parents or carers informed if attendance falls below a certain percentage. In some cases, schools will award certificates to classes or individual pupils for full attendance during a term or half-term.

## How the policies and procedures support children and young people

The policies and procedures of the setting should support children and young people to:

- feel safe
- make a positive contribution
- develop social and emotional skills
- understand expectations and limits.

## Benefits of all staff consistently applying boundaries and rules in accordance with policies and procedures

If all members of the **school community** are using the same principles and strategies when managing behaviour, it is far more likely that the children will respond positively. Pupils will know the scale of rewards and sanctions, and the order in which they will be applied, whoever is speaking to them about their behaviour. Workforce remodelling has had an impact on the number of different professionals who are now working in schools. Support staff and midday supervisors, as well as those running extended school provision, should know the importance and impact of consistent strategies. It is also important that support staff are given status within the school so that they are respected in the same way as teaching staff.

### Key term

**School community** — all personnel contributing to the work of the school including pupils, teachers, support staff, volunteer helpers, parents and carers, and other professional agencies

### Reflect

How do children in your school address teaching assistants and other support staff? Do they use first names or surnames (for example, Mrs Jones)? Do you think this makes any difference to the way in which children in the school perceive the responsibilities of support staff?

## Be able to promote positive behaviour

### Benefits of actively promoting positive aspects of behaviour

It is important for all pupils, but especially for those who tend to be reprimanded more than others, that we recognise and reward positive behaviour. Even as adults, we like to be noticed for something good that we do. Research has shown that we need to be given six positives for every negative in order to balance this out. It is always much easier for us to focus on negative aspects of a pupil's behaviour and react to these. When recognising and rewarding positive behaviour, however, you must not forget to notice those children and young people who always behave appropriately.

### Getting ready for assessment

1. Write a reflective account about how your school manages behaviour. Also examine the expectations of support staff. In your account, you should include references to your school's behaviour policy and state how you have implemented different aspects of this. Why is it important for all school staff to be consistent when applying behaviour management strategies?

2. Restorative justice techniques encourage pupils to take responsibility for their own behaviour. They focus on relationships and work to support children to restore these where there has been conflict or inappropriate behaviour. School councils or buddy schemes support children and young people to reflect on a range of issues and find solutions. Give an example of where restorative justice has been used.

3. Discuss some of the ways in which you have recognised and rewarded positive behaviour in school. Outline the reasons why this is an important aspect of behaviour management.

4. In your role, you may also find that you have to deal with often challenging behaviour from pupils and this may include risks to the safety of both yourself and others. Write a reflective account stating how you reacted to and managed the situation, and if you needed to refer to others within the school. What strategies does your school have in place for meeting the needs of pupils with learning and behavioural difficulties?

These ideas are linked to behaviourist theory, which was developed by B.F. Skinner in the 1940s. He suggested that children will respond to praise and so will repeat behaviour that gives them recognition or praise. This may take the simple form of verbal praise, which is very powerful, or merit marks or house points. Children and young people who receive praise or attention for positive behaviour, such as consideration towards others, are more likely to repeat this behaviour.

Children and young people may also attempt to gain attention through undesirable behaviour, so you will need to be aware of this and try to ignore it where possible, instead giving attention to those pupils who are behaving well.

### CASE STUDY: Promoting positive behaviour

Phillip is in Year 8. He often tries to dominate during group work and does not listen to the views of his peers. One day when supporting the group during an art project, you notice that he has taken into account suggestions of another pupil.

- What will be the benefits of praising Phillip?
- Why is it important to do so?

## Ways of establishing ground rules which underpin appropriate behaviour and respect

Where possible, pupils should be involved in devising school or classroom rules so that they have more ownership of them. You can do this by inviting them to put forward their ideas and to say why, and then ask others to vote for them. Alternatively you can give them a range of different ideas or think about and discuss rules from other schools, so that they can see a range of different approaches. This will be beneficial as you will agree as a group how pupils should behave, and the pupils will understand why ground rules are important. You will be able to say to them, for example, 'As a class we agreed that we would respect other people's property' rather than 'Leave Sajida's things alone'. This will also encourage them to take responsibility for their actions.

### Skills builder

The next time you work with a new group of pupils, make sure you establish ground rules before you start. Encourage pupils to suggest their own ideas and take responsibility for the rules. What difference do you think this will make to the activity?

## Promote positive behaviour, demonstrate realistic, consistent and supportive responses, and provide an effective role model

You will need to demonstrate that you are a good role model in all areas of behaviour within the school. Children and young people will take their lead from adults and need to see that they too are behaving

*How many of these strategies do you apply in your school?*

appropriately and responsibly. We cannot ask them to behave in a certain way if our own behaviour is not appropriate. This is also true for good manners! Be careful when speaking to other adults and pupils that you are showing the same respect that we are asking children to show others.

### Notice when children and young people are behaving well or trying hard

This is important because it will help to build positive relationships and shows that you care about the child. If you do not notice, they may think that it is not worth repeating the behaviour or that it is not important.

### Ensure responses are realistic

When managing behaviour, you should ensure that you do not give children unrealistic targets. They should be able to achieve any requirements which are set, so that they do not become disheartened and stop trying.

### Use positive recognition such as merit marks

Most schools use these kinds of systems and will have assemblies and evenings to celebrate work and behaviour.

### Follow up on important issues .

You should always make sure you follow up, particularly if you have said that you will. There is little point in saying to a child that you will be telling their form or subject teacher how pleased you are with their behaviour if you then forget to do so. The child will then think that you do not really believe it is important.

### Build trust with all pupils to maintain positive relationships

Do all you can to show pupils that you are interested in and value them. As you get to know them, you will remember particular things about them. Giving your trust to pupils encourages them to take more responsibility, for example, helping to set up laptops for use in a lesson.

### Ensure children and young people know why they are being rewarded

You must be clear on exactly what you are praising or rewarding, for example, 'I am giving you this merit mark because you have remained on task and have met your target this morning.'

### Making sure directions are unambiguous

You should make sure that you communicate clearly to children so that they understand what you are asking. If you communicate through questioning, for example, 'Do you have time to complete the next question?', pupils may think that there is some choice involved. If we want children to do as we ask, we need to say things as though we mean them!

### Use of school councils

School councils are also being increasingly used in both primary and secondary schools and are linked to the Citizenship curriculum. In Wales they have become a compulsory part of school life, following legislation by the Welsh Assembly. They discuss a range of issues, but a report by Ofsted in November 2006 cited them as having one of the most positive impacts on whole-school behaviour, as pupils have a voice in managing issues which affect them. Councils comprise an elected representative group of pupils who play an active role in dealing with issues such as bullying. An organisation called School Councils UK has the support of the Department for Education (DfE) and gives advice and guidance for setting up and running councils.

## Be able to manage inappropriate behaviour

### Minimising disruption through inappropriate behaviour

An error which is often made when starting to work with children and young people is to try to befriend them first as a way to gain their approval. This not only does not work, but will make behaviour management very difficult. It is more important to set boundaries and limits first so that pupils know where they stand. This will ultimately make your job easier and you can then build effective relationships. As well as being aware of school policies and any scale of sanctions which you are able to use, you should also be able to show that you mean what you say — never use empty threats, as this will prevent children from listening to you in the future. (See the best practice checklist at the end of this section for more strategies.)

## Managing inappropriate behaviour according to policies and procedures

You will need to demonstrate strategies for managing inappropriate behaviour according to the policies and procedures of the setting.

---

**CASE STUDY:** Managing inappropriate behaviour

Michael is working with a Year 8 group. Today he has been given a literacy group to work with for the first time and some of the pupils have started to talk over him and not listen to what he is saying. Michael asks them to stop and says that if they do not, he will have to send for the teacher. They do not stop and he threatens to keep them in at breaktime.

- Why will Michael's second strategy not work either?
- Do you think he considered the policy of his school in this case?
- What should Michael have done?

---

**Functional skills**

**English: Speaking, listening and communication**
You could share your experiences and responses to the case study in the form of a class discussion. Remember to listen carefully to what others are saying, so that you can respond in an appropriate way.

## Apply rules and boundaries consistently and fairly, according to age, needs and abilities

You will need to be able to adapt how you manage the behaviour of children, as their behaviour will depend on their age and stage of development. Depending upon the age and/or needs of pupils, your rewards and sanctions may be very different – this is to ensure that they are age-appropriate. Pupils in Years 7 and 8 may be happy to receive praise and certificates in front of their friends, but as children mature they may feel that praise is not 'cool' and it may result in them being shunned by their peers.

A quiet word may be more appropriate for some children. Your school should have a scale of sanctions for you to use with pupils when their behaviour is inappropriate.

## Age and ability of children and young people

Children will achieve **milestones** at broadly the same time. From the age of 11 years to 19 years, children and young people experience many changes in physical and emotional development. Hormonal change during puberty can cause mood swings and may affect behaviour. Children at this stage are becoming increasingly independent and developing their self- and sexual identity. Young people may be more likely to be influenced by their peers than other adults – for example, about their dress and behaviour. They need to understand and be reminded regularly of the reasons for rules and boundaries of behaviour.

---

**Key term**

**Milestones** – measurable points in development; the term is usually used to describe stages in children's development where progress can be measured

---

**Functional skills**

**ICT: Developing, presenting and communicating information**
**English: Writing**
You could look at the rules and boundaries in your school and produce two differentiated posters: one for Year 7 and one for Year 11, each outlining what their rules and boundaries are. This would provide you with the opportunity to practise writing for a different purpose and also differentiating your language to include all children.

## Needs of children and young people
### Physical stage of development

You may have to take pupils' physical stage of development into account when managing behaviour. Sometimes if children's growth patterns are very different from those of their peers, this may have an effect on their behaviour. For example children in their first year of secondary school will vary considerably in height. Girls in particular can become much taller than boys and this can put pressure on them to behave differently. If there are physical difficulties, for example, a visual or hearing problem, these may affect the way in which children relate to others and cause a delay in their overall development which you may need to take into consideration.

## Social and emotional stage of development

The social and emotional development of children is directly linked to the way in which they begin to relate to others. Children need to interact with others so that they have opportunities to gain confidence. For example, they may withdraw socially, find communicating difficult or suffer a language delay. All of these could have a negative effect on their developing self-esteem and on their behaviour, and you may need to take this into account. The rate at which a child will develop socially and emotionally will also depend on the opportunities which have been given for them to interact with others. Where a child has come from a large family, for example, there may have been many more opportunities to play with others and form relationships. There also may be less understanding of social codes of behaviour, such as taking turns or waiting for others to finish speaking, or alternatively negative behaviour in order to gain attention (see also page 66, Be able to respond to challenging behaviour).

### Reflect ❓

Write an account of a situation in which you have had to manage pupils' negative or inappropriate behaviour. Did you take into consideration the ages, needs and abilities of the children? Make sure you include your school's strategies and how you have implemented these in stages.

### Functional skills 💬

#### English: Reading

You may need to read round the area in textbooks, policies or the Internet prior to writing your account. Reading to obtain information from at least three different documents will help to develop this area of your functional skills.

### CASE STUDY: Considering pupils' needs

Marc is working as an individual support assistant to Paula, who is in Year 7. She has a developmental disorder which means that she finds it difficult to keep up with her peers intellectually and socially. After lunch, two girls from the same class complain to Marc that Paula keeps following them at lunchtime and asking them if she can join them. They said they don't want her to keep following them.

- How should Marc address Paula's behaviour in this instance?
- What should he say to the other girls?

## Support colleagues to deal with inappropriate behaviour

You should be aware that behaviour management is the responsibility of all adults in the school. This may mean that you are called upon to support colleagues in different situations, or that you will need to act spontaneously if needed. You should always check if you find that you are close to others who are managing behaviour, to see whether they may need assistance. It is also important to back them up if required, for example, if you are passing and a situation is happening where this would be helpful.

### CASE STUDY: Providing support for colleagues

Lizzie is a new teaching assistant who has been working at your school for two terms and is working towards her level 2 qualification. As you walk down the corridor, you notice that she is having to speak to a couple of boys about an incident of bad language. She seems to be managing the situation well.

- Would you do anything as you passed Lizzie?
- What might you do if the children were not responding positively to what Lizzie was saying?

# Sorts of behaviour or discipline problems that should be referred to others

Depending on your experience, confidence and how long you have been in the school, you may feel comfortable in dealing with inappropriate behaviour yourself. However there are some situations in which support staff should always refer to others. These are if:

● pupils are a danger to themselves and/or others

● you are dealing with a difficult situation on your own

● you are not comfortable when dealing with a pupil, for example, if they are behaving unpredictably

● pupils are not carrying out your instructions and you are not in control of the situation.

Depending on the situation, you may have to refer to different people – sometimes it may be enough just to have support from another adult within the school. However, there is also a wider range of specialist support you may be able to call upon:

● within the school:

  • the SENCO or supervisor should be the first point of contact for behaviour support and devising additional strategies for use within the classroom. They will also contact other professionals outside the school

  • other form or subject teachers may also be able to offer support, particularly if they have had to deal with similar behaviour patterns

  • Head Teacher or Deputy – you should be able to speak to those in the Senior Management Team of your school if you have particular concerns about a child or situation

● outside the school:

  • Behaviour Unit – this unit is usually run by the local authority and will offer support and suggestions for dealing with pupils who have behaviour problems. They may also come into schools to observe or work with specific children

● educational psychologists visit all schools regularly to support children and the adults who work with them. They offer help and advice on a variety of special needs problems, and may assess children and devise individual programmes. They are also involved with assessing those children who may need a statement of special educational needs.

## Skills builder

In pairs, look at the scenarios below. Decide which of these you would be comfortable dealing with yourself and which you would need to refer to others.

• A child in Year 7 becomes angry and breaks the ruler he has been using.

• A pupil with ADHD (attention-deficit hyperactivity disorder) is refusing to join in with your group's activity.

• At breaktime, an argument between two Year 8 boys over a football has become aggressive.

• You discover a case of cyber-bullying during your speech and language group activity.

• You come across an incident in the corridor which has left a Year 10 pupil very upset.

• A pupil has reacted uncharacteristically when being told she has to stay and finish her work.

How would you deal with the situations you could manage yourself?

## Functional skills

**English: Speaking, listening and communication**
Answering these scenarios in the form of a whole-class discussion allows you the time to practise your speaking and listening skills. You may also be able to collect some good tips from your peers to support you in your role.

**BEST PRACTICE CHECKLIST:** Managing unwanted behaviour

- Intervene early so that the problem does not escalate. If you are the first to be aware of a situation, intervene straightaway.
- Repeat directions calmly rather than reacting to what the pupil is saying or doing.
- Send for additional help if needed, especially if there are health and safety issues.
- Make eye contact with the pupil who is misbehaving, so that they see an adult is aware of what they are doing.
- Relate any negative comments to the behaviour, rather than the pupil, for example, 'Simon, that was not a sensible choice', is more acceptable than 'Simon, you are not a sensible boy'.
- Remove items that are being used inappropriately. The pupil should then be told why the item has been removed and when they will be able to have it back.
- Use proximity; move closer to a pupil who is misbehaving so that they are aware of an adult presence. You can use this practice in whole-class teaching time, when the teacher is at the front, to calm or prevent inappropriate behaviour by having an awareness of whom to sit beside.
- Use time out if older children or young people are consistently misbehaving and need to be given some time to calm down before returning to a situation. It can be applied within the classroom or elsewhere on school grounds.
- Use an agreed scale of sanctions of which all in the school community are aware.

# Be able to respond to challenging behaviour

## Recognise patterns/triggers for inappropriate behaviour and act to avoid them

As you get to know pupils, you may find that you are able to identify triggers to their inappropriate behaviour. Knowledge of the pupil will also help you when dealing with this, as you will be able to predict what works and what does not. For example, changing the grouping of pupils may be enough to reduce the likelihood of inappropriate behaviour. An awareness of the child's needs will be very important if they have specific behavioural difficulties.

## Use agreed strategies, assess and manage risks to own and others' safety

You will need to know how to manage risks to yourself and others. If you are in any doubt about your ability to do this, you must always refer to another member of staff. Your school's behaviour and health and safety policies should give guidelines for dealing with **challenging behaviour** and also the use of restraint, which may be based on local guidelines.

**Key term**

**Challenging behaviour** — behaviour which may involve verbal or physical abuse, or behaviour which is illegal or destructive

**CASE STUDY:** Identifying triggers

Jason is in Year 8 and is autistic. Carla works as Jason's support assistant. Today the year group are going into the school hall to watch a visiting drama group, instead of attending their usual English lesson. Carla knows that this may be a trigger for Jason to become distressed and to behave inappropriately, as he finds changes in routine difficult.

- Should Jason still go to the hall with the others?
- If you were working with Jason, what might you do and what might you say to him?
- How will an awareness of Jason's needs have helped in this situation?

*What strategies have you used in situations involving challenging behaviour?*

Children will not always be aware of risk and dangerous situations, particularly if they have particular needs or are caught up in what they are doing. Therefore, when speaking to them you should always point out the consequences of their behaviour.

When you are assessing risks to safety, these may be due to:

- a pupil who is violent or aggressive
- a situation which has got out of control, for example, an argument.

### Over to you!

Find out about your school's policy regarding the use of restraint. Are there guidelines from your local authority? Have you ever needed to refer to them?

## Support others to identify the circumstances which trigger inappropriate behavioural responses

When working within classes or with individual children who have particularly negative behaviour on a regular basis, it may be helpful to keep a log of

any situations which they find difficult or triggers to their behaviour. If you become aware of triggers to inappropriate behaviour, you should always mention it to others so that the situation can be avoided if possible. You may need to remove the child from the situation or speak to them if you see the warning signs that they are becoming distressed. If you are supporting a child who has behavioural needs, you should be able to discuss with them the kinds of situations which they find difficult to manage. In this way, you may be able to support them in managing their own behaviour. Alternatively you may discuss the situation with your SENCO and decide to bring in help from an outside professional in order to evaluate different strategies.

## Deal with bullying, harassment or oppressive behaviour according to policies and procedures

Research for Childline and the DfES in 2003 found that 51 per cent of children in primary schools and 54 per cent of children in secondary schools feel that bullying is a 'big problem' or 'quite a big problem' in their school. The NSPCC reported that 31 per cent of children have experienced bullying by their peers during childhood. As you have close contact with children and young people, you may find yourself in a situation in which you need to act straight away in order to deal with bullying and/or oppressive behaviour. This may take place on the playground or in other places outside the classroom, or it may be less obvious. You should, however, know your school's policy for dealing with bullying so that you act appropriately. Bullying can start from a very young age and all schools should have a definite plan of action in order to create an environment in which pupils feel safe. Your school may have a separate anti-bullying policy or this may be linked with the policy for behaviour.

You should also remember that although traditionally bullying has meant issues such as playground name-calling or taunts, it can also mean email, texts or hurtful comments through social networking sites. If a pupil confides in you that they are being sent hurtful or distressing messages, you should not discount the seriousness of this and you should always report it.

The NSPCC have devised a distance learning programme for dealing with bullies in schools which was launched in November 2008 — details of the website are at the end of this unit.

### Functional skills

**Maths: Analysing and interpreting**
You could create a questionnaire and hand it out to children in your setting about whether they feel bullying is an issue to them at school. From the completed questionnaires, you could collate your results in the form of percentages and then produce a pie chart of results. This research will not only develop your mathematical skills, but your findings could also feed into the personal, social, health and economic education (PSHE) programme at school.

# Be able to contribute to reviews of behaviour and behaviour policies

## Supporting children and young people to review their behaviour

Rather than simply reprimanding children and young people, it is likely that you will be asked to support them in reviewing their behaviour and consider why they have acted inappropriately. It is important for

*What kinds of situations have you had to deal with which may constitute bullying?*

children and young people to learn to understand and respect the feelings of others. In many schools, the programme of **restorative justice** is used to ask pupils to sit down with the person with whom they have had a conflict or disagreement so they can learn to understand how their behaviour affects others.

## Link

See also TDA 3.4 on promoting positive behaviour.

Children and young people need to be able to understand how their own feelings may affect their behaviour and you may also need to talk to them about this. For example, saying to a pupil 'I know you are upset because you could not do food technology today' will help them to make the link between emotion and behaviour. In this way, they are more able to understand how to think about others.

## Supporting children and young people to identify and agree behaviour targets

You may need to work alongside your class teacher or SENCO as well as the child concerned to devise targets for **behaviour support plans** or individual education plans. Usually these plans will be specific and outline the steps to be taken by staff to support the pupil when working towards the target, and the resources used.

There may have been suggestions for targets you can work on from outside agencies. When working with and setting targets, you should make sure that they are SMART (specific, measurable, achievable, realistic and time-bound) and that the pupil is aware of why they need to work on them. It is also important to have realistic expectations of both pupils and staff. When working towards the targets, you will then be able to discuss with pupils why they have agreed these and ask them about any issues which arise. You may also be able to help pupils who do not have specific support plans to think about how they can improve their behaviour if this is starting to become an issue.

It can also be helpful with older pupils to draw up a contract for behaviour so that they can recognise and proactively take responsibility for their actions. It will then be clearer to them exactly what they are required to do.

## Key terms

**Restorative justice** — programme in which pupils are encouraged to consider the impact of their actions or words on others by making amends directly to the victim or community that has been harmed

**Behaviour support plan** — plan setting out arrangements for the education of children and young people with behaviour difficulties

---

### Secondary School

Summer Term 2011

Support Began: Jan 2011

Name: Michael Davies

Supported by: Margaret Ross

### Behaviour Support Plan

(School Action) Action Plus

Review date: July 2011

Class: Year 9

**Targets**

1. To come into class without disturbing others
2. To work in a group with peers and remain on task for 20 minutes

Signed: P Smith (teacher) M Davies (pupil) T Davies (parent)

*An example of a behaviour support plan. Is the format different in your school?*

## Provide feedback to relevant people on progress made by children and young people with behaviour support plans

If you have pupils in your school who have specific behavioural difficulties, they should be invited to review their behaviour and any targets they have on a regular basis. This will give them the opportunity to think about and discuss the impact of what they do. If you are involved in reviews with pupils, you should know them well and they should be comfortable working with you. Your role, when reviewing behaviour, will be to encourage pupils to think about what they have done and the consequences of their actions for themselves and for others. This will be in relation to the impact their behaviour has had on themselves and others, and on their learning and achievement. When reviewing targets and asking children about their progress, you will need to be sensitive in the way you approach them and the kind of questioning you use. It is likely that other members of staff and the child's parents will also be involved and that the review will also feed in to developing new targets if necessary.

## Contribute to reviews of behaviour policies and the effectiveness of rewards and sanctions

Evaluation of behaviour policies should be an ongoing process. What works one week with a child or group of children may not always work in another. You should work with the form teacher and other staff to evaluate the kinds of systems which are used within the class and the school as a whole.

## Provide feedback on the effectiveness of behaviour management strategies to inform policy review and development

Behaviour management strategies should be reviewed through careful monitoring of outcomes. You should also be involved in the **review of behaviour management**, which the school should undertake with all staff when reviewing the behaviour policy.

---

**CASE STUDY:** Reviewing behaviour support plans

Gill is working with Neil, a Year 7 pupil who has some social and emotional difficulties. His behaviour has improved slightly since having a support plan and this is reviewed every three weeks, which reminds everyone how he is managing. Just before the latest review is set to take place, Neil has a particularly bad day and his parents have to be called in to take him home.

- What impact will this have on the review?
- Should any different action be taken in your view?
- Outline how you would tackle this issue if you were Gill.

---

**CASE STUDY:** House points system

Hilden Secondary School has recently decided to implement a house points system in order to help promote positive behaviour in the school. Although behaviour is not a serious issue in the school, the staff have decided that it is important to recognise when pupils are making special efforts with their behaviour. The programme has been running for two terms when there is a staff meeting to discuss how it is going. The whole-school staff are invited and are given the date well in advance.

- Why is this meeting important?
- What might it be helpful to do before the meeting?
- Why is it important to invite all members of staff?

## Check your knowledge

1. What policies will be relevant to managing pupil behaviour in school?

2. How does your school make pupils aware of school and class rules? Are these reviewed regularly and how?

3. Think about the ways in which you promote positive behaviour on a regular basis. How does this encourage pupils to behave appropriately?

4. Which of these might you use to manage unwanted behaviour?

   a) make eye contact with a child who is misbehaving

   b) send for additional help

   c) repeat instructions calmly to a pupil who is behaving inappropriately

   d) intervene early

   e) remove any items which the pupil is using to distract someone else

   f) move closer to a pupil who is misbehaving, for example, during assembly.

5. What are the names of other professionals who may be able to support pupils who have behaviour issues?

6. How can pupils be encouraged to discuss their behaviour and identify reasons for continued misdemeanours?

### Websites

**www.dcsf.gov.uk/everychildmatters** – Every Child Matters (Green Paper)

**www.nspcc.org.uk/pbb** – Information on NSPCC Educare programme to prevent bullying

**www.schoolcouncils.org** – School Councils UK

**www.teachernet.gov.uk/teachingandlearning/ socialandpastoral/seal_learning** – Teachernet, Social and Emotional Aspects of Learning (SEAL)

# School life

## My story: Amal

I started working at Maydene Secondary School as a learning mentor, working in Year 7. I am aware of the difficulties and concerns that pupils experience in the first term at their new school, so I was really keen to support the children as much as possible. Many of them come from backgrounds which had led to poor behaviour. I decided to set up a group at lunchtimes where they could come just to have a chat, and to be available every day. I use one of the classrooms and just call it my 'listening ear club', and they know that they can come and talk to me about anything which is worrying them. Over the last couple of terms I have helped to sort out a bullying issue, as well as helping a child who was under pressure at home as he was a carer for his mum, who is ill. As a result of what the children said, I also suggested to my line manager that we had a blitz on behaviour management for this year group, as many children did not seem to know school rules and staff have not been consistent in applying sanctions or rewards. This has been a big success, we have had staff meetings on behaviour management and reviewed our policy, which has led to an improvement in the school and on the playground. It has been great to be a part of this.

## Ask the expert

**Q** What can I do if there is one particular child who always seems to be getting into trouble?

**A** Make sure that you look out for times when the child is trying hard to do the right thing and praise them – in this way they will receive positive rather than negative attention.

### VIEWPOINT

This can be a problem, in particular if different adults apply different rules. Children need to be clear on boundaries and know what the consequences will be if they do not. Do you think there are behaviour issues in your school? How can you work closely with other staff to make sure that pupils know what is expected of them?

# TDA 3.5 Develop professional relationships with children, young people & adults

This unit looks at how you work with others in school and develop professional relationships with them. All five learning outcomes will need to be assessed in the workplace and your assessor will need to see you show how you meet them. However, much of the knowledge you will need for this unit will be found in TDA 3.1 Communication and professional relationships with children, young people and adults and will be cross-referenced to help you.

## By the end of this unit you will:

1. be able to develop professional relationships with children and young people

2. be able to communicate with children and young people

3. be able to develop professional relationships with adults

4. be able to support children and young people in developing relationships

5. be able to comply with policies and procedures for confidentiality, sharing information and data protection.

# Be able to develop professional relationships with children and young people

You may find it easy to explain why you work with children — usually this is because you find communication with them comes naturally to you. However, being able to develop professional relationships so that you can work effectively with pupils can sometimes prove more of a challenge, particularly if the child or group with whom you are working has particular needs or issues which make communication difficult.

## Establish trusting relationships with children and young people and demonstrate supportive responses to their questions

### Link

See TDA 3.1 for more on communication with children.

You will need to ensure that whenever you communicate with children and young people, you are actively listening to what they are saying. In busy situations adults can have a tendency to speak to pupils without doing this, which may make the pupil feel that what they are saying is not valued. Responding appropriately to children and young people reinforces self-esteem, values what they are saying and is a crucial part of building relationships. Making conversation and finding out the answer to questions also builds on the language skills that are vital to a pupil's learning.

Children of all ages need to feel that they are heard. This is particularly true if they have concerns or are distressed about something. You may need to reflect on how you do this and the opportunities you give pupils to talk.

## Support children and young people in making choices for themselves

An important part of learning is for children to learn to make choices for themselves. In the earliest stages of school, making choices is part of the curriculum and they are given opportunities to practise this in their selection of play activities. They are encouraged to have some control within the boundaries of the setting. As they become older, pupils should continue to be encouraged to participate in decision making. This is because a strict and authoritarian structure is likely to cause problems later on, as children will become frustrated by constantly being told what to do. One strategy which is often used with children is discussing targets for work and behaviour and involving them in setting their own, so that targets are not imposed on them without their involvement. Another strategy, which is regularly used with older pupils, is the use of school councils. These work very effectively in encouraging pupils to think about and discuss different sides of an issue and then come to a decision which will then be adopted by the school.

---

**CASE STUDY:** Supporting children's concerns

Marion works with a Year 9 group each morning, supporting learners who are on an intervention programme for English. One day she was approached by Megan, who asked if she could speak to her about something. Marion noticed that she looked upset and not her usual self. She had to rush off to a meeting with the English teacher at lunchtime so told Megan that she would see her after lunch. The meeting went on longer than she thought and then Marion had to prepare resources for an art lesson. She only remembered that she had promised to talk with Megan in the middle of the afternoon.

- What should Marion have done?
- Is there anything she can do now to resolve the issue?

It is the beginning of the new school year. The form teacher and yourself need to speak to the new class about the kind of behaviour you expect to see in the class. You have decided that you will involve the pupils in discussing a set of rules.

- Why might this be a worthwhile exercise?
- What support would you need to give the pupils?
- Have you been involved in similar activities in your own school?

## Give attention to individual children and young people in a way that is fair to them and the group

When you are working with groups of children and young people, you may find it difficult to balance the needs of individuals with those of the group. This will be because often children seem to require different levels of attention: some may be able to work and organise themselves independently, whereas others may need the reassurance of an adult. You will need to arrange the position of different pupils in the group, as well as your own, so that you are able to give this reassurance at times just by your physical nearness. If you encourage pupils to work and make decisions for themselves, they will not need as much adult support and will have more confidence.

**BEST PRACTICE CHECKLIST:** Giving attention to individual pupils

- Encourage all pupils to put forward their own ideas.
- Know the names of all pupils.
- Acknowledge that some pupils will have strengths in a particular area and encourage this.
- Know the needs of all pupils (for example, any special educational needs).
- Enable pupils to express themselves in different ways — for example, through creative activities.
- Sit close to pupils who need more reassurance.
- Be sympathetic if individuals find some things difficult.

# Be able to communicate with children and young people

## Forms of communication to meet the needs of children and young people

It is likely that you will use different forms of communication with pupils on a regular basis. Although spoken language will be appropriate for most children and young people, in school we often need to use body language and gestures to get our point across. This is particularly true in situations where a teaching assistant needs to communicate with a pupil from the other side of the classroom — for example, through making eye contact with them and raising their eyebrows to let them know they have seen them talking! In order to communicate with learners, you may find that in some cases you will need to go for additional training — if a pupil who you support uses British Sign Language or Braille, for example, or uses electronic methods of communication. You may also need to speak to the class teacher or SENCO (Special Educational Needs Co-ordinator) if you have concerns about a particular pupil around issues of communication; even if speech is the most appropriate form of communication, some pupils may have speech and language difficulties and need additional support.

**CASE STUDY:** Using appropriate communication methods

Matthew is working as an individual support assistant in Year 7 for Jessica, who has a range of learning difficulties. Although Matthew is very experienced, because of the range of Jessica's needs, he feels that he is finding it difficult to communicate effectively with her. He has spoken to the SENCO who has given him some ideas, but Matthew still does not feel equipped to support Jessica as effectively as he might.

- Is there anything else Matthew could do?
- Where else might he go for help?

## How to adapt communication

You will need to demonstrate how to adapt communication with children and young people for:

- the age and stage of development of the child or young person
- the context of the communication
- communication differences.

**Link**

See TDA 3.1 for more on communication with children.

## Strategies to promote understanding and trust in communication

As well as building positive relationships with children, you can promote understanding and trust with them in other ways. Where miscommunication occurs, it can affect their confidence and this can be difficult to restore. Strategies and techniques to promote understanding and trust in communication include, for example:

- active listening
- avoiding assumptions
- using questions to clarify and check understanding
- summarising and confirming key points.

### Active listening
You need to show that you are interested in what pupils are saying and that you are actively listening.

It is very frustrating when we are talking to another person and find that they are not listening and we need to repeat what we have said. We can also show that we are listening through the use of body language and the amount of interest we display, including how we respond. It is important for children to gain the approval of adults and most will respond better to a member of staff who is taking the time to listen to them. This also means that pupils are more likely to talk to staff and confide in them if there is anything wrong.

### Avoiding assumptions
You should always ensure that you do not make assumptions when you are speaking to children and young people, as this can cause misunderstandings and sometimes confusion. This means that you should not assume that they know what you are referring to or what you mean when you are speaking to them.

### Using questions to clarify and check understanding
You should always use questions to check that pupils understand key points and know what they are required to do. It also helps if you avoid asking closed questions which require 'yes' or 'no' answers in order to encourage children and young people to respond in more depth.

**CASE STUDY: Using questions to check understanding**

Vijay is in Year 9 and has been in school for six months. He did not speak English when he started in the school, but has picked up quite a lot and is managing well. The teacher has just given the class a complicated list of things to do at the beginning of the session and you notice that Vijay seems unsure what to do and is looking worried.

- Why is it important that you go and speak to Vijay?
- What strategies could you use to help him and others in the class to check their understanding?

## Summarising and confirming key points
It is always worth repeating and summarising key teaching points to pupils when you are working with them, in case they have not picked them up. When giving children and young people instructions, go over what they need to do or ask them to do it for you. In this way you can be sure that they have understood the requirements of the task.

## Making sure you carry out anything you say you will
You should always follow up on anything which you tell learners is going to happen. This may range from telling a teacher about something good or disappointing that a pupil has done to remembering that you said you would pick up their PE kit that their parent has left in the office.

## Being sympathetic and responding to children's needs
You should always take time to make sure that you listen and respond to pupils appropriately when they are speaking to you. In this way you will develop trust and they will feel that you are approachable and be more likely to want to speak to you.

# Be able to develop professional relationships with adults

## Establish rapport and professional relationships

When working with other adults, whether this is within or outside the school environment, you will need to be able to work in an environment of mutual support and openness. In school surroundings you will not be able to work independently of others, nor would it be practicable to do so. Although you will need to maintain your professionalism in a school environment, you should also be able to support other adults in a practical and sensitive way.

The support you will be required to give other adults will be on several levels (which you can remember with the acronym PIPE).

- **Practical:** You may be working with others who are unfamiliar with the classroom or school surroundings and need to have help or advice with finding or using equipment and resources.

- **Informative:** You may need to give support to those who do not have information about a particular situation. Alternatively, you may be asked to prepare and write reports about specific pupils.

- **Professional:** You may be in a position to support or help others with issues such as planning, or you may be asked whether others can observe your work with pupils or discuss your work with them.

- **Emotional:** It is important to support others through day-to-day events and retain a sense of humour!

The school should also support and encourage good lines of communication between all staff as this is one of the most effective ways of maintaining positive working relationships.

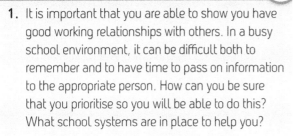

**BEST PRACTICE CHECKLIST:** Establishing and maintaining professional relationships

- Remain professional in the school environment and when communicating with other professionals in contact with the school.
- Treat others with respect.
- Notice the efforts and achievements of others.
- Give practical support where needed.
- Avoid speaking about others in a negative way such as gossiping.

### Getting ready for assessment

1. It is important that you are able to show you have good working relationships with others. In a busy school environment, it can be difficult both to remember and to have time to pass on information to the appropriate person. How can you be sure that you prioritise so you will be able to do this? What school systems are in place to help you?

2. Think about the range of adults and pupils with whom you come into contact as part of your role. Show how you demonstrate to pupils the value and importance of having positive relationships with others, and of respecting individuality, and how this is promoted in your school setting.

3. Outline any areas of conflict between adults which you have experienced during the course of your professional work in school. How have these been resolved? (You will need to remove names or have a professional discussion with your assessor about this so that they do not appear in your portfolio.) Have they helped you to deal with any issues between children as they arise?

4. At level 3, you should be able to be involved in planning alongside teachers and in putting forward your own ideas. How will this kind of activity help to promote positive professional relationships and clear communication? Why is this so important?

## How to adapt communication for cultural/social differences, context and communication differences

### Cultural and social differences

It is likely that you will be aware of any cultural or social differences when communicating with adults and will adapt how you speak to them accordingly. However, there may also be school policies in place where you have a large number of parents who are from a particular culture or speak English as an additional language, and you will have support and guidance from your local authority as to how you might adapt your communication skills accordingly.

You may also find that there are social differences in the way in which some individuals approach certain situations. Where this occurs, you will need to make sure that you respect the views of others.

### The context of the communication

You will adapt your communication skills to the context of the communication when you change the way in which you communicate according to the situation. This may simply mean formal or informal verbal communication, but could also be through other means, for example, written — emails, letters, newsletters, notices and so on. You should ensure that however you communicate, the information is accessible to all those for whom it is intended.

**CASE STUDY:** Context of communication

Pete is setting up an after-school football club for children in Year 7. He has sent letters out to parents both through teachers and via 'parentmail', which is the school email system. However, several parents have complained to the school office that they have not seen the letters. Two pupils were away when the letters were given out. Several children and their parents speak English as an additional language and do not always understand the letters sent from school. As a consequence several children missed the chance to join the club.

- What could Pete have done to ensure that everyone was given a letter?
- How else could he ensure that others for whom English is a second language are able to access communications like this, so that children are not excluded?

## Strategies to promote understanding and trust in communication

Understanding and trust for others is a crucial part of being able to have a positive relationship with them. We cannot do this unless we value others, respect their views and show that we do this. We can do this in a number of ways.

● Actively listen to all adults and let them put their ideas forward – encourage discussion.

● Avoid assumptions about adults, particularly if you know little about them or their backgrounds.

● Find out how individuals like to be addressed and then speak to them in the correct way – for example, Ms Malone, Miss Matharu.

● Use questions to clarify and check understanding when this is unclear.

● Summarise and confirm key points when you have finished speaking to adults to ensure that you are clear on what has been said.

It is important for you to remember that we are all individuals and that you should not expect others to share the same ideas.

## Use skills to resolve misunderstandings and conflicts constructively

Often areas of conflict occur when communication has not been effective. This may be because information has not been passed on or because of a misunderstanding. The best way to resolve areas of poor communication is to discuss them to establish the cause and then find a way forward together. The important thing is not to ignore the problem or talk about it to anyone except the individual or group of people concerned.

**Link**

See TDA 3.1, Communication and professional relationships with children, young people and adults for more on resolving misunderstandings and conflicts.

## When and how to refer others to further sources of information, advice or support

You may find that you need to refer other adults to further sources of information, advice or support. This may be because you work with an individual child and regularly meet with parents, or you are a family support worker and are more regularly asked for advice. You should ensure that you maintain your professionalism and that you are passing on the correct information. If you are at all unsure you will need to say so, or let them know that you will find out and then get back to them. There are a number

**CASE STUDY:** Developing understanding and trust with others

A new learning support assistant in your school, Mary, has come to speak to you because she has had a disagreement with a physiotherapist who has come to visit one of the pupils. She tells you that the physio has given her a long list of exercises to do with the child and that she does not have time to do this and has told the physio so. Moreover, she says that the physio became unhappy when Mary got her name wrong and addressed her incorrectly. Mary says that it is enough to try to remember the names of all the pupils and she should not be expected to learn longwinded surnames of everyone who comes into school.

• What issues need to be considered here?
• What might you say to Mary?
• Should you speak to anyone else about this?

of social services which may be able to help in different situations. If at all unclear, you should speak to your SENCO or another member of the Senior Management Team.

---

**CASE STUDY:** Referring other adults for further support or advice

Linda is working with Raoul, who has **global developmental delay**. His mother also has some special needs. Linda has been working with Raoul for a term when she is approached by his mother. She asks Linda to help her as she wants to take him to swimming lessons, but does not know how to go about it. She tries to give Linda some money and asks her whether she can arrange the lessons for her son. She has sought Linda's help on other occasions too and is often outside the classroom during lesson time or looking through the lost property. She has also asked Linda to do some shopping for her and has asked her to come to the house.

- Should Linda help Raoul's mother in this way?
- Where else could Linda seek help or find out how to support her?

---

**Key term**

**Global developmental delay** — a brain disorder where an individual may struggle with, for example, speech and fine/gross motor skills

# Be able to support children and young people in developing relationships

## Help children and young people to understand the value of positive relationships

As adults working with children and young people, we need to help them to understand the value

and importance of positive relationships. Children will learn about this over time in different ways in school. They will be encouraged to work in pairs, groups and as a class to listen to one another and acknowledge ideas. They will learn to think of others and have respect for others' feelings. They will also find out how positive relationships with others will enhance what they do. By observing our interactions with children and young people and other adults, they should be able to see the effects that positive relationships with others have.

## Provide an effective role model in own relationships

As adults, we need to show children how to get along with one another and model the kind of behaviour we expect from them. If we are able to show them that we value and respect others, they are much more likely to learn to do the same. You should be consistent in your behaviour and relationships so that children learn to do this.

Having positive relationships with others is also important because we will be more likely to communicate information to one another. Parents and other professionals who come into the school will be more likely to offer support if communication is strong and effective. This will in turn benefit the children.

## Encourage children to respect individuality, diversity, feelings and points of view

It is important that schools encourage pupils to learn to value and embrace diversity and individuality. The learning environment should be one in which all cultures, ages and personalities are valued and respected. Often as pupils become older and form friendship groups, they can become nervous about being different and standing up for what they think. Adults need to encourage them to speak confidently and listen to what they have to say.

## CASE STUDY: Respecting others' individuality

It is lunchtime and you are in the dining hall with children from Year 7. You notice that some pupils are huddled around a boy who is not eating. When you go over to find out what is happening, he tells you that he is fasting because it is Ramadan. The other children ask you what this means and why he cannot have any lunch.

- How would you deal with this in the short term?
- Why should you follow this up, and how would you do this?
- What procedures does your school have in place for supporting children who celebrate different religious festivals?

It is important for children to learn to understand and respect the feelings of others. We often speak to them in school about thinking through the consequences of their actions and how they might have affected others. Through the **PSHE** curriculum, visiting speakers, stories, assemblies and role plays we might encourage them to consider the feelings of others.

Children also need to be able to understand how their own feelings might affect their behaviour and you may need to talk to them about this. For example, saying to a child 'I know you are upset because you could not take part in PE today' will help them to make the link between emotion and behaviour. In this way, they will be more able to understand how to think about others.

One effective way of encouraging children to understand and respect the feelings of others is through discussion and activities such as 'hot seating'. Children will benefit from talking through issues as they occur. A whole-class forum is often a good way of doing this.

### Key term

**PSHE** – personal, social, health and economic (PSHE) education

*As you spend more time with pupils, you will get to know their personalities and backgrounds.*

Strategies such as restorative justice programmes are also popular in schools. These are taken from the criminal justice system and have worked well as a method of resolving behaviour issues and learning from what happens. Table 1 below, taken from the Transforming Conflict website, an organisation which promotes restorative justice, shows how you can encourage and support pupils as they learn to understand how their behaviour affects others.

**Portfolio activity**

Write a reflective account of the different ways in which your school supports the development of positive relationships between children.

- How have you been involved?
- What kinds of activities does the school encourage and have you seen benefits of this way of working?

If you have had any specific training, you should also mention this.

**Functional skills**

ICT: Developing, presenting and communicating information
Once you have written your reflective account, you could present your account in the form of an idea-sharing presentation using PowerPoint®. This would give you the opportunity to gather tips from each of your peers to support you in your role.

## Encourage children and young people to deal with conflict for themselves

Conflicting points of view and ideas will be a natural outcome of encouraging children and young people's individuality. We all have our own thoughts and feelings, and children and young people need to learn how to deal with this. They will also have to learn what behaviour is acceptable in the school environment, and be able to listen to and respect the thoughts of others. Children and young people should be encouraged to

| Retributive justice | Restorative justice |
| --- | --- |
| Negative behaviour is 'breaking the rules' | Negative behaviour is adversely affecting others |
| Focus on blame/guilt/who was the culprit | Focus on problem solving and expressing needs and feelings |
| Adversarial relationships | Dialogue and negotiation |
| Imposition of pain/unpleasantness to punish and deter | Restitution leading to reconciliation |
| Attention to rules | Attention to relationships |
| Conflict represented as impersonal and abstract | Conflict identified as interpersonal with value for learning |
| One social injury replaced by another | Focus on repair of social injury |
| School community as spectators | School community involved in facilitation |
| People affected by behaviour are not necessarily involved | Encouragement of all concerned to be involved |
| Accountability defined in terms of punishment | Accountability defined as understanding the impact of the action |

Source: www.transformingconflict.org – restorative justice in schools.
Table 1: Retributive justice versus restorative justice.

have discussions and debates around different points of view, as this will give them perspectives other than their own. Learning to talk through and resolve issues themselves will give them a valuable skill.

## When you should intervene

You will need to recognise that adults should not always intervene when there are areas of conflict and that if we want children to learn to resolve issues, we need to give them opportunities to do so. The best strategy is for them to discuss or negotiate issues themselves. However, there are times when you need to intervene and speak to pupils, for example, if at any time they become aggressive or unkind to others.

Children who are immature or have emotional and social difficulties may find it more difficult to put themselves in the place of others. You may need to point out the rights of others and the importance of considering others' views.

If children have specific needs or abilities, for example, if they are autistic, they may find empathy with others very difficult. You will need to adapt how you respond in order to support them and you may need to ask for specialist advice. Where pupils have limited understanding due to their needs, it may be more difficult to explain to them and you may have to speak to them sensitively to resolve conflict.

**CASE STUDY:** Encouraging children to solve conflict themselves

You are working close to a group of Year 8 pupils who are carrying out an investigative activity. They have to investigate ways that light is reflected. The children have started well but are now arguing about the best method they can use to measure the results of their investigation. You are observing them and decide to wait and see whether they are able to resolve the argument themselves. After some time, one of them suggests that they use a protractor to measure the angles of the light rays, as this will give more accurate angles.

- Do you think that this is the best outcome?
- Would the children have benefited from adult intervention? If so, how?

## Encourage other adults to have positive relationships with children and young people

It is very important for you to support positive relationships between children and other adults in the

*How can you encourage children to consider the feelings and needs of others?*

setting. You are in a position in which children will notice and take their lead from your behaviour and the way in which you relate to others. If they see adults modelling negative behaviour and comments, they will learn to think that this is acceptable. You should always make it clear that you have positive views about others when working with them.

---

**CASE STUDY:** Supporting other adults to have positive relationships with children

You are working to support Year 9 groups during their maths lessons. On one afternoon each week the teacher has planning, preparation and assessment (PPA) time and the children have another teacher, Mr Clarke, who does part-time supply work at the school. Although the class like Mr Clarke, you have noticed that some of them are making negative comments about him and this has started to affect their behaviour during the afternoon session.

- Is there anything you can do to support the teacher both in the session and outside it?
- Why is it important to try to keep the relationship positive?

---

# Be able to comply with policies and procedures for confidentiality, sharing information and data protection

## Apply the setting's policies and procedures for sharing information, confidentiality and data protection

Schools need to keep and use information only for the purpose for which it was intended, to comply with the Data Protection Act 1998. They also need to keep information securely. You should consider all information about pupils as confidential and ensure that you do not share it with others without parental consent. When discussing pupils with others, you should take care to ensure that you only share necessary information.

---

**Link**

See TDA 3.2, Schools as organisations, for more on confidentiality and data protection.

---

## How to report and record information formally and informally

There will be a number of different ways in which you will record information in school, both formally and informally. If you are keeping school records on a child for any reason, you will need to follow school policy for the formal recording and storage of information. You may also need to report to others on something which has happened, for example, on the playground, if information needs to be passed on quickly. However, you must make sure that you also have a formal record and that information is also passed to parents.

---

**CASE STUDY:** Recording and reporting information

Melanie is a teaching assistant supporting pupils in Year 8. One of the children in Year 7 has fallen during lunchbreak and cut her head. Melanie observed the accident; she reports and records the incident in three ways.

1. She takes the child straight to the first aider and tells them what has happened.
2. She writes the incident in the Accident Book so that there is a record in school.
3. She fills in a form with details for the parents and gives it to the child to take home.

- Is there anything else which Melanie could do?
- Why is it important to follow school procedure in this situation?

---

**Knowledge into action**

Find out about your school's systems for recording and storing information, and the responsibilities of staff. When your assessor comes into school, show them examples of any records which you have updated.

## Functional skills

### ICT: Using ICT

It is important to remember that any electronic records that contain confidential information should be password protected. It is important to keep a password as strong as possible. You can do this by ensuring the password contains lowercase letters, uppercase letters and numbers.

## Getting ready for assessment

In order to gather evidence for this unit, you will need to demonstrate how you develop professional relationships with children, young people and adults. Learning outcomes will need to be assessed in the workplace and you should encourage your assessor both to observe you working with others and to interview witnesses who will verify your positive relationships with adults and children. Make sure you set up plenty of opportunities for this to be observed, both formally in the classroom or in a meeting, and informally — for example, in the staffroom during break.

### Websites

**www.direct.gov.uk** – you can find more on the Data Protection Act 1998 here

**www.transformingconflict.org** – Transforming Conflict

## Check your knowledge

1. Give three examples of how you might establish trusting relationships with children and young people.

2. How can we show as adults that we are supportive and respectful of children's questions, ideas and concerns?

3. What can we do to balance the needs of all children when working with them as a group?

4. Which of the following are strategies to promote understanding and trust in communication with children?
   a) active listening
   b) talking to their parents every day
   c) questioning them to check their understanding
   d) being sympathetic to their needs.

5. Give two examples of how you might support other adults in school.

6. What are the main sources of conflict between adults? Give two ways in which you might go about resolving these.

7. Give three ways in which you might demonstrate to children that you are an effective role model.

8. How can you encourage pupils to deal with conflict for themselves?

9. Where would you find your school's policy for confidentiality and data protection?

# School life

## My story: Sandy

I am new at the school and have been put in a class with a real 'old school' teaching assistant. She has been here for ages and thinks she knows it all. I like her, but whenever we talk she seems to think I don't know anything about children and she can be really patronising. I have talked to other TAs about it and they have told me to ignore her and just get on with my job.

## My story: Lynne

I came to my school a long time ago when my children were small – I think it's about 23 years now. I have always really enjoyed my work with the children and like to think that there are a lot of people in school that I get along with. However, recently a few people left that I have been quite close to and some new people came to the school this term. They all have new qualifications (I have never bothered with those as I have plenty of experience which I think counts for a lot) and seem to think that they know better than me as a result. I am starting to feel really uncomfortable in the staffroom as they are always in there and when I walk in it goes quiet.

## Ask the expert

**Q** How can we get along?

**A** These two members of staff want to get on with each other, but each has their own preconceived ideas about the other. They have not tried talking through how they feel and this is likely to continue to be a difficult working relationship unless they do. In this type of situation it is important to think about things from the other person's point of view and try to work together, as it is unlikely that the children will benefit from this kind of animosity among the adults who work with them.

**VIEWPOINT**

How else can this be resolved? Think about what else could be done by other members of staff and by Lynne and Sandy to help them to work together in the best interests of the children.

# TDA 3.6 Promote equality, diversity & inclusion in work with children & young people

You should be aware of national legislation and codes of practice relevant to your work with children and the importance of ensuring that all pupils have equal access to the curriculum. You need to understand the impact of prejudice and discrimination and actively encourage and demonstrate positive relationships within school. When your assessor comes into school, you will need to show that you promote equality and diversity through your work and the way in which you interact with children.

## By the end of this unit you will:

1. be able to promote equality and diversity in work with children and young people

2. understand the impact of prejudice and discrimination on children and young people

3. be able to support inclusion and inclusive practices in work with children and young people.

# Be able to promote equality and diversity in work with children and young people

## Current legislation and codes of practice

Areas of legislation are ever-changing but it is important to be able to identify current and relevant aspects of those which promote equality and value diversity. You are not expected to know the details of each but should be able to identify their main points and their relevance to the school environment, and show that you are aware of them in your practice.

### Every Child Matters 2003 and Children Act 2004

These were put into place to ensure that all organisations and agencies involved with children between birth and 19 years should work together to ensure that children have the support needed to be healthy, stay safe, enjoy and achieve, make a positive contribution and achieve economic well-being. The acronym SHEEP can help you to remember this:

- **S**tay safe
- **H**ealthy
- **E**njoy and achieve
- **E**conomic well-being
- **P**ositive contribution.

### Functional skills

**ICT: Developing, presenting and communicating information**
The Every Child Matters framework lends itself to being converted into a poster that could be displayed within your setting. This also provides a good opportunity to practise a range of different layout techniques including text, images and other digital content.

Following the Every Child Matters framework, the Children Act 2004 required that these recommendations become a legal requirement. The key aspect of the Act was to overhaul child protection and children's services in the UK. Every Child Matters has been further developed through the publication of the Children's Plan 2007 which sets out to improve educational outcomes for all children.

### Link

See also CYP 3.3, Understand how to safeguard the well-being of children and young people.

### Race Relations Act 1976 and 2000

The Race Relations Act places a statutory duty on schools to promote race equality. It makes it against the law for a person to be discriminated against, whether directly or indirectly. Schools are expected to improve the educational achievements of all children and to promote equal opportunities and good relations between different racial groups. Schools are also required to have a race equality policy which is linked to an action plan.

### Disability Discrimination Act 1995 and 2005

This made it illegal for services such as shops and employers to discriminate against disabled people. According to the Disability Discrimination Act, a person has a disability if 'he [or she] has a physical or mental impairment which has a substantial and long-term adverse effect on his [or her] ability to carry out normal day-to-day activities'. It is now a statutory requirement to encourage the inclusion of children with disabilities into mainstream schools.

The Disability and Discrimination Act 2005 builds on the 1995 Act by requiring all schools to produce a Disability Equality Scheme. The DES must set out ways that schools promote equality of opportunity and promote positive attitudes towards pupils, staff and others who are disabled. In addition, there must also be an Accessibility Plan in place which identifies how the school will increase access to the curriculum, improve the physical environment and provide information in a range of ways to meet the needs of individuals with a disability.

### SEN Code of Practice 2001

The Special Educational Needs and Disability Act 2001 (SENDA) strengthened the rights of parents and SEN children to a mainstream education. It made significant changes to the educational opportunities that are available to children with disabilities and special educational needs. This means that it is more likely for these children to be in mainstream schools.

| Inclusion | Separation |
|---|---|
| Equality – all children receive the support they need to build on and achieve their potential | 'Special' or different treatment |
| Learning assertiveness | Learning helplessness |
| Participation of all | Participation of some |
| Involves all members of society | Builds barriers in society |

*Table 1: Advantages of inclusive education.*
(Source: Disability Equality in Education)

## Human Rights Act 1998

The United Nations first set a standard on human rights in 1948 with the Universal Declaration of Human Rights. This was accepted by many countries around the world and highlighted the principle that all humans have the same rights and should be treated equally. In 1998 the Human Rights Act gave a further legal status to this. Your basic human rights are:

- the right to life
- freedom from torture and degrading treatment
- freedom from slavery and forced labour
- the right to liberty
- the right to a fair trial
- the right not to be punished for something that wasn't a crime when you did it
- the right to respect for private and family life
- freedom of thought, conscience and religion, and freedom to express your beliefs
- freedom of expression
- freedom of assembly and association
- the right to marry and to start a family
- the right not to be discriminated against in respect of these rights and freedoms
- the right to peaceful enjoyment of your property
- the right to an education
- the right to participate in free elections
- the right not to be subjected to the death penalty.

*(Source: Direct.gov.uk – Human Rights Act)*

## UN Convention on the Rights of the Child 1989

The UK signed this legally binding agreement in 1990. It leads on from the Human Rights Act and sets out the rights of all children to be treated equally and fairly and without discrimination. (For more on this Act, see CYP 3.4 Support children and young people's health and safety.)

### Over to you!

Choose one area of legislation and show in more detail the impact it has had on provision available for pupils in schools.

### Functional skills

**ICT: Finding and selecting information**
Completing this task may require you to research legislation on the Internet. Try using various search engines to expand results. Remember to check the validity, authenticity and currency of the information you are using. For instance, government sites (.gov) or educational sites (.edu or .ac) will be more reliable.

## The importance of promoting the rights to participation and equality of access

All pupils should be able to fully access all areas of the curriculum. The advent of the Every Child Matters framework and the focus on personalised learning in all sectors of education has also made this high on the agenda. The reasons for this are:

- human rights
  - all children have a right to learn and play together
  - children should not be discriminated against for any reason
  - **inclusion** is concerned with improving schools for staff as well as pupils

### Key term

**Inclusion** – the right for all children to participate fully in the curriculum

- equal opportunities in education
  - children and young people do better in inclusive settings, both academically and socially
  - children and young people should not need to be separated to achieve adequate educational provision
  - inclusive education is a more efficient use of educational resources
- social opportunities
  - inclusion in education is one aspect of inclusion in society
  - children need to be involved and integrated with all of their peers.

All schools should have codes of practice and policies around equal opportunities and inclusion. These sometimes form part of the policy for special educational needs but are usually separate. You should be familiar with these policies and know where to find them in school.

## Functional skills

### English: Reading

You could locate and read the codes of practice and policies around equal opportunities and inclusion for your setting, and then compare them against the policy for special educational needs. Not only will this comparison highlight the relationships between the policies, but it will also give you a good opportunity to develop your reading skills further.

Always be aware of the needs of different pupils, whatever these may be. Remember that these may become more apparent as you get to know particular pupils. Those who may be vulnerable could include pupils:

- who have special educational needs (SEN)
- who speak English as an additional language
- who are new to the school
- who are gifted and talented
- whose culture or ethnicity is different from the predominant culture of the school
- who are in foster care
- whose parents' views are not consistent with those of the school.

## Reflect

- What can you say about inclusion in your school?
- How effective is it, in your experience?
- Do you think that its advantages outweigh any disadvantages that you can identify?

## The importance and benefits of valuing and promoting cultural diversity

Schools will all be aware of the importance of valuing and promoting cultural diversity. Most will actively include a number of strategies to ensure that children from all cultures feel welcome in school. These may be:

- 'Welcome' displayed in a variety of languages in the entrance hall, and other signs in different areas of the school
- other languages spoken in different lessons or during registration
- festivals and celebrations from other cultures discussed and explored
- representations from other cultures found in books and learning resources, and displayed around the school
- parents involved in 'finding out' sessions with children.

Measures such as these will have a number of benefits for children and young people — mainly that they will grow up in an environment which values cultural diversity and enables us to learn from one another. Children and young people will also become used to finding out about other cultures and belief systems from an early age. In this way they will not grow up thinking that their own and their family's culture is the same as everyone else's.

Children from all backgrounds need to know that their culture and status is valued as this helps them to feel settled and secure; this in turn contributes to their being able to learn. If they feel isolated or anxious, it is more likely that learning will be difficult for them.

## CASE STUDY: Valuing and promoting cultural diversity

In their food technology class, Year 9 are working in groups to plan suitable dishes to be offered in a local cafe which will appeal to individuals from a range of cultures. One of the pupils mentions that his father is a chef and uses recipes from India which have been passed down through the family. The teacher invites the parent, Mr Chaudhry, to the school to demonstrate a dish. The teacher arranges an Indian afternoon and displays paintings, clothes, artefacts and photographs and other recipes from India to facilitate discussion about Indian culture.

- In what ways will this be beneficial to the children?
- How might the class extend what they have learned during the afternoon?

## Interact in a way that values diversity and respects differences

You should always ensure that when interacting with children, you value diversity and respect their backgrounds and beliefs. Children and young people will quickly pick up on any discriminatory comments or opinions in the school environment. You should also be aware that your own thoughts and opinions have been shaped by your experiences and background — self-awareness of your own values and beliefs is an important part of your work with others. Make sure that you react and respond to children appropriately at all times.

### Reflect

Consider and discuss how you feel about:

- the movement of several traveller families into the school catchment area
- the request from a parent of a Muslim child that she fasts during Ramadan
- a Catholic pupil who is not allowed to eat any meat on Ash Wednesday
- a request from a Sikh parent that her child is able to wear his Kara (a bangle) at all times, including during PE lessons.

*How can you actively value and respect the diversity of the children you work with?*

## Ways of applying the principles of equality, diversity and anti-discriminatory practice

This assessment criterion will need to be assessed in the workplace.

You will need to be able to show how you apply these principles within your day-to-day practice in school, so that all children are included in all aspects of school life. When working with pupils who have additional needs, you may need to ensure that they have equal opportunities to others in a number of ways, which may include:

- adapting and modifying learning materials for them so that they can fully access the curriculum.

- using additional resources or specific equipment such as new technologies

- going for specific training – this may be learning to sign or use Makaton or PECS (Picture Exchange Communication System, relating to autism), or how to use a Braille machine

- giving them extra time to complete tasks if required

- adapting assessment methods or giving additional time

- working with them on intervention programmes.

**Anti-discriminatory practice** forms the basis of an environment in which there is no discrimination towards individuals on the basis of race, ability, gender, culture or ethnicity. No children should be the victims of discrimination and fair treatment should be given to all individuals. The term 'inclusion' is often used when referring to children who have special educational needs, but it is also used in a wider sense to describe equal opportunities for all in the learning environment. It is through the development of trust and positive relationships that children will learn to respect one another. You can apply the principles of anti-discriminatory practice through the way in which you form relationships in school, both with adults and children, and through acting as a role model at all times. However, you should also challenge any discriminatory comments or behaviour made by others.

*What sort of support will children with special educational needs require?*

# Understand the impact of prejudice and discrimination on children and young people

## Ways in which children and young people can experience prejudice and discrimination

There are many ways in which children can experience prejudice and discrimination in school. There are so many pressures on children to fit in and to conform with expected appearances and behaviour that they may be discriminated against and bullied if they do not. Staff in schools need to be vigilant to ensure that children respect and embrace diversity. Children can experience prejudice and discrimination in the same way as adults due to race, religion, age, sex, culture or ethnicity.

In particular look out for:

- comments about a child's appearance or clothes

- children not interacting with others who may be 'different'

- children being excluded because they are boys or girls

- children only socialising with others of the same race or ethnicity.

## The impact of prejudice and discrimination

Although it may sound obvious, an environment of prejudice and discrimination will have a very negative impact on children. Depending on how long it goes on and the form it takes, a negative atmosphere will have an effect on the following for a child.

### Self-esteem and social and emotional development

A child who is discriminated against for whatever reason will feel that they are not valued as a person and will start to lose confidence in themselves. This may mean that they start to withdraw socially, becoming less able to join in with activities with their peers, as they will not want to draw attention to themselves.

### Learning

A child who does not feel part of the class and their peer group due to discrimination or prejudice will not be happy and settled in school. This will mean that their learning will be affected and they will find it difficult to focus on their work.

## Relationships with others

A child who lacks confidence and who does not want to participate in activities with others as a result is likely to develop fewer positive relationships with their peers or with adults.

### Skills builder

Many secondary schools have a school council. Suggest ways to introduce the subject at a meeting. Think about and list ways that a school's council, or group of pupils, could become involved in reducing incidents of prejudice and discrimination.

## Evaluate how own attitudes, values and behaviour could impact on work

There is nothing wrong with having your own beliefs and values — everyone has them, and they are a vital part of making you the person you are. But you must be aware of them, and how they may affect what you do at work.

## How to promote anti-discriminatory practice in work

You must practise in an anti-discriminatory way with colleagues and pupils. Your day-to-day practice and attitudes are important in how effective your anti-discriminatory practice will be. You should be interested in learning about other people's lifestyles, cultures and needs. Finding ways of meeting individual needs can also contribute to job satisfaction.

## How to challenge discrimination

You must always challenge discrimination whenever you come across it and in many schools you will also need to record and report discriminatory behaviour and comments. Children will sometimes say things without understanding the implications, in particular if they have heard them said by others. It should be made clear to them that their comments are not acceptable and that everyone in school should be treated fairly and with respect.

*What effects does low self-esteem have?*

CASE STUDY: Challenging discrimination

Chris is working in an inner-city school which has very few children who are from white British backgrounds. Although the school has an inclusive policy and has a 'no tolerance' view on any form of discrimination, Chris has sometimes had to deal with some incidents of bullying and racial discrimination. On one occasion, a white child who was new to the school approached him and said that a group of girls told her that she could not go with them to the computer club because she was not 'one of them'.

- What should Chris do?
- What should he say to the group of girls?
- Should he follow up the incident in any way?

# Be able to support inclusion and inclusive practices in work with children and young people

## What is meant by inclusion and inclusive practices

As already identified, pupils all have an equal right to education and learning. Equal opportunities and inclusion should take account not only of access to provision on school premises, but also to facilities outside the school setting, for example, on school visits. Schools and other organisations that offer educational provision must by law ensure that all pupils have access to a broad and balanced curriculum. The school should ensure that inclusive practices are a matter of course within day-to-day provision and that any barriers to inclusion are identified and removed.

## Barriers to children and young people's participation

Barriers to participation may include:

- physical barriers – lack of access, equipment or resources

### Key term

Barriers to participation – anything that prevents the pupil participating fully in activities and experiences offered by the setting or service

- organisational barriers – school policies, lack of training, lack of diversity within the school curriculum

- attitudes within the school community – staff, parents, other pupils.

### Physical barriers

These include lack of equipment or resources which may be needed by the child to enable them to participate fully. Physical barriers may also be present in the school environment if it has not been properly adapted to cater for the needs of all pupils. Examples of these adaptations are ramps, disabled toilets, lifts for wheelchair users and hearing loops for hearing-impaired pupils. As a result of the amendments made to the Disability Discrimination Act in the Special Educational Needs and Disability Act 2001, all schools built from 2001 need to have physical access for all pupils.

### Organisational barriers

These mean that policies within the organisation have been not set up effectively to ensure that all pupils are included effectively. Reasons may be lack of training within the school, insufficient use of support which may be available or lack of understanding.

### Attitudes within the school community

There may be barriers within the attitudes of staff, parents, governors or other pupils. This means that they may hold views which are inconsistent with those of the school and which mean that pupils may be discriminated against. Attitudes such as these can mean that children become confused about the school's values, as they will be receiving conflicting messages. This may also give them a reason to behave in a way which the school does not agree with.

**CASE STUDY:** Barriers to participation

You support Charlotte, a wheelchair user, who is in Year 9. A residential trip has been arranged to an activity centre. You know that there are suitable facilities and that there are a range of activities which will include Charlotte. Following letters to parents, her father comes to the school and tells you that the visit will not be suitable for her as 'that kind of place doesn't cater for children like her'. You are concerned about the attitude of the parent and by the possibility that Charlotte may not be able to take part with her friends.

• What would you do?
• How can schools go about removing social barriers such as these if they exist?

## Ways of supporting inclusion and inclusive practices

This assessment criterion will need to be assessed in the workplace.

**Link**

See also TDA 3.5, Develop professional relationships with children, young people and adults.

You will need to be able to show that you support inclusion within your school and that you are committed to inclusive practices. This will principally affect your work with children but you should also be aware of it in your dealings with adults. Your school will in all likelihood already demonstrate positive policies for supporting inclusive practice, but you should know how it does this and what it means for the school community.

You can support inclusive practices by:

● knowing and following your school's inclusion or equal opportunities policy

● demonstrating positive relationships with all children and adults

● actively showing that you respect and value individuals through your day-to-day communication with them

● supporting pupils who have additional needs

● respecting individuality and encouraging pupils to do the same

● challenging any discrimination when it occurs.

### Knowing and following your school's inclusion or equal opportunities policy

You can show that you do this by reading and highlighting your school's policy and showing it to your assessor to demonstrate that you know and understand key points.

### Demonstrating positive relationships with all children and adults

You should be approachable and show sensitivity in your relationships with others, in particular if you notice something where others do not seem to be aware that there is anything wrong.

**CASE STUDY:** Supporting inclusive practice

Kwakye is a male teaching assistant in a secondary school. He enjoys his job and working with his female colleagues, and is a valued member of staff. However, you have noticed that he is often teased and almost bullied in the staff room by female colleagues. They often say that he is a man, so is unable to multitask, or that as a man he won't be able to deal with sensitive issues. You have noticed that lately he seems to be spending less and less time in the staffroom.

• Do you think that these kinds of comments matter?
• Would you say anything to Kwakye?
• Why is it important that these kinds of issues are addressed?

# Inclusion Policy

## Introduction

(To be read in conjunction with the following school policies: English as an Additional Language; Equal Opportunities; Gifted and Talented Children; Racial Equality; Special Educational Needs.)

In our vision for our school we talk about creating an attractive and exciting learning environment in which our children are stimulated to learn. Importance is placed on high self-esteem as we are committed to giving all of our children every opportunity to achieve the highest of standards. We do this by taking account of pupils' varied life experiences and needs. We offer a broad and balanced curriculum and have high expectations for all children. The achievements, attitudes and well being of all our children matter. This policy helps to ensure that this school promotes the individuality of all our children, irrespective of ethnicity, attainment, age, disability, gender or background.

## Aims and Objectives

Our school aims to be an inclusive school. We actively seek to remove the barriers to learning and participation that can hinder or exclude individual pupils, or groups of pupils. This means that equality of opportunity must be a reality for our children. We make this a reality through the attention we pay to the different groups of children within our school:

- girls and boys
- minority ethnic and faith groups
- children who need support to learn English as an additional language
- children with special educational needs
- gifted and talented children
- children who are at risk of disaffection or exclusion
- travellers and asylum seekers.

We offer a broad curriculum which meets the specific needs of individuals and groups of children. We meet these needs through:

- setting suitable learning challenges
- responding to children's diverse learning needs
- overcoming potential barriers to learning and assessment for individuals and groups of pupils
- providing other curricular opportunities outside the National Curriculum to meet the needs of individuals or groups of children (such as work-based learning, personal, social, health and economic education)
- working with other agencies to provide additional advice and support such as speech and language therapy and mobility training.

We achieve educational inclusion by continually reviewing what we do, through asking ourselves these key questions.

- Do all our children achieve their best?
- Are there differences in the achievement of different groups of children?
- What are we doing for those children who we know are not achieving their best?
- Are our actions effective?
- Are we successful in promoting racial harmony and preparing pupils to live in a diverse society?

*Part of a school's inclusion policy.*

## Actively showing that you respect and value individuals through your day-to-day communication with them

You should be self-aware and think about the impact your words and behaviour will have on others. This may be in your interactions but can also be through other forms of communication such as letters, emails, texts and notices. It may be that you say something which you had intended as a joke but which others might take to heart – it is better not to do it in the first place.

## Supporting pupils who have additional needs

You may need to do this through differentiating work, modifying materials and resources, or in the way which is most appropriate to the child and their needs. You will work alongside your SENCO and class teacher in order to establish what will be in the child's best interests.

## Respecting individuality and encouraging pupils to do the same

When you find that issues of individuality come up in your day-to-day work with children, it is worth discussing and thinking about it with them. In this way any questions can be answered and children who may feel 'different' from others will have an opportunity to talk about their beliefs if they would like to.

**CASE STUDY:** Respecting individuality

You are supporting a group of pupils discussing the similarities and differences of the main religions. One of the pupils starts to talk about the differences in diet and says that he is only able to eat halal meat, which is not available in school, so he sticks to a vegetarian diet. Another pupil said that he thinks it is silly if religions dictate what you can or can not eat.

- Why is this a useful learning opportunity?
- How could you make the most of this opportunity to respect individuality in the classroom?

## Challenging any discrimination when it occurs

Whether this has been reported to you or if you have heard or seen it yourself, you must always ensure that you challenge anyone who is discriminatory towards others. This will occur rarely, but incidents of discrimination should not go unchecked.

## Getting ready for assessment

Think about the ways in which your school supports inclusion and celebrates diversity. You may want to look at policies, discuss particular aspects of your school and its catchment area, look at the assembly timetable, or show how the school involves parents and the community. You can then show your assessor when they come into school or write up a reflective account and use it for your portfolio.

## Functional skills

ICT: Developing, presenting and communicating information
ICT: Using ICT

Using PowerPoint®, you could create a new presentation entitled 'Supporting Inclusive Practice', then link it to your role in school through examples of your day-to-day work. You could try to include relevant digital pictures, film or images that you have scanned in to your presentation. As you develop your knowledge and skills, you will take on more responsibilities and you can add these to your presentation at a later date.

## Websites

**www.dcsf.gov.uk/everychildmatters** – Every Child Matters framework
**www.direct.gov.uk/surestart** – government programme to deliver the best start in life for every child
**www.institute.nhs.uk/building_capability/breaking_through/race_relations.html** – Race Relations Act
**http://nationalstrategies.standards.dcsf.gov.uk/node/84335** – this site explores the importance of key messages on inclusive practice in the Early Years Foundation Stage (EYFS)
**www.ncb.org.uk** – National Children's Bureau, supporting parents and children

## Check your knowledge

1. Identify three areas of legislation which have impacted on the promotion of equality and diversity in schools.

2. Why is it important for schools to have policies in place with regard to equal opportunities?

3. How would you define the term 'inclusion'?

4. Outline how schools can show that they value diversity in the learning environment.

5. Why is it important to promote and value diversity in schools? (Choose all that apply.)

   a) It makes all children feel valued.

   b) It keeps everyone happy.

   c) It enables children to learn from one another.

   d) It means that we can find out about other cultures.

   e) It shows the importance of inclusion in society.

6. Why should we think about our own values and attitudes when considering anti-discriminatory practice?

7. Name four ways in which you as an individual have demonstrated that you promote equality and diversity.

8. What impact might prejudice and discrimination have on a child?

9. How can you support inclusive practices in school?

# School life

## My story: Jackie

I am a very experienced bilingual assistant working in a school which has a high number of speakers of other languages. I support the children in several subjects including maths and science. During these sessions I adapt the materials and help children to understand the instructions and record information. In the science lesson, the teacher asked me to also help two pupils with special educational needs. As there was a large group, this put quite a lot of pressure on me and I felt that I could not carry out my role effectively in supporting children in the group with English as an additional language. I also felt that this was a form of indirect discrimination, as these children had good knowledge and skills but they were put in a lower set.

I decided to speak to her, but had to be careful how I approached the issue as I did not want her to feel that I was criticising or undermining her; also, as I am not in the class all the time, I do not have much chance to speak to her outside lessons. I was able to arrange to meet up with her and said that all three children had achieved their targets easily but required support so that they could understand the instructions and discuss and record their findings. I said that my role was to support children with English as an additional language, and I found that I wasn't able to do this properly as well as supporting the children with special educational needs. To be fair to the teacher, she was fine about it and thanked me for bringing it to her attention. She said that she would request additional support for the class – it's hard to keep tabs on everything with a class of 33!

## Ask the expert

**Q** Can I tell the teacher what I think?

**A** It's fine from time to time to say what you think to the teacher, as long as you are not overtly critical, and in particular if they ask you what you think – you are working as a team and you have close contact with their class. However, you should also bear in mind that there are likely to be reasons for them to work in a particular way and you may not always be aware of these. However, if you have ongoing concerns about anything, you should always say something, either to the teacher or to your own line manager.

### VIEWPOINT

In any work situation you may find that there will be people you get on with better than others, and schools are no exception. You should remember that it is unlikely that you will work with the same teacher for more than a year and that all relationships will be about compromise. You may also find that you get on better than you had anticipated and that you learn a lot from the experience! Remember to remain professional and that communication is very important.

# TDA 3.7 Support assessment for learning

Assessment for learning involves encouraging pupils to take responsibility for their own learning and being active participants through thinking about their progress towards meeting learning objectives. As part of the assessment for learning process, you will need to know the kinds of strategies that teachers use to inform assessment. You will then need to show how you involve pupils in checking and reviewing their progress, and enable them to apply self-assessment strategies to check their learning as they work.

## By the end of this unit you will:

1. understand the purpose and characteristics of assessment for learning

2. be able to use assessment strategies to promote learning

3. be able to support learners in reviewing their learning strategies and achievements

4. be able to contribute to reviewing assessment for learning.

# Understand the purpose and characteristics of assessment for learning

## Compare the roles of the teacher and the learning support practitioner

One of the main responsibilities of the teacher is to monitor and assess pupil achievement. They will need to know how all children in their class are progressing and be able to report back to parents and other staff. Assessment is an ongoing process which will take different forms and in your role as a teaching assistant, you will need to be able to support teachers with the process.

### Functional skills

**Maths: Interpreting**
Thinking about one of the subjects that you support a group of children with, you could apply a number of mathematical skills to do the following.

- Find out what fraction and percentage of the class are on, above or below target in this area.

- Investigate the ratio of boys to girls on, above or below target, and then link to any research around gender and this subject.

- Create a graph to track targets on visually in order to show how over time the children have moved on with your support.

Teachers will plan lessons and schemes of work which should set out clear objectives so that learner progress can be measured. Both children and adults in the class will need to be clear about what these objectives are and it is good practice for teachers to set out and display the learning objective at the start of each session. In this way you will be sharing with all children what they are going to learn as well as having a clear understanding of what you are supporting.

## The difference between formative and summative assessment

### Formative assessment strategies

As pupil learning takes place, you will need to measure it against these objectives using ongoing methods of assessment. These are known as formative assessment methods and can be used to check the learning in any lesson.

- **Using open-ended questions** – this will encourage children to put their ideas forward without being 'led' by adults, for example, 'Tell me how you are going to…'

- **Observing pupils** – we will gather much of our knowledge of how pupils are achieving through watching them work and noticing the kinds of strategies they are using to work things out or what they find more difficult. This can take place on a daily basis or can be carried out more formally through direct observations.

- **Listening to how pupils describe their work and their reasoning** – through doing this we hear about the methods which pupils use.

- **Checking pupils' understanding** – we can do this through questioning pupils about their learning and asking them what they know.

- **Engaging pupils in reviewing progress** – this should take place throughout each session, when pupils should be encouraged to think about what they have learned and measure it against learning objectives, and how they might apply this knowledge in the future.

### Summative assessment

The other main form of assessment which teachers use to check learning is summative assessment. This occurs at the end of a term or scheme of work when it is important to know what pupils have achieved at a particular time. It could take the form of end of Key Stage SATS or an end of year school report, and informs a range of people about the level of a pupil's work. It could really be called assessment *of* learning.

# The characteristics of assessment for learning

**Assessment for learning** informs and promotes the achievement of all pupils, as it encourages them to take responsibility for their own learning. The process involves explaining learning outcomes to pupils, giving them feedback on their progress and enabling them to develop their self-assessment skills so that they are ultimately able to reflect on and recognise their own achievements. This will usually start with pupils taking part in peer assessment to build up these skills and discuss their work before moving on to thinking about their own work. Pupils will need to be able to consider their learning carefully throughout the process and keep coming back to the learning objective or what they are expected to learn.

## Key term

**Assessment for learning** – using assessment as part of teaching and learning in ways which will raise learners' achievement

## Reflect

How are pupils encouraged to think about their learning during the process? Are they clear about learning objectives? Do they review this at the end of each lesson?

## Functional skills

**ICT: Developing, presenting and communicating information**

Using a suitable software package on the computer (Word® or Publisher®), you could have a go at devising a self-assessment sheet that you could use with the children that you work with. This could include symbols to record how they feel about their work and maybe bullet points to say how they could improve.

*How do you ensure pupils learn to reflect on and assess their own learning?*

## The importance and benefits of assessment for learning

Research has shown that there is a clear relationship between being part of the process of assessment and pupil motivation. Children who are actively engaged with their progress will feel empowered to improve their performance, as they will feel more ownership of their learning. This will in turn develop their self-esteem and motivation — children who feel that they are not part of the learning process are far more likely to become disengaged and consequently lose interest. Effective feedback also ensures that adults are supporting more able as well as less able learners by giving them the tools to achieve to the best of their potential. Assessment for learning is a device to enable pupils to understand the aim of what they are doing, what they need to do to reach that aim and where they are in relation to it.

## How assessment for learning can contribute to planning for future learning

Assessment for learning must by definition contribute to future planning for all who are involved in the learning process. As such it is a valuable tool, and it will mean that all concerned will learn from the experience.

### For the teacher

For the teacher, effective assessment for learning will enable them to pass on the responsibility to the pupil over time for managing their own learning, so that they will become more actively involved in the process.

### For the pupil

For the pupil, the process will inform them about how they approach learning and tackle areas on which they need to work. They will be able to consider areas for improvement by looking at assessment criteria and develop their ability to self-assess. Their increased awareness of how to learn will develop their confidence and help them to recognise when to ask for support.

### For the learning support practitioner

For you, assessment for learning will inform how you approach pupil questioning based on what you have discovered about how they learn. You may need to pace the progress of learners depending on their needs, so that less able pupils are given opportunities to revisit areas of uncertainty.

# Be able to use assessment strategies to promote learning

## The information required to support assessment for learning

Information required includes:

- the learning objectives for the activities
- the personalised learning goals for individual learners
- the success criteria of the learning activities
- the **assessment opportunities and strategies** relevant to own role in the learning activities.

### Key term

**Assessment opportunities and strategies** — the occasions, approaches and techniques used for ongoing assessment during learning activities

At the start of any activity, pupils will need to be clear about what they are going to learn and how they will be assessed. For assessment for learning to be effective, pupils will need to know what they are learning, why they are learning it and how assessment will take place. Pupils should discuss these with you at the start of each session and will need you and the class teacher to give them specific criteria against which their learning will be measured. As pupils take on more responsibility for their learning, they will find it easier to look at learning objectives to see whether these have been met. A simple example of this might be a literacy activity in which pupils are learning to use apostrophes and then writing a report using apostrophes to check their knowledge (see below). You may or may not make pupils aware of the success criteria for the activity, which will be how they apply the learning objective in their subsequent work.

As well as knowing the learning objective, pupils will need to think about their own personalised learning goals, if they have these, so that they can integrate them in the process. For example, if a pupil's learning goal for literacy is to produce clear and fluent joined handwriting, this will tie in well with the literacy activity listed below. However, if the goal does not tie in, it can still be part of the process, as thinking about their target will still encourage them to be aware of their learning needs.

- **What pupils are learning** — where apostrophes need to be applied.
- **Success criteria** — pupils able to use apostrophes for possession and contractions consistently.
- **Why they are learning it** — to enable them to use the correct form of written English.
- **How assessment will take place** — teacher and teaching assistant will check that pupils are using apostrophes consistently in their written work.

It may be helpful to give pupils exemplar pieces of work which show what they need to do in order to meet the success criteria. In this way they will start to see what is being asked for.

As you support learners through the process, you will also need to use a variety of assessment opportunities to guide them in thinking about their work and their progress — for examples of these, see page 106.

### Portfolio activity

Using examples from your own experience, describe how you have supported pupils to enable them to take on more responsibility for their own learning and become more active learners.

### Functional skills

ICT: Developing, presenting and communicating information
You could convert individual targets into charts so that the individuals have a visual target grid that they can use to help them to see their own progression. As each pupil you support achieves a target you can record this on the grid and use it to discuss their progress.

## Personalised learning goals and criteria for assessing progress with learners

It is likely that all pupils in secondary schools will have **personalised learning goals** or targets for each of their subjects. These may be updated on a termly or half-termly basis, depending on school policy. The subject teacher will usually agree similar targets with children who are of the same ability, so that work can be tailored for their needs as a group. Pupils will usually have them printed out in the front of their books.

Children who have additional needs will also have personal targets, but these may be recorded on an individual or personalised learning plan which will have been agreed and signed by pupils, parents and teachers.

Before starting work on an activity, you will need to discuss and ensure that pupils know and understand their own learning targets as well as the learning objectives.

### CASE STUDY: Clarify personalised learning goals for assessing progress

Karen is working with Helen in Year 7, who has dyslexia and **dyscalculia**. Helen is aware of her needs and discusses and agrees each target with her teacher. She does not have an individual education plan (IEP). One maths target this term is to carry out calculations on a calculator using more than one step, using brackets and the memory. Today Helen is working in Karen's group and the learning objective is to calculate the surface area of cubes and cuboids. There are opportunities to tie in her learning target with the objective.

- How might Karen approach this with Helen?
- Should Karen focus on the learning objective or Helen's personal learning goal?

### Key terms

**Personalised learning goals** — goals which reflect the learning objectives of activities and take account of the past achievements and current learning needs of individual learners

**Dyscalculia** — a learning disability or difficulty involving innate difficulty in learning or comprehending mathematics

## Use assessment opportunities and strategies to gain information and judge learners' participation and progress

In order to help you to review pupils' progress, it may be helpful for you to follow a checklist like this.

- Ensure pupils understand the learning objectives and any individual learning targets so that they can assess their own progress to meeting these as they proceed.
- Talk to pupils about what they have to do and whether they need to hand work in.
- Inform pupils how they will be assessed and ensure they understand.
- Give examples of work produced by other learners if possible, so that pupils can see how the assessment criteria are applied.
- Provide individual support and oral feedback as pupils are working, praising learners when they focus their comments on their personalised learning goals for the task.
- Ensure that there are opportunities for either peer or self-assessment.
- Encourage learners to review and comment on their work before handing it in or discussing it with the teacher.
- Provide written feedback.

For further assessment strategies to use with pupils, see 'Formative assessment strategies' on page 102.

You do not need to use all the points above, but they are indicators for you to make sure you have not missed any of the opportunities to support assessment for learning.

### Portfolio activity

Using the list above as a guide, reflect on how you have supported either an individual or a group of pupils through a learning activity.

## Provide constructive feedback to learners

For assessment for learning to be effective, it is essential that children receive constructive feedback from adults which focuses on strengths as well as supporting and guiding pupils through any difficulties they may have.

You will need to give feedback which:

- gives information to a pupil which focuses on performance
- is delivered positively
- is not personal, but based on facts.

There are different types of feedback which we should give pupils during and following learning activities.

- **Affirmation feedback** should be delivered as soon as possible: 'Well done, you have remembered to include all the points we discussed!' This type of feedback helps to motivate pupils.
- **Developmental feedback** will suggest what to do next time: 'Nathan, try to remember to get all the equipment you will need before starting the activity.'

Both types of feedback can be written or oral, but for feedback to be effective, it should be given as promptly as possible. If feedback is given too long after an activity has been completed, children will find it harder to apply it to their learning. This may be particularly true in the case of marking, which should be done as soon as possible after an activity is completed, if possible with the child present.

### Reflect

Think about and discuss in groups some feedback you remember from when you were at school. It is possible that you have received some feedback which focused on negative rather than positive points. What effect did this have on you as a learner?

English: Speaking, listening and communication
In order to develop your confidence in this area, you could role-play giving and receiving feedback in pairs. This will support you in the classroom with the children if you have tried some suitable phrases out first.

## BEST PRACTICE CHECKLIST: Providing feedback

- Remain non-judgemental.
- Focus on strengths.
- Work through one thing at a time.
- Give constructive advice where needed and guidance on how a child can improve.
- Link feedback directly to what has been observed or written.
- End positively.

## CASE STUDY: Encouraging through feedback

You have been working with a group who is finding a task quite difficult. You have tried praising them for the work they have done so far, but they are continuing to struggle and you are concerned that they might not want to continue.

- What kind of feedback should you be giving the group?
- Outline the steps you might go through to encourage them back on task.

## Provide opportunities and encouragement for learners to improve upon their work

An important aspect of assessment for learning is that children's progress will be measured against their own previous achievements rather than being compared with those of others. Pupils' learning should be set at a level which ensures that they are building on what

they learn. This means that they should be starting from a point of previous understanding and then extending their learning to take in new information. Pupils will benefit from discussing previous learning experiences to consolidate what they know and reinforce their understanding before moving on to take in new concepts and ideas. You will need to encourage and motivate pupils, in particular if they are finding it difficult to understand or there are other factors which are impacting on their learning. It is important that you show them that you believe in them and are able to support them as they start from what they know.

If you have pupils with low self-esteem, or who have tried to learn in a particular way before which has been clearer to them, you may need to adapt or modify what they have been asked to do in order to help them.

## Knowledge into action

Ask learners to think about a piece of work that they have completed well and which they feel proud of. Encourage them to think about the learning objectives and success criteria of the session, and evaluate it against their targets. They should then be able to feed back to others about their learning.

# Be able to support learners in reviewing their learning strategies and achievements

## Help learners to review their learning strategies and future needs, and encourage them to communicate needs and ideas

When we talk about reviewing learning, we sometimes assume that it is going to be at the end of a session or unit of work. However, the learning process is such that we should be reviewing learning with children throughout learning sessions. It is good practice during any session for adults to review with pupils what they are learning, but this can be harder for you to do in some learning situations than in others. This may be due to time but might also be due to the way in which the activity has been presented to pupils. If you are involved in planning activities, try to build in time for review so that pupils can consider their work at each stage. Pupils should be encouraged to take responsibility for their own learning. You can support this process through open-ended questioning which helps pupils to recognise their progress in relation to their own previous achievements, rather than against that of their peers. They should also be encouraged to measure their progress against the learning outcomes and to think about their future learning based on this. This may be part of a whole-class discussion, in groups, with a partner or with yourself. There may also be whole-school strategies which are used to check on pupil learning. Some examples are listed below.

- **Traffic light system** – this could be used by pupils who have special educational needs, or those with less confidence to ask for help, to indicate if they are stuck or unsure at any stage of the lesson.

- **Foggy bits** – pupils are given the opportunity to write down or articulate the parts of the session or activity which have not been clear.

- **Write a sentence** – pupils are able to put in a sentence the key points of their learning at the end of a unit of work or learning activity.

- **Talk partner review** – pupils talk to their partner about their learning and parts that they enjoyed or found difficult. They can also do this at the beginning of a session to see what they already know.

*How do you check pupils understand the purpose of the task?*

- **Post-it® Notes™/whiteboards** – children can write down on Post-it® Notes™ or whiteboards what they have learned, what they found easy and what they found hard.

## Support learners in using peer assessment and self-assessment

When supporting pupils during self-assessment, you will need to structure learning activities so that their purposes and outcomes are very clear. However, if pupils understand why they are doing something, it is far more likely that they will want to learn. The outcomes need to be clear and written in language which is appropriate for the age and ability of the children. Self-assessment can be difficult even for older pupils. They often view assessment as summative and something that only happens at the end of the process. It is important that they understand that assessment is part

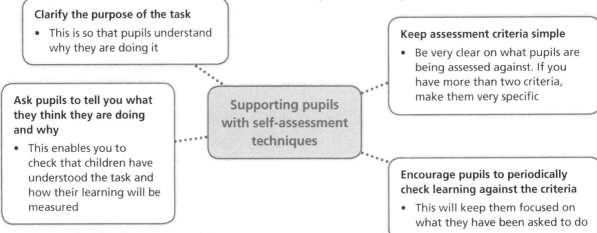

**Clarify the purpose of the task**
- This is so that pupils understand why they are doing it

**Ask pupils to tell you what they think they are doing and why**
- This enables you to check that children have understood the task and how their learning will be measured

**Supporting pupils with self-assessment techniques**

**Keep assessment criteria simple**
- Be very clear on what pupils are being assessed against. If you have more than two criteria, make them very specific

**Encourage pupils to periodically check learning against the criteria**
- This will keep them focused on what they have been asked to do

*Supporting pupils with self-assessment techniques.*

of a process which they need to be involved in. It may be helpful to start by using peer assessment, to encourage them to think about learning aims and recognise what makes a 'good' piece of work (see below).

## Keep assessment criteria simple

You need to be very clear on what pupils are being assessed against. If you have more than two criteria, you will need to make them very specific. Clarify the purpose of the task so that pupils understand why they are doing it. Ask pupils to tell you what they think they are doing and why. This enables you to check that children have understood the task and how their learning will be measured. Encourage pupils to check learning periodically against the criteria – this will keep them focused on what they have been asked to do.

## How to promote the skills of collaboration in peer assessment

Pupils will build up their assessment techniques through working with adults and their peers so that they can ultimately begin to assess their own learning against learning outcomes and to look more objectively at their achievements. Peer assessment is not supposed to compare the achievements of children or cause them to grade one another according to their performance. For this reason, it is very important that children are clear on what they will be assessed against. Pupils should look at one another's work and notice how it relates to the assessment criteria. They can discuss what they have been asked to do and how their work reflects this. In this way it will start to bring their attention to what teachers are looking for when measuring achievement.

Through looking at the work of others, they may be able to see more easily how assessment criteria can be used to measure learning.

### Skills builder

Discuss with a group of learners what they know about assessment. At the beginning of an activity find out if learners know:

- what the learning objectives are, and if not, why this might be
- how they will be assessed
- why they are assessed and how the information will be used.

Following the activity, ask learners to reflect on their learning. They could:

- work in pairs to carry out peer assessment against learning outcomes
- discuss reasons for the decisions.

You could write up your findings in a report and share with the teacher or manager. Think of two strategies you could use to support children to self-assess.

## Support learners to reflect on learning, identify progress, needs, strengths and weaknesses

### Reflect on their learning

When you are supporting learning, you will need to encourage pupils to think about and reflect on their

### CASE STUDY: Promoting skills of collaboration

You have been asked to work with Year 7 and support them as they critically evaluate their own work against a list of assessment criteria during an art session. During a visit to a historical building, learners will be looking at architectural features. They must consider architectural features such as windows, doors, chimneys and archways.

The assessment criteria have been defined as follows.

1. Identify architectural features of the building.
2. Record features using a digital camera.

3. Make connections between design and purpose of the features.
4. Justify your choice of features.

- How would you introduce the activity so that pupils understand how their progress will be measured?
- How could this start as a peer assessment and then move on to a self-assessment activity?
- How would you ensure that you did not emphasise children's weaknesses and damage their self-esteem?

learning throughout the process, and not just when they have finished their work. This is because they may need to think about the approach they are taking and whether this is the best way to tackle the task. You will need to do this through effective questioning and checking their understanding of the objective against what they are doing. You may also like to use the kinds of tools suggested on page 108.

### Identify the progress they have made

You will need to check that the children are able to assess the progress that they have made when working. They might do this through peer or self-assessment, as already discussed, or you may need to question them about their learning by asking them to:

● put their hand up if they have a question about the activity and then asking if any of the others can answer it for them rather than answering yourself

● write down any areas which they still feel unsure about

● tell you what they have learned during the session.

### Identify emerging learning needs, the strengths and weaknesses of their learning strategies, and plan how to improve them

As children reflect on their learning, they will start to be able to identify what they need to do to improve. Where they are used to doing this, they may find it straightforward, but children who have a fear of 'getting it wrong' may find the process challenging and you may need to support them though it. One way of doing this is to use misconceptions or incorrect ideas as a discussion point so that pupils can talk about how they approached the task and what led them to their answer. This can lead to a more positive approach to learning from mistakes and seeing it as an opportunity rather than something to be feared.

Another way of supporting pupils might be to keep a record of their learning through a journal or diary in which they have the opportunity to think about their learning. They could also use this as a place to write or keep any of their own personalised targets.

# Be able to contribute to reviewing assessment for learning

## Provide feedback to the teacher on learners' participation and progress

When using assessment for learning techniques, you need to work closely with the teacher so that you can discuss and review how you present learning activities to pupils and the kinds of opportunities which are available for assessment for learning. You will need to consider how pupils have responded to the process and which strategies you have found useful and thought-provoking for pupils. In this way you will be able to develop the opportunities available for use in the future.

As you will need to give feedback to the teacher, it is important to consider the different aspects of assessment to learning. The teacher will need to be aware of pupil engagement in the process and any difficulties which they have. It is likely that you will be giving the teacher feedback on learner participation and progress in the learning activities in any teaching and learning activity. This may be done verbally or using a feedback sheet, but you need to include all aspects of the learning process. It can be useful to note down either on Post-it® Notes™ or small pieces of paper any interesting or useful comments which pupils make during the learning process so that these can also be fed back. It will be useful to observe and feed

---

**CASE STUDY:** Supporting learners to reflect on their learning

You are supporting a group of pupils in Year 10 who are studying health and social care. The group has just completed a learning activity where they have been required to measure body temperature, breathing rate and heart rate. They are expected to go on to analyse their findings in relation to normal measurements and to record the information. They have worked collaboratively to collect

measurements and have discussed their results. Although the investigation has gone well, they are uncertain how to interpret and record their findings.

• Why do you think the pupils might be confused about their learning?

• How might you support the learners through assessment for learning?

• What might you do differently next time?

back whether assessment for learning makes pupils more eager to participate in the learning activities and whether it makes a difference to pupil engagement.

An alternative way of giving feedback to teachers is through group feedback, in which the learners discuss the results of peer assessment with adults. In this way you will find out about their learning and feed back to the teacher at the same time.

## Reflect ?

How do you feed back to teachers when carrying out assessment for learning tasks? Do you ever change the way in which you do this? Does it work well both for you and for the teacher?

## Functional skills

**English: Speaking, listening and communication**
This 'Reflect' provides a useful discussion opportunity for you to share good practice with your peers and maybe collect some good tips for yourself. Perhaps you have come across some barriers that you could discuss further in order to help you to resolve them.

## Use the outcomes of assessment to reflect on and improve own contribution

Following learning activities, you will need to look at the outcomes of assessment for learning so that you can judge whether the way in which you have approached the process has been successful. In other words, you should be able to check that it has enabled pupils to take more responsibility for the learning experience and has influenced what they have learned. You will also need to be able to reflect on your own learning and experience when supporting pupil learning, so that you can adjust your approach if necessary. You should think about:

● how you questioned pupils and encouraged them to look closely at the assessment criteria

● how you gave feedback to pupils

● how you supported both peer and self-assessment.

It may help to look again at the checklist on page 107 so that you can see whether different strategies may have worked better with pupils.

You will also need to discuss with the teacher the pupils' responses to the process, as some will have found it easier to manage than others and teachers may have suggestions as to how this may be developed. Depending on the ages and needs of the pupils, the use of peer or self-assessment may need to be altered.

## Getting ready for assessment

As learning outcomes 2–4 need to be assessed in the workplace, it would be helpful if your assessor could witness you planning and carrying out an assessment for learning lesson in which you encourage pupils to look at their progress against learning objectives and their own personal targets. If you can also encourage pupils to review their work, this will enable you to gather evidence for many of the assessment criteria.

## Check your knowledge

1. How would you define assessment for learning?
2. How can assessment for learning help pupils when they are carrying out learning activities?
3. What is the difference between formative and summative assessment?
4. What kind of information do we need in order to carry out assessment for learning?
   a) the teacher's long- and medium-term plans
   b) information on the child
   c) learning objectives for the lesson
   d) success criteria for the objectives.
5. What kinds of assessment strategies might you use to find out how well learners are participating in the session?
6. How would you use peer assessment in a lesson?
7. How can we encourage pupils to feed back to us about their learning?
8. How might we develop opportunities for assessment for learning in the classroom?

### Websites

**www.teachers.tv** – Teachers' TV
**www.tes.co.uk** – the *Times Educational Supplement* (TES) website also has some useful ideas on assessment for learning

# School life

## My story: Jess

Our school recently had a blitz on assessment for learning and all staff were asked to ensure that it was implemented in classes. The teachers were all sent on training and the Head emphasised its importance and the need for a 'whole-school' approach. However, I really did not feel able to implement the requirements and did not really understand what it was all about. I found some clips on Teachers TV which were good and also an article in the *Times Educational Supplement*, but did not really think I was getting enough support from the school for something that we were all supposed to be doing. I spoke to my head of year as I get on well with her and said that a few of us didn't feel able to implement something which was clearly a priority without more information and training. She apologised and said that it was a misunderstanding as she had thought that teachers were going to pass on the information to support staff, whereas in reality this had not been organised. We were then able to set some time aside for training and now I am getting used to the process, I think it is very beneficial to the pupils, as it builds on what we were doing anyway.

## Ask the expert

**Q** What should I do when I am not sure about what I have been asked to do, but no one has time to talk to me?

**A** You must always speak out if you do not know what you are required to do – you will not be able to support children effectively if you are not clear about what you are to do with them. In a similar way the children may also be confused or unclear about their work, which will affect their learning. Although staff in school are always busy, there will be someone who will be able to listen to you and hear your concerns. Choose your moment carefully though – sometimes it is not possible to drop everything!

### VIEWPOINT

In the situation above, do you think the responsibility for passing information on lies with the Head Teacher or the staff below them? Remember that your colleagues have their own priorities and pressures, and if information has not been passed on to you, you may need to approach the relevant person for it in a tactful manner, rather than suggesting they are not doing their job properly.

# SfCD SHC32
# Engage in personal development

There will always be changes taking place in education which will have an impact on you and the work you carry out in schools. This unit is also about how to engage in your own continuing professional development. You will also need to have some form of professional appraisal which includes thinking about your practice and setting targets for development. Appraisals will usually be carried out by your line manager, and some schools are asking their higher level teaching assistants (HLTAs) to appraise other assistants.

## By the end of this unit you will:

1. understand what is required for competence in the learner's own work role within the sector

2. be able to reflect on practice

3. be able to evaluate own performance

4. be able to agree a personal development plan

5. be able to reflect on how learning opportunities contribute to personal development.

# Understand what is required for competence in the learner's own work role within the sector

## Duties and responsibilities of own role within the sector

To support pupils effectively, you should have a very clear idea about the school structure and your role within it. You should have an up to date job description which is a realistic reflection of your duties. A starting point for thinking about your role will then be to look through it and think about any changes which have taken place over the past year.

> **Link**
>
> See also TDA 3.2 for more on how schools are organised and the roles of different members of staff.

---

**London Borough of Lewisham**
**Job Description**
**Title: Teaching Assistant**
**Post: Level 3**

**Main purpose of the job:**

Under guidance of teaching staff: implement work programmes to individuals/groups (this could include those requiring detailed and specialist knowledge in particular areas); assist in whole planning cycle and management/preparation of resources; provide cover for whole classes for short periods under an agreed system of supervision.

**Summary of responsibilities and duties:**
**Support for pupils**

- Use specialist (curricular/learning) skills/training/experience to support pupils.
- Assist with the development and implementation of individual education plans (IEPs).
- Establish productive working relationships with pupils, acting as a role model and setting high expectations.
- Promote the inclusion and acceptance of all pupils within the classroom.
- Support pupils consistently while recognising and responding to their individual needs.
- Encourage pupils to interact and work co-operatively with others, and engage all pupils in activities.
- Promote independence and employ strategies to recognise and reward achievement of self-reliance.
- Provide feedback to pupils in relation to progress and achievement.

**Support for teacher**

- Work with the teacher to establish an appropriate learning environment.
- Work with the teacher in lesson planning, evaluating and adjusting lessons/work plans as appropriate.
- Monitor and evaluate pupils' responses to learning activities through observation and planned recording of achievement against predetermined learning objectives.
- Provide objective and accurate feedback and reports as required to the teacher on pupil achievement, progress and other matters, ensuring the availability of appropriate evidence.

---

*An example of a level 3 teaching assistant job description. What are the similarities and differences from your own?*

Sample teaching assistant job descriptions are also available on www.teachernet.gov.uk; click on management, staffing and staff development, job descriptions.

As well as a job description, there may also be a person specification, which should set out personal qualities which are relevant to the particular post. It may include some of the strengths listed below. You do not have to use these for your performance review, but it may be worth looking at them and bearing them in mind.

### Knowledge into action

Find a copy of your own job description. Has this changed at all since you started in your role? If so, write a short paragraph describing the changes and ask your line manager to sign it. What are your main duties and responsibilities? Copy the job description and changes if necessary to put in the front of your portfolio.

### Be a good communicator/enjoy working with others
It is vital that an assistant is able to share thoughts and ideas with others, and is comfortable doing this.

### Use initiative
Assistants will need to be able to decide for themselves how to use their time if the teacher is not always available to ask. There will always be jobs which need doing in a classroom, even if this just means checking display boards or making sure that resource cupboards are tidy.

### Respect confidentiality
You should remember that in a position of responsibility, it is essential to maintain confidentiality. You may sometimes find that you are placed in a position where you are made aware of personal details concerning a child or family. Although background and school records are available to those within the school, it is not appropriate to discuss them with outsiders.

### Be sensitive to children's needs
Whether an individual or classroom assistant, it is important to be able to judge how much support to give while still encouraging children's independence. Pupils need to be sure about what they have been asked to do and may need help organising their thoughts or strategies, but it is the learner who must do the work and not the assistant.

### Have good listening skills
A teaching assistant needs to be able to listen to others and have a sympathetic nature. This is an important quality for your interactions, both with children and other adults.

### Be willing to undertake training for personal development
In any school, there will always be occasions on which assistants are invited or required to undergo training; these opportunities should be used where possible. You may also find that your role changes within the school due to movement between classes, year groups or departments. You will need to be flexible and willing to rise to different expectations.

### Be firm but fair with the children
Children will quickly realise if an adult is not able to set fair boundaries of behaviour. Adults should always ensure that when they start working with children they make these boundaries clear.

### Enjoy working with children and have a sense of humour
Assistants will need to be able to see the funny side of working with children and young people; a sense of humour is often a very useful asset!

### Functional skills
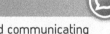

ICT: Developing, presenting and communicating information
English: Writing
These are all key skills that teaching assistants need to have. You could produce an information booklet on the computer outlining these skills and why they are important. This information booklet could be used to give to other people who are considering a career in this area. Make sure you present the information clearly and concisely.

## Expectations about own role in relation to relevant standards

Each work role will have its own set of **standards**; there is a list of standards for classroom teachers and there are also standards for school support staff, depending on their role. You will need to look at these together with your line manager as well as your assessor, as you will need to meet the standards in order to gain your qualification.

The National Occupational Standards for Teaching Assistants offers guidance on the wider aspects of competent performance. It also forms the basis for the NAPTA (National Association of Professional Teaching Assistants) Profiles, which some schools are asking their teaching assistants to complete (see www.napta.org.uk). The Support Work in Schools qualifications at levels 2 and 3 are also based on the National Occupational Standards. Other models of performance which are accessible to assistants include local and national guidelines for codes of practice, provided by government bodies such as the DfE and Ofsted. These are often available in school or through the DfE and Ofsted websites (www.education.gov.uk and www.ofsted.gov.uk).

It is important to be able to look through the standards and think about how they are relevant to you in all areas of your role. For example, each mandatory unit in this book relates to national standards against which you will need to be assessed. You will then need to choose those optional units which are more closely relevant to your own role by looking through and considering the requirements of each one.

### Over to you!

Choose one aspect of the standards for supporting teaching and learning (for example, those for personal development) and compare them with the corresponding standards for classroom teachers which may be found on the Training and Development Agency for Schools (TDA) website (www.tda.gov.uk). What similarities and differences do you notice?

### Functional skills

**English: Reading**
Read through the standards for teaching assistants at level 2 and level 3. Summarise the difference in the role, responsibilities and expectations for teaching assistants working at level 3.

# Be able to reflect on practice

## The importance of reflective practice in improving the quality of service provided

The role of the teaching assistant has in recent years become that of a professional. As part of any professional job role, it is important to be able to carry out reflective practice. This will be especially important when working with children, as your personal effectiveness will have a considerable impact on them and their learning.

**Reflective practice** means thinking about and evaluating what you do and discussing any changes which could be made. It relates not only to your **professional development** but also to how you carry out individual activities with children and other aspects of your role. You will need to reflect on a regular basis and should have opportunities to discuss your thoughts and ideas with your colleagues. By doing this you will be able to identify areas of strength as well as exploring those which need further development. Teaching assistants have quite diverse roles within schools and inevitably you will find that you are more confident in some situations than others. By reflecting on your practice and how you work with others, you will come to be more effective in your role and gain in confidence.

### Key terms

**Standards** – statements about how tasks should be carried out and the minimum acceptable quality of practice that should be delivered

**Reflective practice** – the process of thinking about and critically analysing your actions with the goal of changing and improving occupational practice

**Professional development** – ongoing training and professional updating

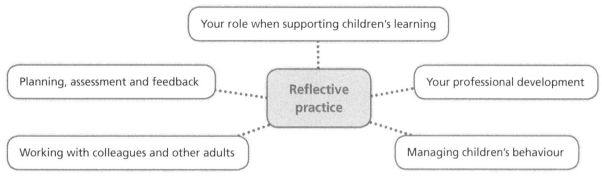

You will need to reflect on different aspects of your role.

## The ability to reflect on practice

Reflecting on your work will give you opportunities to improve your practice and therefore will empower you, as you are using skills which you have developed yourself. It is important to take time out to think about what you are doing in your work with children; you have a professional duty to consider the impact of what you do. By thinking about this and knowing why particular strategies or approaches have worked, you will then be able to repeat them. In identifying aspects which have been less successful, you will be able to ask for more support. Remember that it is not a question of whether you got it 'right' or 'wrong', but making sure you can build on all the positive aspects of the work you do as a positive means of developing your career. Effective questioning of your experiences will help you to find a starting point for your reflective analysis. As a tool, it enhances your experiences as it enables you to take more control over what you do and develops your confidence.

In all aspects of your role, you will need to be able to think about your practice. Your school will be able to offer you support and will provide you with the experience you need. Taking a step back and looking at things from a different point of view is often an enlightening exercise – the important thing to do is to ask the right questions so that you are learning from the experience. You may also have the opportunity to benefit from other tools such as observations of your practice, peer assessment and feedback from your assessor. These are all useful ways of helping you to think about how your practice comes across to others. You may find that some of your reflections come as a surprise and you were not expecting to find out some things. If the school has an ethic of

reflection anyway, it will be easier for you to engage in personal reflection, as you will be more used to the process. This is particularly true when it comes to uncovering the difference between words and actual practice – if the school has an open and accepting ethos where everyone is engaged in reflection and expects to learn through mistakes, the process will be less threatening.

### Functional skills

**English: Speaking, listening and communication**
Prior to your appraisal, it is always effective to spend a short time completing some personal reflection of your own practice. When you do this, make some notes to remind you. You can then discuss these in a formal situation at your appraisal with your line manager. Always try to collect your thoughts together before answering so that you present your information clearly and concisely.

Why is it useful to discuss your reflections with others?

It is important to remember that in your work with learners, you are part of a whole school. If you are reflecting on your practice and find that you need to change or develop the work that you are doing, you will need to discuss this with others with whom you work, as this will also affect them. This could mean that if you are in a school which is less receptive to change or where staff do not reflect on their work as a matter of course, it may be difficult for you to approach others. You may need to be very tactful and sensitive in order to put your ideas across in a way which does not appear threatening.

A good starting point might be speaking to the form or subject teacher or line manager, as they may be able to advise you on your ideas. Staff or year group meetings may also be an opportunity for you to put forward proposals, and this will also give others the chance to respond. You will need to think about how you communicate your thoughts so that you do not appear to be criticising the way others operate. Always ensure that you build in a means of reviewing and evaluating any changes which are considered.

## Functional skills

**English: Speaking, listening and communication**
This paragraph contains some really useful information that will support you in developing your speaking, listening and communication skills.

> **BEST PRACTICE CHECKLIST:** Reflective analysis
>
> - Be honest with yourself and others.
> - Make sure you evaluate successes as well as failures.
> - Include all areas of your work.
> - Ask a colleague for help if required.

## How own values, belief systems and experiences may affect own working practice

As you examine your existing practice, you may find that the process is challenging and sometimes hard. You will need to reflect not only on the practical side of your work with children, which can be a difficult process in itself, but also on your own attitudes and beliefs. Reflection can lead you to reconsider issues which you may not even have thought of as relevant. When you start to think about all aspects of your role, you may find this hard, as beliefs can be very difficult to change. You may also come across parents who have very different views from yourself or from those of the school. You will need to maintain your professionalism at all times.

*How often do you take the opportunity to discuss your ideas with the class teacher?*

**Reflect**

Think about how you have changed since starting in your role. Have any of your own opinions been altered since working in school? How do you think this has helped you in your professional development?

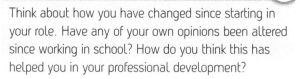

# Be able to evaluate own performance

Once you have understood the requirements of your role and started to reflect on your practice, you will need to consider what you have done and evaluate it against the relevant standards.

## Evaluate own knowledge, performance and understanding against relevant standards

You should be able to think about activities you have carried out with individuals or groups of children and evaluate how the sessions went. Even if you always work in a particular way which seems to go well, you should consider different ways of approaching work you do with children. Questions you can ask yourself at the end of a session could include the following.

- What went well?

- What did not go as well as anticipated? Why?
- Did the children achieve the learning objectives for the session?
- What would I change if I did the activity again?

In this way your evaluation will encourage you to develop and change what you are doing if needed, to ensure that you are working effectively with the children. It may be helpful, if you have not evaluated your work before, for the subject teacher or line manager to observe you working with children. They may then go through the evaluation with you afterwards and be able to offer suggestions and help you work though ideas.

**Reflect**

How often do you think about work you have done with children and evaluate it? How much do you think it would benefit you in practice? Make a point of thinking carefully about at least one activity you complete with children each week.

**Functional skills**

ICT: Developing, presenting and communicating information
If you complete any planning on the computer for the work that you do with the children, it is always a good idea to add an additional column on to the plan for evaluation. By saving these documents, you can revisit them after the session and add your evaluation for future reference.

By going through different aspects of your work in school, you will start to identify areas in which you are not as successful as others. Your reflections will enable you to draw conclusions about your work which may not be easy. Remember that this is a process and that by working through and addressing areas of your performance, you will improve your practice in the long run.

**Link**

See pages 116–18 of this unit for more on evaluating your practice.

## Portfolio activity

Gather together all the notes and evaluation forms you have on your performance and put them in date order. You can then put these in your portfolio as evidence.

## Use feedback to evaluate own performance and inform own development

You will also need to be able to show how feedback has helped your own development. It may be useful for you to use assessment forms from your assessor visits in order to show how you have progressed since the start of your qualification. You will then be able to think about how you would like to move on in the future.

## Portfolio activity

As part of your qualification, your assessor will need to come into school and observe your work with children. They will then give you feedback on what they have seen and your work with the children and relationships with adults, and give you areas for development.

When you have received your feedback, think about any areas in which development issues have been raised, or where you have been given particular credit. Answer the following questions fully and use them in your portfolio.

- Are these areas different from what you had expected?
- Did any issues come up as part of your observation that surprised you?
- Why is it important for everyone working with children to reflect on their practice?

## Functional skills

### English: Writing

Answering these questions will form a very useful reflective account. Consider your layout and the audience for this writing so that you can ensure that the information is presented clearly and concisely.

## Be able to agree a personal development plan

### Sources of support for planning and reviewing own development

In your school, there will be a number of sources of support which you are able to draw on to help you to plan and review your own development. Sources of support may include formal and informal support, appraisal, and may be within or beyond the organisation. You may choose to speak to a member of the Senior Management Team informally about your development if you do not have a formal procedure in your school. Alternatively, your school may undertake formal appraisals with all members of support staff. If you are undertaking a college course, you should also have a mentor or tutor who is able to advise and support you as you consider your performance and professional development.

---

**CASE STUDY:** Sources of support for planning and reviewing own development

Following redundancy from his job in industry, Adam has decided to begin a new career in education. He has started working as a learning support assistant in the secondary school in a nearby town. At present he is unsure who his line manager is in school as nobody has told him, and there are several issues which he would like to discuss with a more experienced member of staff to support his practice. He is also aware that he needs to gain a qualification, and has noticed that there are courses run by the local college which he thinks would be helpful. However, he does not know whom to ask, as everyone always seems too busy in school.

- What should Adam do first?
- How could this situation be avoided? Think about it from both the school's and Adam's point of view.

## Work with others to review own learning needs and agree own personal development plan

The appraisal system is designed to help members of staff to consider their own professional performance on a regular basis. This should ensure that they think about their performance and continuing professional development.

The main consideration is that the **appraisal** process is a positive and non-threatening one. Each member of staff, including head teachers, will be appraised by the person who has responsibility for managing them. In the case of the Head Teacher, this will usually be done by governors. With teaching staff, the process is an ongoing cycle which takes place annually. As an assistant, you may be appraised by your line manager or a member of staff with responsibility for teaching assistants. Higher level teaching assistants often take on this role. In the case of individual support assistants, this may be done by the school's Special Educational Needs Co-ordinator (SENCO).

### Key term

**Appraisal** – a regular meeting to discuss your development progress

You may find that the appraisal process is a good opportunity to discuss issues which may not otherwise be approached. It is also useful for discussing with your line manager anything you have done which you feel has been more or less successful than you had anticipated. In a similar way, you should also discuss any areas in which you would like to have further training due to your own professional needs or interests.

You will usually be able to find out through your school the different courses and development opportunities which may be available. You may find that the school invites people from different outside agencies to speak to staff about particular subject areas during staff meetings, and these may be optional for support staff. Your line manager or supervisor should be able to give you information about training and help you to decide on the best courses and meetings to attend. The SENCO may be able to give you details about specific special educational needs courses, such as those run by the Sensory Support Service, or the Behaviour Management Unit.

If you have difficulty finding help, the local authority should publish details of courses which are run for teachers and support staff. You may also be able to contact the local borough for information about professional training for assistants, as this is undergoing a period of national change. Most local authorities will offer the induction training for teaching assistants which has been devised by the DfES (now the DfE) and is aimed at those who are completely new to the role. It is fairly comprehensive and covers areas such as behaviour, literacy and numeracy, and special educational needs (SEN). These courses should be free of charge to assistants in local schools. The borough's education department should have a member of staff responsible for support staff training who will also be able to advise you.

### Over to you!

What development opportunities are available in your local area for support staff? How do you find out about these and are there regular opportunities for you to attend additional courses?

### Functional skills

**ICT: Using ICT**
Completing this task is a great way of making time to look further into continuing professional development (CPD) opportunities. Your local education authority's website may be a good starting point. When you find a good website that provides you with the relevant information, bookmark the page so that you can locate it again easily in the future.

### BEST PRACTICE CHECKLIST: Areas for development

- Make sure you are aware of when and where courses are run for support staff.
- Look out for opportunities for development as they become available and ask about them.
- Read information boards and magazines in your school.
- Speak to your line manager or the class teacher about particular areas of interest.
- Join any secondary school cluster groups or networks.

## How the appraisal system works

The general appraisal form below gives some idea of how the initial discussion with your line manager might be structured. However, this is a basic outline and further ideas such as whether you would like a more formal observation of your work may be recorded. If this is the case, the focus and timing of the observation should be decided at the initial meeting. An observation may take place if you or your manager feel that you would benefit from some feedback concerning your work: for example, if you are not sure that your methods for giving children praise are as effective as you would like. You will then agree on any action to be taken and new targets for the coming year. Following the meeting, copies of the appraisal form will be given to you and to a senior teacher for record keeping, but will be confidential.

**BEST PRACTICE CHECKLIST:** Preparing for your appraisal

- Check through your job description before the meeting.
- Be prepared by having some ideas of strengths and successes.
- Think about areas you may wish to develop before going to the meeting.

**Getting ready for assessment**

1. Reflect on your own role, if you have not done so already as part of your own professional development. Note down any areas which you feel satisfied with over the past year and see whether you are able to identify any areas for development.

2. Are there any parts of this process which you find difficult? Why?

If you use a copy of your appraisal, which has been signed by your line manager, this will count towards the assessment criteria of this unit. Speak to your assessor about how much it will cover, based on what it says.

## How to develop and set targets

When thinking about areas for development, it may help to divide your knowledge and experience into sections. As an example, these might be knowledge and experience of:

- the curriculum
- behaviour management
- ICT

# General self-appraisal

It would be useful if you could bring this information with you to your initial meeting, to help you to identify your needs as part of the appraisal process.

1 Do you feel that your job description is still appropriate? Do you feel that there are any changes that need to be made?

2 What targets were set at the last appraisal/when you started your job? Have you achieved your targets?

3 What are the reasons for not having achieved your targets?

4 What aspect of your job satisfies you the most?

5 What aspect of your job has not been as successful as you had anticipated?

6 Are there any areas of your work that you would like to improve?

7 What training have you received? Has it been successful?

8 What are your current training needs?

*If you have not been given one, suggest to your line manager that you complete a form such as this before your initial meeting.*

- relevant or new legislation
- health and safety
- working with or managing others
- record keeping
- special educational needs.

You will then need to think about your level of confidence in each of these areas so that you can begin to see areas of strength and those which may need further development. You will need guidance in order to turn these into targets.

Your line manager should be able to work with you to set personal development targets which are SMART (see the following table).

| Specific | You must make sure your target says exactly what is required. |
|---|---|
| Measurable | You should ensure that you will be able to measure whether the target has been achieved. |
| Achievable | The target should not be inaccessible or too difficult. |
| Realistic | You should ensure that you will have access to the training or resources which may be required. |
| Time-bound | There should be a limit to the time you have available to achieve your target. This is because otherwise you may continually put it off to a later date! |

Table 1: SMART targets.

When thinking about these targets, you should not usually set more than three or four, so that they will be achievable. You should also ensure that you check between appraisal meetings to make sure that you are on course to meet your targets. There is little point in setting them if you have the meeting and then put the paperwork away again until next year.

You may find that because of the school development plan there are already training programmes planned over the next 12 months, for example, on the use of the interactive whiteboard in the classroom (see below), and that you will be attending this anyway. This will therefore form one of your targets. You may also like to think about training courses which will be useful to attend.

# Be able to reflect on how learning opportunities contribute to personal development

You will constantly be coming across learning opportunities in school which will help you to develop professionally. Whether these are just through talking informally with others, your own experiences, or through more formal training or INSET, your learning will shape the way you manage future situations and contribute to your personal development as you think about and reflect on what has happened. It is therefore useful to take time to think about how these learning opportunities have affected your own practice.

New targets for professional development:

1 To attend whole-school training on developing interactive whiteboard skills

2 To attend course on supporting children with challenging behaviour

3 To complete level 3 qualification in Supporting Teaching and Learning in schools.

Part of a completed appraisal form.

## How learning activities have affected practice and how reflective practice has improved ways of working

### Classroom management

You may pick up new information on classroom management in different ways. In the course of your work and through experience you may gather information which you can integrate into your practice. Alternatively you might have been on a course which suggests that you try a new approach. You can also be more proactive by asking to observe other teaching assistants who may have more experience than you, or who manage children in a particular way.

### Meetings

You will find that you pick up new information during whole-school meetings or those which are run for assistants. Sometimes, colleagues may pass on details of training which they have attended or give handouts if they have found something which may be useful to others. If you find something useful, it is always worth mentioning this to others for their benefit.

### INSET/training

It is likely that you will need to attend whole-school training and INSET, which usually takes place at the start of a new term. You may be required to implement new ways of working if the whole school are taking on a new initiative, for example. You may then be asked to evaluate how things are going and whether the changes have been beneficial to the children.

**Skills builder**

Keep a list of all the INSET and training you attend each time you do it. This will be valuable to you when you are filling in job applications or reflecting on your own professional development.

### New legislation

New legislation is brought in from time to time which will affect the way we work in schools. It is likely that if there are legal implications, the school will be obliged to offer training so that the requirements can be explained in detail. You may find that this affects your practice on a daily basis, or that the changes to you are very slight.

**Portfolio activity**

How do the headings above support you in thinking about the way in which your learning has affected your practice? Give examples of the ways in which your practice has been enhanced as your own experiences have developed.

**Functional skills**

**ICT: Developing, presenting and communicating information**
You could create a document on the computer that contains a table where you can track and record any learning opportunities that you take part in. Make sure that you save this document so that you can edit it again and add to it when necessary.

### Curriculum changes

During the course of your career, there will be regular changes to the way in which different subject areas are taught and in particular the way in which support staff are deployed to deal with them. You will be given information and training as the need arises and these will affect your practice as you will be required to implement them. It is likely that you will also form your own opinions about whether they have had a positive effect.

### Informal conversations with others

You might find that just through chatting to others, you pick up on new information which may affect your work with children. You should make the most of breaks and other times which give you the chance to catch up and discuss your practice with others.

### Working with a child who has specific needs

You will gain a great deal of experience through working with pupils who have specific educational needs. This may be learning about dyslexia, for example, or how to support a pupil who has a hearing impairment. It is useful to keep information or helpful ideas for your own benefit, as you may need to refer to them again at a later date.

## CASE STUDY: Improved ways of working

As part of her qualification in Supporting Teaching and Learning, Helen needs to have a professional review meeting with her line manager so that targets can be set for review. She has discussed this with her assessor and is keen to identify areas for development, as she has started to reflect on her practice. She asks her line manager whether this is possible, as at present, teachers in the school have professional development meetings but not teaching assistants. Her line manager is not enthusiastic about the idea as she says it will make more work for her, but says that she will speak to the Head Teacher. In case there is no comeback, Helen starts to talk to her assessor to find out whether there are other ways for her to gather this evidence.

Three weeks later, the Head Teacher asks Helen about the evidence she needs to gather. The Head says that it would be good practice for all the teaching assistants in the school to have performance management meetings and tells Helen it will be an item for discussion at the next staff meeting.

* How did Helen show sensitivity in her request for professional development?
* Should she have gone straight to the Head Teacher, in retrospect?
* How might the school benefit from Helen's request?

## How to record progress in relation to personal development

Make sure you keep any paperwork from your targets and personal development plans so that you can refer to them later. They will also be useful as they will show how you have progressed professionally during your time in school. You should also always keep a record of all courses, qualifications and other ways in which you develop professionally during the course of your career. Your school may be able to track those you have attended since starting, but it is worthwhile keeping your own record. This will be a good aide-memoire for you but will also be useful when applying for jobs or further qualifications. You should list courses in date order and keep a record of who was running it, and whether there were any qualifications or credits attached, in case you need this information later. The quickest and easiest way is to keep a file which you can add to and also a Word® document on your computer with a list such as the one below. Always keep handouts and other paperwork, certificates or letters of attendance, as you never know when these may be useful.

### Portfolio activity

If your school does not usually carry out a professional appraisal for teaching assistants, you may like to use the example on the next page. You can then use this in your portfolio.

---

**Alison Jamison – Record of courses attended**

September – December 2008: DfES Induction Training for teaching assistants (12 sessions on Monday afternoons)

January 2009: whole school INSET on managing behaviour

May 2009: maths course – twilight 4–6pm with local maths co-ordinator

September 2009: Interactive whiteboard training for teaching assistants – afternoon as part of INSET

September 2009 – June 2010: Level 2 NVQ for support staff in schools at Petersfield College

October 2009: one day whole-school ICT INSET with Jenny Williamson

November 2009: whole-school Ofsted preparation

January 2010: safeguarding training – two-day course at local authority

*You will need to keep your own record of professional development.*

# Professional Review Meeting

Name: ........................................... Date: ..............

Line manager: ...........................................

Areas discussed:




Review of last year's targets:

1 ......................................................... target met/not met

2 ......................................................... target met/not met

3 ......................................................... target met/not met


New targets for professional development:

1 .........................................................

2 .........................................................

3 .........................................................



To be reviewed on: ...........................................


Signed ...........................(TA)

...........................(Line manager)

*An example of a professional review meeting form.*

## Getting ready for assessment

The appraisal meeting as a whole should cover many of the learning outcomes and assessment criteria for this unit *if they are all discussed*, although you should check with your assessor to make sure that your awarding body will accept this. If your assessor can be present at your appraisal interview and witness it, this will be even better evidence for your portfolio, although this can be difficult to arrange.

### Target setting examples

1. Some candidates choose to have one of their targets as completion of their award by a set date.

2. Include any INSET training that your school will offer during the next 12 months, for example, whole-school training on the new curriculum in 2011. In this way, you are including something you will be doing anyway, rather than setting additional work for yourself.

3. Include any training you have requested specifically for yourself, for example, a sign language course or a qualification to upgrade your maths or English skills.

Remember that targets will all need to be SMART (specific, measurable, achievable, realistic and time-bound). If your line manager has written a target which is not clearly achievable within the timescale, or which is not clear, it is important that you point this out.

If you are having some difficulty in setting a meeting in your school, speak to your assessor. You may be able to set and review some targets of your own through your college course.

## Check your knowledge

1. Why is it important to have an up to date job description?

2. What kinds of strengths should a good teaching assistant have in addition to professional knowledge?

3. Which of the following might a member of support staff be asked to do?
   a) carry out a playground duty
   b) work with a child who has specific learning difficulties
   c) clean classrooms
   d) put up displays
   e) take assemblies
   f) work on speech and language targets with individuals
   g) carry out first aid.

4. Why is it important to keep track of your own professional development?

5. What kinds of things should you consider when setting targets for the following year?

6. How can you find out about professional opportunities which may be available to you?

### Websites

www.education.gov.uk – Department for Education
www.learningsupport.co.uk – *Learning Support* magazine (for teaching assistants in primary schools)
www.napta.org.uk – National Association of Professional Teaching Assistants (NAPTA)
www.ofsted.gov.uk – Office for Standards in Education, Children's Services and Skills (Ofsted)
www.teachernet.gov.uk/teachingassistants – Teachernet: information about support staff
www.tda.gov.uk – Training and Development Agency for Schools (TDA), National Occupational Standards for Teaching Assistants
www.tes.co.uk – the *Times Educational Supplement* (TES) website

# School life

## My story: Nicola

I am a new member of staff and came to my current school last term after six years at a smaller school. I really needed to change and move on as I had been unhappy in my previous role. But it took me a while to get the confidence to start applying for other things, even though I am quite experienced. I decided to go for it and started applying with the support of my friends and family. Now I have moved on and things are so different here. We have a large staff and regular meetings, and I really feel as though I am part of a big team. Everyone has been really welcoming and I am wondering what took me so long to make the change. I have also been able to take on a slightly different role from that in my previous school and am currently working on my level 3 in Supporting Teaching and Learning in Schools. If possible, after this I am hoping to go on to qualify as a higher learning teaching assistant. Things are great!

## Ask the expert

**Q** I am always asking to go on courses but never seem to be able to – what should I do?

**A** You should be entitled to some courses through your school, although head teachers can sometimes be reluctant to allow support staff out on a regular basis. Do not ask too often – if you can find one or perhaps two each year that are of particular interest to you or that are linked to your role, this is plenty as you should also be attending staff development days in your school.

# CYP 3.4 Support children & young people's health & safety

This unit requires you to know about procedures which exist in your school for keeping children safe in the learning environment. You may also be required to help in outdoor environments or on school visits or journeys. You will need to have a clear understanding of the expectations of your role, what you should do in different situations and how to assist with the safety and protection of children. You should know and understand your responsibilities for maintaining a safe environment and ensuring that risks and hazards are dealt with appropriately. For your role and responsibilities with regard to child protection and safeguarding issues, see CYP 3.3.

## By the end of this unit you will:

1. understand how to plan and provide environments and services that support children and young people's health and safety

2. be able to recognise and manage risks to health, safety and security in a work setting or off-site visits

3. be able to support children and young people to assess and manage risk for themselves

4. understand appropriate responses to accidents, incidents, emergencies and illness in work settings and off-site visits.

# Understand how to plan and provide environments and services that support children and young people's health and safety

Planning and providing environments means that you will need to be aware of how to take into account the health and safety requirements of pupils when setting up learning activities. Before starting any learning activity, you should always make sure that the environment is free of any **hazards** and that children will be able to work safely.

## Factors when planning healthy and safe indoor and outdoor environments

### The function and purpose of environments and services offered

Rooms should be organised safely and there should be adequate space so that the number of people who will be using them can move around comfortably. Everyone should be able to access materials and equipment as required without causing **risk** to others. There should be sufficient light for the children to work without discomfort. You should also be aware that harsh lighting (for example, from fluorescent bulbs) can sometimes be uncomfortable after a prolonged time and cause headaches for some people. You may also find that an area which you had thought was suitable in which to work with children is too noisy or too dark and therefore not suitable for use. You should consider the following aspects.

- **Specific risks to individuals.** You should take any specific risks to individuals into account. These may include pregnancy, sensory impairment or other needs which will impact on the way in which you plan the environment or carry out activities.

- **The individual needs, age and abilities of the children and young people.** You should take the specific needs of pupils into account when setting up the environment – for example the age, abilities and needs of the children with whom you are working. You should in particular take note of any pupils who have special educational needs

(SEN). Furniture should be an appropriate size for the age of the children so that they are able to sit comfortably when working. Children should not be hunched over tables which are too small or have difficulty in sitting normally.

- **The duty of care.** As we have a duty of care towards pupils, we should ensure that they are comfortable and safe and that the environment is secure and conducive to learning. Equipment should be stored safely so that it does not present a hazard. Drawers and storage should be clearly marked so that it is clear where different equipment is kept and pupils are able to find it easily.

- **Outdoor spaces.** Outside areas to be used by children should be secure and boundaries regularly inspected to ensure that they are safe. Outside areas should be checked regularly to ensure that they are tidy and any litter, broken glass or animal mess has been cleared up. If you are responsible for putting out equipment, make sure that children are aware of how it is to be used; reinforce rules wherever possible to remind them how to behave. The long jump pit should be covered when not in use, as when left uncovered it can attract foxes and dogs, and can also be hazardous. Any equipment should always be appropriate to the space available and should be put away safely. Plants can also be dangerous – thorns or nettles should be kept back and any poisonous plants noted and/or removed.

- **Safety equipment.** Staff will need to ensure that safety equipment which is provided for use when carrying out activities is always used. This will include safe use of tools which are used for subjects such as design and technology, or gloves or goggles when handling materials in science activities. There should be guidelines in the school's policy for the safe use and storage of safety equipment.

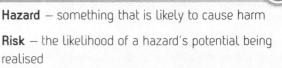

## Key terms

**Hazard** – something that is likely to cause harm

**Risk** – the likelihood of a hazard's potential being realised

*You will need to be aware of safety issues in all learning environments.*

## CASE STUDY: Planning healthy and safe environments

Rehana supports pupils in Year 7 during Food Technology. Part of her responsibility is to prepare the classroom before the lesson and to supervise pupils as they work and when they put equipment away. She has found that the layout of the room and organisation of equipment is not as it might be. To reach equipment, pupils sometimes have to pass others as they are removing food from hobs or ovens. The problems in layout are made worse for one of the pupils, who has a visual impairment and mobility difficulties. This pupil finds difficulty in accessing her work space and also relies on Rehana as she is unable to reach some of the equipment.

- What could Rehana do in this situation?
- Have you experienced these kinds of issues? If so, how have you managed them?

### Functional skills

**Maths: Representing**
You could draw a scale plan of a practical classroom to show how you consider the needs of all the learners in your setting.

## How health and safety is monitored, and how people are made aware of risks and hazards

The person responsible for health and safety in your school should carry out safety checks routinely or make sure that these take place on a regular basis. There should be regular walk-rounds or other means of making sure that hazards are not being left unreported. Where hazards are discovered — for example, items stored on top of cupboards which could fall down when the cupboard is opened — these should be recorded and reported immediately.

Safety checks should also be made on all equipment which could be hazardous if neglected. All electrical items which are used in school should have annual checks carried out by a qualified electrician. Equipment such as fire extinguishers should also be checked annually, and the date of each check should be recorded on the outside of the extinguisher. Health and safety should also be a regular discussion point at any meetings which you attend in the school, and staff should be regularly reminded about any issues. If a specific hazard has arisen and all staff need to be notified quickly, there should be a procedure for doing this.

## Over to you!

Consider how health and safety is monitored in your own school. How are staff made aware of risks and hazards and encouraged to work safely?

## Sources of current guidance and how legislation, policies and procedures are implemented

The Health and Safety at Work Act (1974) was designed to protect everyone at work through **procedures** for preventing accidents. Although it applies to all environments, it is very relevant to school settings and all staff will need to be aware of its main points.

## Key term

**Procedures** – steps your setting says you must follow

## Report any hazards

Everyone should be alert to any hazards which are likely to cause injury to themselves or others in the school. The school is required to carry out an annual risk assessment to determine which areas and activities of the school are most likely to be hazardous, the likelihood of specific hazards occurring, and those who are at risk. Children and staff need to be vigilant and immediately report any hazards which they notice to the appropriate person. This may be the school's health and safety representative, the head teacher or another member of staff. You should be

aware of the designated person to whom you should report health and safety matters (see also page 139).

## Follow the school's safety policy

The school needs to have a safety policy, which should give information to all staff about procedures within the school to ensure that it is as safe as possible. All new staff joining the school should be given induction training in safety procedures and what to do in case of emergencies. Safety should be a regular topic at staff meetings and staff should sign the health and safety policy to state that they have read it.

## Knowledge into action

Look at a copy of your own school's health and safety policy. What references can you find to current legislation? How does your school ensure that all staff have read and implement correct procedures?

## Functional skills

**English: Reading**
**English: Writing**
You could read three different health and safety policies, then compare the content. Using the information you have read, you could select certain aspects from each policy to write your own health and safety policy.

## Make sure that their actions do not harm themselves or others

Staff also need to ensure that any actions which they take are not likely to harm or cause a danger to others in the school. This will include tidying up and putting things away after use. You also need to consider the effects of not taking action – for example, if you discover a potential danger, it is your responsibility not to ignore it but to report it as appropriate.

## Use any safety equipment provided

Staff will need to ensure that safety equipment which is provided for use when carrying out activities is always used. This will include safe use of tools which are used for subjects such as design and technology, or gloves when handling materials in science activities. There should be guidelines in the school's policy for the safe use and storage of equipment.

## Ensure equipment is safe and appropriate

All materials and equipment used in schools will need to fulfil recognised standards of safety. The most widely used safety symbol is the Kitemark, which shows that an item has been tested by the British Safety Institute. Products are not required legally to carry a Kitemark, but many do so in order to show that they meet these requirements. However, European regulations require that many items must also meet legal requirements before they can be offered for sale within the European Union. These items will carry a CE symbol (this stands for *Conformité Européenne*, 'European conformity') to show that they meet European rules.

Always make sure that equipment you are offering for use to children is age- and ability-appropriate. The guidelines given by manufacturers are intended to be a realistic means of checking that equipment is not misused. A child who is too young or too old

may be unable to use the equipment, and may hurt themselves and others as a result.

All staff working within a school have a responsibility to ensure that children are cared for and safe. The Children Act 1989 and Children (Scotland) Act 1995 also require that we protect children as far as we can when they are in our care. This includes preventing any risks which may occur.

*How many of these safety symbols do you recognise?*

# Be able to recognise and manage risks to health, safety and security in a work setting or off-site visits

You will need to be able to identify a number of hazards in all situations, both in your setting and when managing children off site. This means that you should be vigilant both when working with others and when planning off-site visits. It is also a legal requirement that schools complete a specific risk assessment form before carrying out some activities or taking pupils off site — for more on this, see page 136.

## Identify potential hazards to the health, safety and security of others

When supervising children, you should be aware of the kinds of risks to which they are exposed and how likely these are to happen, bearing in mind the age and/or needs of the child. If you are working with children who have learning difficulties, they may also be less likely to have a fully developed awareness of danger. You will need to modify your supervision according to the needs of the children and their level of awareness.

### Identifying on-site hazards

- **Physical** — physical hazards will be varied and will range from objects being left lying around to more serious ones such as equipment not being checked. As you spend more time in school, you will get to know the kinds of hazards which you are likely to come across.

- **Security** — potential security hazards may be around unidentified persons on the premises and children being able to go off site. Make sure that you are always vigilant as regards security issues and do not be afraid of challenging any individuals if you do not recognise them (see also page 139).

- **Fire** — ensure that you are aware of fire procedures, particularly if you are new to the school. Hazards are increased in science laboratories, food technology classrooms or the school canteen.

- **Food safety** — you should be a good role model for children and always follow good practice yourself with regards to hygiene. This will include washing of hands before any activity involving foodstuffs, such as at lunchtime or prior to cooking activities. Instruct children how to handle sharp knives, use hotplates and ovens and monitor their use.

- **Personal safety** — you should have an awareness and be vigilant when alone with other adults, or if for any reason you are in an isolated part of the school and working alone.

---

**CASE STUDY: Managing personal safety**

Zara undertakes support work at her local specialist college. It is the end of term and she has been helping out with the end-of-term musical production. On the last night, she stays behind to help to clear up. Some of the props are stored in a Portakabin across the other side of the school car park. She has been asked by the head of music and drama to return some props and to lock up the Portakabin before she leaves. She is uncomfortable about this, as it is getting quite late and almost everyone else has left.

- What could Zara do in this situation?
- What do you think the school could do to ensure that staff are not left in positions of vulnerability?

---

### Identifying off-site hazards

You will need to be aware of safety issues when taking children out of the school. If you are taking children on an educational visit, a member of staff should always go and look at the site, and undertake a risk assessment beforehand. This means that they will check what kinds of risks there might be and the likelihood of the risk occurring. This will depend upon the type of visit which may be a day, adventure activity or residential visit, including travelling abroad. The level of risk may be dependent on:

- the adult–child ratio
- where you are going
- how you will get there
- your planned activities.

The group leader will look at the facilities and check that they are adequate for the needs of the children and young people — for example, if there is a pupil who is

*Can you identify potential hazards in this learning environment?*

disabled in the group. As well as a risk assessment, preparation will need to include other considerations. You must be familiar with the plans so that you are prepared for whatever happens. For educational day visits, the lead person will need to:

- seek and gain parental consent

- provide information for parents and children and obtain information on emergency contact/additional needs

- arrange for suitable safe transport

- confirm insurance arrangements are in place

- make sure there is a first aid kit and a first aider travelling with the group

- advise on and check that pupils have appropriate clothing for the activity or weather

- make lists of adults and the children for whom they will be responsible

- give information sheets and hold briefings for all supervisors, including timings and any additional safety information

- ensure that the rules of behaviour are understood by pupils, parents and supervisors, including rules for remote supervision.

The information will depend upon the type of visit; for more hazardous activities or residential visits, more detailed information will be required.

## Skills builder

Think about the areas of risk for the following groups. How does the risk involved balance with the learning experience?

- Taking a group of pupils with learning difficulties to the park.

- Working with a Year 8 group to maintain and improve an area used for natural study in the school grounds.

- Accompanying a Year 10 group to a careers fair in the local town.

- Supporting pupils in Year 7 with a design and technology project using craft knives and hot glue guns.

- Accompanying pupils who are taking part in adventure activities such as abseiling or canoeing.

- Accompanying pupils to compete in football matches after school.

## Deal with hazards in the work setting or in off-site visits

If you come across a hazard whether you are in school or off site, you should act immediately to make sure that others are not put in danger. This includes making sure that any other individuals are warned and directed away from the area straight away. If you can, you should deal with the hazard but if this is not possible, you may need to direct others away from the area and/or send for another adult. Children in particular are naturally curious and if they see something happening they will want to have a look!

### Portfolio activity

Write a reflective account showing how you have dealt with a hazard, either in your school environment or on an educational visit. You will need to describe, in order, the steps you took and how you ensured that the needs of all individuals were taken into account.

### Functional skills

**English: Writing**
When writing your reflective account above, it is important to consider the layout, content and audience of the text. Take particular care with your spelling, grammar and punctuation.

## Undertake health and safety risk assessments and explain how they are monitored/reviewed

In the normal course of your practice, it is likely that you will be involved in risk assessment at some stage, whether this is because you have some responsibility for health and safety or because you are going on an educational visit. There will usually be a member of staff responsible for ensuring that all risk assessments are carried out and the paperwork completed in good time before the visit or activity is carried out. This will then need to be

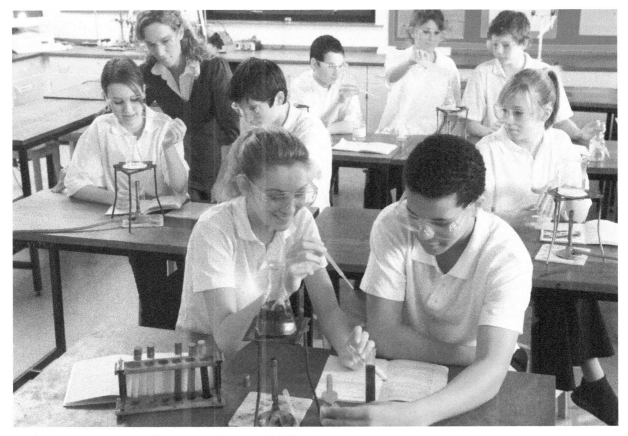

*How can you encourage pupils to asses and manage risks?*

checked and signed by the representative and by the Head Teacher to show that it has been completed correctly. For visits including hazardous activities, residential or visits abroad, the school governors or the local education authority will be required to give consent.

You may be involved in risk assessment activities, in particular if you are taking children off school premises. Always encourage children and young people to talk and think about any risks when they are working with you, so that they develop their own consideration of danger.

## Knowledge into action

When it is appropriate, for example, when you are going on an educational visit, carry out a risk assessment alongside the person in your school who would normally be responsible for completing it. Ensure that you follow the normal procedures and that all staff who are required to see the forms have done so and that the forms are signed. These will then need to be copied and stored correctly so that they can be found quickly if needed and are on file for future reference.

- How will the risk assessment reduce the risk in this instance?
- How are risk assessments monitored and reviewed in your school?

| Risk Assessment – Transport (Contract Vehicle) | | | |
|---|---|---|---|
| Hazard | Who may be affected? | Control measures | Further Action |
| Condition of vehicle/driver | All | If the condition of either the vehicle or the driver is considered to be dangerous the venture is not allowed to proceed. | Ask the company to confirm that vehicle to be used has appropriate documentation, is roadworthy and drivers hold relevant qualifications and experience prior to booking. |
| Unexpected movement/ braking of vehicle | All | Pupils sitting in seats with seat belts fastened at all times when the vehicle is in motion. Pupils must not distract the driver when the vehicle is in motion. All baggage stowed securely. | Staff supervision to ensure that this is complied with throughout the journey. |
| Road Accident | All | **If the accident is not serious** On normal road keep pupils on the vehicle if it is safe to do so. If not then move the pupils to a safe location protected from traffic. When moving follow the highway code and use staff to supervise the pupils to avoid danger. **If the accident is serious** Move those able to walk away from the scene of the accident keeping them safe throughout. This will have to be assessed at the time. Deal with casualties as best as you can until emergency help arrives. | Control communication between pupils and parents/carers. Contact school as soon as possible. Control communication between pupils and parents/carers Contact school and Emergency Contact at the LEA as soon as possible. Co-operate with the emergency services At least one member of staff should accompany any injured young people to hospital and remain there until parents or guardians arrive. |

*A risk assessment form.*

# Be able to support children and young people to assess and manage risk for themselves

## A balanced approach to risk management and the dilemma between the rights/choices of children and safety requirements

It is important for all children and young people to have opportunities to take some risks and most activities will carry some element of danger. Many educationalists now believe that the current tendency for many parents to keep their children indoors and take them everywhere by car is detrimental and overprotective, as it does not allow children and young people to explore and discover the world for themselves or assess elements of risk. If children's experiences are limited due to adults' anxieties, it is likely that they will find it difficult to assess and manage risk as an adult. When a more **balanced approach** is taken and children and young people are given more independence, they are more likely to grow in confidence. They should be encouraged to think about risks which may arise and act accordingly.

### Key term

**Balanced approach** – taking into account child's age, needs and abilities, avoiding excessive risk taking, not being risk averse and recognising the importance of risk and challenge to a child's development

In school, while it is important to be vigilant and not put pupils in direct danger, we can help them to think about risks in the environment and what we can do to avoid these risks. Although you are making sure that learning environments in which pupils can work and play are safe places, you can also encourage them to think about why certain courses of action, such

as playing cricket or football close to other pupils, may not be sensible. As pupils grow older, they should have more opportunities, both in school and through extra-curricular activities, to consider how their decisions will impact on themselves and others. They should also have opportunities to discuss potential risks and problems with their peers and adults.

### CASE STUDY: Taking a balanced approach

The geography teacher called a meeting to discuss the possibility of taking a group of Year 7 children on a field trip to the coast to study coastal processes. It is a large group and two of the pupils concerned have behavioural difficulties. At the meeting, another teacher and teaching assistant raised concerns about health and safety, as the area has a reputation for being hazardous and, in the spring term, the weather can be quite changeable.

- What do you think about this situation?
- Why is it important to discuss this as a group before planning to take the children?

### Functional skills

**English: Speaking, listening and communicating**
Discussing the case study would lend itself well to developing your speaking, listening and communicating skills. Try adopting different roles within the discussion, in order to take everyone's views into consideration. Try to make sure that you respond appropriately and move the discussion along.

## Supporting children or young people to assess and manage risk

You will need to be able to give examples from your own practice of how you have supported children and young people in assessing and managing risk to themselves. This will show that you have an awareness of the kinds of situations in which you should be vigilant, but also how you are able to pass this awareness on to children.

**Portfolio activity**

Give an example of a time when you have given pupils an opportunity to discuss and evaluate risk within your setting or on an educational visit. Show how you have supported them in the activity and what you consider the benefits to have been.

# Understand appropriate responses to accidents, incidents, emergencies and illness in work settings and off-site visits

In any environment where pupils are being supervised, it is likely that there will be incidents or injuries at some time. You may find that you are first on the scene in the case of an accident or in an emergency and need to take action. If you are the only adult in the vicinity, you will need to make sure you follow the correct procedures until help arrives. It is vital to send for help as soon as possible. This should be the school's qualified first aider and an ambulance if necessary.

You will also need to support and reassure not only the casualty but also other children who may be present. Children and young people may become quickly distressed and, depending on what they have witnessed, may be in shock themselves. You should also ensure that you and any others on the scene are not put at unnecessary risk.

You must remember that if you are not trained in first aid, and if you are at all unsure about what to do, you should only take action to avert any further danger to the casualty and others.

**Over to you!**

Find out who your school's first aiders are. Was it easy to find the information? Is it displayed around the school?

## Policies and procedures in response to accidents, incidents, injuries, signs of illness and other emergencies

All schools need to ensure that they take measures to protect all adults and pupils while they are on school premises and on off-site visits. This means that there will be procedures in place for a number of situations which may arise. These include the following.

- **Accidents and first aid** – there should be enough first aiders in the school or on the trip at any time to deal with accidents. First-aid boxes should be checked and refilled regularly, and there should be clear lines of reporting so that accidents are recorded correctly. If you are off site, you should know where the first aider is.

- **School security and strangers** – this includes making sure that all those who are in school have been signed in and identified. Schools may have different methods for doing this – for example, visitors may be issued with badges. If staff notice any unidentified people in the school, they should be challenged immediately. If you are on playground duty and notice anything suspicious, you should also send for help. Schools may also have secure entry and exit points which may make it more difficult for individuals to enter the premises.

- **General health and safety** – health and safety should be a regular topic at staff meetings and during assemblies, so that everyone's attention is drawn to the fact that it is a joint responsibility.

- **Control of Substances Hazardous to Health (COSHH)** — anything which may be harmful should be stored out of the reach of pupils or locked in a cupboard, for example, cleaning materials or medicines. COSHH legislation gives a step-by-step list of precautions that need to be taken to prevent any risk or injury.

- **Procedures for fires** — schools may need to be evacuated for different reasons — for example, fire, bomb scare, or other emergencies. Your school is required to have a health and safety policy which should give guidelines for emergency procedures and you should be aware of these. The school should have regular fire drills — around once a term — at different times of the day (not just before breaks for convenience!) so that all adults and pupils are aware what to do wherever they are on the premises. Fire drills and building evacuation practices should be displayed and recorded, and all adults should know what they need to do and where to assemble the children. If you are on a school visit, you should have been briefed as to what to do in case of fire or evacuation of the building.

- **Missing children** — fortunately it is extremely rare for pupils to go missing, particularly if the school follows health and safety guidelines and procedures. On school visits you should periodically check the group for whom you are responsible. If for some reason a child does go missing, you should raise the alarm straight away and make sure that you follow school policy.

## The correct procedures for recording and reporting accidents, incidents, injuries, signs of illness and other emergencies

Even if you are not a first aider, you should know the correct procedures for recording and reporting injuries and accidents in your school, as you may be called upon to do this. Remember that following all injuries or emergencies, even minor accidents and near misses, a record should be made of what has happened and the steps taken by staff who were present. You should also report verbally to senior management as soon as possible.

*Is this fire notice similar to those in your setting?*

## Secondary School
## Accident report form

Name of casualty .........................................................................................................

Exact location of incident ...........................................................................................

Date of incident ...........................................................................................................

What was the injured person doing? ..........................................................................

How did the accident happen? ....................................................................................

What injuries occurred? ...............................................................................................

Treatment given ...........................................................................................................

Medical aid sought .......................................................................................................

Name of person dealing with incident .......................................................................

Name of witness ...........................................................................................................

If the causualty was a child, what time were the parents informed? .......................

Was hospital attended? ................................................................................................

Was the accident investigated? ........................... By whom? ...................................

Signed ............................................................... Position.......................................

*Find out where accident forms are kept in your school and the procedures for completing them.*

### Functional skills

**ICT: Developing, presenting and communicating information**
**ICT: Using ICT**
Have you got electronic copies of all the relevant paperwork that your setting uses? If not, you could produce electronic versions that you could email out as attachments to all staff for ease of completion.

In addition to recording accidents, your school also needs to monitor illnesses which are passed around the school, as in some cases these will need to be reported to the local education authority. It is likely that your school office or sick bay will have a Department of Health poster showing signs and symptoms of some common illnesses so that staff will know what to look for. All staff need to be alert to physical signs that pupils may be incubating illness. **Incubation periods** can vary between illnesses, from one day to three weeks in some cases. General signs that children are 'off colour' may include:

- pale skin
- flushed cheeks
- rashes
- different behaviour (for example, quiet, clingy, irritable)
- rings around the eyes.

### Key term

**Incubation period** — the length of time between initial contact with an infectious disease and the development of the first symptoms

| Illness and symptoms | Recommended time to keep off school and treatment | Comments |
|---|---|---|
| **Chickenpox** – patches of itchy red spots with white centres; nausea; high temperature; muscle aches | For five days from onset of rash. Treat with calomine lotion to relieve itching | It is not necessary to keep the child at home until all the spots have disappeared. Chickenpox may pose an extra risk for pregnant women |
| **German measles (rubella)** – pink rash on head, trunk and limbs; slight fever, sore throat | For six days from onset of rash. Treat by resting | After being infected it usually takes between 14 and 21 days for symptoms to appear. Keep the child away from pregnant women. This illness is prevented by the MMR injection |
| **Impetigo** – small red pimples on the skin, which break down and weep | Until lesions are crusted and healed or 48 hours after commencing antibiotic treatment. Treat with antibiotic cream or medicine. | Antibiotic treatment may speed up healing. Wash hands well after touching the child's skin |
| **Ringworm** – contagious fungal infection of the skin. Shows as circular flaky patches | None. Treat with anti-fungal ointment; it may require antibiotics | It needs treatment by the GP |
| **Diarrhoea and vomiting** | Until diarrhoea and vomiting has settled and for 48 hours after. No specific diagnosis or treatment, although keep giving clear fluids | |
| **Conjunctivitis** – inflammation or irritation of the membranes lining the eyelids, red, watering or sore eyes; sticky coating on eyelashes | None (although schools may have different policies on this). Wash with warm water on cotton wool swab. Lubricant eye drops can be purchased over the counter. GP may prescribe antibiotics | |
| **Measles** – fever, watery eyes, sore throat, cough; red rash, which often starts from the head, spreading downwards | Four days from onset of rash. Give rest, plenty of fluids and paracetamol or ibuprofen for fever | This is now more likely with some parents refusing MMR inoculation |
| **Meningitis** – fever, headache, stiff neck and blotchy skin; dislike of light; symptoms may develop very quickly | Get urgent medical attention. It is treated with antibiotics | It can have severe complications and be fatal |
| **Tonsillitis** – inflammation of the tonsils by infection. Very sore throat, fever, earache, enlarged red tonsils, which may have white spots | Rest; ibuprofen or paracetamol may be taken to ease pain and fever; in some cases antibiotics can be taken. Ensure the child continues to eat and drinks plenty of fluid. | It can also cause ear infection |

*Table 1: Childhood illnesses and their characteristics.*

Children and young people often develop symptoms of illness more quickly than adults, as they may have less resistance to infection. Most schools will call parents and carers straight away if their child is showing signs or symptoms of illnesses. If a pupil is on a course of antibiotics, most schools will recommend that they stay off school until they have completed the course.

## Getting ready for assessment

A good way of producing evidence for this unit is to go for a health and safety walkabout in your school with your assessor during one of your setting visits. You can point out any hazards and carry out your own safety check of facilities and equipment in all areas of your school. This could include fire extinguishers and exits, first aid kits, access to first aid, how the school routinely checks equipment and prepares for school visits including risk assessment, and how accidents are recorded. If you are a first aider or have dealt with any incidents or illnesses, you could show the evidence to your assessor. They may also ask witnesses in your school whether you follow health, safety and security procedures yourself, and how you encourage pupils to do the same.

## Check your knowledge

1. Name three factors you might take into account when planning healthy and safe indoor and outdoor environments.

2. Where would you find guidance and procedures for health and safety in your school?

3. What are your responsibilities regarding hazards?

4. What kinds of situations are potentially hazardous?

5. List the types of risk you might encounter when taking children off site.

6. Give an example of when you might need to undertake a risk assessment.

7. Why do children and young people need to learn to be able to manage risk themselves?

8. Should only first aiders record and report accidents?

### References and websites

www.actionforchildren.org.uk – Action for Children
www.barnardos.org.uk – Barnardo's, a children's charity
www.bbc.co.uk/health/treatments/first_aid – first aid guide
www.hse.gov.uk – Health and Safety Executive
www.kidscape.org.uk – Kidscape, a charity to prevent bullying and child abuse
www.nspcc.org.uk – NSPCC: Helpline 0808 800 5000 or help@nspcc.org.uk
www.redcross.org.uk – British Red Cross
www.sja.org.uk – St John Ambulance
www.teachernet.gov.uk – TeacherNet, which also gives a list of charities that work together with schools
www.unicef.org – UNICEF

# School life

## My story: Paul

I work in a secondary school in my local town. The pupils are often taken on educational visits to support the curriculum. Recently a visit had been arranged to the local museum and art gallery, and I had been asked to accompany the group. In addition to myself there was one other teaching assistant and two parents. At the last minute the teacher was unwell and unable to accompany the group. The other teachers were all teaching so unable to come, and health and safety requirements state that visits off site should be taken by a qualified teacher. I checked with the Deputy (the Head was off site), who said that we would have to postpone the visit as it was important to comply with regulations. One of the parents had taken the morning off work to come with us; they were quite annoyed and said that we had enough adults to meet the adult–pupil ratio so should be able to go. As it turned out, we postponed the visit until the following week. I think we did the right thing, as I would not like to have been in charge if there had been any accidents or incidents while we were off site.

## Ask the expert

**Q** What happens if a supervising adult is unwell before or during a planned visit?

**A** Your school's risk assessment should outline what to do in this situation, but if an adult is unwell before setting off, it would be best to have another on standby. If the adult is a teacher it is important that the replacement adult is also a teacher, as the group leader should be suitably qualified and know about the expectations of the trip. If the trip has already been paid for, there should be another member of staff who can be sent instead – in the situation above it was easy to postpone the visit.

> **VIEWPOINT** 💬
>
> **How does your school prepare for educational visits and school journeys? What plans do they have in place in these kinds of situations?**

# CYP 3.1 Understand child & young person development

This unit requires you to have knowledge and understanding of the different areas of development of children and young people from the ages of birth to 19 years. You will also need to be aware of the factors which have an impact on children and young people's development and how various theories of development will influence current practice.

## By the end of this unit you will:

1. understand the expected pattern of development for children and young people from birth to 19 years

2. understand the factors that influence children and young people's development and how these affect practice

3. understand how to monitor children and young people's development and interventions that should take place if this is not following the expected pattern

4. understand the importance of early intervention to support the speech, language and communication needs of children and young people

5. understand the potential effects of transitions on children and young people's development.

# Understand the expected pattern of development for children and young people from birth to 19 years

## Explain the sequence and rate of each aspect of development from birth to 19 years

Although you may be looking at and discussing different aspects of child development separately, it is important to remember that development is **holistic**, and that each child is unique and will develop in their own way. Many of the skills and areas of development overlap with one another. A child does not learn the skills needed to play football, for example, which may be considered a physical skill, without having social, communication and cognitive skills as well. Aspects of development include physical, communication and language, intellectual/cognitive, social, emotional and behavioural, and moral.

### Physical development

This is an important area of children's overall development and one which can often be assumed will take place automatically as they grow and mature. Although children do develop many skills naturally as they get older, it is imperative that they have the opportunity to develop them in a variety of ways and they will need support in order to do this.

- **0–3 years.** This is a period of fast physical development. When they are first born, babies have very little control over their bodies. Their movements are dependent on a series of reflexes (for example, sucking, grasping) which they need in order to survive. In their first year they gradually learn to have more control over their bodies so that by 12 months, most babies will have developed a degree of mobility such as crawling or rolling. In their second year, babies will continue

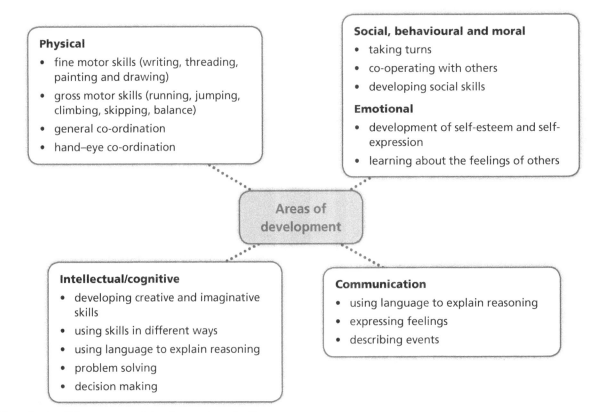

**Physical**
- fine motor skills (writing, threading, painting and drawing)
- gross motor skills (running, jumping, climbing, skipping, balance)
- general co-ordination
- hand–eye co-ordination

**Social, behavioural and moral**
- taking turns
- co-operating with others
- developing social skills

**Emotional**
- development of self-esteem and self-expression
- learning about the feelings of others

**Areas of development**

**Intellectual/cognitive**
- developing creative and imaginative skills
- using skills in different ways
- using language to explain reasoning
- problem solving
- decision making

**Communication**
- using language to explain reasoning
- expressing feelings
- describing events

*How do the different areas of development overlap?*

to grow and develop quickly and it is at this stage that most children will start to walk. Their ability to control their movements will mean that they start to use their hands for pointing, holding small objects and start to dress and feed themselves. They will also be able to play with a ball and will enjoy climbing, for example, on stairs or furniture. In their third year, children will start to have more control over pencils and crayons, and will enjoy looking at and turning pages in books. They should be able to use cups and feed themselves. They will be starting to walk and run with more confidence, and will be exploring using toys such as tricycles.

- **3–7 years.** At this stage, children will be able to carry out more co-ordinated movements and will be growing in confidence as a result. They will be refining the skills developed so far and will have more control over fine motor skills such as cutting, writing and drawing. They will also become more confident in activities such as running, hopping, kicking a ball and using larger equipment.

- **7–12 years.** Children will continue to grow and develop, and will now be refining many of their skills. They may start to have hobbies and interests which mean that they are more practised in some areas, for example, sport or dance. They may also be able to make very controlled finer movements, such as those required for playing an instrument or sewing. Girls in particular will start to show some of the early signs of puberty from the age of 10 or 11. In boys, puberty usually starts later, when there will be another period of rapid physical growth.

- **12–16 years.** At this stage of development, young people will be growing stronger. Boys will be starting to go through puberty and many girls will have completed the process and have regular periods. Girls will experience breast enlargement and increased fat layers. Boys will experience an enlargement of their testes and penis and muscle strength. Their voice will break and become deeper. Between these ages there can be a great variety in height and strength. Boys and girls may experience a growth spurt at this time, although at the end of this stage, most boys will be taller than most girls, on average.

*What signs of physical development have you observed in babies and small children that you see in everyday life?*

- **16–19 years.** This is the stage at which young people become adults and often at the peak of their physical performance. Although many girls may have reached physical maturity, boys will continue to grow and change until their mid-20s.

## Communication and language development

- **0–3 years.** From the earliest stages, adults will usually try to communicate with babies even though they are not yet able to understand what is being said. This is because it is important for babies to be stimulated and have an interest shown in them. In cases where babies are neglected and do not spend time with adults, they will find it very difficult to learn the skills of effective communication later. At this age, babies will be listening to language from those around them and will enjoy songs and games. Most will start to try to speak at around 12 months, although pronunciation will not be clear and words will usually be used in isolation. Between 1 and 2 years they will start to put words together, and their vocabulary will start to increase fairly rapidly so that by 2 years, most children will have about 200 words. Between 2 and 3 years, children will be starting to use negatives and plurals in their speech. Although their vocabulary is increasing rapidly, they will still make errors in grammar when speaking — for example, 'I drawed it.'

- **3–7 years.** As children become more social and have wider experiences, they will start to use an increasing number of familiar phrases and expressions. They will also ask large numbers of questions and will be able to talk about things in the past and future tenses with greater confidence.

- **7–12 years and upwards.** By this stage, most children will be fluent speakers of a language, and will be developing and refining their skills at reading and writing. Their language skills will enable them to think about and discuss their ideas and learning in more abstract terms.

## Intellectual and cognitive development

Children's intellectual development will depend to a wide extent on their own experiences and the opportunities they are given from the earliest stages. It is also important to understand that children will learn in a variety of ways and that some will find particular tasks more difficult than others due to their own strengths and abilities. There have been a number of theories which outline the way in which children learn and it is important to bear these in mind when thinking about stages of learning.

- **0–3 years.** Babies will be starting to look at the world around them and will enjoy repetitive activities in which they can predict the outcome. They will start to understand, for example, that objects are still here even when hidden. At this stage, babies and young children will be learning to identify different items and be able to point to them. They may start to recognise colours.

- **3–7 years.** This will be a period of development in which children are becoming skilled at aspects of number and writing, as well as continuing to learn about their world. They will still be looking for adult approval and will be starting to learn to read.

- **7–11 years.** Children will start to develop ideas about activities or subjects which they enjoy.

*How can you encourage pupils to develop their language abilities during discussions?*

They will still be influenced by adults and will be becoming fluent in reading and writing skills. They will be developing their own thoughts and preferences, and will be able to transfer information and think in a more abstract way.

- **12–16 years.** Young people will usually now have a clear idea about their favourite subjects and activities, and will usually be motivated in these areas. They will be reflecting on their achievements and choosing their learning pathway. They may lack confidence or avoid situations in which they have to do less popular subjects, to the extent that they may truant. It is particularly important to teenagers that they feel good about themselves and want to belong.

- **16–19 years.** By the time they come to leave school, young people will be thinking about career and university choices based on the pathway and subjects they have selected. They will be able to focus on their areas of strength and look forward to continuing to develop these as they move on.

## Social, emotional, behavioural and moral development

This area of development is about how children and young people feel about themselves and relate to others. They need to learn how to have the confidence to become independent of adults as they grow older and start to make their way in the world.

- **0–3 years.** Very young children will be starting to find out about their own identities. They will need to form a strong attachment, the earliest of which will be with parents and carers. In nurseries, children are usually given a key worker who will be their main contact. At this stage of development, children may start to have tantrums through frustration, and will want and need to start doing things for themselves.

- **3–7 years.** Children will still be developing their identities and will be starting to play with their peers and socialise using imaginative play. This will help them to develop their concept of different

roles in their lives. It is important that they are able to learn to understand the importance of boundaries and why they are necessary. They will also respond well to being given responsibility, for example, class helpers, and will need adult approval.

- **7–12 years.** Children's friendships will become more settled and they will have groups of friends. They will need to have the chance to solve problems and carry out activities which require more independence. They will continue to need praise and encouragement, and will be increasingly aware of what others may think of them.

- **12–16 years.** At this stage, the self-esteem of children and young people can be very vulnerable. Their bodies will be taking on the outer signs of adulthood but they will still need guidance in many different ways. They will want to be independent of adults and spend more time with friends of their own age, but can continue to display childish behaviour. They can find that they are under the pressures of growing up and of increasing expectations, and may be unsure how to behave in different situations.

- **16–19 years.** Young people enter adulthood but will still sometimes need advice and guidance from other adults. They will lack experience and individuals will vary in emotional maturity and the way in which they interact with others.

### Functional skills

English: Reading
ICT: Developing, presenting and communicating information
You could summarise the main points of the stages of development and put the information into a booklet. This is a good way of developing your reading skills. If you produce your booklet on the computer, you could also develop your ICT skills by inserting relevant images.

**BEST PRACTICE CHECKLIST:** Supporting social, emotional, behavioural and moral development

- Make sure you are approachable and give children and young people your time.
- Give fair but firm boundaries and explain the reasons for these.
- Ensure children and young people feel valued and are given praise and encouragement.
- Give children the chance to develop their independence.
- Be aware of each child's overall development and sensitive to their needs.
- Encourage them to think about the needs of others.
- Act as a good role model.

## Portfolio activity

In order to gather evidence for this assessment criterion, you may have to use a range of methods to show that you know and understand the stages of development for each age group. You can do this in a variety of ways including those suggested below.

- Write a reflective account, based upon your own observations of children at key stages of development, referring to their actual and expected milestones.
- Have a professional discussion with your assessor to show that you know and understand the milestones of each particular age and stage.
- Your assessment centre may prefer to provide an assignment to cover the learning outcomes.

## Functional skills

**English: Writing and Speaking and Listening**
Completing the tasks in this portfolio activity will allow you to develop your English skills. Take care with your spelling, punctuation and grammar in the reflective account. When having the discussion, make sure you listen carefully to what is being said so that you can respond in an appropriate manner.

## The difference between sequence of development and rate of development

Each child is unique and will develop at their own rate. However, while children will usually follow the same **pattern of development**, the ages at which they reach them may vary depending on the individual. Milestones of development are given as a broad average of when children may be expected to reach a particular stage. You may notice in particular classes or year groups some children who stand out because they have reached milestones in advance of or later than other young people.

### Key term

**Pattern of development** — usual rate of development (usual time frame in which development takes place) and sequence of development (usual order in which development occurs)

Sometimes, if a young person's growth pattern is very different from those of their peers, this may have an effect on their behaviour. For example, the onset of puberty can vary by as much as three years between children of the same sex and even longer between boys and girls. Some pupils may be very tall or very small for their age, or develop unwanted physical signs of puberty such as acne or body odour. This can sometimes affect how young people are treated by their peers. Their emotions can be affected and they may experience mood swings. It can also impact social development. During puberty a young person is developing their independence, self-identity and sexual identity. They may be more influenced by peers than by their parents or teachers. You should therefore look at the patterns of development discussed here as a guide to help you to draw up an overall idea of these different stages.

Although development is often divided into different areas, it is important to remember that they are interconnected and link with one another. For example, developing physically and refining these physical skills will also affect children's ability to become independent, socialise and grow in confidence.

When planning or thinking about activities which you are going to carry out with children and young

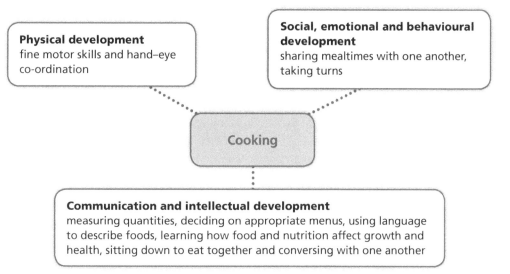

**Physical development**
fine motor skills and hand–eye co-ordination

**Social, emotional and behavioural development**
sharing mealtimes with one another, taking turns

Cooking

**Communication and intellectual development**
measuring quantities, deciding on appropriate menus, using language to describe foods, learning how food and nutrition affect growth and health, sitting down to eat together and conversing with one another

*Can you think of another activity that would develop a range of skills?*

people, you should try to think not only in terms of specific areas, but also in terms of the broader picture. Many activities will stimulate children's interest and encourage them to develop skills in different areas. For example, an activity such as cooking (or food technology for older pupils) will develop a range of skills.

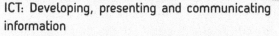

**Functional skills**

**ICT: Developing, presenting and communicating information**
Thinking of an activity that you have done with the children, you could create a PowerPoint® presentation that demonstrates all the different areas of development that the activity promoted. Delivering this presentation to your peers is a great way of sharing good practice and ideas.

# Understand the factors that influence children and young people's development and how these affect practice

## How development is influenced by personal and external factors

Children's development will be influenced by a wide range of factors. Their background, health and the environment in which they are growing up will all have an impact, as each will affect all areas of development. You will need to have an awareness of some of these, as you will need to know how pupils may be affected and encourage them to participate and develop as far as possible.

### Personal factors
#### Pupils' health
If pupils suffer from poor health or a physical disability or impairment, this may restrict their developmental opportunities. For example, a child who has a medical condition or impairment may be less able to participate in some activities than other children. This may initially affect physical development but may also restrict social activities, for example, participating in sports. The child's emotional development may also be affected, depending on their awareness of their needs and the extent to which they are affected. It is important that adults in school are aware of how pupils may be affected by these kinds of conditions and circumstances, so that we can support them by ensuring that they are included as far as possible.

### Learning difficulties
A child who has learning difficulties should be encouraged to develop in all areas to the best of their ability and as much as they can. If you are supporting a pupil who has learning difficulties, it is likely that you will have advice and guidelines from other professionals as to how to manage their needs while encouraging their development.

## External factors

### Pupils' background and family environment

Pupils will come from a range of different family environments, cultures and circumstances. Many families go through significant changes, during the child's school years, which the schools are not always aware of. These may include family break-up or the introduction of a new partner, bereavement, illness, moving house or changing country. Any one of these may affect children's emotional and/or intellectual development, and you may notice a change in pupil behaviour and ability to learn as a result.

### Poverty and deprivation

Poverty and deprivation are likely to have a significant effect on pupil development. Statistics show that children who come from deprived backgrounds are less likely to thrive and achieve well in school, as parents will find it more difficult to manage their children's needs, which will in turn impact on all areas of their development. These will all affect the way in which pupils are able to respond in different situations.

### Personal choices

The personal choices of pupils will affect their development as they grow older, as they decide on friendship groups, extra-curricular activities, academic involvement and so on. They may need advice and support from adults to enable them to make the choices which are right for them.

### Looked after/care status

If a child is looked after or in care, this may affect their development in different ways. However, they will usually be monitored closely and there will be regular meetings with the school to ensure that they are making expected levels of progress. Where there are any issues, these will then be addressed straight away.

### Education

In some cases, children may come to school without any previous education — for example, if they are from another country where formal education may begin later. Alternatively they may come from a home schooling environment or a different method of schooling, so they may need to have some additional support until they become settled.

## Theories of development and frameworks to support development

There have been a number of theories of development and many of them will influence the way in which we approach our work with children. Many psychologists have different ideas about how children learn — some feel that a child's ability is innate and others that it depends on the opportunities that they are given. This is often called the 'nature versus nurture' debate.

### Cognitive/Constructivist

Piaget believed that the way children think and learn is governed by their age and stage of development, because learning is based on experiences which they build up as they become older. As children's experiences change, they adapt what they believe; for example, a child who only ever sees green apples will believe that all apples are green. Children need to extend their experiences in order to extend their learning, and will eventually take ownership of this themselves so that they can think about experiences that they have not yet developed.

### Psychoanalytic

Freud stated that our personalities are made up of thee parts — the id, the ego and the superego. Each of these will develop with the child and each will develop in a subconscious way, driven by psychological needs.

- The id is the instinctive part of our personality; in other words, it is based on biological needs, such as hunger. A baby will cry if it is hungry and will not consider the needs of others around it.

- The ego starts to develop as the child realises that its behaviour may affect how its needs are met. For example, if it is hungry, it may decide not to cry for its food but to wait, as food will come anyway.

- The superego develops later on in childhood and is based on the development of the conscience. The superego may develop conflicting views to that of the ego, and may punish the individual through guilt. Alternatively, if the ego behaves well, the superego will promote pride.

## Operant conditioning

Operant conditioning theory states that our learning is based on a consequence which follows a particular behaviour. In other words, we will repeat those experiences which are enjoyable and avoid those that are not. This is as relevant for learning experiences as it is for behaviour. For example, a child who is praised for working well at a particular task will want to work at the task again. B.F. Skinner called this positive reinforcement. His work is closely linked to that of John Watson, discussed below, although it differs from Watson's in that individuals are more active in the process of learning and will make their own decisions based on the consequences of their behaviour.

## Behaviourist

Watson believed that we are all born with the same abilities and that anyone can be taught anything — it does not depend on innate ability but on watching others. His idea was that of 'classical conditioning' and was born out of Ivan Pavlov's research using dogs. Pavlov devised an experiment by ringing a bell when the dogs were about to be fed, which made them salivate, as they associated it with food appearing. The bell was then rung repeatedly with no food and gradually the dogs stopped salivating. Watson discounted emotions and feelings while learning, and based his theories purely on how individuals can be 'trained' to behave in a particular way.

## Social learning

Bandura's approach was also one of behaviourism; in other words, it accepted the principles of conditioning. However, Bandura stated that learning takes place through observing others rather than being taught or reinforced. Children will sometimes simply copy the behaviour or activities of adults or their peers without being told to do so, meaning their learning is spontaneous.

## Humanist

Maslow was originally interested in behaviourism and studied the work of Watson. He also acknowledged Freud's belief in the presence of the unconscious — however, he did not think that individuals were driven by it. He felt that a knowledge of ourselves and our own needs was far more important. Humanistic psychology is based on our own free will, although we have a hierarchy of needs without which we will be unable to continue to progress.

*Can you think of examples that you have seen of Skinner's theory of operant conditioning?*

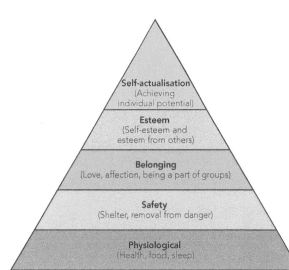

*Maslow's hierarchy of needs. Children will be unable to reach their full potential without their needs being met*

## Social pedagogy

Social pedagogy is a humanistic framework to support development. It refers to a holistic approach to the needs of the child through health, school, family and spiritual life, leisure activities and the community. Through social pedagogy the child is central through their involvement and interaction with the wider world. The framework is socially constructed and may vary between cultures, contexts and the time at which it takes place.

### Portfolio activity

Find out a little more about the learning theories of Freud, Maslow, Bandura, Skinner and Watson. Use the information to create a reflective account for your portfolio.

### Functional skills

**English: Reading**
Researching these theorists is a great way to develop your reading skills. Try finding a book to support your research and a good Internet website. Take care when using the Internet that you are aware of any copyright restraints.

# Understand how to monitor children and young people's development and interventions that should take place if this is not following the expected pattern

## Monitor development using different methods

Different methods of monitoring include:

- assessment frameworks
- observation
- standard measurements
- information from carers and colleagues.

You will need to use different methods and opportunities to monitor the development of children and young people in the course of your work with them.

It is important to understand the purpose of observations as part of your role. This is because you will need to report back to the teacher, who will in turn report to parents and carers on pupil progress. Parents and teachers should share information about pupils to enable them to work together in the pupil's best interest. These observations may be carried out both formally and informally, and there are advantages and disadvantages to each.

Informal observations will be those which you carry out each day as you work with pupils. These may be small but over time will enable you to build up a picture of each pupil. You may notice, for example, that an individual is able to understand new concepts very easily, or is unsure of how to use the calculator to work out a maths problem. It is likely that you will discuss your observations with teachers as part of the feedback process after your work with pupils. A disadvantage to informal observations is that they may not be recorded and you might forget to pass on what you have seen to others.

You may also be asked to carry out formal observations on pupils to support the teacher in assessing pupils' levels of development (see TDA 3.3, page 51, for more on formal observations).

Standard measurements are used to measure a child's physical development and to determine whether they are growing at the expected rate for their age. It is unlikely that you will be required to carry out this kind of check, as it will be done by health practitioners.

The Assessment Framework or Assessment Triangle is the term given to the way in which a child is assessed, to determine whether they are in need and what the nature of those needs is. In this way the child's best interests can be planned for with regard to their stage of development. It is looked at in more detail in CYP 3.3 on safeguarding children. Standard measurements and assessment frameworks will be useful in deciding on whether the child is reaching expected milestones of development in different areas. You should not be required to use these without the guidance and support of the form teacher or Special Educational Needs Co-ordinator (SENCO).

# Reasons why development may not follow the expected pattern

Children do not always follow a smooth developmental pathway or meet their expected milestones in all areas at the same time. They could be advanced in physical development, but delayed in language development, for example. Expected patterns of development may be affected by:

- **personal factors** such as health status, presence of any disability, genetic inheritance, disposition
- **external factors** such as economic, environmental, family circumstances, trauma.

Refer to the personal and external factors explored on pages 151–52, and the potential effects of transitions on pages 160–62. If you have concerns about a child's development, you should always speak to the form tutor or your manager in the first instance.

## CASE STUDY: Concerns about a child's development

Ania is in Year 9. Although she requires additional support for her reading and maths, she has made good progress during the first two years at secondary school. She has a wide circle of friends and enjoys taking part in many of the after-school activities. You know that she lives with her father and a younger sister who is at primary school. You have recently noticed that she is often alone at lunchtime and appears to be avoiding Lucy, who is her close friend. When you mention the new drama club to Ania, she shrugs and says she has to go straight home every day. During the last few days, you have become aware that Ania has not handed in her homework for maths or English.

- Would you say anything to Ania?
- Would you do anything else?
- Why is it important that you do something about what you have seen?

## How disability may affect development

Disability may affect development in a number of ways. Depending on the pupil's needs, it may cause a delay in a particular aspect of their development – for example, a physical disability may affect their social skills if they become more withdrawn, or their behaviour if they become frustrated. Development may also be affected by the attitudes and expectations of others – if we assume that a disabled person will not be able to achieve and do not allow them the opportunity to take part, we are restricting their development in all areas.

When you are working with pupils who have special educational needs (SEN), you will find that many professionals and parents speak about the danger of 'labelling' pupils. This is because it is important that we look at the needs of the individual first, without focusing on the pupil's disability or impairment. In the past, the medical model of disability has been used more than the social model (see the following table) and this kind of language has promoted the attitude that people with disabilities are individuals who in some way need to be corrected or brought into line with everybody else. This has sometimes led to unhelpful labelling of individuals in terms of their disabilities rather than their potential.

| Medical model | Social model |
|---|---|
| Pupil is faulty | Pupil is valued |
| Diagnosis | Strengths and needs defined by self and others |
| Labelling | Identify barriers/develop solutions |
| Impairment is focus of attention | Outcome-based programme designed |
| Segregation or alternative services | Training for parents and professionals |
| Ordinary needs put on hold | Relationships nurtured |
| Re-entry if 'normal' or permanent exclusion | Diversity is welcomed and pupil is included |
| Society remains unchanged | Society evolves |

Table 1: Medical and social models of disability, from *Disability Discrimination in Education Course Book: Training for Inclusion and Disability Equality.*

You should also be realistic about the expectations you have of pupils and consider their learning needs. For some, although not all, the curriculum will need to be modified and pupils may need support. However, it should not be assumed that SEN pupils will always require extra help and you need to encourage them to be as independent as possible.

## How different types of interventions can promote positive outcomes

As a teaching assistant, you are likely to be involved in intervention groups or other group work in order to support pupils who are not progressing at the same rate as others. This is likely to be advised by either the SENCO or another professional who will have links with the school. Any of the professionals below may come into school in order to discuss a child's progress or to advise teaching staff on next steps.

- **Social worker** – a social worker might be involved if a child has been a cause for concern in the home environment or if parents have asked for support. They will also liaise with the school regarding Looked After Children (LACs). Occasionally schools may contact social services directly if they have concerns about a child and their home environment.

- **Speech and language therapist** – see page 158 on supporting communication needs. See also page 159 on supporting speech, language and communication.

- **Psychologist** – see page 158 on supporting communication needs.

- **Psychiatrist** – a psychiatrist may be asked to assess a child if there are serious concerns about their emotional development. Children will usually have been referred through a series of assessments before this takes place.

- **Youth justice** – this form of intervention is a public body which aims to stop children and young people offending. The youth justice team may be involved in partnership with schools and the community where there are cases of offending behaviour. It also acts in a preventative way by running youth inclusion programmes, which are targeted towards those who may be at high risk of offending.

- **Physiotherapist** – a physiotherapist will advise and give targets for pupils to work on around the development of their **gross motor skills**. They may give exercises for school staff and parents to work on each day, depending on the needs of the child.

- **Nurse/health visitor** – these medical professionals may be involved in supporting the development of some children where they have physical or health needs. They will usually come into school to advise and speak to staff, generally with parents present.

### Key term

**Gross motor skills** – control of the larger muscles, typically those in the arms or legs – for example, kicking a ball

### Skills builder

Children with speech, language or communication needs often have difficulty in reading and understanding text. Investigate reading materials which are available in school and which are used to support children who have reading difficulties. This may be a reading scheme or other materials. Evaluate the materials in relation to their effectiveness in supporting children. For example:

- Is the material varied?
- How is it used?
- Is it age-appropriate?
- Is it flexible?
- Does it include different genres?
- Is it likely to inspire children to read and discuss the materials?

You could ask children who use the materials for feedback. What do they particularly like or not like about the materials?

● **Assistive technologies** – these are technologies which enable pupils who have specific needs to access the curriculum. They may range from computer programmes to specific items such as a speech recognition device or a hearing aid, and will give the individual an increased level of independence.

In all of these cases, positive outcomes will be more likely to be achieved, since the child will be working with a specialist who will then advise teachers and support staff. Their progress will then be measured through setting and reviewing targets on a regular basis.

# Understand the importance of early intervention to support the speech, language and communication needs of children and young people

## The importance of early identification and the potential risks of late recognition

Language is crucial to learning, as it is linked to our thoughts. It enables us to store information in an organised way. If children have difficulties in communicating with others due to a speech and language delay or disorder, they will be working at a disadvantage, as they will be less able to organise their thought processes and express themselves. As children become older and the curriculum becomes more demanding, the use of rational and abstract thought will become more important. The earlier the diagnosis of delayed language acquisition, the easier it will be for professionals and others to target the child's needs so that they are able to give support, and the more beneficial for the child, as the early years are a time of rapid learning and development.

Pupils with language delay may also find it harder to form relationships with others. As a result they may become frustrated, leading to possible behaviour problems and isolation. Very young children in particular will not have the experience to recognise the reason for their feelings. If you are working with a child who has a communication delay or disorder, you should be sent on specific training or given additional support and strategies to help you in your work with them.

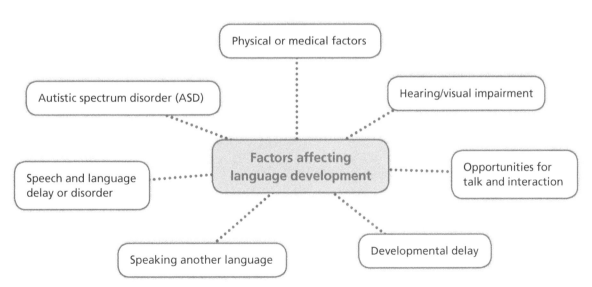

*Consider the impact one of these factors might have on a child's holistic development.*

**CASE STUDY:** Identifying speech and language delays and disorders

Neil is working in Year 7 as a teaching assistant and often supports a small group of children who are not making expected levels of progress. Sophie is in his group and is a bright and enthusiastic child, but her comprehension of the texts is limited and she finds it difficult to express what she wants to say. He has noticed recently that she seems increasingly quiet even in the small group. Neil has registered his concern once with Sophie's form teacher and SENCO, but so far nothing seems to have happened, and he does not like to be pushy as he knows they are busy.

- What should Neil do?
- Can you think of any other ways in which he could support Sophie?

## How multi-agency teams work together to support speech, language and communication

There will be a number of other professionals with whom you may come into contact if you support a pupil with communication and interaction needs. They may also come together as a team in order to discuss and plan out how the child's needs can be best met. Those involved will depend on the specific needs of the child, but may include some of the following.

### Speech and language therapist

This therapist will sometimes be based in schools but is usually external. They will give a diagnosis of a particular communication delay or disorder and will also advise school and parents about ways in which they can support the child. Speech and language appointments will usually be delivered in blocks, followed by activities for pupils to work on before they are next reviewed. Parents and teachers will be closely involved in the monitoring and review of pupils' progress.

### SENCO

The SENCO will co-ordinate the work of the other professionals who work with the child and will ensure that paperwork and appointments are up to date. They will encourage communication between agencies which work with the child and may organise meetings at the school to discuss progress.

### Other support staff

You may work alongside other support staff to deliver learning programmes to a particular child. You will need to ensure that you have opportunities to meet with them regularly in order to discuss the child's progress.

### Sensory support teacher

This teacher from the local authority may come to school regularly to advise on how best to support pupils who have a visual or auditory impairment, which will also have an impact on their communication skills. They may also provide resources to support pupils with their learning.

### Autism advisory teacher

This support teacher may come into school to advise on how best to support a child who has a diagnosis of autism. Two aspects of autism are that individuals will have an impairment in the areas of social interaction and communication.

### Educational psychologist

The educational psychologist may become involved if, following intervention and action from speech and language therapists and teaching staff, the child is still not starting to make some progress. They will carry out an assessment and suggest the next steps.

You may be invited to contribute to a multi-agency meeting alongside other professionals to discuss the needs of the child and to draw up targets for them.

**Knowledge into action**

Talk to your SENCO about which of the above professionals come into school on a regular basis and the children for whom they give advice and guidance.

## Functional skills

### Maths: Analysing

While talking to the SENCO, you could do some research to develop your maths skills. Try to calculate:

- what percentage of the children in school come under the care of the SENCO
- what the ratio is for these children when they access their support
- what percentage of their working week is spent with further support and how it has impacted on their achievement.

# How play/activities are used to support speech, language and communication

You need to encourage children and young people to develop language and communication skills as much as possible, as this is a key area of their development. Adults will need to give all children and young people opportunities to take part in speaking and listening for different purposes and in different situations. It is important that pupils use language both in whole-class and small-group activities and that you encourage them by asking them to talk about their own ideas.

In early years, play experiences can enhance all areas of development and can be directed specifically to address individual areas such as speaking and listening, or can be used more generally to support all. Through play, children will learn both about themselves and about others, and will be using their speech, language and communication skills in order to interact in a non-pressured environment.

As they grow older, their play takes on rules which require skills of negotiation. Children and young people still need to receive the chance to enjoy self-directed activities and equipment which support their creative and investigative skills. It is important that they have opportunities to use their own initiative and at times to work collaboratively. Project work, particularly when it involves problem solving, can support children and young people to develop their personal, learning and thinking skills.

A great deal of our communication with others is expressed non-verbally. It is important for children and young people that they are able to recognise and respond to non-verbal signals from others. Children and young people who are autistic, for example, may well have difficulty in recognising and interpreting non-verbal signs. It is likely that, if you are working with a pupil who has communication and interaction needs, you will be using different non-verbal strategies to support them. Through using this form of communication, you will be giving pupils an additional aid to understanding. The kinds of strategies you could use include:

- **using gestures** – this could be something as simple as a thumbs up or beckoning the pupil to come over

- **pointing to objects** – you can help pupils to understand by giving concrete examples of what you are discussing, and encouraging pupils to point to different objects in a similar way

- **through facial expressions** – a smile or nod can show approval, while you can also indicate excitement, disapproval, happiness and other emotions

- **through the use of body language** – you can show that you are giving the pupil your attention through the way in which you sit or stand.

You may also need to be specific and ask children and young people what particular gestures or signals from others might mean if they are unable to interpret them.

A number of visual and auditory approaches can also be used to enhance communication.

- **Pictures** can be used to initiate or supplement conversation, as they are a good starting point. The pupil can also use pictures to illustrate their ideas.

- **Games** are often used successfully to initiate pupil's speech and involve them in social interactions with others.

- **Signs** are used to support pupils who are unable to communicate verbally. However, they should not be used exclusively by these pupils; other children will enjoy learning different signs as well as teaching them to one another.

- **Technology** such as CDs, computer programs and interactive whiteboards are useful means of stimulating pupil's communication skills.

- **Modelling language** is important, as it gives children the chance to hear the correct use of language.

- **Music and singing** are excellent ways of reinforcing language for all age groups.

- **Drama and movement activities** can provide alternative ways to communicate ideas.

## Functional skills

### ICT: Using ICT

It is important to remember when using tape recorders, CDs, DVDs, whiteboards and other electrical items such as a roamer in your classroom that they are all different forms of ICT. Maybe you could list all the different forms of ICT you use or take some pictures that you could share with your colleagues.

## CASE STUDY: Support the development of speech, language and communication

Claire transferred to the secondary school last term. She found the transfer difficult as her close friends now attend a different school. She will respond to other children in the class, but only when they initiate discussion. She does not participate in any class discussion or volunteer answers to questions. When you try to start a conversation, she looks uncomfortable and only nods in reply.

- What strategies might you use to encourage Claire to communicate, both verbally and non-verbally?
- How could you work with others to support Claire in school?

Communicating with others is an important aspect in the development of self-esteem. As we grow up, we interact with others, which in turn reinforces our understanding of who we are and how we fit into our own families and the wider community. It is important for children as they develop that they have opportunities to socialise and work with others, and to feel part of different situations. Pupils who have communication and interaction needs will require support and encouragement, and should be included in all activities alongside other children.

## Reflect

How do you think it would affect your own social and emotional development if you were unable to communicate effectively?

# Understand the potential effects of transitions on children and young people's development

Whatever age group you are supporting, at some stage you will be working with children or young people who are going through a transition phase. The term 'transition' is applied to different situations in which children and young people pass through a period of change. As well as the more obvious school-based transitions, such as starting school, changing classes or key stages, or passing on to secondary school, children will pass through other periods of transition which may be long or short term. These may include changes in personal circumstances or experiences, passing through puberty, or simply a change in activity in the classroom.

## How different types of transitions can affect development

## Link

See pages 151–52 for information on factors that influence development.

When it comes to times of change and transition, children should be given every opportunity to talk about what is going to happen so that they are prepared for it. In some cases, such as bereavement, this may not be possible. However, where they are given some warning or opportunity to ask questions about events, any negative or harmful effects on their development can be reduced.

Types of transitions may be:

- emotional – for example, bereavement, entering/leaving care
- physical – for example, moving to a new educational establishment, a new home/locality, from one activity to another

- physiological — for example, puberty, long-term medical conditions
- intellectual — for example, moving from pre-school to primary or post-primary.

## Emotional

Pupils' emotions will be affected by their personal experiences and their relationships with others. If these experiences or relationships are unsettled or traumatic, it is likely that children's emotional development will be affected. They may find it harder to form trusting relationships with adults. Alternatively they may be more immature than their peers or seek attention. In younger children, emotions may be affected for some time by incidents which are seemingly insignificant to adults, such as the loss of a favourite toy or the death of a small pet.

## Physical

This kind of change may mean simply that the child is being asked to move on to a different activity, which can be difficult for some children if they are absorbed in what they are doing. If this is a consistent problem with some children, their development may be affected if they are not then taking part in other activities or widening their experiences. Another example of a physical change can be changing schools or moving house; you should have advance notice about changes like these and be able to discuss and prepare for them with children.

## Physiological

Physiological transitions may be harder to manage for pupils, as they will be happening over a longer period of time. Some children cope well with the changes they experience during puberty, while others require support and reassurance. Children and young people may not be aware of the underlying effects of physiological transition and they may also be more sensitive to discussing them.

## Intellectual

This type of transition may be because children are moving between key stages or need to change settings, for example, from Nursery to school or primary to secondary. Transitions may also be between year groups within one school which, if not handled well, can be traumatic for some pupils. As you get to know the pupils in the age range in which you work, you will

find out about routines which schools use to familiarise children with new environments before moving to them. Examples of this may be home visits for children who are moving to Nursery, or opportunities to visit secondary schools and meet teachers and pupils before transferring to Year 7. When managing the needs of older children, you should have opportunities to discuss with them the kinds of choices they will need to make. This may be the selection of GCSE's, A levels or diplomas. They must also begin to consider their career options. Opportunities to take part in external activities such as work experience, voluntary work and enterprise can be beneficial as they will support young people to develop their confidence, decision-making skills and self-reliance.

## The effect of having positive relationships during periods of transition

It is important for children to have positive relationships during periods of transition, as they will need to feel secure in other areas of their lives. They may need to talk to someone about how they are feeling and you should make sure that there are opportunities for them to do this. If you have advance notice that a child or group of children will be going through a period of change, this will give you an opportunity to plan how you will support them.

### CASE STUDY: Supporting periods of transition

Your role is to support children during their first term at secondary school. It is now the summer term and a meeting has been called to discuss the needs of the children who are due to transfer to the school from the local primary schools. You have been asked to contribute your ideas to support the smooth transfer for children and reduce their anxiety.

- What kinds of issues do you think there will be as the pupils prepare for secondary transfer?
- What are likely to be the main worries of children when they transfer?
- What differences are children likely to experience between their primary and secondary school?

# Primary/Secondary School Transition Policy

**Statement of Intent**

At Western View Secondary School we recognise that the transition from primary school to secondary is an important step in a child's school life and it is our intention to make this a positive experience for every child.

**Aims**

We endeavour to provide our children with a smooth transition from Year 6 (primary school) to Year 7 (secondary school). We ensure that the pace and quality of learning is sensitively maintained through the transition period so that children can continue to make good progress and develop the skills they will need to succeed in Key Stage 3.

**Procedures**

Transition to secondary school may be a stressful time for some children. We have built excellent relationships with local primary schools. The school also has procedures which will minimise difficulties or concerns and help children to settle into the new school environment as quickly as possible by:

- holding open days each October for Year 6 pupils and their parents.
- liaising with Year 6 primary teachers to discuss the strengths of individual children and any difficulties or specific needs they may have
- Year 7 teachers visiting primary schools in the spring term to speak to groups of pupils and answer any questions they may have
- the school holding one information evening and one information morning in May for parents with opportunities to speak to teachers and visit classrooms and specialist areas
- inviting Year 6 pupils in June to spend a day at the secondary school and take part in 'taster' sessions.

**Additional support**

We understand that some pupils may take longer to find their way around, feel part of their new school and come to terms with the new curriculum and learning and teaching methods. We aim to support pupils by:

- providing a buddy system – an older child is paired with each Year 7 child to give advice and support
- assigning a teaching assistant to each Year 7 classroom for each lesson during the first term, to provide support for the curriculum and pastoral support
- having a senior teacher with specific responsibility for transition who is available to answer children's or parents' concerns.

*An example of a transitions policy.*

## BEST PRACTICE CHECKLIST: Supporting transitions

- Work to ensure positive relationships during periods of transition.
- Be sensitive to pupils' needs and think about how the transition may be affecting them.
- Ensure pupils are given opportunities to talk about and discuss what will be happening and to ask any questions.
- Give pupils the opportunity to visit new classes or schools.
- Liaise with pupils who are already in the year group in order to build relationships and encourage questions from the children who are moving on.

### Portfolio activity

Write a reflective account of how you have supported a pupil or group of pupils during a period of transition. For instance, during their first term in Y7, support for a pupil after an extended absence or support for a new pupil joining a class.

### Functional skills

**English: Reading**
Use the reflective account from your portfolio activity. Read through relevant school policies for supporting inclusion and highlight the relevant parts to show how you followed policy and procedures when you supported individual children or groups. You might go on to make further suggestions of what else could be included in the policy.

## Getting ready for assessment

For this unit you will need to show your awareness both of children's development and also of the kinds of monitoring which takes place to ensure that they are making expected levels of progress.

Carry out two case studies on different children in your school who have been the subject of intervention due to their developmental levels. You will need to change the children's names due to confidentiality and obtain permission from parents and teachers. Give a short account of their backgrounds and describe the kinds of factors which may have influenced their development. Write about the way in which the school has monitored their development and the different professionals who have been involved with each, including how this has made a difference to their progress.

### Websites and references

**www.makaton.org** – Makaton information
**www.autism.org.uk** – National Autistic Society
**www.pecs.org.uk** – information on the Picture Exchange Communication System
**www.yjb.gov.uk** – Youth Justice Board

Donaldson, Margaret (1986) *Children's Minds*, HarperCollins

Hughes, Cathy and Pound, Linda (2005) *How Children Learn: From Montessori to Vygotsky – Educational Approaches and theories Made Easy*, Step Forward Publishing

Lindon, Jennie (2005) *Understanding Child Development Linking Theory and Practice*, Hodder Arnold

Lovey, Jane (2002) *Supporting Special Educational Needs in Secondary School Classrooms*, David Fulton Publishers

Sudbery, John (2010) *Human Growth and Development*, Routledge

## Check your knowledge

1. Explain the difference between sequence of development and rate of development. Why might children develop at different rates in different areas?

2. Explain how the emotional development of a child in Year 7 may be different from that of a child in Year 12.

3. What kinds of factors will influence a child's development?

4. Why is it important to have a basic understanding of some of the theories of child development? How will this help you in your practice?

5. What kinds of resources are available to support staff in schools when working with pupils who have developmental needs?

6. Which of the following are true? We monitor children's development by:
   a) observing them
   b) speaking to their peers
   c) carrying out assessments
   d) letting them make their own choices about their learning
   e) speaking to parents.

7. What are the differences between the medical and social models of disability?

8. Why is it important to act early when monitoring children's speech and language development?

9. Give three different types of transition.

# School life

## My story: Anita

I have been working to support the special educational needs department of a secondary school for three years now. Most of my work is with pupils in Year 7, so I have developed a good understanding of their needs during their first year in the school. I became concerned about Liam by the end of the first term. Initial assessments, and reports from his primary school, showed that Liam has dyslexia and would benefit from additional support with his reading and written work. His maths assessment showed that he was meeting the expected level of progress for his age. Liam worked hard in class and appeared to make progress in English lessons, but he was withdrawn and did not socialise with the other children. I was aware that some children do take a while to settle in but they usually do this within the first term. I began to observe Liam more closely and noticed that he did not join in with the games of other children, and if he had the opportunity he would go to the library or computer suite.

I spoke to Liam's personal tutor and SENCO to discuss my concerns. We looked at his records which had been passed on from the primary school and found that with additional support, Liam had made good progress in most subjects. His personal tutor suggested that I arrange a meeting with Liam's primary school teacher to discuss the concerns. During the meeting I found that during Liam's final year at primary school, he had experienced bullying. This had been dealt with and it was felt that Liam had put it behind him. The information had not appeared in the records which were passed on. If this had been known, support and reassurance could have been put into place earlier. The bullying had clearly had a longer-term effect than had been realised. We now ensure that we request an overview of each child's holistic development from the primary school and speak to parents before their transfer. I also suggested a buddy system which has now been introduced for all new pupils.

## Ask the expert

**Q** There seems to be a lot of focus at my school on intellectual development but far less on the social and emotional – why is this?

**A** Schools should focus their attention on all areas of a child's development – it may seem that more emphasis is placed on the academic, but it is not usually true to say that it is all that children learn. There will, for example, be Personal, Social, Health and Economic education (PSHE) and Citizenship activities which are carried out on a regular basis and are part of the curriculum. Pupils will also learn how to behave through socialising with others and through finding out the expected norms of behaviour and school rules.

**VIEWPOINT**

Reflect on the development of different children. You may, for example, want to think about a child who is very able academically. Are they also mature in other areas of their development?

# CYP 3.3 Understand how to safeguard the well-being of children & young people

This unit is about the way in which you safeguard the well-being of children and young people. You will need to be aware of health and safety issues as well as those around e-safety and child protection. You will need to have a clear understanding of your role and what you should do in different situations, and of the roles and responsibilities of others both within and outside the school.

## By the end of this unit you will:

1. understand the main legislation, guidelines, policies and procedures for safeguarding children and young people

2. understand the importance of working in partnership with other organisations to safeguard children and young people

3. understand the importance of ensuring children and young people's safety and protection in the work setting

4. understand how to respond to evidence or concerns that a child or young person has been abused or harmed

5. understand how to respond to evidence or concerns that a child or young person has been bullied

6. understand how to work with children and young people to support their safety and well-being

7. understand the importance of e-safety for children and young people.

# Understand the main legislation, guidelines, policies and procedures for safeguarding children and young people

## Current legislation, guidelines, policies and procedures affecting safeguarding

The Children Act 1989 introduced comprehensive changes to legislation in England and Wales surrounding the welfare of children. As well as ensuring that the welfare of the child is paramount, the Act identified the responsibility of parents and of those who work with children to ensure the safety of the child. Its main aims were to:

● achieve a balance between protecting children and the rights of parents to challenge state intervention

● encourage partnership between statutory authorities and parents

● restructure the framework of the courts, in particular with regard to family proceedings

● redefine the concept of parental responsibility.

It remains an important piece of legislation due to its focus on safeguarding children and the duties of local authorities.

The Every Child Matters guidelines, which led to the Children Act 2004, came about as a direct result of the Laming Report following the death of Victoria Climbié. The report was highly critical of the way in which the Climbié case was handled and made 108 recommendations to overhaul child protection in the UK. The main points which emerged were that:

● there should be a much closer working relationship between agencies such as health professionals, schools and welfare services

● there should be a central database containing records of all children and whether they are known to different services

● there should be an independent children's commissioner for England to protect children and young people's rights (a children's commissioner for Scotland had been in post for several years)

● there should be a children and families board, chaired by a senior government minister

● Ofsted will set a framework which will monitor children's services.

The Children Act 2004 required that these recommendations became a legal requirement. As a result the Every Child Matters framework was introduced to implement the Act and the wider reform programme. In addition to this, the document 'Working together to Safeguard Children' set out how organisations and individuals should work together to safeguard children and local safeguarding children boards (LSCBs) were established through local authorities.

### Link

See also TDA 3.6 on promoting equality, pages 88–89.

### The United Nations Convention on the Rights of the Child (1989) (UNCRC)

The UNCRC is an international human rights treaty which sets out the rights of all children to be treated equally. Under the treaty there is a list of rights to which every child under the age of 18 should be entitled. These include the full range of human rights – civil, cultural, economic, social and political – through articles such as:

● the right to services such as education and health care

● the right to grow up in an environment of happiness, love and understanding

● the right to develop their personalities, abilities and talents to their own potential

● the right to special protection measures and assistance.

The UK signed this legally binding act in 1990 and ratified it in 1991, which means that the UK is required to implement legislation to support each of the 54 articles. In 2008 the government attended a hearing in Geneva and reported on the progress that the UK has made since the implementation. The UK nations are continuing to work together and are also addressing the UN Committee's recommendations. For more on the UNCRC, see www.unicef.org/crc

The Common Assessment Framework, or CAF, is used across children's services in England and is a way of finding out about their additional needs and how these can be met. It aims to identify children's needs at an early stage and to provide a way of looking at a method of support which is appropriate for the child. A CAF should be used where practitioners feel that a child will not make progress towards the five outcomes of Every Child Matters without intervention. However, it should not be used in cases where you are worried that a child has been harmed or is at risk.

The Department for Education (DfE) also produces guidance and supporting documents for schools and local authorities regarding safeguarding and child protection. See www.education.gov.uk

## Functional skills

ICT: Finding and selecting information
ICT: Developing, presenting and communicating information
There are a number of websites highlighted throughout this unit. You could list them all in a document and produce a reference leaflet with a short summary of what each website provides information on.

## Portfolio activity

Go to the DfE website (www.education.gov.uk) and search for the following document: Working Together to Safeguard Children: A guide to inter-agency working to safeguard and promote the welfare of children (March 2010). You may find a copy of it in your school.

What are the responsibilities of schools under this document? What reference does it make to the Children Acts of 1989 and 2004? Identify one chapter which is of interest to you and make a short presentation about it to your group.

## Functional skills

English: Speaking, listening and communication
It is important to remember, when presenting to the group, to speak clearly and use language appropriate for the audience.

## Child protection within the wider concept of safeguarding

The term 'child protection' is increasingly being replaced by that of 'safeguarding'. Safeguarding has been described as a broader definition of the range of ways in which adults and professionals working with the child need to act when managing child protection issues. These are designed to prevent risks of harm to the welfare of children and young people rather than react to them. The term child protection tends to be used for policies and procedures which should be followed in the event of suspected harm or abuse.

## How guidelines, policies and procedures for safeguarding affect day-to-day work

Day-to-day work involves, for example:

- childcare practice
- child protection
- risk assessment
- ensuring the voice of the child is heard (for example, providing **advocacy** services)
- supporting children and young people and others who may be expressing concerns.

You will need to be aware of local and national guidelines for safeguarding in your work with children

## Key term

**Advocacy** — putting forward a person's views on their behalf and working for the outcome that the individual wishes to achieve on a day-to-day basis. The kinds of issues which may arise in schools may vary – however, you should always be alert to any safeguarding concerns and ensure that you are acting appropriately and within the appropriate guidelines.

## Childcare practice

The term childcare practice applies to all those who work in schools, nurseries and other early years settings, childminders and children's homes. All professionals working with children will need to be fully trained and CRB (Criminal Records Bureau) checked. Those in childcare practice are required to ensure that they demonstrate the correct safeguarding procedures and follow the policy of the organisation when working with children and young people, and in reporting any concerns.

## Child protection

Child protection is the responsibility of all who work with children and young people and you need to be aware of your school's policy for reporting and recording suspected abuse. As well as observing policies and ensuring that children are secure when on site, child protection records will need to be kept of what pupils have said, as well as notes, dates and times of any meetings that have taken place between the school and other agencies. If a pupil reports anything which is a cause for concern, the school needs to make sure that it is followed up. For child protection purposes, parents must be notified if any photographs of children are to be taken which are likely to be used or seen outside the school environment.

## Risk assessment

Individual risk assessments will need to be carried out prior to any activities where children or young people are undertaking an activity which has the potential to cause harm. This may be a school trip or visit but may also be in day-to-day practice where there are items of equipment or areas which carry potential risk. The school will have a procedure for risk assessment which it will need to carry out annually on the school buildings and grounds.

**Link**

See CYP 3.4 page 137 for an example of a risk assessment form.

### Functional skills

**English: Writing**
**Speaking, listening and communication**
When planning your next acitivity, produce a risk assessment. Describe ways you will minimise any identified risks for children or yourself when implementing the activity. Discuss your assessment with the teacher or manager.

### Ensuring the voice of the child is heard

In cases of child protection, all agencies concerned will need to ensure that the voice of the child is considered. Advocacy services (for example, the National Youth Advocacy Service) should be provided in order to support the child or young person during a time which will be difficult and often traumatic for them.

### Supporting children and young people and others who may be expressing concerns

The initial response when considering child protection and safeguarding issues should always be to listen carefully to what the child says. After reassuring the child and clarifying what has happened, and explaining what action will be taken, it is important not to press for any further information or to tell them that what they say will remain confidential. This is important, as the child may need to talk to other adults about what has happened.

### LSCB (local safeguarding children board)

This body will have been set up by your local authority to ensure the safeguarding and welfare of children. If your school does have concerns about a child, the local authority will also act alongside to follow guidelines and ensure that all agencies work together.

### Over to you!

Find out about your local LSCB and the work it does.

## When and why inquiries/reviews are required and how sharing findings informs practice

According to the LSCB Regulations 2006, serious case reviews (SCRs) will be required in situations where a child has died due to known or suspected abuse or neglect. In some situations, reviews may also be carried out where a child has been seriously harmed or has suffered life-threatening injuries. The purpose of an SCR is for agencies to discuss the case together and to determine the lessons which are to be learned about the way in which professionals have worked and can work together in the future. A report will then be written which will be made public so that recommendations are known. The DCSF publication 'Working Together to Safeguard Children 2010' sets out the processes which should be followed when undertaking SCRs.

## How processes used comply with legislation covering data protection, information handling and sharing

The way in which the school handles information will be covered by the Data Protection Act 1998. Under this Act, information which is gathered by the school in the context of safeguarding and child protection must be used only for that purpose. If any individuals concerned wish to know the information which is held about them, they have a right to access to it. They are also entitled to see their own educational record. There are only a few main exceptions to this, namely:

● information which may cause serious harm or risk of abuse to the health of the pupil or another individual

● information given to a court or in adoption or parental order records

● copies of examination scripts or marks prior to their release

● unstructured personal information, or information which is held manually and not in school records.

For more guidance on this and in particular how processes used by the school need to comply with legislation in different UK countries, see the website for the Information Commissioner's Office (www.ico.gov.uk), which deals with the Data Protection Act and Freedom of Information Act.

### Knowledge into action

Find out and write a reflective account about how the processes used in your own school comply with data protection and information handling legislation.

### Functional skills

**ICT: Using ICT**
You could complete this task by holding a discussion with someone involved in this role within the school. Maybe you could use ICT to record the conversation, so that you could write up the response later or refer back to it at a later date.

# Understand the importance of working in partnership with other organisations to safeguard children and young people

## The importance of safeguarding children and young people

All adults, and in particular those who work with children, have a responsibility to safeguard children and young people from harm. As professionals, we have a duty to ensure that children and young people are protected while they are in our care and that where we have other concerns outside school, these are investigated fully. School policies and procedures need to be such that parents and governors are aware of them and that staff are fully trained with regard to safeguarding. Schools will need to consider and include in their policies:

● children's physical safety and security on the premises and on off-site visits

● children's safety when in the home environment

● e-safety and security when using the Internet

● staff awareness and training

● monitoring and record keeping

● partnership and involvement with other agencies.

## The importance of a child- or young person-centred approach

It is also important that schools develop children's awareness with regard to acceptable and unacceptable behaviour. This encompasses both in school and off site, and also when using the Internet (see also page 179). Those who are known to be on the 'at risk' register, or those who have been identified as being at greater risk, should be supported by the school and by outside agencies where appropriate. All agencies will need to consider the ways in which their approach is child-centred, for example, involving the child in meetings and asking for their opinion when discussing matters relating to them as much as possible.

### Skills builder

Find a copy of your own school's child protection or safeguarding policy. What measures does the school have in place for ensuring that a child-centred approach is employed during any safeguarding issues? Who is the named member of staff responsible for safeguarding?

## The meaning of partnership working in the context of safeguarding

As there are a number of different agencies which may be involved when working in the context of safeguarding, it is important that they communicate and work closely to ensure the safety and protection of children. Each area of expertise may need to have an input in any one case and each should be considered when discussing issues around safeguarding. A working party or 'team around the child' meeting may be called involving a number of agencies in order to discuss how to move forward in the best interests of the child.

## Roles and responsibilities of different organisations involved when a child or young person has been abused or harmed

Different organisations involved in safeguarding are:

- social services
- the NSPCC
- health visitors
- GPs
- the probation service
- the police
- schools
- the psychology service.

### Social services

Social services will be concerned with the immediate care of the child and in ensuring that they are safe from harm. They will work in partnership with parents and other agencies in order to do this. In extreme cases, schools may need to contact social services directly where there are serious concerns about a parent or carer. Social services may then take the child into care.

### The NSPCC

The NSPCC (National Society for the Prevention of Cruelty to Children) is a charity which works to protect children from harm. However, it is the only charity which has a statutory power to take action where there are cases of child abuse. The NSPCC as a charity also provides services to support families and children through its helplines and draws attention and public awareness to the safety and protection of children.

### Health visitors and GPs

Health professionals may be involved in order to examine children to determine whether any injuries which have been sustained are accidental. They will also always be alert during the course of their practice to any injuries which they suspect are signs of child abuse and inform other agencies as appropriate.

### The police and probation service

The police work closely with other agencies in order to ensure that children are free from harm. All police forces have a Child Abuse Investigation Unit (CAIU); these units have been set up to gather information and to determine whether the police should begin a criminal investigation or take other immediate action.

### The psychology service

The psychology service may be called in to carry out an assessment of a child in cases of harm or abuse. They will make recommendations and suggest a course of action appropriate to the child's needs.

# Understand the importance of ensuring children and young people's safety and protection in the work setting

## The importance of ensuring that children and young people are protected from harm

As adults in positions of responsibility, we should all be aware of the importance of protecting children and young people from harm. While children are in school, we are acting 'in loco parentis', which means that we take over responsibility from their parents while they are in our care. This can be seen within all contexts, from health and safety issues to those around safeguarding, Internet safety and safety on school trips.

## Link

For more on health and safety issues and procedures, see CYP 3.4.

## Policies and procedures to protect children and young people and adults working with them

Policies and procedures for safe working include, for example:

- working in an open and transparent way
- listening to children and young people
- duty of care
- whistle-blowing

- power and positions of trust
- propriety and behaviour
- physical contact
- intimate personal care
- off-site visits
- photography and video
- sharing concerns and recording/reporting incidents.

Under the Health and Safety at Work Act, it is the responsibility of everyone in the school to ensure that safety is maintained and in particular that vulnerable groups such as children are safeguarded. Standards for safety are also set by the government department in each country responsible for education and are monitored by the body responsible for school inspections, for example, Ofsted in England and HMIE (Her Majesty's Inspectorate of Education) in Scotland. As well as having an awareness of safety issues, all routines should be planned carefully with safety in mind so that incidents are less likely to occur. Pupils should also be encouraged to think about safety in the learning environment so that they start to develop their own awareness. Your school will have health and safety policies as well as safeguarding policies, which will set out the procedures which you should follow as a member of staff.

It is likely that your safeguarding policy will give you guidelines about how you should work with children

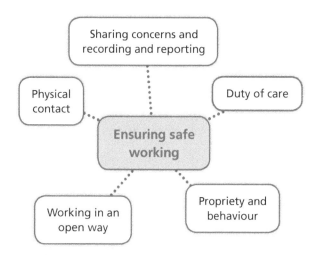

*How does your school ensure that staff and pupils are safeguarded?*

in a way which protects both them and you. This is important, as the school will need to be aware of and pass on to staff how they should best protect themselves against incidents of alleged abuse or inappropriate working practices.

## Physical contact

Although it may be appropriate to put an arm around a child when working with a younger age group, it would not be so acceptable for children and young people in secondary schools. There are some situations in which physical contact cannot be helped, for example, if you are working with a child who has special educational needs and you need to attend to their personal care. You should make sure that you follow school policy at all times when you are doing this.

## Sharing concerns/recording and reporting

If you have any concerns about a safeguarding issue, due to what a child has said or because of your own observations, you should always share these concerns and ensure that you record exactly what has happened. In this way you will protect yourself if later on the child says that they have told you or that you knew previously. You should also inform managers if you have any concerns about other members of staff due to poor practice (see section below on whistle-blowing).

## Propriety and behaviour

In your capacity as a professional working in a school, you should ensure that you act in a professional way at all times. When working with children, we are required to behave appropriately and make sure that children and young people also understand what is expected of them. As adults we are role models and are required to set an example through our own behaviour and our interactions with others.

## Duty of care

Adults in schools have a duty of care towards children and young people, and should always act in a way which ensures their safety. We should remember that we are in a position of trust and always listen to children and reassure them about issues which concern them.

## Working in an open way

Your working practice should be such that you always work in an open way. This includes:

- ensuring that you are not left alone with pupils if at all possible. Try to keep doors open and ensure that there are other people around

- being clear about why you are acting in a particular way

- keeping other staff informed about any concerns.

## How to report concerns about poor practice

Staff in your school should all be aware of the way in which suspected poor practice, concerns or any illegality can be reported. It is important that those who are concerned about issues around safeguarding should be able to report them. This should be done confidentially and with no concerns for any repercussions towards the individual who reported the incident or those whose practice is being questioned; the process is known as whistle-blowing. All members of staff should feel that they are able to raise concerns without any fear of discrimination or victimisation as a result.

### BEST PRACTICE CHECKLIST: Whistle-blowing

- Speak to your line manager or a senior manager about any concerns.

- If the concern is to do with your line manager, go to the next level. In the case of a head teacher, go to the chair of governors.

- Investigate your school or local authority's whistle-blowing policy.

- If you belong to a union, find out if they give any advice about whistle-blowing.

### Portfolio activity

Find out about what your school would do in cases of whistle-blowing. Speak to others in your group about how their school or local authority's policy protects those who may be involved in whistle-blowing. Alternatively, there are a number of exemplar whistle-blowing policies available online which you may compare.

## How practitioners can take steps to protect themselves in the work setting and on off-site visits

All schools are required to have a clear health and safety policy. You should know where to find this in your school so that you are able to refer to it when necessary. Although each school will have a slightly different policy, each will need to outline its purpose and aims, and the responsibilities of staff.

### Link

For more on this, see Policies and procedures on pages 167–68.

# Understand how to respond to evidence or concerns that a child or young person has been abused or harmed

## Signs, symptoms, indicators and behaviours that may cause concern

As an adult working with children, you need to have an understanding of the different signs that may indicate that a child is being abused. Although you will need to do your best to ensure a child's safety while they are in your care, you also need to look out for any signs that they are being mistreated while they are out of school. The signs may include both physical and behavioural changes. There are four main types of abuse:

● physical abuse

● emotional abuse

● sexual abuse

● neglect.

### Physical abuse

This involves being physically hurt or injured. Physical abuse may take a variety of forms and be either spasmodic or persistent. Injuries may come from children being hit, punched, shaken, kicked or beaten.

The signs of physical abuse are often quite straightforward to spot and can include bruises, cuts, burns and other injuries. However, you should be aware that such injuries can also be caused by genuine accidents. If you notice frequent signs of injury or if there appear to be other signs of abuse, it is important to take action. Less obvious signs of physical abuse may include fear of physical contact with others, reluctance to get changed for PE, wanting to stay covered up, even in hot weather, and aggression.

### Emotional abuse

This involves the child being continually 'put down' and criticised, or not given love or approval at a time when they need it the most. It includes bullying, discrimination and racism, which may also take place outside school. This could take the form of name-calling, humiliation or teasing. Increasingly, it can also take place through social networking sites and mobile phones (see pages 175–76 for more on cyber-bullying).

The signs of emotional abuse are that the child is withdrawn and lacks confidence, shows **regression** or is 'clingy' towards adults, and has low self-esteem. Children who suffer from emotional abuse are likely to be anxious about new situations and may show extremes of behaviour or appear distracted and unable to concentrate.

### Key term

**Regression** – going backwards in terms of development to an earlier stage

### Sexual abuse

Sexual abuse involves an adult or young person using a child sexually, for example, by touching their bodies inappropriately or by forcing them to look at sexual images or have sex.

The signs of sexual abuse may include sexual behaviour which is inappropriate to the child's age, genital irritation, clinginess or changes in behaviour, regression and lack of trust of adults. Sexual abuse can be almost impossible to identify and its signs can be caused by other forms of abuse. It is therefore important that any signs are seen as possible, rather than probable, indicators.

## Neglect

This means that the child is not being properly cared for and not having its basic needs met by parents or carers. Basic needs include shelter, food, love, general hygiene and medical care. The signs of neglect may include being dirty, tired, hungry, seeking attention and generally failing to thrive.

## Actions to take in line with policies and procedures of own setting

As a teaching assistant, you are in a good position to notice changes in pupils' behaviour which may be a possible sign of abuse. Children or young people may also confide in you or allege that abuse has taken place. If you have been told something by a child or you are at all concerned, speak to either your class teacher or the school's Child Protection or Safeguarding Officer. They will need to follow the school's safeguarding policy and, if necessary, local authority guidelines for informing social services. Always keep a note of exactly what happened and when, exactly how you reported it and whom you told.

---

**CASE STUDY:** Actions to take when a child alleges harm or abuse

Amir works at the local secondary school. He supports pupils in Year 8. For the past two weeks, he has noticed a change in the behaviour and attitude of one of the pupils. On several occasions he has observed Matthew responding quite aggressively to other pupils in the class. Amir tried to speak to Matthew at lunchtime, but he would not engage in conversation. Amir has mentioned his concerns to the form teacher and they agree that Amir should keep a close eye on Matthew.

Each week Amir accompanies the class to the local baths. During one visit he noticed a bruise right across Matthew's back. When he asked Matthew what had happened, the boy broke down and said that his uncle had hit him with a belt having arrived home drunk. He asked Amir not to say anything, as it would only make things worse. He added that his uncle was only staying with him and his mum for a short time, and would be leaving soon.

- What should Amir do now?
- Discuss with others in your group the order in which things might happen and who else should be involved.

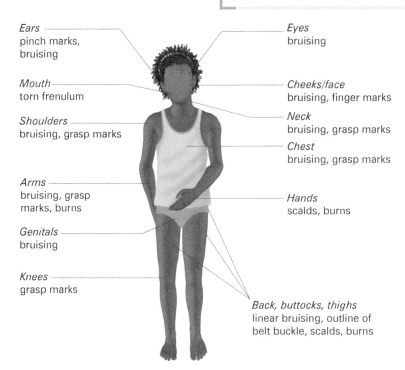

Ears
pinch marks, bruising

Mouth
torn frenulum

Shoulders
bruising, grasp marks

Arms
bruising, grasp marks, burns

Genitals
bruising

Knees
grasp marks

Eyes
bruising

Cheeks/face
bruising, finger marks

Neck
bruising, grasp marks

Chest
bruising, grasp marks

Hands
scalds, burns

Back, buttocks, thighs
linear bruising, outline of belt buckle, scalds, burns

*You will need to look out for the signs and symptoms of abuse.*

## Functional skills

**English: Speaking, listening and communication**
This case study provides a good opportunity for a class discussion. Not only could you share your ideas on how you would deal with this situation, but you could also develop your speaking and listening skills. Take care to listen to what other people are saying, so that you can respond in an appropriate way.

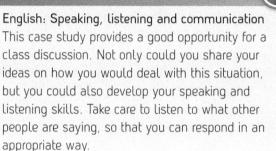

## The rights of children, young people and their carers

In situations where harm or abuse is suspected or alleged, it is important to remember that all individuals need to be treated with respect and have their own rights. In any case of harm or abuse to children all parties will have a right to be investigated through the correct channels and the outcome documented accordingly. They also have a right to confidentiality and those involved in any investigation should be reminded of this.

## Understand how to respond to evidence or concerns that a child or young person has been bullied

It is likely that at some stage you will need to deal with bullying in some form. This may be because you notice children picking on another child, or are asked to 'keep an eye' on a particular situation following concerns by parents or the class teacher. Alternatively, you may find that children confide in you if they feel that they are being bullied by others. You will need to know the course of action you should follow and the school's policy for dealing with bullying.

## Types of bullying and potential effects on children and young people

Children and young people may be victims of different types of bullying. There are a number of ways in

which bullies can target children and the increasing use of cyber-bullying is of particular concern since this type of bullying is 'invisible'.

Bullying may be:

- **physical** (pushing, kicking, hitting, pinching, other forms of violence or threats)
- **verbal** (name-calling, insults, sarcasm, spreading rumours, persistent teasing)
- **emotional** (excluding, tormenting, ridicule, humiliation)
- **cyber-bullying** (the use of Information and Communications Technology, particularly mobile phones and the Internet, deliberately to upset someone else)
- **specific bullying** which can relate to all of the above. This may be homophobic, gender-based, racist or relating to special educational needs or disabilities.

### Physical
This may take place in the school grounds or on the way to or from school. You may need to speak to children about isolated incidents of violence; however, you should be alert to situations in which some children seem to be picked on more than others.

### Verbal
Children can bully one another through verbal insults, teasing and targeted comments towards a particular child. You will need to investigate all allegations of bullying as soon as they are made.

### Emotional
This kind of bullying can be particularly difficult to discover, and in particular if is carried out through cyber-bullying (below). Children may be subjected to ridicule or humiliation at the hands of others, which over a period of time will cause extreme emotional distress.

### Cyber-bullying
This type of bullying is relatively recent due to the increased use of mobile phones and the Internet by children. This form of bullying is particularly distressing as it reaches into the homes of children and young people. Children who bully feel disassociated from the act so may be more extreme

in their comments. There may also be sharing of inappropriate photographs through social websites. Girls are more likely to cyber-bully. Cyber-bullying can be very difficult to find out about and children should be reminded about the consequences of their actions and the need to discuss any concerns with an adult.

## Functional skills

**ICT: Developing, presenting and communicating information**

You could create a poster for the pupils all about Internet safety that you could display in your computer room/area. Remember to think about the age of the children reading the poster. Try to use an appropriate layout and have a go at including images and a variety of different text.

### Specific bullying

This can relate to all or one of the above and may be based on, for example, racism, disability or gender. Children who are in a minority may be the object of this kind of bullying and they should be encouraged to report any incidents straight away.

## Policies and procedures in response to bullying and why they are in place

Head Teachers are obliged to draw up procedures to prevent bullying in schools under the School Standards and Framework Act 1998. All staff, parents and pupils need to be aware of the procedures that should be followed and the consequences of bullying.

When dealing with any situations of bullying in your school, you will need to make sure that you follow your school's anti-bullying policy. Although you may need to deal with a single incident on your own, you should also ensure that you are not acting alone in dealing with any ongoing situation and have discussed your actions with a member of the school's Senior Management Team. It is likely that you will have to follow a series of steps, for example:

- deal immediately with any incidents of bullying

- record or report to the Head Teacher the named person with safeguarding responsibility or a member of the Senior Management Team, according to school policy
- notify the form teacher
- if bullying persists, parents will be informed
- measures will be introduced following discussion with all concerned.

## Link

See also TDA 3.4 for more on policies and procedures on bullying.

## CASE STUDY: Dealing with bullying

Paula is a teaching assistant working in the school's Special Educational Needs Department. One day, after supporting Caitlin in the English class, Paula noticed her hanging around the doorway after the others had left. The girl asked Paula if she could talk to her. Caitlin then said that she was having problems with a group of girls in the class. She said that they were telling other pupils lies about her and a boy in the class. She also said that on the way to school that morning, she had received a text message to say that the girls would be waiting for her. Paula found the three girls at lunchtime and spoke to them, but did not take further action. Two days later, Paula noticed that Caitlin was not in class. Paula was worried because of what she had been told.

- What should Paula do now?
- Why is it important to follow school policy?

## How to support a child or young person and/or their family

As part of the school's policy, there will be guidelines on how to support a child or young person and their family when bullying is suspected, and also what is available through the local authority. You will be working as part of a team and clearly each case will be different, although step-by-step procedures will be the same. You should work with your school and follow school procedures to manage the situation and reassure the child and their parents. There are also a large number of websites and organisations available to support both the child and their family in coping with the distress which is caused by bullying (see the end of this unit).

# Understand how to work with children and young people to support their safety and well-being

## Support children and young people's self-confidence and self-esteem

Children's self-confidence and self-esteem are directly linked to the way in which they relate to others. Self-esteem can be high or low, positive or negative. It is how we feel about ourselves and leads to our self-image, or how we think about or perceive ourselves. Children develop positive self-esteem when they feel good about themselves and when they feel valued. They need to have the opportunities to develop positive relationships and participate in a range of activities, which will in turn impact on their social and emotional development. Where children do not have these opportunities, or are unable to find out about themselves and develop their communication skills through social activities, their confidence and self-esteem will be affected. This will also have an impact on their learning as they will be less likely to attempt tasks when they do not have confidence in their abilities.

In a safeguarding context, children need to be confident enough to be able to tell others if they are unhappy about something which is happening to them. This may be a situation in which they are being bullied, or forced into something which they do not agree with. A child who has a negative self-image or does not feel valued may not think that anyone will listen to them and may be reluctant to talk about

*How do you help children and young people to develop a positive self-image?*

something which is worrying them. The way in which we treat children has a direct effect on this, so it is important that we:

- encourage and praise them
- allow them to feel independent
- value each child as an individual
- celebrate differences and similarities.

## The importance of supporting resilience in children and young people

Children who are going through a difficult period or who are lacking in confidence or self-esteem may need your support in order to help them to remain resilient in dealing with this. You may need to be sensitive when managing their emotions at times and in helping them when maintaining their confidence in difficult situations. You should do this by remaining approachable and facilitating opportunities for pupils to discuss any issues as they arise. You should also encourage them as much as possible and give them reassurance as they learn to manage their emotions.

## Why it is important to work with the child or young person to ensure they have strategies to protect themselves

All children have a right to be safe and feel protected. The UN Convention on the Rights of the Child, which was signed by the UK in 1990, sets out the rights of all children to be treated equally and fairly. These include the rights to:

- grow up in an atmosphere of happiness, love and understanding
- be as healthy as possible
- grow and develop to the best of their ability
- live in a safe environment.

Children and young people may also need your support in devising strategies to protect themselves and to maintain their own safety. Children will need to learn not to put themselves in a position of risk.

## Ways of empowering children and young people to make positive and informed choices

As well as encouraging their awareness of health and safety issues, you should also support their development by helping them to have a positive self-image. Young people are particularly vulnerable emotionally during puberty, as they are developing their sexual identity. Children need to have plenty of opportunities and encouragement as they grow up in order to develop their independence and learn about their likes and dislikes. They should also be aware that they have a right to be safe and know what to do if they do not feel safe. It is difficult for children to tell someone what is happening, as they often feel that it is their fault. Older children may just hint that something is wrong, so it is important that you listen and give time to pupils. The curriculum should include giving pupils information about organisations that exist to protect them, such as the NSPCC, ChildLine and Kidscape.

---

**BEST PRACTICE CHECKLIST:** Supporting children and young people to empower themselves

- Ensure that pupils are taught to keep themselves safe.
- Encourage pupils to talk about their worries and speak to others.
- Use age-appropriate language when speaking to pupils.
- Never promise to keep it secret if a pupil discloses that they have been abused.
- Set an example by encouraging co-operation and positive behaviour.

---

### Functional skills

**English: Writing**
You could plan a set of short activities that would promote keeping safe, which you could deliver over a few weeks to the children. This will provide you with the opportunity to practise writing for a different purpose.

# Understand the importance of e-safety for children and young people

As adults, we have a responsibility towards children and young people to make them aware of the dangers which they may face in the outside world. In school, this awareness has historically been around issues such as road safety, stranger danger and how to treat and respond to others. However, as well as being an additional resource, the emergence of the Internet has opened up a wide range of additional threats to children in the virtual world.

The Internet has brought with it a large number of benefits which outweigh the drawbacks. However, it is important to stress to children that anyone can set up a website, which means that there may be places on the Internet which represent extremist views or are disrespectful to others.

## Risks and possible consequences of being online and of using a mobile phone, and reducing risk

All adults working with children and young people need to be aware of the increasing risks to children from being online and from the use of mobile phones. E-safety is gaining a higher profile as technology advances and schools are now required to have more policies and guidelines in place for staff, parents and children. Children and parents may also be required to sign an Internet safety agreement to show that they have discussed Internet safety and agree with the school's policy for safe Internet use. However, it is likely they will also use the Internet at home and they should be aware of the risks and possible consequences of using different technologies. This will also usually be discussed in school as part of pupil's ICT lessons.

### Social networking sites

The tragic case of Ashleigh Hall's murder in 2009 after befriending her attacker on a social networking site has led to a heightened public awareness of the dangers of the Internet and in particular social networking sites. Children and young people should be reminded not to put personal information such as

telephone numbers, photographs or email addresses online. They should also limit other information such as school name, clubs they attend, where they meet up and so on, as this kind of information can easily be pieced together to gain an insight into their lives. Children may not have considered that by putting their personal information online it also becomes accessible to individuals other than their friends. Social networking sites can easily be accessed by others and parents should check that privacy settings are not open to all. It is also important that you do not share your own personal information or allow pupils to add you to their social network page.

### Internet use

Pupils in school will be unable to access any material that is inappropriate due to filters which school computers are required to have. However, if home computers do not have filters or settings such as the Child Safety Online Kitemark to protect children, they may not be safe online. Schools are increasingly running information workshops for parents about the importance of ensuring that children are Internet-aware and protected as much as possible.

# Key Stage 3
## Pupil ICT Acceptable Use Agreement

➤ I will only use ICT in school for school purposes.

➤ I will only use my class email address in school.

➤ I will make sure that any ICT contact I have with adults and children is polite and friendly.

➤ I will not deliberately look for, save or send anything that could be unpleasant or nasty. If I accidentally find anything like this, I will turn off my monitor and tell my teacher immediately.

➤ If I see anything I am unhappy with or I receive a message I do not like, I will not respond to it but I will tell a teacher or a responsible adult.

➤ I will not open an attachment or download a file unless I have permission and I know and trust the person who has sent it.

➤ I will not give out my own details such as my phone number or home address.

➤ I will never arrange to meet someone I have only ever previously met on the Internet or by email unless this is part of a school project approved by my parent/carer and my teacher, and a responsible adult comes with me.

➤ I will be responsible for my behaviour when using ICT because I know that these rules are to keep me safe.

➤ I know that my use of ICT can be checked and that my parent/carer will be contacted if a member of school staff is concerned about my e-Safety.

My Name: _____

My Signature: _____

We have discussed these rules and _____ (child's name) agrees to follow the e-Safety rules and to support the safe use of ICT at Kingswood Secondary School.

Parent/Carer Signature: _____ Date _____

*A Pupil Acceptable Use Agreement.*

## Email

Children and young people should be aware that they should only open emails and files sent from people that they know, as they will not know the contents. They could contain a virus or an inappropriate image. Pupils should also be told that if they are sent anything hurtful or unpleasant, they should tell an adult.

## Buying online

Children and young people will need to be careful if they are using the Internet for purchases. It is possible that older children may have debit cards or they may ask parents for their card information or use online vouchers in order to pay for items over the Internet. In this situation they should be warned about the possibilities of identity theft and of putting information online where others may see it.

## Using a mobile phone

Most children now have mobile phones. Phones can be the cause of muggings and theft, in particular if the equipment is very up to date. They can also be a means of bullying, in the same way as email and social networking sites.

## Getting ready for assessment

For your assessment in this unit, you will need to show that you understand the purpose and process of safeguarding and child protection. If you have been involved in a safeguarding or bullying incident and have attended meetings to this effect, you should speak to your assessor about what happened. If you have not, find out about school policy and speak to staff about how such an incident would be managed in your school. While you should not record names or circumstances, you may be able to write a reflective account or have a professional discussion about the actions which were followed. Look carefully at the assessment criteria and include as many points as you can so that you can cover as much as possible, for example, procedures or policies that you followed and how the child and their family were supported.

## Check your knowledge

1. What are the main areas of legislation and guidelines in your home country which affect the safeguarding of children and young people?

2. Name some of the agencies which may help and support schools in cases of suspected child abuse. What are their roles?

3. Why should children and young people be given guidance about use of the Internet? What kinds of risks and consequences might there be of unfiltered Internet use in schools?

4. What should you do in cases where you suspect a child may be at risk of harm or abuse? How will you be protected against any repercussions?

5. Name some of the policies your school might have in place to deal with issues around child safety and safeguarding.

6. Name three ways in which adults in schools can empower children and young people, when supporting their safety and well-being.

## Websites

**www.abs-kids.co.uk** – information and support for children on bullying
**www.anti-bullyingalliancetoolkit.org.uk** – guidance and practical ideas to help tackle bullying
**www.antibullying.net** – established by the Scottish Executive for parents, teachers and young people
**www.beatbullying.org** – information on and support for bullying
**www.bullyfreezone.co.uk** – raises awareness of alternative ways of resolving conflict and of reducing incidences of bullying
**www.bullying.co.uk** – Bullying UK, the UK anti-bullying charity
**www.ceop.police.uk** – Child Exploitation and Online Protection Centre, an organisation which aims to provide information to parents, children and education professionals around safety online
**www.coastkid.org** – anti-bullying website with helpful advice and information
**www.education.gov.uk** – guidance and supporting documents from the Department for Education (DfE)
**www.ico.gov.uk** – the Information Commissioner's Office
**www.keepingchildrensafe.org.uk** – the Keeping Children Safe (KCS) toolkit is available through their website to support those working in child protection and offers training materials as well as a CD-ROM to support agencies in putting child protection into practice
**www.kidscape.org.uk** – Kidscape, charity to prevent bullying and child abuse
**www.nspcc.org.uk** – the NSPCC is the UK's only free, online, specialised child protection resource for practitioners, researchers, trainers, policy-makers and other professionals working to protect children providing information on child abuse, child protection and safeguarding in the UK. NSPCC helpline: 0808 800 5000 or help@nspcc.org.uk
**www.nyas.net** – National Youth Advocacy Service: UK charity to provide children's rights and give children and young people a voice
**www.teachernet.gov.uk/wholeschool/behaviour/tacklingbullying** – Teachernet advice on tackling bullying
**www.unicef.org/crc** – the United Nations Convention on the Rights of the Child (1989) (UNCRC)

# School life

## My story: Anna

I have worked as a support assistant in a large community college for several years. Part of the week I support individual pupils in a range of curriculum subjects. I also support small groups who require additional support with their reading. I had concerns about one of the girls in Year 10 last year. She had become withdrawn and did not take the usual care in her appearance. On one occasion, when I engaged in a conversation with her, she became very distressed and said that she'd had some 'problems' at home with her older brother. She said she hated him and wished he would leave. When I asked how I could help, she appeared to be on the verge of saying more, when we were interrupted by a friend.

I felt that there was something serious concerning her, so I went to the named person in the school with safeguarding responsibility. He thanked me for passing on the information and that he would act on my concerns. It emerged that the girl was being sexually abused by her older brother.

Although it will have a lasting effect on her, the abuse has now stopped and she receives counselling. She is now making good progress with her academic work and I notice that she has a close group of friends. I like to think that my observations have helped her to turn her life around.

## Ask the expert

**Q** There are quite a few pupils in my school that I think are neglected – do I report all of them?

**A** It may be that in some areas there is a higher proportion of pupils who suffer abuse or neglect – you should still say something even if there are several pupils as each case should be looked at individually. It will be the role of your Senior Management team and those responsible for safeguarding in your school to follow these up.

### VIEWPOINT

Do you think it is better to speak up with concerns about a child even if they turn out to be unnecessary concerns? You should always say something, even if it turns out that you are wrong – if you have told someone else, you have passed on your concerns, which is the important thing.

# TDA 3.10 Plan & deliver learning activities under the direction of a teacher

You will need to reflect on how your own role complements the work of the teacher. Each learning outcome from this unit focuses on your own skills, so as you work with learners you must reflect on ways that you use your own knowledge and expertise to support, extend and where necessary adapt activities. You will also explore the role of assessment, considering the importance of observing and reviewing learners' response to the planned activities and their progress towards the learning objectives. Information in this unit overlaps with other units, particularly TDA 3.3, TDA 3.7 and TDA 3.13, so you may find that you are able to cross-reference some of your evidence.

## By the end of this unit you will:

1. be able to plan learning activities under the direction of the teacher
2. be able to deliver learning activities
3. be able to monitor and assess learning outcomes.

# Be able to plan learning activities under the direction of the teacher

## Objectives, content and intended outcomes of learning activities

It will benefit yourself, the teacher and the pupils if you are involved at the beginning of the planning stage. If you are not usually invited to planning meetings, you should ask when these take place and if you can attend. Long-term planning will be in place well before the school year begins, with regular planning meetings throughout the term to agree on the detail of the content and delivery strategies. Before each lesson, you should receive a detailed plan of the learning objectives for the activities being undertaken.

Long-term planning outlines the scheme of work for each year group across the school year for each statutory and non-statutory curriculum area. It will show units of learning and how these will be sequenced.

Medium-term planning usually covers a term or half-term. It will include an overview of the subject and **learning outcomes**. There will be links to any cross-curricular learning, particularly if taught through a topic, and information on additional activities such as visits or visitors.

Short-term planning provides information on the week's lessons, broken down into the activities for each day. The planning will be detailed and include:

- **learning objectives**
- activities
- organisation, for example, timing, groupings
- inclusion/differentiation
- resources
- assessment opportunities
- role of other adults.

An example of an outcome may be that the majority of learners in the class are 'able to recognise the equivalence of percentages, fractions and decimals by the end of the term'. The learning objective for an individual lesson (which will support pupils to achieve the outcome) is for them to be able to 'change percentages into fractions'.

### Key terms

**Learning outcomes** — broad statements of what pupils will know, understand and be able to do at the end of a topic or period of study

**Learning objectives** — statements of intentions, what pupils are expected to do and achieve by the end of the activity

## How the learning activities relate to statutory and non-statutory frameworks

The curriculum includes both statutory and non-statutory frameworks. The National Curriculum provides the statutory part of the whole-school curriculum and applies to pupils at compulsory school age from 5 years to 16 years. With the exception of religious education, which is planned locally, each subject area sets out what must be taught in programmes of study.

| Key Stage | Statutory subjects |
|---|---|
| Key Stage 3 | • Art and Design<br>• Citizenship<br>• Design and Technology<br>• English<br>• Geography<br>• History<br>• Information and Communication Technology<br>• Mathematics<br>• Modern Foreign Languages<br>• Music<br>• Physical Education<br>• Science<br>• Religious Education |
| Key Stage 4 | • Citizenship<br>• English<br>• Information and Communication Technology<br>• Mathematics<br>• Physical Education<br>• Science<br>• Religious Education |

Table 1: National Curriculum Key Stages 3 and 4.

At Key Stage 4, pupils also have an entitlement to study subjects from the arts, design and technology, humanities and modern foreign languages.

The non-statutory framework is an essential element of the whole-school curriculum. It includes areas of learning which support pupils' overall development and improves their achievement in other areas of the curriculum. Non-statutory subjects include:

● personal well-being, including sex and relationship education

● economic well-being and financial capability

● careers education.

When supporting pupils in class, you may also find that the outcomes identified for the lesson relate to areas beyond the subject you are supporting. For example, it is important to become familiar with the outcomes for **functional skills** and **personal, learning and thinking skills**. There is also a statutory requirement across the secondary curriculum in relation to:

● inclusion of all learners

● use of language

● use of ICT

● health and safety.

The programmes of study from both the statutory and non-statutory framework provide the basis for lesson planning. Attainment targets describe the knowledge, understanding and skills expected of individual learners when they reach the end of each key stage. As each key stage covers more than one year, this means that these expected targets or outcomes must be broken down into steps within the schemes of work.

● Key Stage 3: Years 7,8, and 9 (aged 11–14 years).

● Key Stage 4: Years 10 and 11 (aged 14–16 years).

● Post-16 education: Sixth form (16–19 years).

### Link

At post-16 there is no statutory curriculum. For more information on the qualifications and programmes of study for this phase and for Key Stage 4, refer to TDA 3.14.

The secondary frameworks for mathematics, science, English and ICT support whole-school planning. The frameworks provide objectives, guidance and assessment information. The curriculum for Scotland is non-statutory but provides a framework for schools. More information can be found at www.ltscotland.org.uk — Learning and Teaching Scotland (LTS).

### Portfolio activity

In geography the outcome for Year 8 pupils is to understand the causes and effects of flooding. They have recently taken part in a field trip to a river valley. During the visit they studied maps and took a series of digital photographs. The teacher wants pupils to develop their literacy skills through their geography topic. She has asked you to plan and prepare the following.

1. An ICT activity for a group of pupils with above-average ability which will enable them to develop their writing skills.

2. An activity to support an individual pupil who is easily distracted to develop his speaking and listening skills.

• Research the relevant curriculum framework and use this to plan two activities demonstrating how each activity supports the needs of children.

### Key terms

**Functional skills** — essential knowledge of English, Mathematics and ICT to prepare pupils for future learning and work

**Personal, learning and thinking skills** — essential skills for successful learning and personal development, set out in six areas: independent enquirers, team workers, effective participants, self-managers, reflective learners, creative thinkers

Teachers must ensure that all aspects of the separate subjects or areas of learning are covered at each stage of learning. This is achieved through long-term planning. Schemes of work may be in relation to individual subject areas or cross-curricular.

## Planning and preparing learning activities, as directed by the teacher

You may be asked to plan learning activities for a group or an individual pupil. If you have been involved in the long-term and medium-term planning, you will have an understanding of the outcomes and specific learning objectives which you need to consider. The activity you devise will need to take into account:

- the number of pupils
- previous learning
- the environment
- resources which are available to you
- time available.

If you work regularly within the class, you will know what pupils have learned previously and so be able to build on this knowledge.

### Personalised learning

A personalised approach requires teachers and teaching assistants to take into account not only different academic levels of achievement, but also pupils' individual needs and interests. Individual targets or learning objectives will support children and young people to reach their full potential. Planning must take into consideration ways that pupils learn. Planning for the needs of each individual learner may seem daunting, but children of similar abilities and interests can be grouped together and work towards the same targets.

## Using knowledge to contribute to planning partnership working with the teacher

Although your role is to work under the direction of the teacher, this should be viewed as a partnership. It is essential that you develop a rapport with the teacher you support. In order to make an effective contribution at the planning stage, it is important that you:

- become familiar with the programmes of study for the key stage you support.
- understand the achievements, needs and interests of individual children in the class
- reflect on your own knowledge, expertise and interests.

As you become more experienced you will begin to contribute your own ideas at each stage of the planning process. If you are asked to plan and deliver activities, you will need a range of information about the individual learners from:

- records of learners' achievements
- individual learning plans
- information provided by the teacher
- your own observations.

You should consider the strengths you have that can enrich the learning experiences for children. You may have particular skills that you can bring to activities, for example, ICT skills, an interest in literacy or the ability to play an instrument. You should also reflect on areas where you lack confidence and take opportunities to seek advice or undertake training to develop these.

### Knowledge into action

Build up evidence of ways that you have contributed at each stage of planning. You could keep a diary or annotate meeting minutes or planning information to record your own contributions. For example, what suggestions have you put forward for activities? What ideas do you have for the resources or strategies you could use?

### Functional skills

**English: Writing**
You could write a reflective account of what your role was in the last planning meeting that you had with your department or team. In your account you could include what your role was, how well the planning went and what you would do in the future to improve it. Plan your account first so that you can organise it into paragraphs.

### Key term

**Partnership working** — working with the teacher to support teaching and learning towards shared goals, for example in whole-class plenary sessions

## CASE STUDY: Supporting mathematics to meet attainment targets

Chris is working in Year 9 to support mathematics. The learning objective from the Mathematics Framework is 'identify reflection symmetry in 3D shapes'. She has been asked to support a group of four pupils. The teacher has informed her that the children have already investigated the symmetry of 2D shapes and can confidently identify symmetry in these. The children are of similar ability. Chris knows the following information from her observations.

1. Paul loses concentration easily and often distracts others. He works best when he is actively involved.

2. Roshan is very quiet and withdrawn, and is often reluctant to take part in group activities. She is very creative.

3. Maisie can articulate her findings but has difficulty in recording information on paper.

4. Sean enjoys working with others. He responds particularly well when he is challenged.

- How will the characteristics and needs of the individual children affect Chris's planning?
- How can she use the children's previous experience and knowledge to support learning?
- What other information would help her to plan an activity?

# Be able to deliver learning activities

## The use of teaching and learning methods

Before you consider the teaching and learning method, you must know and understand the learning objectives for the group or individual. Whatever methods you use, it is essential that pupils are actively involved in their own learning. As they get older they will develop a preferred learning style, although it is still important that they are allowed

time to explore and talk about what they have learned. Children and young people are more likely to understand and develop concepts and skills if they are allowed to discover things for themselves.

Your own role should be viewed as **facilitator**. Lev Vygotsky stressed the importance of the adult to provide activities which are both achievable and challenging. He called the stage when children had achieved their target by reaching a level of understanding or had mastered something the 'zone of actual development'. At this stage children are able to work independently. The stage when children are working toward their targets he called the 'zone of proximal development'. At this stage they are able to achieve with some help and support from an adult.

### Key term

**Facilitator** — someone who supports the process of learning

Jerome Bruner built on Vygotsky's theory. He used the term 'scaffolding' to describe the assistance given to children to support them to achieve the next level of learning. As children begin to understand a concept or master a new skill, the scaffolding or assistance can be gradually removed as they begin to work independently. At this stage there is a review of learning and children will begin to work toward a new set of targets.

## Meet agreed learning objectives and intended outcomes

Planning is not restricted to the content to be delivered and the activities to be carried out. For you to support learning effectively, you must know everything that will happen in the classroom so that you are able to give the same messages and work towards the same goals as the teacher. Before each lesson you should have agreed the strategies that will be used to:

- support pupils to meet their individual targets or learning objectives
- maintain their interest
- challenge pupils' thinking
- observe individual pupils' progress and achievements.

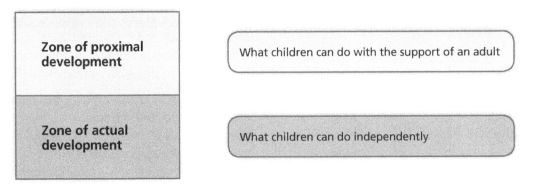

*Vygotsky's theory describes what children can do with and without help.*

> ## BEST PRACTICE CHECKLIST: Achieving learning objectives
>
> - Share the learning objectives and individual targets with pupils.
> - Build on what pupils already know and can do.
> - Give children time to talk about the activity and what they have learned.
> - Provide focused support to help pupils to move to the next level of learning.
> - Encourage independence.
> - Provide challenges.
> - Have high expectations.

## Maintaining learners' motivation and interest

To maintain learners' interest, it is critical that they are motivated, or enthusiastic, to learn. There may be a number of reasons why pupils want to take part in an activity and maintain their interest. Many pupils do so because they wish to please you by completing the task or because of a reward such as house points. This is called **extrinsic** motivation. The pupils are likely to progress but are not taking part because they want to learn or realise 'what's in it for them'.

Learning which gives children and young people personal satisfaction will be more enduring. This is referred to as **intrinsic** motivation. To support learners to develop this 'inner' motivation, it is essential that you tap into their natural interest in the world about them. Children and young people who are eager to

learn will feel good about themselves and begin to recognise their own progress.

Children and young people are naturally curious and want to find out about the world around them. When planning an activity, it is essential that you tap into this natural interest. As the activity develops, consider ways that you can maintain learners' interest. Children and young people can easily lose concentration and become bored in a learning activity, so it is important that the learning objectives are realistic and achievable. Learners need challenge but will soon lose interest where the learning activity is beyond their ability and skill. The converse is also true where learners have already met their targets and are not 'stretched'.

## Supporting and challenging learners

When planning an activity, you could think about ways that you can vary the tasks, such as keeping pupils moving, and varying the pace and groupings. **Passive learning** – sitting and listening to instructions or information – should be reduced to a minimum, as children and young people can soon become bored and 'turn off'. Providing learning experiences which ensure that learners are actively involved will help to support

### Key terms

**Extrinsic** – outer or separate from

**Intrinsic** – something natural or belonging to

**Passive learning** – learners do not interact or engage in the learning process and challenge their thinking. **Active learning** does not necessarily mean that pupils are moving around the classroom, but interacting with new ideas and information. This could be through group discussions, using information in new ways, quizzes, interactive activities or designing and producing something.

## Promoting independence

Sharing the learning objectives with children will support them to be in control of their own learning. This will have a direct impact on their self-esteem. The ways that you do this will depend upon the age and stage of development of the child. Strategies may include:

- involving children in identifying and reviewing their own learning targets
- giving children choices about their own learning
- storing and labelling resources and equipment so that children can access them easily
- teaching self-help strategies, for example, **mnemonics**, checking own work, how and where to find information
- pairing children with work buddies.

### Functional skills

**English: Speaking, listening and communication**
You could prepare a presentation to share with your colleagues or peers on how you have helped the children you care for promote their own independence. Presenting this information in a group is a good way of developing your confidence and sharing good practice.

### Functional skills

**English: Speaking, listening and communication**
The case study opposite provides a good opportunity for discussion. When discussing the points, listen carefully to what others have to say so that you can respond in an appropriate way.

### Key terms

**Active learning** — learners are involved and interact in the learning process

**Mnemonics** — systems for improving and aiding the memory

### CASE STUDY

Martin works at his local secondary school supporting children in Key Stage 3. He recently supported a group of Year 7 children investigating environmental issues in their local area. He is fully involved at each stage of planning, so when the teacher asked him to prepare an activity supporting children to plan and produce written information, he suggested making this an open-ended activity as the group he supports are mixed ability. One of the children has dyslexia and another has hearing loss.

Martin introduced the activity by showing the group information about a local town; the information was in different genres including brochures, leaflets, newspaper articles and a DVD. He then suggested that the learners identify their own audience and choose their own method to present information. All the learners met their learning objectives which related to knowledge and understanding of local history and literacy skills.

- In what ways will the activity meet the needs of all the learners?
- How will this activity help to maintain interest?
- How could Martin extend the activity for a pupil who is gifted and talented in English?

## Gather feedback on progress and achievements

As you support children and young people it is important that you monitor, not only whether they have achieved the learning objectives of the activity you are supporting, but also their level of interest and motivation so that at the end of the session you are able to feed back on each pupil's progress with the teacher. Ways to do this will be explored more fully on pages 195–97 and in TDA 3.7.

**CASE STUDY:** Meeting pupils' needs in a history topic

Gill supports a group of pupils in Year 8 with writing. Following a visit to a local heritage site for their history topic, Gill has been asked by the English teacher to plan an activity which requires pupils to produce information for visitors. The pupils are of mixed ability.

1. Tom is confident in writing and can structure his work well. He enjoys working independently and is reluctant to contribute to group work.

2. Chetan is of average ability. He moved to the UK last year and although he has made good progress in his spoken English, he continues to require some support.

3. Sally is inconsistent with work. She is beginning to make good progress but lacks concentration. She has excellent ICT skills.

4. Claire has dyslexia. She has a good imagination and is creative, but finds structuring her ideas difficult.

- How can Gill ensure that her planned activity meets the pupils' needs across the different levels of ability, interests and skills?
- How can she help to maintain each learner's interest and motivation?
- What opportunities are there for assessment?

Your own role is critical to support learners to ensure that they are included and feel valued. When working with individual or small groups of pupils you will be able to observe individual needs and any barriers, either long term or temporary, that they encounter and which prevent them from participating. For example, you might:

- provide physical help with tasks
- support communication, for example rephrasing teacher's instruction or using picture aids
- break down the task into smaller chunks of learning
- provide additional or assistive technology or resources
- adapt resources or the activity to meet pupils' individual needs.

**Over to you!**

Obtain and familiarise yourself with policies and procedures which work to break down any barriers to participation within your school.

**Functional skills**

**English: Reading**
Finding and reading the policies and procedures for your setting in this 'Over to you!' activity is a good way of expanding your knowledge of your setting. You could swap with a peer and then compare the similarities and differences between the different settings.

## Promoting and supporting the inclusion of all learners

Inclusion is concerned with ensuring that all learners, whatever their background or ability, are given the opportunity to participate fully in the school curriculum. You will be aware of the children and young people with special educational needs (SEN) or disabilities and the additional support they require. However, inclusion is not only concerned with children with SEN. There is a range of reasons why children may be more at risk of exclusion. Children and young people who have particular problems such as health conditions or family problems, and those who have become disengaged or are from minority ethnic groups, are also more vulnerable.

## Organising and managing learning activities to ensure the safety of learners

The health and safety of pupils is paramount. Although there will be someone with overall responsibility for health and safety, under the 1974 Heath and Safety at Work Act, all those working in the school have a duty to ensure the health and safety of children in their care. You must also be mindful of your own health and safety, and that of colleagues and any visitors. When planning and supporting learning activities, you need to ensure that the classroom is prepared and maintained with health and safety in mind.

**CASE STUDIES:** Supporting children and young people experiencing barriers to participation

1. When taking part in the School Council a group of boys tended to dominate the meeting. Two girls, who are quiet and withdrawn, wanted to take part but found that the boys did not take their suggestions seriously.

2. Jimmy is 11 years old. He has just started the school mid-term. He is from a traveller family and has already moved schools four times. He finds it difficult to make friends and other pupils tend to shun him and not invite him to join their games or choose him for their teams.

3. Sian is in Year 7 and has communication and language difficulties caused by hearing loss. She does have a hearing aid, but at times this does not appear to be working effectively. She often finds that she is unable to grasp the information when the teacher introduces the lesson. You have noticed that other children are reluctant to include her in the conversation during group activities.

- How might each pupil feel in these scenarios?
- How might it affect their academic progress and personal development?
- What strategies could you use to ensure that all pupils are included?

When planning an activity, you need to consider if the space is adequate and if you require access to particular facilities. As you prepare the area to carry out your activity, you need to check that the area is free from hazards such as bags or trailing wires. Learners with mobility or visual problems are at particular risk, so you need to pay particular attention to lighting, sound levels and accessibility. You must also consider the age and stage of development of learners.

As you supervise the learners, you must continue to be vigilant so that you can deal with any safety issues as they arise — for example, mopping up spilt water or reminding learners of how to handle tools and equipment safely. The pupils should also be aware of risks and have an understanding of any dangers associated with the learning activities. You can support children by discussing the activity and ways they should work safely, using age- and stage-appropriate language.

*Supporting a safe and healthy environment.*

## Risk assessment

Risk assessments are carried out in schools to prevent accidents or ill health. Assessments must take into account any hazards, the likelihood of harm, who may be at risk and what form the risk may take. Hazards will be identified in relation to:

● the learning environment

● the activities which take place

● where there may be additional or particular risks to individual pupils, for example, children who are disabled.

Following any risk assessment, it will be decided what precautions will be taken to reduce any risks. You must be aware of the policies and procedures for the environments where the children learn. There will also be procedures for reducing risks in relation to the learning activities which take place. Some activities, such as design and technology, physical education or science activities, will have greater risk associated with them, particularly where equipment and tools are used. Some activities may be carried out off site. In this situation, the teacher responsible should have visited the site to assess any potential risks.

*How experienced are you at working in partnership?*

**Functional skills**

**ICT: Developing, presenting and communicating information**
Creating a table on the computer is a good format for a risk assessment. There is also the benefit that if you have your risk assessment in an electronic format, you can return to it at a later date to make any necessary alterations or evaluate what you did.

## Working in partnership with the teacher to support learning activities

A report commissioned by the Training and Development Agency for Schools (www.tda.gov.uk) suggests that an increase in the number of teaching assistants is strongly associated with improved school attainment. School attainment relies upon effective teamwork where roles are understood. There is a range of strategies that teaching assistants can use when working alongside the teacher, as shown by the following diagram.

## Be able to monitor and assess learning outcomes

Assessment should be integral to the day-to-day delivery of learning activities. You may hear the term **assessment for learning** used to describe this process. At the end of each topic or series of activities, the teacher may carry out a formal assessment of what children have learned. This is **assessment of learning** or summative assessment.

**Key terms**

**Assessment for learning** — using assessment as part of teaching and learning in ways which will raise learners' achievement

**Assessment of learning** — an evaluation of what learners know, understand and can do at a particular stage

**Link**

See TDA 3.7, Support assessment for learning, for more on this area.

*How many ways do you work?*

## Monitor learners' responses to activities

As learners undertake the activities, it is essential that their responses are monitored. Their responses will tell you whether the activity you have planned is appropriate and likely to support them to achieve their targets. This may be evident from their:

- **level of interest and engagement** – are they immediately interested, do they continue to stay on task and contribute their own ideas?

- **behaviour** – do they appear interested by the activity and immediately get involved, or are they distracted and even display inappropriate behaviour?

- **verbal responses** – do they ask pertinent questions and make interesting and appropriate suggestions or comments to yourself or peers?

- **level of independence** – how far are they relying on yourself or peers to support them as they work?

- **use of resources or equipment** – are they appropriate for the age and stage of development, and do they support the learning process?

## Ways of modifying activities to meet learners' needs

You may modify learning activities:

- before the activity, as you know the individual needs of pupils and have taken account of these during the planning stage

- during the activity, as when monitoring responses you observe that pupils are experiencing difficulty in some aspect of the activity.

Lesson plans should include differentiated activities for pupils who have special educational needs, disabilities or specific learning difficulties. You may be asked to support the teacher by modifying activities for a particular learner or group of learners. Modifications may be through providing additional support, changing the teaching and learning method or strategy, or adapting learning materials.

Materials may be adapted for a number of reasons. Learners with reading difficulties may require information to be simplified and broken down into smaller steps. Adding illustrations or diagrams will also aid understanding. Learners with visual impairment will require information to be produced using a larger font. Learners with dyslexia often find that white backgrounds on paper or screens make reading text more difficult so pastel-coloured paper or overlays can be helpful. They may also benefit if a larger or different font, such as Comic Sans, is used.

Some learners with motor difficulties may require activities to be adapted through the use of technical aids or more appropriate resources. Consider the equipment and resources that you have chosen and decide if they are suitable for all the children. In PE, for example, learners with motor difficulties may require a lighter bat and one with a different grip. A learner with visual impairment may be able to take part if a brightly coloured ball is selected.

For some learners a different approach may be required. Children learn by using all their senses. As children get older, planned activities are usually presented requiring learners to rely on their sense of hearing and sight. Some children, particularly those with learning disabilities, dyslexia or **dyscalculia**, will benefit if a **multi-sensory approach** is used; others may work best when they are physically active.

### Key terms

**Dyscalculia** – a learning disability or difficulty involving innate difficulty in learning or comprehending mathematics

**Multi-sensory approach** – activities which require children to use a range of senses – auditory, visual and kinesthetic (touch) to receive and express information

### Reflect

Reflect on ways that activities have been adapted to meet the needs of individual pupils.

## Monitor learners' participation and progress

Before you deliver an activity, you will have agreed with the teacher the objectives for the activity and will know the learners' individual targets. You need to share these targets with learners at the start of the activity. As well as the academic achievement targets, learners should also understand exactly what they need to do and the expectations of behaviour.

### Peer assessment

When planning an activity, it is good practice to allow some time, usually at the end of the session, for reviewing the learning and participation of individual pupils. This may be done individually or as a group review. For example, a group of Year 8 pupils have been researching African masks and producing their own designs. At the end of the activity they presented their designs and discussed their work with peers. Discussing their progress in the group helped learners to assess whether they had met their targets and helped them to develop ideas and focus on the next stage of the project.

### Informal records

As learners work and you observe their progress, you will make a mental note of an individual's participation and progress. It is helpful also to jot down any specific information regarding progress or concerns which you need to feed back to the teacher. You may use a section on the activity planning sheet for this or have a small notebook with you. Remember, however, to observe confidentiality at all times and ensure that information written about learners is stored securely.

In the example of peer assessment in the Skills builder activity above, the teaching assistant also made notes on each pupil's progress. The following page is a section from their notebook.

It is important to feed back on individual learner's progress to the class teacher.

### Skills builder

Negotiate a time when you can observe a small group or individual child as they take part in a learning activity. Before you start, prepare for the observation by identifying individuals you will observe and any special educational needs or specific needs they may have. Also identify the objectives of the lesson. Note what you see happening as the children take part, including their reactions. After the observation, take time to reflect and interpret what you saw. Identify what you have learned about each child and how this will help you in future planning.

## Providing learners with focused support and feedback

Assessment can only be effective where pupils receive specific information on their progress and their achievements. Feedback can be in relation to what has actually been achieved so far. It must be specific so that the learner knows which target they have met or how they have improved. It is not constructive just to say, 'Well done, Adam you've worked hard today.' In contrast, saying 'Well done Adam, you have remembered to use punctuation throughout your writing' tells the learner what he has achieved and will help to motivate him.

Feedback should be continuous and constructive, focusing on the positives and ways to progress. For example, 'You have collected the information and have the correct labels for your graph, Charlotte, but remember to take more care when drawing your graph too so that the lines are drawn clearly.'

You should give feedback as learners work or as soon as possible after the activity has taken place. If you are marking work, you may give written feedback, but it is only meaningful if you discuss this with learners before they move on with work.

## 10th Feb                           Art and Design Y8

Objectives:

- Research traditional African masks
- Develop ideas on paper in preparation for mask making
- Discuss ideas with peers

C.W.  Was able to research masks independently using the Internet. He had clear ideas for his own design and described how he intends to approach the task.

L.M.  L needed support to find examples of masks. He produced a plan for his own mask but had to be reminded on two occasions of the objectives for the lesson. He has produced basic plans for making the mask but at this stage is unsure of the materials he will use. He described his plans briefly to the other pupils.

M.S.  M used books and the Internet to research masks. He has produced a detailed sketch and has identified the materials he will need. He presented his ideas confidently and made suggestions to L on ways he might develop his plans.

*Handwritten notes are a useful reference for tracing pupils' progress.*

# Assessment techniques to support the evaluation of learners' progress

Earlier in this section you read about assessment for learning, which is ongoing, and assessment of learning, which takes place at the end of a period of learning. There is a range of ways to assess children's learning and development, but there will be a greater understanding of children's progress where several techniques are employed during each learning activity.

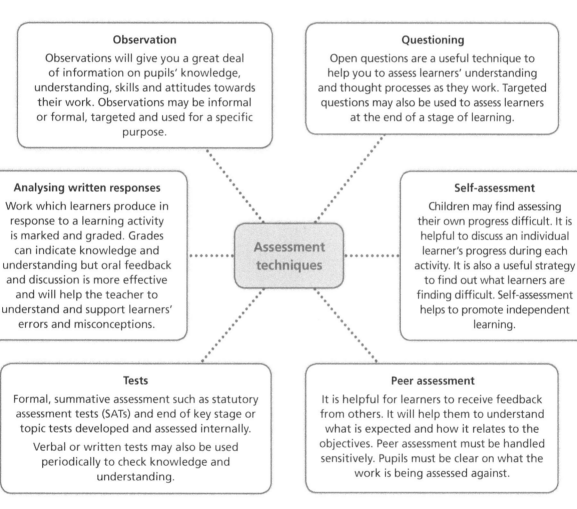

**Observation**
Observations will give you a great deal of information on pupils' knowledge, understanding, skills and attitudes towards their work. Observations may be informal or formal, targeted and used for a specific purpose.

**Questioning**
Open questions are a useful technique to help you to assess learners' understanding and thought processes as they work. Targeted questions may also be used to assess learners at the end of a stage of learning.

**Analysing written responses**
Work which learners produce in response to a learning activity is marked and graded. Grades can indicate knowledge and understanding but oral feedback and discussion is more effective and will help the teacher to understand and support learners' errors and misconceptions.

**Self-assessment**
Children may find assessing their own progress difficult. It is helpful to discuss an individual learner's progress during each activity. It is also a useful strategy to find out what learners are finding difficult. Self-assessment helps to promote independent learning.

**Assessment techniques**

**Tests**
Formal, summative assessment such as statutory assessment tests (SATs) and end of key stage or topic tests developed and assessed internally.
Verbal or written tests may also be used periodically to check knowledge and understanding.

**Peer assessment**
It is helpful for learners to receive feedback from others. It will help them to understand what is expected and how it relates to the objectives. Peer assessment must be handled sensitively. Pupils must be clear on what the work is being assessed against.

*Assessment techniques.*

## Check your knowledge

1. What are the statutory subjects at Key Stage 3?

2. How does religious education differ from other subjects?

3. Vygotsky describes a stage where children can do something with help. What is this called?

4. Suggest three ways to promote independent learning.

5. Name the legislation which underpins health and safety in schools.

6. What is meant by risk assessment?

7. What is the difference between assessment of learning and assessment for learning?

8. What is meant by a multi-sensory approach?

## Websites

**www.dcsf.gov.uk/everychildmatters** – the five outcomes for Every Child Matters

**www.education.gov.uk** – Department for Education

**www.ltscotland.org.uk** – Learning and Teaching Scotland

**www.nicurriculum.org.uk** – National Curriculum, Northern Ireland

**www.scotland.gov.uk** – curriculum guidance for Scotland

**www.tda.gov.uk** – Training and Development Agency

**www.teachernet.gov.uk** – education site for teachers and teaching assistants

**www.wales.gov.uk** – gives information about the National Curriculum in Wales

# TDA 3.13 Support teaching & learning in a curriculum area

How you are deployed will depend on the size and organisational structure of the school, the number of teaching assistants and your own skills. In secondary schools the role of the teaching assistant is becoming more specialised and so you are likely to support teaching and learning in a particular curriculum area. Teaching assistants may be assigned to particular departments or faculties to support teaching and learning in a subject area such as mathematics or English, or to support a cross-curricular area such as personal, social, health and economic education (PSHE). Whichever area you work in, this unit will support you to develop the necessary knowledge and the skills to contribute effectively to teaching and learning.

## By the end of this unit you will:

1. be able to use subject knowledge to support teaching and learning in a curriculum area

2. be able to develop own subject knowledge

3. be able to contribute to developing teaching and learning in a curriculum area.

# Be able to use subject knowledge to support teaching and learning in a curriculum area

Before considering subject knowledge within the curriculum area you support, it is important to understand how it fits in with the school curriculum. The secondary curriculum is organised into different stages:

● Key Stage 3 – ages 11–14 years (Years 7–9)

● Key Stage 4 – ages 14–16 years (Years 10 and 11)

● post-16 – ages 16–18 (sixth form).

Schools are also organised in departments or faculties. Each department is responsible for a particular part of the **curriculum area**.

## Aims of learning provision in a curriculum area

Within a secondary school the curriculum comprises a wide range of subjects, both statutory and

### Key term

**Curriculum area** – all forms of organised learning experienced across the curriculum. For example, thematically structured work in the primary phase, single subjects, vocational subjects and cross-curricular work in the 14–19 phase

non-statutory. English, mathematics and science are core subjects so it is likely that your role will be to support pupils in these curriculum areas, but you may support one of the range of subjects taught in Key Stages 3 and 4 or even in post-compulsory education. You could be required to support vocational subjects, particularly if you have experience of a particular industry or work sector. Although teaching through a topic is more common within a primary school, there will be aspects of cross-curricular learning in all areas of learning. For instance pupils will develop their skills in ICT and English through many other subject areas.

## The National Curriculum

The National Curriculum forms a central part of the whole curriculum and is a statutory requirement at Key Stages 3 and 4. The National Curriculum has recently been revised and is subject to review and development, so it is important that you keep abreast of curriculum developments, particularly in the subject area you support. Although the National Curriculum provides schools with the concepts, content and scope of information which must be taught within each subject area, there are opportunities for schools to develop a whole-school curriculum to meet the needs of their pupils. Specialist schools, for example, will have a requirement for pupils to follow a particular curriculum area alongside statutory subjects. Wales and Northern Ireland follow a similar national curriculum framework although in Wales the Welsh language is also a core subject. In Scotland the curriculum is non-statutory though guidance is provided by the Scottish Executive Education Department.

| Statutory subjects at Key Stage 3 | English Mathematics Science Geography Music Citizenship Modern foreign languages Art and Design History Physical Education Design and technology Religious Education Information and Communication Technology (ICT) |
|---|---|
| Statutory subjects at Key Stage 4 | English Mathematics Science Physical Education Citizenship Religious Education Information and Communication Technology (ICT) |

*Table 1: The statutory curriculum at Key Stages 3 and 4.*

At Key Stage 4 there is also an entitlement for young people to study other subject areas including work-related learning.

Although included within the National Curriculum, the following two subjects are treated differently.

1. **Religious education** is a statutory subject but the programme of study is devised locally to meet the needs of the pupils and reflect the school and the community.

2. **Personal, social, health and economic education** is a non-statutory area of the curriculum. This curriculum area, which includes economic well-being and financial capability and personal well-being, supports pupils to reach the outcomes from Every Child Matters which all organisations working with children must aim towards.

### Link

Each outcome from Every Child Matters is described in TDA 3.2, Schools as organisations.

### Link

For more on this topic see TDA 3.14, Support delivery of the 14–19 curriculum.

### Post-16 education
Not all secondary schools provide a post-16 curriculum. Although there are plans for all young people to stay in education or training until they are 19, this stage is non-compulsory. At this point young people will begin to specialise. They may choose an academic route such as A levels or a work-based path such as an Apprenticeship or a vocational subject.

### Disapplication of the National Curriculum
For some pupils with a statement of special educational needs, the National Curriculum programme of study may not be appropriate. The Head Teacher, following consultation with the teacher and parents, may request to disapply all or some areas of the curriculum to meet the needs of the individual child.

## The relevant school curriculum and age-related expectations of learners

The curriculum area you support will depend upon the needs of the school and also your own particular skills and knowledge. Whichever curriculum area you support, it is important for you to understand the programme of study or subject content and the age-related expectations. You will find the following information in each National Curriculum subject:

- the importance and aims of the area of study
- a **programme of study**
- attainment targets
- level descriptions
- links to other subjects or areas of study.

### Key term

**Programme of study** — outlines the knowledge, understanding and skills that children and young people are expected to acquire for each National Curriculum subject

### Skills builder

Consider ways that skills in the use of language and/or ICT could be integrated in the following activities.

1. In Year 7 the RE class is investigating the diverse beliefs and religions and cultures in the local area and finding similarities and differences in aspects such as food and dress, and rituals related to birth, marriage or death.

2. In Year 8 the art class is studying African art and is designing and making masks based on their research.

3. In Year 9 the geography class is studying the effects of human activity on the environment.

4. In Year 10 the history class is studying a crime and punishment module towards their GCSE. They are researching how crime and punishment has changed since the Middle Ages.

Below is the structure for the programme of study for mathematics at Key Stage 3. You will find that each National Curriculum subject is organised in the same way.

Some curriculum areas may have different terms to describe the programme of study. For example, in vocational or work-based programmes, the term 'specification' may be used. This includes the expected learning outcomes and links with other curriculum areas. Whichever term is used, you will find there is information for teachers on the purpose, the scope of content, aims and expected attainment levels included.

## Age-related expectations

For each curriculum area there are expectations of what learners should know, understand and be able to do. In National Curriculum subjects these are called **attainment targets**. These relate to each aspect of the subject. There are also **level descriptions** which describe what children typically know, understand and are able to do at the end of each key stage. For example, most pupils at the age of 11, as they transfer to secondary school, would be expected to be at level 4. At the age of 14 they are likely to have reached a level between 5 and 6. Some pupils will be below average and will not reach the expected level for their age and others will be working at a level above the expected level. In other subjects different terms may be used, such as assessment criteria or grading descriptions, so it is important that you understand these key terms used for any subjects areas you support.

At the end of Key Stage 3 pupils will be assessed formally by the teacher against level descriptions. At Key Stage 4 young people will take part in national tests or assessments such as GCSEs or vocational qualifications. The level description opposite describes a child who is working at level 5 in National Curriculum English in writing. These descriptions are not age related and could describe a child who is 12 years old who excels in English or a pupil at the end of Key Stage 3 who is working at the same level as the majority of their class.

### Key terms

**Attainment targets** — set out the knowledge, understanding and skills that children are expected to reach by the end of each key stage

**Level descriptions** — descriptions for each subject of what pupils characteristically achieve at that particular level. There are eight level descriptions with an additional level which describes exceptional performance

| The key concepts | • Competence, for example, applying, communicating<br>• Creativity, for example, imagination, reasoning<br>• Applications and implications of mathematics, for example, the way knowledge is used, asking questions<br>• Critical understanding, for example, as an abstract tool, knowing limitations and scope |
| --- | --- |
| The key processes | • Representing<br>• Analysing<br>• Interpreting and evaluating<br>• Communicating and reflecting |
| The range and content | • Number and algebra, for example, rules of arithmetic, ratio and proportion, linear equations<br>• Geometry and measures, for example, properties of shape, surface areas and volumes<br>• Statistics, for example, handling data |
| Curriculum opportunities | • Links with other subjects, for example, analysing data in geography<br>• Personal learning skills, for example, working collaboratively |

Table 2: The structure for the programme of study for KS3 mathematics. Source: http://curriculum.qcda.gov.uk

*'Pupils' writing is varied and interesting, conveying meaning clearly in a range of forms for different readers, using a more formal style where appropriate. Vocabulary choices are imaginative and words are used precisely. Sentences, including complex ones, and paragraphs are coherent, clear and well developed. Words with complex regular patterns are usually spelt correctly. A range of punctuation, including commas, apostrophes and inverted commas, is usually used accurately. Handwriting is joined, clear and fluent and, where appropriate, is adapted to a range of tasks.'*

*(Source: Level descriptions for English, QCDA)*

### Portfolio activity

Find out the level descriptions for the subject area you are supporting or expectations of performance if you are supporting a curriculum area which is not a part of the National Curriculum.

### Intervention strategies

Intervention is specifically designed to support pupils who are not meeting their full potential in English and mathematics rather than for those with special educational needs (SEN). Intervention at an early stage is critical so that children do not fall too far behind.

This usually happens in Year 7 when well-targeted support will help to motivate children. At Key Stage 4 intervention is also used to support pupils to reach their potential in GCSE mathematics and English. Targeting English in particular benefits pupils across all areas of the curriculum. Teaching assistants have an important role to play in intervention programmes.

### Link

Check out the information on study plus approach at Key Stage 4 in TDA 3.14, Support the delivery of the 14–19 curriculum.

## The relationship between the role of the teacher and own role

Whichever curriculum area you are supporting, the subject teacher has overall responsibility for the planning, preparation, delivery and assessment of the curriculum area. Your own role is critical at each stage of the process to support the teacher, the pupils and the area of the curriculum. A report commissioned by the Training and Development Agency for Schools suggests that an increase in the number of teaching assistants is strongly associated with improved school attainment (www.tda.gov.uk). It is important that you are involved at all stages of planning and delivery

---

**CASE STUDY:** Identifying pupils who would benefit from the intervention programme

Salma is a teaching assistant working in the English department. She provides support in Key Stage 3. Ben has recently transferred to the school and is in the first term in Year 7. His records show that he is an able child and achieved level 4 in his SATs tests at the primary school. Salma observed that Ben took a while to settle into the secondary school and that in class he is easily distracted. When supporting Ben's group, she noticed that he took a long time to start his written work. Although he appears confident when reading, and can discuss what he has read, Salma also noticed that Ben finds difficulty in

organising his ideas when writing. Following a meeting with Ben and his parents and the head of the English department, it was agreed that Ben would benefit from the intervention programme. Salma now provides one-to-one support to help Ben to improve written skills for two sessions each week.

- Why is it important to identify Ben's specific difficulty early?
- How might the intervention support Ben's progress in other areas?
- Where can Salma find the expected level of attainment for Ben at Key Stage 3?

and assessment within your own curriculum area. The diagram below shows each of these stages.

Effective support is reliant on the relationship between you and the subject teacher. Communication is key to building an effective relationship. This is to some extent affected by the personality of the teacher and their own working methods. You can, however, through your own actions, help to promote and maintain a successful working relationship. Your role may be to provide:

● whole-class support alongside the teacher

● support for a group within the class under the direction of the teacher

● support for a group withdrawn from the class

● support for an individual pupil with special educational needs (SEN).

## Using your subject knowledge to contribute to activity planning, delivery and evaluation, and supporting learners

You will need to use your own subject knowledge to:

● contribute to the planning, delivery and evaluation of learning activities or lessons

● support learners in developing knowledge, understanding and skills in the curriculum area

● help learners address errors or misconceptions in understanding the principles and concepts of the subject area.

## Contribute to planning, delivery and evaluation

To be able to provide effective support it is essential that you are involved in planning for the curriculum area you support. Planning will take place at different stages:

● long-term planning — for the year

● medium-term planning — termly or half-termly

● short-term planning — for a week or individual lesson.

Being involved at the early stage of planning will help you to prepare. You will have time to become familiar with the subject matter and the opportunity to ask questions about anything you do not understand. Planning should include not only the content of the lesson, but the activities which will take place, how pupils will be grouped, timing, resources, equipment and any differentiated work for individuals or groups. Even if the subject content in

*You should be involved at all stages when planning a curriculum area.*

planned activities is new to you, you will be able to contribute to planning meetings. It is likely that you know the needs of individual children and can advise on how they could be grouped to work effectively, ways that the activities could be presented or how the resources could be adapted. At the planning stage it is important that you are also involved in risk assessments relating to any activity and are clear about the safe use of any equipment or materials which will be used.

Your role in planning may include:

- attending planning meetings
- preparing by researching the concepts and content to be covered before meetings
- providing information on individual learning needs or disabilities of children you work with
- offering suggestions relating to content, organisation and strategies for individual children.

### Over to you!

Find out when long-, medium- and short-term planning meetings take place for your own curriculum area.

## Supporting preparation

The teacher will identify before the lesson what needs to be in place and the resources to be used. Your role may be to prepare all or some of the resources ready for the lesson. You may also be asked to adapt some of the resources, for example, by enlarging a photocopy of a poem in preparation for an English lesson for a pupil who has visual problems. Being prepared for the lesson is important. Having the resources and equipment in place for pupils before the lesson begins can save time and ensure that pupils begin their lesson promptly. It will also minimise the risk of inappropriate behaviour. Preparation is about ensuring that you understand your own role in the lesson and are equipped with the necessary knowledge and understanding of the concepts to be taught so that you can support the pupils.

Your role in preparation may include:

- agreeing your role in obtaining and setting up the classroom
- researching information and asking questions to ensure an understanding of the concepts and information to be covered
- checking that the resources are available (for example, textbooks, equipment, DVDs)
- photocopying worksheets and information
- checking availability of equipment/booking specialist equipment and setting this up
- setting up interactive whiteboards/DVD players/ laptops and so on
- adapting materials or providing additional or alternative equipment for individual pupils with particular needs.

## Delivery

The delivery of the lesson is about the organisation, pace and activities which take place. Lessons are usually organised in the following way:

- **Introduction:** reflecting on previous learning and giving pupils information on the aims and objectives of the lesson.
- **Lesson development:** pupils undertaking activities to promote their learning.
- **Plenary:** reviewing what has been achieved, checking understanding and answering questions.

You need to be clear on your role during the lesson. At one end of the scale you may just listen to the introduction and take no specific role, or you could take an active role, for example, writing up points on the whiteboard as the teacher introduces them, taking part in a role play or introducing the objectives to a group of pupils in a separate area.

### Key term

**Plenary** — a session, usually at the end of the lesson, when all pupils come together to discuss what they have learned and achieved

## CASE STUDY: Supporting learners who need more explanation

Mike works in Year 9 to support pupils in science. He supports a small group of pupils in the class giving particular support to Jamie, who has dyslexia. Jamie is doing well in science but lacks confidence to speak out in class and also finds difficulty in written work. During the teacher's introduction to the lesson on energy, Mike observed Jamie and the group he supports. Mike noticed that Jamie looked a bit puzzled as the teacher explained how he wanted the children to record their evidence. Mike felt that the teacher had not made this clear and so spoke for the group, asking the teacher if he could go over this information again.

- Did Mike take the correct action?
- How does this support:
  a) Jamie
  b) the rest of the pupils
  c) the teacher?

## BEST PRACTICE CHECKLIST: Strategies to support children's learning

- Encourage more reticent pupils.
- Help pupils to make choices and select suitable resources.
- Provide challenges.
- Encourage pupils to review their own learning.
- Adapt the activity if necessary.
- Give pupils strategies to enable them to work independently.
- Suggest alternative ways to find answers or solutions to problems.
- Help children to remain focused on their task.
- Partner or join group discussions.
- Observe and assess individual achievement.

## Supporting the development of knowledge, understanding and skills

As the lesson develops you will support the class generally or support small groups or individuals. In some lessons you may be asked to support the class while the teacher works with a targeted group. Look at the Best Practice Checklist (top right) and consider which of the following strategies you use to support children's learning.

For some children with specific needs or disabilities, you may need to provide more specific support such as acting as a scribe, providing physical help with tasks, translating or using alternative forms of communication.

## Supporting evaluation

Planning, delivery, and evaluation must be seen as a cycle. What happens in the lesson should inform the planning for the next session, so it is important to think about what went well and what could be improved. Evaluation should include all aspects of the lesson including the following.

- Were the lesson objectives achieved?
- Was the pace and timing appropriate?
- Did pairs or groups work together effectively?
- Were there any behaviour problems?
- Were the resources and equipment appropriate and sufficient?
- Were all pupils included?

### Functional skills

**English: Writing**
You could write an evaluation for the last session that you did with the children. Thinking about the questions above, organise and plan your evaluation before you begin, to ensure that you cover every aspect.

**CASE STUDY:** Working with a supply teacher

Alana is employed in the mathematics department of a specialist technology college. She works with a group of pupils in Year 7 who require additional support. Last week she was informed that the teacher she usually works with was off sick and a supply teacher would be taking the class. Alana had been involved in planning and had a copy of the lessons for the week. The pupils were continuing their work on data. Alana made sure that she got to the classroom early to introduce herself to the supply teacher and to give a brief overview of what had been planned. She explained her role to support two pupils with special educational needs within the class. The textbooks, graph paper and calculators were kept in the resource cupboard near the classroom, so Alana had collected these on her way to the room. The supply teacher asked Alana if she would remind the class of their previous activity where they had collected data on traffic flow. He then introduced the activity on processing and presenting the data in a graph. During the lesson Alana noticed that two pupils were distracting each other. She spoke to the supply teacher to inform him that they usually worked in separate groups and suggested that one of the pupils join her group. Before the next session, Alana met with the mathematics teacher to provide feedback on the pupils' achievements.

- In what ways did Alana's role change because the usual teacher was absent?
- How did Alana's actions before and during the lesson support the flow of the lesson?
- What might have happened if Alana had not been involved in lesson planning with the subject teacher?

## Addressing errors or misconceptions

When supporting or assessing pupils' work, you may notice that they have made errors or have misconceptions. Some misconceptions are common, so it is important that you are aware of these in the curriculum area you support. For example, in science it is often believed that the sun moves around the earth or that heavy objects fall faster than light ones. It is sometimes useful to ask pupils to complete a **concept map** at the beginning of a new topic to discover if there are any misconceptions. Misconceptions may also be linked with specialist terminology so it is important that pupils understand new words as they are introduced.

Although you should help learners to address errors and misconceptions in children's work, it is important that it is dealt with sensitively. They should understand that learning is a process and not 'right' or 'wrong'. Rather than providing pupils with the answer,

*What misconceptions have you come across?*

### Key term

**Concept map** – a diagram showing relationships between different ideas or concepts

| Strategy | Example |
|---|---|
| Ask pupils to look at previous work | During a mathematics lesson Charlotte has made a mistake in her calculation. The teaching assistant asks her to look back at her work from last week where she had used the formula correctly. |
| Ask pupils to read through information again | Jamie has made grammatical errors in his work. The TA asks him to read it aloud. As he does this, he recognises his own errors and corrects them. |
| Model or provide learners with an example which they can apply to their own work | During an ICT lesson Claire has forgotten how to produce a graph. The TA demonstrates using basic data and Claire then goes on to produce her own graph using her own data. |
| Ask pupils to discuss a principle or concept in pairs or small groups | In her health and social care class, Amina had misunderstood the concept of the social model of disability. The TA asked pupils to work in a group to discuss the principle and to agree a definition with examples. |
| Ask questions or explain thought processes | During a mathematics lesson Darren has difficulty in converting fractions to decimals. The TA asks Darren to explain how he has arrived at the answer. |
| Produce a model or drawing to represent a concept | During a science activity two pupils found difficulty understanding that matter is made of particles. The TA drew a diagram of particles representing solids, then asked the pupils to complete the drawing to show a representation of liquids and gases. |

*Table 3: Strategies to help pupils develop their understanding.*

try to use strategies which help them to reach their own understanding. This Chinese proverb provides a useful reminder:

> *I hear, I forget.*
> *I see, I remember.*
> *I do, and I understand.*

# Be able to develop own subject knowledge

It is important that you develop your own knowledge, understanding and skills within the curriculum area you work in so that you can support children more effectively. As you become more confident, you will find that you are developing more and more expertise. This can lead to you becoming more involved and being able to take on additional responsibilities such as mentoring new teaching assistants and taking a bigger role in planning, delivery and assessment.

## Self-evaluation of your own subject knowledge and skills

Whether you have some experience or are just starting to support a particular area of the curriculum, a good starting point is to evaluate your knowledge and skills. You should start by assessing your own knowledge in relation to the particular curriculum area. Initially write down any qualifications and experience that you have. This could be through other jobs so you should also consider the knowledge and skills that you transfer to this role. Even if you have good knowledge and skills in a particular area, you may find that you have a greater understanding of some aspects of the curriculum than others. For example, if you are supporting ICT you may feel particularly confident and have good experience in organising and formatting information in different types of documents but be unsure how to format numerical information, or you may feel confident in using different strategies to support children in reading but be unsure on how to assess their progress.

### Knowledge into action

The National Association for Professional Teaching Assistants (www.napta.org.uk) provides an online Professional Development Review which will help you to identify your own knowledge and skills against National Occupational Standards.

# Feedback from teachers and others to identify subject knowledge and skills

It is important that you reflect on feedback you receive from others; this may be informal or formal. Informal feedback may come from different sources, not only the teacher you support. Feedback may be given by:

- the children and young people
- other teaching assistants
- the teacher
- parents
- senior managers.

It may not always be explicit or obvious when informal feedback is given, but you should take note of comments you hear. For example, a child may say, 'I understand how to work out that problem now you have explained it again.' You could overhear the Special Educational Needs Co-ordinator (SENCO) telling the subject teacher that she has noticed that a child you have supported with reading appears far more confident in all his subjects. You should also be prepared for any informal advice on any weaknesses you have.

Formal feedback can take place in different ways. This would normally be provided by your manager, a senior manager or the subject teacher. Formal feedback will include:

- classroom observations – reference will be made on the role and support provided by teaching assistants during regular internal classroom observation

- an Ofsted inspection – reports often include information about the role and effectiveness of teaching assistants in the school (although individuals are not named in the report)
- feedback from the subject teacher(s) when reflecting on each lesson and your own role
- feedback from your tutor relating to your knowledge, understanding and skills in relation to occupational standards
- appraisal.

## Appraisal and performance management
Each school should have an appraisal or performance review procedure. This is when you have the opportunity to sit down with your manager and discuss your progress. If you have agreed targets during a previous appraisal, these will be reviewed to see if you have met them. An appraisal should be viewed as an opportunity. You can discuss your strengths and ways you have supported the pupils, the teacher, curriculum and school. You can also discuss your own professional development and agree ways that you can overcome any areas of weakness.

Before you attend an appraisal, you should prepare by considering:

- your own role – this should be outlined in a job description
- evidence to show that you have met or are working towards any previous targets
- your strengths in relation to your role and occupational standards
- any weaknesses in your knowledge or skills
- ideas on INSET activities, training opportunities or other strategies to support your professional development.

## Functional skills

**ICT: Developing, presenting and communicating information**
Completing this Skills builder exercise on the computer not only allows you to develop your ICT skills by using tables and different layouts, but you could also save it in a folder titled CPD so that you can come back to it at a later date to edit it and add more targets.

## Link

Further information and an example of a performance review meeting is in SfCD SHC 32, Engage in personal development.

## Opportunities to improve your own subject knowledge and skills

It is sometimes difficult to find additional time to develop your subject knowledge and skills. Attending department meetings is a good way to keep abreast of curriculum and subject developments, so you should try to attend these regularly. Schools organise regular staff development days for teachers and teaching assistants. It is helpful to find out the dates for these and consider ways to use your time, for instance obtaining journals and research materials relating to the curriculum area you support or attending an external development programme. You might even request a school-based session to be led by a teacher or an experienced teaching assistant. If you have preparation time on your timetable, think about how you could use this to develop specific knowledge or skills. This time could be used to observe the strategies used by teachers and teaching assistants during lessons. There may even be opportunities to study a GCSE or GCE alongside pupils at the school.

## Over to you!

Schools regularly receive information on available training. This information may be circulated in the staffroom or within departments. Find out what training is available which would support your own knowledge and skills. Also find out who you need to approach to request training opportunities. There may be someone at the school with specific responsibility for professional development.

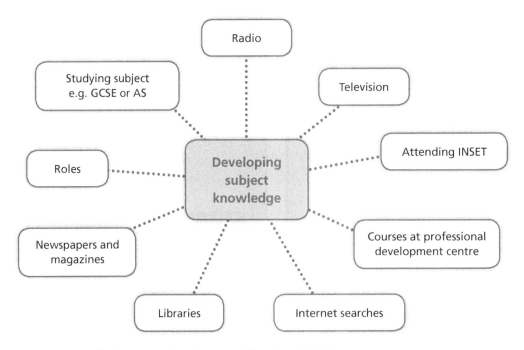

*Can you think of other ways to develop your subject knowledge?*

## Working with others

One effective way of developing both subject knowledge and skills is to work alongside others. When you start work within a new curriculum area, it is useful if you can take time initially to observe how the class is organised and the strategies used to support pupils. You could work shadow a more experienced teaching assistant who works within your curriculum area. There is an increasing number of **HLTAs** working in secondary schools who have a central role in teaching and learning.

### Key term

**HLTAs** — higher level teaching assistants, who act as specialist assistants within a particular curriculum area

## Demonstrate how new subject knowledge and skills have been incorporated

When you become confident in the area of the curriculum you are supporting, you will be able to demonstrate your knowledge through your practice. This may be at the planning stage, when preparing resources or when you are supporting children in class. Evidence can be provided through observations of your practice carried out by others or your own reflections.

### Reflect

Following a lesson or sequence of lessons, ask yourself the following.

- Did I make any contributions during planning meetings?
- Have I been able to suggest resources?
- Am I using vocabulary and terminology relating to the subject?
- Am I able to rephrase the teacher's instructions for pupils?
- Can I answer pupils' questions confidently?
- Am I able to use and demonstrate equipment?

## Be able to contribute to developing teaching and learning in a curriculum area

In the first section of this unit, you considered the different aspects of the planning cycle. You will contribute to all stages of this cycle from the initial planning to the review of learning. Subject knowledge is important for you to be able to contribute to the teaching and learning, but you also need to understand how pupils learn to be able to use effective strategies for support.

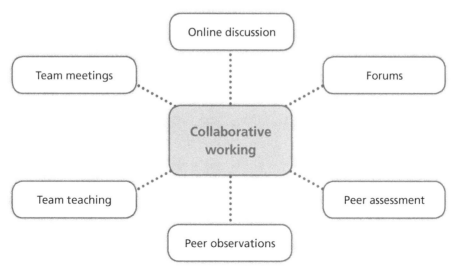

*An effective way to develop skills is by working collaboratively.*

## Monitoring advances relevant to the curriculum area

There is a continuous cycle of practice and review in each subject area. This is important to ensure that the curriculum is relevant so that children and young people are supported to reach their full potential.

The programmes of study in the National Curriculum are reviewed and revised regularly. The National Curriculum at Key Stages 3 and 4 was revised in 2000 and again in 2007 for first teaching in 2008. The GCSE content and method of assessment were also revised and introduced between 2009 and 2010. There are a number of reasons why the subject matter must be under constant scrutiny, including:

- technological advances
- new research
- new processes and techniques
- economic, social and environmental changes
- new priorities, for example, sustainability, global warming
- government priorities.

Curriculum developments may be made in response to outside organisations such as the **Sector Skills Councils**, universities and experts within each field. Organisations also take part in the advances and curriculum development – for example, the Association for Science Education (ASE) responded and advised in relation to the proposed Science Curriculum for Key Stage 3.

### Key term

**Sector Skills Councils** – independent, UK-wide, employer-led organisations which aim to drive improvements in knowledge and skills.

### Over to you!

New qualifications and teaching and learning strategies are often piloted before they are rolled out across all schools. You could find out if your school has been involved in any pilot programmes.

## Reflecting on effectiveness of support for teaching and learning

Observation is an important skill when reflecting on the effectiveness of your support for teaching and learning. It will also help if you are able to observe and consider the skills of others. When focusing on support for teaching and learning, you should consider:

- the range of strategies you use
- how you involve pupils in their own learning
- your questioning skills
- how you encourage independence.

*What strategies might you use when supporting these pupils?*

## Making suggestions for improving support for teaching and learning

As you become more experienced in supporting your particular curriculum area, you will find that you become more confident in making suggestions for improving teaching and learning. Remember that it is important that you know and understand not only the subject matter and content of a lesson but also ways that the concepts are presented to the children. You may be working closely with individual children or small groups, so will be able to observe strategies which work well or do not work. Suggestions for support may include:

- ideas for teaching and learning activities
- suggestions for educational visits
- suggesting materials, resources or equipment to support learning
- suggesting strategies to support understanding
- ways to adapt materials or activities for pupils with special educational needs or disabilities
- ways to incorporate other areas of the curriculum.

## Sharing subject knowledge and expertise with colleagues

You may have subject knowledge through previous studies, a previous job or have gained this through your experience and training within the subject area you support. You may have developed very specific skills or knowledge which will support others to improve teaching and learning. This could be, for example, supporting pupils with special educational needs such as autism or dyspraxia.

This may seem daunting but you should consider that you have been asked because you are considered to have a particular area of expertise. There are many ways that you can share your knowledge and expertise with others in the school. This can be done formally or informally — for example:

- directing others to useful resources, for example, texts, websites, DVDs
- mentoring less experienced teaching assistants
- team teaching with another teaching assistant
- providing INSET for subject areas or specific issues
- cascading information from training courses
- taking part in online discussion forums.

### CASE STUDY: Making suggestions

Peter works in a secondary school in the ICT department. He supports Key Stage 3 classes in ICT lessons and also provides cross-curricular support. Last week Peter attended a planning meeting for geography. The theme next term is weather and climate change. Peter suggested that pupils could become involved in collaborative work with pupils from a school in another part of the country. He then suggested that he could set up a webcam to allow this to happen. During the discussion on pupil achievement Peter also commented that he had noticed that a new pupil with cerebral palsy had difficulty in controlling the mouse and suggested that a tracker ball be purchased.

- How will Peter's contribution support teaching and learning?
- How is Peter demonstrating his subject knowledge?

## Getting ready for assessment

Throughout this unit you must demonstrate your skills in supporting children and young people in a curriculum area. It will be helpful if you start a log or portfolio of evidence of the support that you have provided at the beginning of the unit. Try to take a few moments each day to reflect on ways that you have used your knowledge and skills. Information which will support you to demonstrate your knowledge and skills could include:

- meeting minutes which you have attended (highlight or annotate with your own suggestions or contributions)

- copies of curriculum planning (annotate to include your own role)

- samples of pupil work (with permission)

- evidence of attendance at training/INSET sessions relating to your curriculum area

- reflections on lessons and ways you have supported pupils

- support and/or advice you have given to others relating to your curriculum area.

## Check your knowledge

1. What are the statutory National Curriculum subjects at Key Stage 3?

2. Which year groups are children in when following the Key Stage 4 curriculum?

3. Which subjects are taught in a cross-curricular way?

4. Why might children be disapplied from the National Curriculum?

5. What is a level description?

6. Suggest three strategies to support children who have made errors in their work.

7. What is the term used for a formal review of your work by a manager?

8. Suggest three reasons why subject content may need to be updated.

### Websites

**www.education.gov.uk** – Department for Education
**www.dcsf.gov.uk/everychildmatters** – the five outcomes for Every Child Matters
**www.nicurriculum.org.uk** – National Curriculum (Northern Ireland)
**www.scotland.gov.uk** – curriculum guidance (Scotland)
**www.tda.gov.uk** – Training and Development Agency for Schools
**www.teachernet.gov.uk** – education site for teachers and teaching assistants
**www.wales.gov.uk** – National Curriculum (Wales)

# TDA 3.14 Support delivery of the 14–19 curriculum

This unit will help you to develop your understanding of compulsory and post-compulsory education for 14- to 19-year-olds offered by schools and other organisations. You will explore approaches to working and strategies that you can use to support young people. You will also need to consider ways that different organisations work together to provide educational opportunities to enable young people to progress to higher education, employment or further training. You must demonstrate your own skills to support pupils' learning and promote achievement. You will also need to show how you work with colleagues and external agencies to plan, deliver and review education and training opportunities.

## By the end of this unit you will:

1. understand educational policy and practice for the education and training of 14- to 19-year-olds

2. be able to support teaching and learning for 14- to 19-year-olds

3. be able to work collaboratively to support delivery of the 14–19 curriculum.

# Understand educational policy and practice for the education and training of 14- to 19-year-olds

## Current provision for 14- to 19-year-olds

In 2008, following a review of the 14–19 curriculum, the government published the discussion paper 'Promoting achievement, valuing success: A strategy for 14–19 qualifications'. The intention was to streamline qualifications for pupils in Key Stage 4 and post-16 education. The curriculum is being introduced in stages and it is planned that four main routes will become an entitlement by 2013:

- GCSEs and A levels
- Diplomas
- Apprenticeships
- Foundation Learning.

### GCSEs and A levels

There is a wide range of available subjects in GCSEs; most are academic but there is an increasing number of applied subjects such as engineering or health and social care. GCSEs follow the programme of study from the National Curriculum. They may be achieved at **level** 1 (grades D–G) or level 2 (grades A\*–C). Functional skills are integrated within each GCSE course of study.

---

### Key term

**Level** – the levels of qualification relate to the National Qualification Framework and the Qualification and Credit Framework (for vocational and work-related qualifications). These frameworks group together qualifications which are of similar difficulty

---

A levels provide qualifications at level 3. They are studied in two parts as an AS and A2. An AS is half an A level and may be studied as a free-standing qualification. In the second year of study, pupils progress to the A2. A levels are offered in a wide range of subjects and as with GCSEs there are also a number of applied A levels.

In Scotland there are similar academic qualifications called Highers or Advanced Highers.

### Diplomas

Diplomas are academic qualifications with an applied learning element which helps learners to prepare for employment. Diplomas have been gradually introduced since 2009. There are now 14 lines of learning covering a range of subjects and sectors such as Construction and the Built Environment, Business, Administration and Finance, and Public Services. In each line of learning there are three levels including Foundation (level 1), Higher (level 2) and Advanced (level 3). Diplomas are made up of:

- principal learning – the knowledge, understanding and skills required for the main subject
- additional and specialist learning – pupils choose an additional subject to study, for example, a language
- generic learning – functional skills and personal, learning and thinking skills
- the project – pupils select an issue or aspect to study in depth relating to their main subject or a personal interest
- work experience.

### Apprenticeships

Young Apprenticeships are available for young people aged 14–16. Learning is linked to a particular sector or industry. Pupils undertake 50 days' work experience over two years alongside their studies.

Apprenticeships are available for young people post-16. These provide opportunities to study while working in a specific industry or sector. Young people must also study a work related qualification including WorkSkills and functional skills.

Advanced Apprenticeships are also available with relevant study at level 3.

### Foundation Learning

The Foundation Learning Programme has been introduced to provide flexible curriculum at entry level and level 1. Its purpose is to provide a personalised programme for young people who may be disengaged or have a specific learning difficulty or disability.

It comprises a range of programmes including subject and vocational learning, personal and social learning, and functional skills. Foundation Learning leads to nationally recognised qualifications.

## The relationship between the compulsory and post-compulsory education sectors

Children must attend full-time compulsory education between the ages of 5 and 16 years. In Year 8 or Year 9, pupils will begin to think about and make choices in preparation for their progress to Key Stage 4. There are compulsory subjects which young people must continue to follow to ensure that they receive a broad education. The choices made will be dependent upon:

● the school curriculum on offer

● pupils' ability

● pupils' interests and career aspirations.

At the age of 16, young people will specialise and make their own choices about their preferred route. Not all schools provide post-compulsory education, or particular subjects or routes, so young people may choose to transfer to a different organisation.

### Portfolio activity

Obtain the prospectus at the school or college where you work. Research the provision available for young people aged 14–19 in your own setting.

### Key Stage 4

Key Stage 4 includes pupils from 14 to 16 years in Years 10 and 11. In this phase of education, the National Curriculum continues to form part of the whole school curriculum. The National Curriculum is frequently reviewed so it is important that you keep abreast of developments. Although there are compulsory elements, there is also flexibility for schools to design a curriculum to meet the needs of their pupils. There is a number of statutory subjects but examinations are only compulsory for English, mathematics and science at the end of the key stage. Cross-curricular themes help pupils to make links between subjects and to apply skills and learning in a range of contexts.

In Key Stage 4, young people will be working towards national qualifications. For many this will include General Certificates of Secondary Education (GCSE) but there is an increasing number of young people who study other qualifications such as Diplomas or BTECs. A traditional route for young people was to select eight to ten GCSE subjects, but nowadays many will select more than one type of qualification as part of their studies. They may, for example, follow a GCSE course of study in English, mathematics and science alongside a Higher Diploma.

Integral to each route are functional skills and personal, learning and thinking skills (PLTS). Functional skills, which include mathematics, English and ICT, can also be studied as separate qualifications at levels 1 and 2. They include skills which have been identified as essential for everyday life and the workplace. PLTS are not assessed separately but are demonstrated within other curriculum areas.

| Statutory subjects | Non-statutory subjects | Entitlement to a subject from each of the areas |
|---|---|---|
| English<br>Mathematics<br>Science<br>Information and Communication Technology (ICT)<br>Physical Education<br>Citizenship<br>Religious education | Personal well-being (including sex and relationship and drugs education)<br>Economic well-being and Financial capability<br>Careers education | Creative arts (art and design, music, dance, drama or media)<br>Design and technology<br>Humanities (geography, history)<br>A modern foreign language |

**Cross-curricular dimensions:** identity and cultural diversity; healthy lifestyles; community participation; enterprise; global dimension and sustainable development; technology and media; creativity and critical thinking.

Table 1: Statutory subjects, non-statutory subjects and entitlements.

## Post-16

Choices at Key Stage 4 will affect the choices which will be made in post-compulsory education. Young people will be expected to have a good level of achievement at level 2, perhaps the equivalent of five GCSEs at A*–C before progressing to an advanced level. At 16, young people will begin to specialise in a particular area, usually following the equivalent of four to five A levels. At this stage it is important that young people have information on available choices at 19 and know the entry requirements for higher education, training or work.

At 16, pupils also have a wider choice of where they study. If their chosen course is available at their present school they may choose to continue there until they are 19. Alternatively pupils may apply to study at a different organisation such as a further education college or sixth form centre. Others may choose to follow work-related learning.

Although different routes and qualifications have been outlined in relation to compulsory and post-compulsory phases of education, there is a degree of overlap. Qualifications and training are not restricted to a particular phase so those available at Key Stage 4 will continue to be available. It has been estimated that at least 25 per cent of children will not have achieved at level 2 by the time they leave school, so it is important that there are real choices at entry and level 1. For a minority of young people, who excel in certain subjects, there will be opportunities to study subjects at a higher level at Key Stage 4. Many young people do not achieve at the same level across all areas of study so may study subjects at different levels.

### Functional skills

**ICT: Developing, presenting and communicating information**

You could design a presentation for the learners you support that talks about progression. Cover what options are open to them and how they would benefit from each option. You may be able to share this with your manager once you have completed it.

### Over to you!

Find examples in your own school or college of pupils who are studying qualifications from different pathways and at different levels.

### CASE STUDIES: Personalising learning

1. Michael is 14 and has just transferred to Year 10 where he is presently studying the Higher Diploma in Travel and Tourism. He is also studying GCSEs in English, science and ICT, but as Michael experiences difficulty in mathematics, he is following an entry level course in that subject.

2. Charlotte is in the sixth form at her school. She is studying five AS levels this year and plans to continue these and complete them at A2 next year. Her teachers recognised that Charlotte was gifted and talented in English so she studied and achieved her GCSE a year early. This year she is also studying the Diploma project as a free-standing qualification. This will allow her to select and research a subject, which interests her, in more depth.

3. Kieran has experienced difficulty at school. He had a period when he was absent and it was difficult for him to become engaged with any of his studies. Last year he began a Young Apprenticeship course in car maintenance. He attends a further education college where he has the opportunity to undertake real work experience. This has changed his attitude toward learning. He continues to attend school and is working toward his GCSEs in mathematics, English and science. He admits that he does not really enjoy studying but realises that it is important if he wishes to pursue a career in car maintenance.

- How will Michael, Charlotte and Kieran benefit from a more personalised course of study?
- What options are open to each pupil at the next stage of their education or training?

# Progression opportunities and routes for 14- to 19-year-olds

Progression opportunities for learners include the following.

## Higher education

Young people who have achieved at level 3 may apply for a place to study a higher-level course of study at university. Their success will depend upon the **UCAS points** they achieve at level 3. Higher-level study is not restricted to degrees but includes Higher National Diplomas (HND) or a Diploma in Higher Education (DipHE). Some degrees also give young people the opportunity to spend one year in industry before their final year. Specialised degrees or Higher Diplomas will lead to a specific career, such as nursing or teaching.

It is difficult for young people to decide on a course which is suitable for their own needs. This may depend on:

● a subject they wish to follow at a higher level

● a career they wish to follow

● their particular interests and abilities.

## Further education

At 16, young people may choose to transfer to continue with education or training at a further education (FE) college or training centre. FE colleges offer a range of courses from higher education such as HNDs, or foundation degrees, vocational courses or work-based study. This choice may be

### Key term

**UCAS points** – points or tariffs allocated to different qualifications. They help universities to differentiate between applicants when offering a place on an undergraduate course

more flexible for students who want to progress to a higher level or broaden their education, providing opportunities to study closer to home and to study part-time. For young people who have not yet attained a level 2 qualification, there will be a range of choices at Foundation level and level 2. Training centres tend to focus on work-based and vocational qualifications.

## Advanced Apprenticeships

Young people can select or progress to an Advanced Apprenticeship at 18. This is equivalent to two A levels. Young people will work in a specific industry and attend a day release course to work toward a work related qualification at Level 3, for instance WorkSkills and a Diploma or NVQ.

## Work

At 16 or at 19, young people may choose to seek employment. At 16 it is likely that young people will receive training and in the future young people will have to undertake training if they choose a work option. This may involve day release, although some organisations now offer their own accredited qualifications.

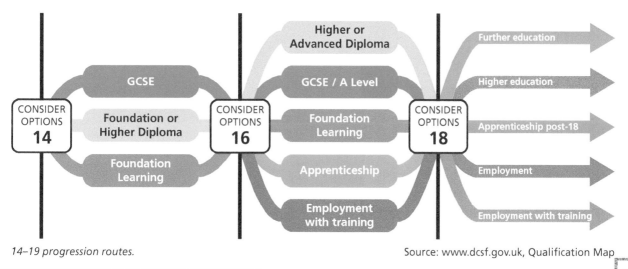

*14–19 progression routes.*

Source: www.dcsf.gov.uk, Qualification Map

## Progression for pupils with special educational needs

Children with special educational needs (SEN) require additional help to make choices about their progression. Foundation Learning provides a wide range of choices at entry and level 1. During Year 9 a **transition plan** is put into place to support young people to progress. Some pupils may progress to supported employment or independent living.

### Key term

**Transition plan** – a review carried out with the child, their family and relevant agencies to support young people with special educational needs to move to their adult stage of education, training or work

### Functional skills

**English: Speaking, listening and communication**
If you are working with young people who have already produced a transition plan, you could plan some questions that you could use in a discussion with them about what they want to do next. This will allow you to be prepared and your discussion will flow. Remember to listen carefully so that you can respond in an appropriate way.

# Be able to support teaching and learning for 14- to 19-year-olds

## Approaches to teaching and learning

Before considering different approaches to learning and ways that you can support strategies for 14- to 19-year-olds, it is helpful to observe ways that young people learn. This is sometimes considered to be the acquisition of knowledge or facts about a subject and then storing information so that it can be recalled. An alternative definition is being able to use the acquired knowledge and understanding and apply it to new contexts and situations.

There are two main theories of learning: the behaviourist theory and the cognitive theory. Those who follow the behaviourist theory believe that learning happens through stimulus, response and reward. This is based on Skinner's 'conditioning' theory which focused on the importance of repeated practice and the use of rewards. An alternative theory is a cognitive approach. This theory is based on a belief that people learn through experience and through solving problems.

Kolb (1984) suggested that most of what we learn we do from experience. This approach focuses on the importance of young people applying their learning and being able to use information in different contexts and situations. Research supports this view that young people learn more effectively when they are actively engaged in their own learning.

### Knowledge into action

Write down something that you have learned and feel confident about. Go on to write down how you developed your knowledge, understanding or skill. Share your thoughts with peers and write a list of things that made learning successful. You might go on to think about an area of learning or a skill that you tried to develop which you found really difficult or you found that you could not master and the reasons for this.

Influences on approaches to learning include:

- the environment – for example, is there space to work effectively in groups or to carry out practical work?
- learning outcomes – what should pupils know, understand or be able to do by the end of the session?
- the pupils – what do they already know or understand or what can they do?

It is also important to know pupils' preferred learning styles, ensuring that approaches are varied to meet the needs of all pupils.

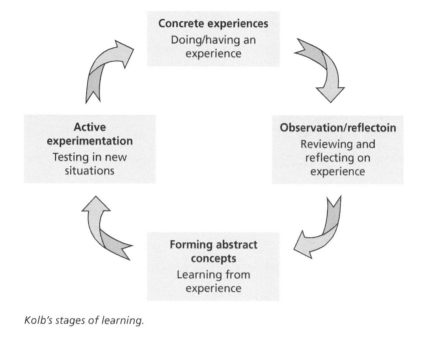

*Kolb's stages of learning.*

## Functional skills

### Maths: Representing

What are the learning styles of the children who you work with? You could produce a chart or graph to show the different learning styles in your class. How do you adapt the materials that you use to suit each of these learning styles?

## Motivation

You only have to watch young children playing to understand that learning is a natural activity. They show curiosity and interest in a wide range of activities. As children get older, they sometimes appear to lose their motivation to learn. You could consider why this might be and the strategies which work well to capture young people's imaginations. A starting activity should be challenging and interesting but be linked to something that the pupils already know and can do, so they have a sense of achievement. Think about ways to involve all pupils so that individuals do not feel left out. Interest could be promoted by:

● posing a short problem or question

● passing round an artefact, showing a picture or playing a short DVD extract.

For learning to be successful, the learning objectives must be shared with pupils so they know what they are expected to achieve and/or produce by the end of the session. The outcomes will be linked to what the young people are expected to know, understand and be able to do by the end of the lesson or period of learning. Different subjects or types of qualification may require a different approach to teaching and learning. Work-based qualifications will be balanced towards what young people are able to do, underpinned with knowledge, while academic qualifications may require more evidence of knowledge and understanding.

## Knowledge

Young people may need to know particular facts or information. Direct teaching may be used to impart the information such as dates, names, symbols or formulae. For some young people, who are kinaesthetic or visual learners, direct teaching can be less effective, so should be accompanied by strategies such as questioning, or asking them to highlight key words and information in text to ensure that they are more actively involved in their own learning.

*Have you used questioning strategies with pupils?*

## Understanding

A different approach will be necessary if we want young people to understand concepts, processes and principles. Being able to repeat facts does not necessarily demonstrate that learning has taken place as pupils need to digest information. Approaches which enable young people to use and apply learning to new situations will be more effective in developing understanding.

- Explaining to others — this will help pupils to consolidate learning and bring to light any misconceptions.

- Case studies — these are useful for supporting pupils to relate their knowledge to different situations, consider events and consequences or to use knowledge to resolve problems.

- Making models/drawing diagrams — by converting ideas and concepts to a model or drawing, pupils will need to think more deeply about the information.

- Reorganising or summarising information — rewriting information shows only basic understanding, but using information helps learners to think more critically.

- Concept mapping — concept maps will help pupils to see and understand connections between different ideas and concepts.

- Collaborative work — this supports development of ideas and concepts through discussion and solving problems.

## Skills

Some skills which must be acquired by young people are quite clear, such as using a piece of equipment, carrying out a task or using particular software. Other skills which are required may not be so obvious, such as the ability to listen and respond during discussions or a debate, or to write in a particular genre. Skills can be developed through the following strategies.

| Teaching and learning strategy | Example |
| --- | --- |
| Simulation | A group of learners who are studying the Advanced Diploma in Travel and Tourism carry out a role play to develop skills in resolving a customer service issue. |
| Real experience | Drama students are involved in planning and producing an end-of-term production. |
| Case studies | A level biology students are provided with a newspaper article relating to an ethical issue of an individual's rights to refuse treatment, to stimulate debate. |
| Modelling | During a textile technology lesson, the teacher demonstrates techniques for screen printing. As she demonstrates, she provides a commentary (thinks aloud) at each stage of the process. |

*Table 2: Teaching and learning strategies.*

## Learning support strategies to meet the needs of 14- to 19-year-old learners

When selecting learning support strategies, you need to consider the age and ability of individuals and the expected outcomes for the session. If you work regularly with individuals, you will have a good understanding of strategies which work particularly well. Support strategies should be agreed with the teacher before the lesson, although it is sometimes necessary to adapt strategies if it is clear that these are not working for individuals. You are likely to use a range of strategies within an individual session.

Consider the strategies you use to:

● involve young people in their own learning (through active learning techniques, self-assessment strategies)

● challenge pupils' thinking (questioning, posing problems and setting challenging activities)

● ensure success (starting from learners' own knowledge and experience, breaking down activities into smaller steps, rephrasing instructions or information)

● motivate (giving positive feedback, varying activities, including strategies which support individual different learning styles, using a range of resources, providing hands-on activities)

● support knowledge and understanding (explaining vocabulary, rephrasing teachers' instructions, questioning, directing towards information or resources)

● support the development of skills (modelling, giving time to practise, giving constructive feedback)

● manage behaviour (building effective relationships, giving clear messages, using reward systems)

● promote independent learning (giving choice, for example, methods to record information, resources to use)

● support inclusion (adapting materials and teaching strategies, breaking down barriers, using resources which reflect the diversity within the setting).

## Questioning

Questioning is an important strategy to encourage pupils to reflect on and discuss what they have learned. Questioning will also challenge pupils to think more deeply about their learning.

Consider the types of questions you ask when supporting young people. Two main types are open and closed questions. For example, you might ask, 'Can you tell me the name of the instrument which measures wind speed?' This is an example of a closed question. It is useful for finding out what pupils know, but this type of question does not promote higher-order thinking skills. An example of an open question might be, 'You said that the artist has been influenced by the impressionist movement. What led you to think that?' This type of question would lead to the pupil considering reasons for their conclusions. Reflect on how you might use open questions when supporting pupils in order to:

● develop ideas

● motivate and promote curiosity

● stimulate discussion

● draw pupils back on task

● encourage deeper thinking.

Questioning can support pupils to develop their higher order thinking skills which are shown in Bloom's taxonomy (see below). As pupils progress to more advanced levels, it is important that strategies and methods used support them to reach the higher-order skills.

● **Knowledge** – recall of information such as listing dates or labeling a diagram.

● **Comprehension** – being able to explain ideas or concepts.

● **Application** – understanding abstract ideas and being able to apply them to a new context.

● **Analysis** – being able to break down information and distinguish between different concepts or ideas to show relationships, for example, strengths and weaknesses of an idea or process.

● **Synthesis** – being able to bring together different ideas to apply to other contexts such as a research project.

● **Evaluation** – being able to justify and make judgements and recommendations, for example, through a debate or written report.

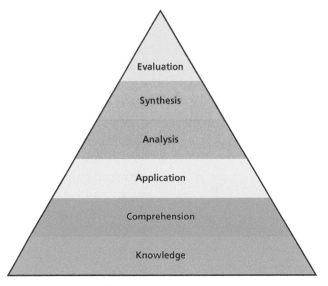

*Bloom's taxonomy of learning.*

## CASE STUDY: Questioning strategies

Leon works in the special needs department of a secondary school supporting pupils who have difficulty in concentration and often lack motivation. Last week Leon supported a group of six pupils in Citizenship. They were considering what was meant by fair trade. The teacher had introduced the concept. The class then broke into groups to discuss their ideas. Leon began by challenging the pupils to tell him how much a kilo of bananas would cost and what percentage the growers would get. He used the outline of a banana which he cut up to illustrate the small amount the growers receive compared with others in the chain. Leon asked pupils to work in pairs, challenging them to list as many goods which were fair trade as they could in one minute. He then showed a poster which had examples of foods and other goods which were fair trade. Leon gave each pair five Post-it® Notes™ and allowed them five minutes to discuss and write one reason why people should buy fair trade goods on each note. As they

worked, Leon discussed their ideas and asked open-ended questions. The pupils then came together as a group, discussing and prioritising each idea then displaying them on a board. Leon gave each pupil positive feedback in relation to their ideas. He developed the lesson by asking pairs to think about ways that consumers could be encouraged to buy more fair trade goods. They were asked to choose a medium to advertise the importance of buying fair trade, for example, posters, a short film for the Internet or TV, a radio advertisement (which they would produce over the following weeks). At the end of the lesson, each pair was asked to explain and justify their ideas to the group.

- List all the strategies that Leon used.
- What questions might he have asked?
- How will the strategies used:
  a) support their learning
  b) motivate learners?

### Functional skills

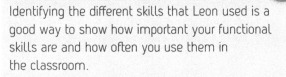

Identifying the different skills that Leon used is a good way to show how important your functional skills are and how often you use them in the classroom.

## Select, develop and use learning resources

### Select resources

Your school or educational setting will have a range of resources to support different learning strategies. When selecting resources, it is important to consider:

- learning outcomes
- individual needs of pupils.

Ask yourself how the resource will support pupils to develop particular knowledge, learning or skills. You may require specialist resources, for example, science, ICT or PE equipment, or general resources such as stationery or recording equipment. Some resources, such as specific pictures or natural materials, may not be available within the setting but you may be able to obtain them yourself. You might also contact external organisations who may be happy to loan resources for specific purposes. Museums often loan artefacts to schools and universities may allow pupils to access specialist resources.

You will need to consider if resources are suitable for all pupils. Pupils with difficulty in fine motor control will require specialist IT equipment or tools for design and technology. For pupils with visual impairment, tactile markers can be purchased to use on measuring equipment for science and talking calculators for mathematics. Organisations such as the Royal National Institute of Blind People or the Council for Disabled Children provide useful information on suitable resources to support learning.

### Over to you!

Check out the specialist resources in the department where you work and those available for cross-curricular work.

### Develop resources

When you have made a decision about suitable resources to support teaching and learning, you may find that they need to be adapted to:

- relate to a particular curriculum area — by changing diagrams, graphs or illustrations or examples and so on
- meet the needs of individuals — by changing the media, language level, breaking down into steps, increasing font size, changing the colour of paper and so on.

You may have to simplify information for pupils working at entry or level 1, but you must consider the age group and interest level. Illustrations and layout should be appropriate for pupils. Resources designed for younger children should not be used for Key Stage 4 and post-16 pupils.

Adaptations are not restricted to paper-based information. PowerPoint® presentations, for example, may also be unsuitable for some pupils within the group. These may need to be adapted by reducing the animation, or changing the colour contrast to ensure that all pupils can follow the information. Adaptations can also be made to the methods of presentation. Podcasting is increasingly used and can be effective for pupils who have difficulty in reading and/or understanding the printed word.

### Use resources

It is important that you understand how resources and equipment are used in preparation for lessons. If resources or equipment need to be set up, this should be completed before pupils arrive so that the lesson is not disrupted or delayed. You may need to demonstrate to pupils how resources or equipment should be used and remind them of any safety considerations and rules.

---

### BEST PRACTICE CHECKLIST: Using resources

- Check that resources are available well before the lesson and book them if necessary.
- Know how to use resources.
- Know how to set up large equipment.
- Consult with relevant staff when selecting specialist resources and equipment.
- Return resources immediately after use.
- Know and use stock control systems and, if necessary, how resources are ordered.
- Check resources and equipment for safety and report any concerns, for example, loose wiring.
- Ask a colleague to proofread or check any resources that you have produced or adapted.
- Use resources which reflect the diversity in society.
- Consider the effectiveness of resources used as part of the lesson evaluation.

## Supporting learners to transfer learning to other areas of life

The wider 14–19 curriculum includes cross-curricular learning which underpins the five outcomes from the Every Child Matters framework. Activities support young people to work toward these outcomes to transfer their learning to all areas of life including social, personal, home, working life and education. These areas of learning include:

- developing independent learning skills
- acquiring knowledge, understanding and skills that can be applied to everyday activities
- developing positive attitudes
- promoting health and well-being.

### Developing independent learning skills

Integrating personal, learning and thinking skills supports young people to develop strategies to manage their own time and work independently and with others. They are helped to think more creatively and reflect on their own development.

### Acquiring knowledge, understanding and skills that can be applied to everyday activities

Cross-curricular learning includes functional skills in English, mathematics and ICT, and economic well-being and financial capability. This learning supports young people in their educational development, personal life and future work by including the knowledge and skills that we all use in everyday life, such as managing personal finances.

### Developing positive attitudes

Citizenship and aspects of personal, learning and thinking skills support learners to think more critically and challenge their attitudes about a range of issues.

### Promoting health and well-being

Personal, social and health education including sex education supports young people to develop appropriate relationships, become self-aware and develop self-esteem. Young people gain knowledge of heath issues and how to safeguard themselves and stay healthy.

### Reflect

Research the five outcomes from the Every Child Matters framework. In what ways could you support young people to meet the outcomes through the curriculum area you work in?

# Be able to work collaboratively to support delivery of the 14 to 19 curriculum

## Roles of services and agencies in providing education and training

The local authorities take a strategic role in ensuring that young people aged 14–19 are able to access education and training routes to which they are entitled. The delivery of the 14–19 curriculum has become quite complex and its success relies upon effective partnership between the different services and agencies. How education and training is delivered will depend upon the current provision in each locality. In some areas the majority of schools may have sixth forms while in others, post-16 curriculum is mainly delivered in further education colleges. In all areas, however, there needs to be increasing collaboration between services and agencies which deliver and support education and training. No single educational or training organisation can provide the range of subjects and progression routes on offer. A co-ordinated approach will:

- give a wider choice
- provide for the needs of individual young people
- broaden experience
- promote inclusion
- provide access to essential resources
- support disengaged young people.

### Services and agencies which provide education and training

There is a wide range of **state schools** within the mainstream sector. Some schools are funded differently and develop particular specialisms; others, such as academies, are funded by and have closer links with the business sector. All state schools provide education for young people in the compulsory education sector from 14–16 years. Some also offer post-compulsory education to 19 years.

## Link

For more about state schools see TDA 3.2, Schools as organisations.

**Sixth form centres** may be part of an FE college or within a school. Sixth form centres offer education for young people aged 16–19. Courses will include GCEs, Diplomas and vocational qualifications. Pupils may choose to transfer to the sixth form at another school if their own school does not offer post-16 education or does not offer the courses which the individual would like to study.

**City Technology Colleges** are state-funded schools which provide education and training for young people aged 11–19. City technology colleges deliver the National Curriculum but specialise in technology-based subjects. They have close links with industry and business.

**Further education (FE) colleges** are usually much larger and offer a wide range of courses. FE colleges work closely with local schools and many offer education and vocational and work-based training for pupils in Key Stage 4. At 16, pupils may decide to transfer to an FE college to study a course on their chosen pathway. They may continue on the academic GCSE route, vocational or work-based programme.

**Training centres** work closely with industry to offer work-based training for young people aged 14 and over. They support practical work skills and deliver work-based qualifications.

**Specialist colleges** provide education and training in a specific field of study such as the arts or agriculture. There are also specialist colleges for young people who have specific needs such as sensory impairment.

## The role of employers

Employers and industry underpin the 14–19 reforms. There is an increasing number of employers across the private and public sectors of all different sizes who play a critical role in the education and training of young people. Their role in supporting the Apprenticeship route is clear, as many young people undertake real work experience in a range of different sectors. There is also a critical role for employers to play in supporting each of the 14–19 routes.

The role they play can vary and may include:

● supporting professional development

● providing Apprenticeship opportunities

● providing short-term work experience

● providing sponsorships

● organising visits

● supporting projects

● giving expert talks.

Some employers including McDonalds, Flybe and Network Rail now have awarding body status. They have developed and had accredited their own qualifications. McDonalds, for example, offers a level 3 diploma in shift management.

Connexions is an agency which works closely with educational and training providers to supply information and guidance to young people on progression routes.

## The importance of effective team working with colleagues within and external to the setting

Your role as a teaching assistant requires you to become part of a wide network within and external to your own educational setting. Teamwork has many advantages for organisations and staff, but it should have at its heart the achievement and well-being of individual pupils. These aspects can be promoted when staff:

● share knowledge and skills

● share information about the needs and preferences of individual pupils

● pool ideas in planning and delivery

● draw on a wide range of expertise

● support the delivery of cross-curricular learning such as functional skills.

**CASE STUDY:** Effective teamwork

Cathy has worked in the special educational needs department at the local secondary school for the last three years and reports directly to the Special Educational Needs Co-ordinator (SENCO). She has developed knowledge and expertise to support pupils with a range of specific learning needs and disabilities. She works with colleagues across the school and from agencies and other educational settings. Cathy is required to attend meetings in a number of departments as well as her own department. She supports and advises subject teachers on the needs of individual pupils and adapts learning materials. Cathy attends review meetings for pupils with special educational needs, which are attended by parents and specialists such as speech therapists and health professionals. Cathy supports pupils to make choices as they transfer to Key Stage 4 and the post-compulsory phase, which requires her to liaise with colleagues and employers from local educational settings and businesses.

- How does Cathy promote pupils' achievement through effective teamwork?
- How can effective teamwork support the well-being of the pupils she supports?
- How does Cathy support the school?

## Ways of contributing to collaborative and cross-sector working

If your role includes supporting pupils aged 14–19, you will be required to work collaboratively with colleagues from both the compulsory and post-compulsory education sectors. A pupil studying a Diploma combined with GCSEs may study at an FE college, school and also undertake work experience in a local business or industry. There are a number of ways that you may contribute to cross-sector working.

### Portfolio activity

Draw a diagram which illustrates ways in which you work within and across different sectors. Add information on ways in which you communicate and share information and the benefits for pupils.

## Using knowledge to provide colleagues with feedback

An essential part of your role as a teaching assistant is to provide your colleagues with feedback on all aspects of each learner's progress and participation. Assessment should take into account whether learners are engaged with their learning as well as any academic progress. Assessment is a continuous process and you will find yourself making **formative assessments** about learners each time you provide support. As you become more experienced you will find that you are able to use more focused questions and observations. This is only possible where you have knowledge of:

- the learners – their prior knowledge, age and stage of development, additional learning needs or disabilities and/or individual targets
- the requirements of the curriculum – for example, learning objectives, attainment targets.

It would be helpful to have a notebook with you at all times to jot down information on pupils' progress and ways that they respond to activities or use equipment or resources.

### Skills builder

Negotiate a time during a lesson when you can just observe pupils as they work. Focus your observation on two or three pupils, relating to specific aspects of their learning and participation. This could be, for example, on their engagement with the activity, their involvement in group work or their skills in using equipment.

### Key term

**Formative assessment** – ongoing assessment of pupils' progress, such as understanding skills and participation. This does not provide any final grade

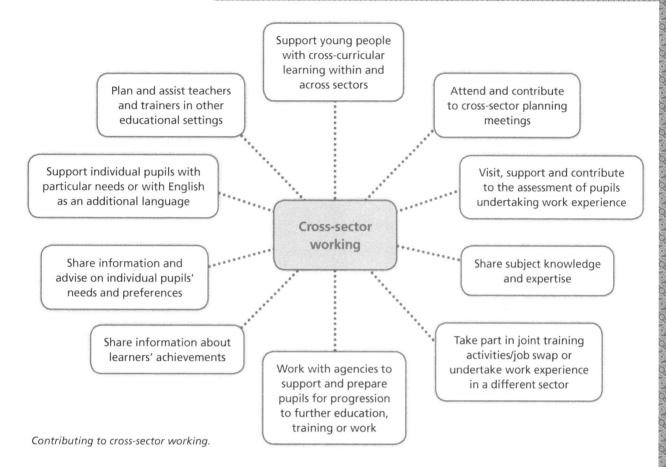

*Contributing to cross-sector working.*

## Sharing information on the progress of young people

Information may need to be shared with colleagues within or external to your setting, so it is important that you understand ways to record and share the information on progress and participation. Within your own setting you may provide informal feedback verbally after each lesson, but this will not be possible where feedback must be shared with colleagues external to the setting. This may happen where young people study and undertake work experience across more than one setting. Diplomas, for example, are planned and delivered by a consortia of partner organisations, so you may be part of the team contributing to the overall assessment of individual pupils. You may also need to share information about the progress and participation of pupils who have special educational needs with

professionals from a range of external agencies. There will be protocols on ways achievement is to be recorded and how this is shared internally and externally. Many schools have electronic systems for recording academic achievement. When recording and sharing information, you must observe confidentiality at all times.

### Functional skills

#### ICT: Developing, presenting and communicating information
When producing a document on the computer that contains confidential information about a pupil or member of staff, it is important that you password-protect that document. A secure password is one that contains a mixture of upper and lower case letters, and numbers.

## CASE STUDY: Contributing to assessment

Amina is studying the Higher Diploma in Business, Administration and Finance. She attends a partner school as her own school does not offer this particular line of learning. Functional skills and personal, learning and thinking skills are integrated within the units she studies, but some aspects are taught at her own school and supported by Mike, who is a Higher Level Teaching Assistant. Amina also studies the project and English and mathematics GCSE at her school, and has chosen German as her additional and specialist learning.

Last term Amina undertook two weeks' work experience at a local business. She was also supported and observed in the workplace by Mike.

- In what ways will Mike contribute to the overall assessment of Amina's progress?
- What does Mike need to know about Amina's previous achievement and the expected outcomes?
- What barriers might exist to prevent the effective feedback of Amina's progress and participation?

## Getting ready for assessment

Throughout this unit you must demonstrate your knowledge, understanding and skills in supporting delivery of the 14–19 curriculum. It will be helpful if you start a log or portfolio of evidence. Try to take a few moments each day to reflect on ways that you have demonstrated your knowledge and skills. You need to show that you understand education and training provision for 14- to 19-year-olds, providing learning support appropriate to this age range, and working collaboratively to support planning, delivery and review of education and training for 14- to 19-year-olds. Teaching and learning strategies, the curriculum and opportunities for work-related learning are under constant review so it is important that you keep abreast of developments.

## Check your knowledge

1. Identify the four main routes at 14–19.
2. Compulsory education covers which age groups?
3. What is the curriculum at entry and level 1 known as?
4. What is the partnership which works together to plan and support Diplomas known as?
5. Identify the five outcomes from the Every Child Matters framework.
6. What is meant by open-ended questioning?

### Websites

**www.apprenticeships.org.uk** – Information about apprenticeships
**www.dcsf.gov.uk/everychildmatters** – Every Child Matters outcomes
**www.direct.gov.uk** – Diploma information
**www.education.gov.uk** – The Department for Education
**www.nationalcurriculum.co.uk** – National Curriculum
**www.ssatrust.org.uk** – Specialist Schools and Academies Trust (SSAT)
**www.tda.gov.uk** – Teacher Development Agency
**www.teachernet.gov.uk** – TeacherNet

# TDA 3.17 Support bilingual learners

This unit is for staff who support bilingual learners in the target language (English or Welsh) and looks at the way in which children develop their language skills. You will need to identify and demonstrate strategies for promoting pupils' development in speaking and listening, reading and writing in the target language.

## By the end of this unit you will:

1. be able to interact with bilingual learners
2. be able to support bilingual learners to develop skills in the target language
3. be able to support bilingual learners to access the curriculum.

# Be able to interact with bilingual learners

## Interact with bilingual learners in a way that demonstrates respect, shows sensitivity and reinforces positive self-image

You will need to show when you are interacting with **bilingual learners** that you take account of and respect each individual and their needs. This means that you should ensure that you are sensitive to their background, culture and beliefs. In order to do this you will need to find out about their home, language and educational backgrounds. Although there will be systems in place in your school for finding out some initial pupil information, you should also take time to get to know the children and young people with whom you are working and their families, particularly when they first start at the school or when you first start working with them.

### Key term

**Bilingual learners** – pupils who have been exposed to two languages, both those newly arrived and new to the language used to deliver the curriculum, and those more advanced bilingual learners who can communicate confidently but need further support in academic contexts

The pupil's home background is important as this will have the greatest influence on the child. Children whose home backgrounds have been traumatic, such as refugees, may have had wide and varied educational experiences. The school needs to obtain as much information as possible and if possible seek the help of an interpreter so that discussions can take place directly with parents. The experiences a pupil has had may also affect their behaviour; for example, if they are non-responsive, this may be because they have suffered a trauma. Children and young people who come from backgrounds with a different culture or religion from the majority of others in the school may feel isolated, and it is important for them that the school values cultural diversity in different ways.

Children's self-image will be directly affected by their perception of how others see them and in their confidence when using language. Their self-esteem must stem from an acknowledgement and acceptance of themselves, whatever race, language, ethnicity or religion they may have. Children and young people also need to experience a sense of belonging in their surroundings so that they are able to grow in confidence. If their parents do not speak English, this may be a child's first experience of having to communicate with others in a language other than their own. It is important for the pupil to be able to communicate in school and, although children will usually pick up language reasonably quickly, this can be a difficult time for them. If you notice that any pupils are finding it hard to make friends, it is important to discuss this with the form teacher. You may also be able to help them to socialise with others during lunch breaks or during after-school activities.

### Reflect

How do you ensure that you find out about what is important, such as the preferred name which is used by pupils?

### Knowledge into action

What kind of information does your school gather when pupils transfer to the school? How do they obtain information from parents and what is the procedure for doing this if parents do not speak English themselves?

A child's language background and how much exposure they have had to the target language are also useful things to know. If staff know that the pupil has never been exposed to the target language before, this knowledge can help them to devise an educational or language plan. Each learner will need an education plan that takes age, individual background and learning needs into account, including appropriate targets. Home visits may also be helpful at this stage for getting to know parents and valuing their input, and to involve them as much as possible in their child's learning from the start. Bilingual staff may also be involved so that the mother tongue can be used in the school where needed.

When interacting with bilingual pupils, it is also important that you support and encourage what they are saying through your communication skills.

### Link

For more on this see TDA 3.1, Communication and professional relationships with children, young people and adults.

## Use language and vocabulary which is appropriate to the learner's age, understanding and proficiency

As you get to know the bilingual and multilingual pupils you support, you will need to think about the language that you use with them, to ensure that it is appropriate to the child's age and level of understanding. A pupil's age may make a difference to how they learn a **target language** — older pupils may be more self-conscious, and as a result less likely to speak, or be hindered by the higher demands of the curriculum. However, another view is that older children are more experienced at using language and this may make the process easier for them. A younger child may be more relaxed and less anxious about acquiring a new language — for children to attempt to initiate language, they need to feel relaxed and confident that their contributions will be valued.

However, the process may take longer, particularly if they are learning two languages at the same time.

If the teacher is talking to the class and has used language which is difficult to understand, you may need to clarify for pupils what has been said. You should also check regularly that they understand — in some cases, pupils may seem to know what is happening or what is being said when they have not really followed it.

### Key term

**Target language** — the additional or second language needed by bilingual learners, for example, English as an additional language (EAL), or Welsh or Gaeilge as a second language

## Be able to support bilingual learners to develop skills in the target language

### The organisation's policy and procedures for supporting bilingual learners

According to government statistics, 15.2 per cent of primary school children and 11.1 per cent of secondary

*How can you tell if a pupil really understands what has been said?*

school children speak English as their second language. Over 200 languages are spoken by children who attend British schools. When supporting bilingual and multilingual pupils, all staff will need to think about how they can promote the development of the target language while valuing the child's home language and culture. This is particularly important if the child is an isolated learner in the target language. The school should therefore have its own policies and practices for how children with English as an additional language (EAL) are supported. The different types of strategies which the school has in place may therefore include:

- school policies to promote positive images and role models
- school policies and practices on inclusion, equal opportunities and multiculturalism
- identification of bilingual/multilingual children
- providing opportunities for pupils to develop their language skills
- having established school and class routines
- finding opportunities to talk with parents of bilingual children and encourage links with the school
- celebrating linguistic and cultural diversity.

## Functional skills

**English: Writing**
You could write a report that explains the different strategies that your school promotes for supporting EAL. You could do this in the style of a newspaper article so as to practise writing for a different purpose. Think carefully about the layout of your article and the spelling, punctuation and grammar.

Many schools also now have a governor and/or teacher in the school with overall responsibility for EAL pupils. The role of the teacher would be to advise other staff on the kinds of strategies which will be the most effective.

## Portfolio activity

Find out what policies your school has which may be relevant to children from bilingual or multilingual backgrounds. How are bilingual pupils and their families supported within your school community?

## Functional skills

**ICT: Developing, presenting and communicating information**
You could produce a leaflet of different services available locally for bilingual learners. You may need to research this on the Internet or through contacting your local borough.

# Theories of first language acquisition and additional language acquisition and learning

There have been a number of theories put forward about how children learn or acquire language. Although there are many, there are still no definite answers about how language development takes place. However, most linguists agree that children will pass through two stages — the pre-linguistic and the linguistic stage.

The pre-linguistic stage is during the first 12 months, when babies begin to learn basic communication skills. During this time they will start to attract the attention of adults and repeat back the different sounds that they hear. This is true of any language, but although babies worldwide are born with the potential to make the same sounds, by the age of 12 months they can only repeat back the sounds that they can hear around them.

The linguistic stage is when babies start to use the words that they hear and learn how to make sentences. Children develop this stage gradually over the next few years so that by the age of about 5 years, they are fluent in their home language. Children who learn more than one language may learn to speak slightly more slowly as they absorb different language systems. This should not, however, affect their overall language development.

Table 1 (right) shows the stages of language development in children. Adults need to support children through all these stages in order to encourage and promote language development. At each stage, the role of the adult may be different. For example, a baby needs positive recognition of their attempts to communicate through eye contact and speech. A 5- or 6-year-old child may need adults to help them to extend their vocabulary through the use of open-ended questions or 'what if?' strategies. Where children's language progresses more slowly through these stages, there may be other factors involved, such as:

- learning more than one language
- a communication difficulty, such as autism
- a speech difficulty, such as a stutter
- lack of stimulation from others
- a hearing impairment.

In the early part of the twentieth century, there were a number of theories with the same broad idea. This was that children acquire language by learning a word together with the thing it means or stands for. Through interacting with adults, they will begin to develop sounds which have meaning and which will gain a positive response. This is called the associationist theory.

Noam Chomsky, an American linguist working in the 1960s, claimed that we are all born with an innate knowledge of the system of language, or a 'Language Acquisition Device'. In this way, whatever language we need to learn and the accompanying grammar will be decoded by the child. This theory helps to explain how children will often apply grammatical rules which they have heard, sometimes wrongly, because they have not yet learned exceptions to these rules. An example of this might be, 'I bringed my drink.'

John Macnamara, working in the 1970s, proposed that children are able to learn language because they have an ability to make sense of situations.

This means that they will understand the intention of a situation and respond accordingly. For example, if a child sees that an adult is beckoning towards them and holding out their hand, they will know that the adult's intention is for the child to come towards them. This will be the case even if the child does not understand the words that the adult is saying.

Additional research has taken place into the language acquisition of bilingual children. Patton O. Tabors, an American researcher, states that there is a particular sequence which children will pass through when learning an additional language.

1. At the first stage of learning a new language, children may continue to use their home language in the setting. It is likely that this stage will not last for long.

2. Children may then be silent for a while when they realise that their home language is not being used by others. They may take some time thinking about the new language and 'tuning in' to the new sounds. They may also start to rehearse the sounds to themselves as they build their confidence.

3. Children will start to experiment with individual words and phrases. They will often use lots of repetition or memorised sequences, or routine language and words used together, such as 'good morning' or 'happy birthday'.

4. Children will develop their use of the second language and start to use more complex constructions.

| Age | Stage of development |
|---|---|
| 0–6 months | Babies try to communicate through crying, starting to smile and babbling. They start to establish eye contact with adults. |
| 6–18 months | Babies start to speak their first words. They begin to use gestures to indicate what they mean. At this stage, they are able to recognise and respond to pictures of familiar objects. |
| 18 months–3 years | Children start to develop their vocabulary rapidly and make up their own sentences. At this stage, children enjoy simple and repetitive rhymes and stories. |
| 3–8 years | Children start to use more and more vocabulary and the structure of their language becomes more complex. As they develop their language skills, they are able to use language in a variety of situations. |
| 8+ years | Children become more confident in their use of language and can adapt their speech for different purposes. Their language is becoming increasingly complex. The attainment targets in the English National Curriculum set out the skills expected at each key stage. |

Table 1: Ages and stages of language development.

When learning a second language, some of the stages of language acquisition will be the same, and others different. For example, learners will be starting the process again but will already have knowledge of a linguistic system. This will help them as they will be able to apply 'labels' to objects they already know. In addition, knowledge of many concepts and aspects will already have been instilled. Their first language will therefore help them in the acquisition of the second. If the first language knowledge is not fully developed, however, it can be difficult to add a second language successfully, and there may even be negative consequences.

Further research has shown that pupils who are bilingual or multilingual must be able to relate their home language to individuals when they are first learning language. For example, if a child speaks Arabic with their parents, it is important for the child to speak only Arabic with them and not to switch languages when first learning to talk. This is because for the child, it is important to develop a distinction between languages; this is easier for them if they relate to different people.

## Knowledge of language acquisition theories and the needs and interests of learners to support development of the target language

An awareness of language acquisition theories is helpful when supporting the learning and development of the target language. You will need to be aware of the different stages, in particular the silent stage, as pupils may need additional thinking time. Research suggests that it may take a year before pupils are able to cope in the classroom, two to three years to develop conversational target language and five to seven years to work at the level of their peers using the target language.

The National Association for Language Development in the Curriculum (NALDIC) provides an outline of the role of the EAL teacher, including the following ways to take into account the needs and interests of learners:

- sharing opportunities to draw on pupils' prior experience and first language

- analysing the language demands of the lesson

- identifying and planning for language learning opportunities within the lesson

- sharing and agreeing teaching strategies which address the pupil's needs including collaborative work between pupils

- providing or developing differentiated resources to ensure pupils' access to the curriculum

- enabling pupils with EAL to transfer skills from one topic or subject to another.

It will help you to develop pupils' skills in the target language if you are aware of their needs and interests, as you will be able to encourage them through the inclusion of specific issues which motivate them.

### Functional skills

**ICT: Using ICT**

If you work with a child who has English as an additional language, you could ask for permission to voice-record one of your support sessions. You can then play it back and reflect on your own practice. This will help you to set targets that you need to work towards.

### CASE STUDY: Being aware of the needs and interests of learners

Sobiga is new to the school and speaks very little English. Although you do not work in her class, your daughter who is at the same school says that she has seen Sobiga at her dancing class in the town and that she is a very good dancer.

- How might this information be useful if you spoke to Sobiga's class teacher or teaching assistant?
- What could be done to encourage Sobiga to interact more with other children?

## Ways of introducing learners to new words and language structures to extend their vocabulary and structural command

Children and young people from all backgrounds, whether they are learning one or more languages, need to be given opportunities to develop their language skills in a variety of different ways. However, bilingual learners will need additional support when learning new words and language structures in order to extend their vocabulary. You will need to encourage them and develop their vocabulary in a variety of ways, including through topic-based activities and the use of stories. In addition, if you are working with younger pupils or in intervention groups, you may be focusing on specific vocabulary at different times, for example, positional language (above, below, behind, between, next to and so on). You may need to work with pictures or other resources to help pupils to develop their understanding of these words.

It is also important to remember that there is a difference between the social language in which pupils may be starting to gain fluency and classroom language. This is because in social situations the meaning of what is being communicated is often backed up by visual cues. Classroom language is frequently more abstract and it can be difficult for pupils to tune in to the kinds of functional language required in some learning situations — for example, hypothesising, evaluating, predicting or inferring. It is likely that there will be less visual demonstration to support learning: if you have access to plans, this will be helpful as you may be able to provide support for this.

## Be able to support bilingual learners to access the curriculum

### Develop learning resources to meet the needs of bilingual learners

If you are responsible for supporting EAL pupils in your school, you should have access to appropriate resources. Your school or local authority (LA) will be able to put you in touch with sources of additional materials and you may have some already in school. The Internet is also an excellent resource, although you may need to have time to look for appropriate sites and programs to use with learners (see the end of this unit for a list of websites). You may also be asked to produce resources, in particular if you are a bilingual assistant, in order to support pupil learning. These might include development of displays or wordbanks for pupils, as well as dual-language texts. If you find additional resources, you should always check with the teacher before using them with pupils.

---

**BEST PRACTICE CHECKLIST:** Working with bilingual learners

- Create a secure and happy environment where the pupils and their families feel valued and part of the class and school.

- Raise cultural awareness in school for all pupils.

- Involve parents of bilingual and multilingual pupils as much as possible.

- Use strategies that develop self-esteem and confidence.

- Reinforce language learning using resources such as dual-language texts.

- Reinforce language learning by giving pupils immediate verbal and non-verbal feedback and praise.

- Make sure that pupils are given time to think about questions before they respond.

- Create more opportunities for speaking and listening. These could include opportunities such as paired conversations with other learners.

- Provide visual and physical supports to aid understanding.

## Portfolio activity

Complete the table below to show the kinds of resources you have used or produced with bilingual and multilingual pupils. An example has been given.

| Type of resource | Source |
|---|---|
| Bilingual reading program for computer | Local EAL advisory teacher |
| | |
| | |
| | |

1. After filling in the table above to show the kinds of resources available to you when supporting EAL pupils, think about where you might look for additional resources when required. As well as specific resources to support these pupils, what kinds of strategies do you use to ensure that teaching and learning experiences are engaging and purposeful for them?

2. As well as having language needs, children and young people with English as a second or third language can sometimes come from backgrounds or circumstances which have had an impact on other areas of their development. How might you obtain and interpret this information? Give examples of the kinds of issues these pupils may have experienced and outline how these may affect their learning. How might you respond to these issues as part of your role?

## Teaching, learning and assessment methods to support learning and language development

You will need to be able to demonstrate that you use a variety of teaching and learning methods with bilingual pupils. This is because you will need to maximise the opportunities for them to use language in different contexts. You will also need to ensure that there is a mixture of speaking and listening, reading and writing, so that pupils are able to develop in all areas.

### Allowing time for learners to adjust and become familiar with structure and pace of lessons

When first arriving in school, bilingual and multilingual pupils will need to have additional time to adjust to the way in which lessons are structured. They will need additional time to absorb and become used to the way in which teaching and learning takes place as their previous educational background may have been very different.

### Explaining learning objectives clearly through visual supports

You should always make sure that pupils are clear on learning objectives and this is particularly important for bilingual pupils. You may need to explain in more straightforward language or use visual representations, and check that pupils understand the purpose of what they are doing.

### Introducing, explaining and using key vocabulary related to subject content

A knowledge and understanding of key vocabulary is vital for all pupils but especially for those who are bilingual. Make sure you know the topic for the term or half-term for the subjects you support, and have a list of key vocabulary so that you are prepared and able to explain specific language.

### Providing key visuals and displays

These are particularly helpful for bilingual pupils as you will be giving them a visual representation of the process they will need to go through and the steps they should take when working through tasks.

### Scaffolding writing and oracy tasks

Scaffolding refers to the process of gradually building up what pupils need to do. For example, in a writing task this may be providing a model so that they have something to work on to support their written work.

### Modelling oral and written language

This refers to your role in demonstrating the correct form of written or spoken language to pupils. It is likely that you will do this subconsciously but you may need to work on specific vocabulary or text together.

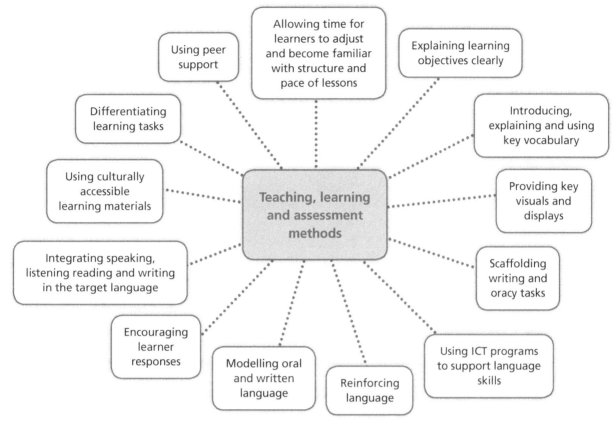

*Teaching, learning and assessment methods.*

## Using ICT programs to support language skills

You may find that there is a range of ICT programs which will support the specific language skills which you need to work on with pupils – for example, when working on comprehension activities. For ideas, you may need to ask your SENCO (Special Educational Needs Co-ordinator) or others in school who support bilingual pupils.

## Integrating speaking, listening, reading and writing in the target language

Bilingual pupils who are learning to speak English or Welsh as an additional language need to have opportunities to read, listen to and discuss a range of texts in the target language so that they can associate their developing verbal and written skills with the printed page. During English lessons they will be able to share texts with the whole class and smaller groups, although you may need to use additional strategies to maximise learning opportunities. Pupils may also need more support during guided reading sessions, but should benefit from these as they will be able to model good practice from other pupils. As with all pupils, they

need to experience a wide variety of texts, both fiction and non-fiction, in order to maximise their vocabulary. If a pupil is able to read and understand more than has been expected, you should always continue to extend their vocabulary by discussing the text further.

## Reinforcing language

In most classroom situations, you will be reinforcing language as you are working and interacting with bilingual pupils. However, specific strategies to reinforce language include:

- repeating what the teacher is saying and in particular key vocabulary
- explaining what has been said
- highlighting key vocabulary
- rehearsing with pupils before they respond to a question
- acting as their talk partner
- encouraging them through smiles, nods, gestures and body language
- summarising and recording what has been learned
- revisiting key concepts through questioning.

Consider the ways in which you reinforce spoken language with pupils when working with them. If you need support with this, ask a colleague to observe you and to note the ways down as you are working.

**English: Speaking, listening and communication**
Once you have been observed, you may want to hold a discussion in order to get your feedback. Before you meet to discuss your observation, you could consider how you think the session went and what you would have done differently. Listen carefully to the feedback so that you can use it effectively to develop your own practice.

## Encouraging learner responses and promoting interaction using different forms of questioning

In order to encourage learner responses and interactions, you will need to think about the kind of questioning you use with pupils and how you use it. You should vary this according to the needs of the pupils and their level of confidence. For example, a pupil who does not understand what is being said may need you to model rather than persist with questioning, whereas a pupil whose second language skills are more developed will be more confident and able to answer more open questions.

Outline how you would promote interaction in the following cases.

1. A bilingual child is not speaking.
2. A bilingual child does not appear to understand your questioning.
3. A bilingual child does not socialise with others in the class.
4. A group of children from the same community are reluctant to mix with others.

## Using culturally accessible learning materials

Bilingual pupils need to be able to use learning materials which offer a broad cultural representation. You should work with others in school to ensure that pupils have access to resources and materials which do this.

## Differentiating learning tasks

It is important to remember that teaching and learning should be differentiated by ability and that bilingual pupils should not always be grouped with pupils of a lower ability or put together with each other. In order to develop their language, they will benefit from being in groups with pupils who are of the same or mixed ability and who are modelling the correct form of the target language. You should also ensure that learning tasks such as homework are set at a level which is manageable for bilingual pupils.

## Using peer support to promote thinking and talking in first language

Strategies such as using a partner who speaks their first language may help bilingual pupils to gain understanding and develop their ideas. This will in turn increase their confidence as they will have clarified what they need to say.

---

**CASE STUDY:** Supporting pupils of mixed ability

David is working with a group of three Year 7 pupils, who all speak Gujarati. Although they have the language in common, their needs are all different.

1. Rashid speaks very little English and has just entered the country.

2. Harpal has lived in the UK for two years but always speaks Gujarati at home and needs extra support with his English. He is of average ability.

3. Aasha is bilingual and able to converse well but is still very anxious when producing written work.

- Would you approach the support you give these pupils differently even if you had to group them together?
- How could you balance the needs of the children while supporting them effectively?

## Deal with the challenges of the language demands in ways that maintain confidence and self-esteem

The demands of the target language may cause challenges when supporting bilingual/multilingual pupils. If a group or pupil is finding a particular word or activity too challenging, you may need to modify or change what you are doing or saying to accommodate this. You can rephrase what is being asked, so that it is easier for the pupil to understand. If they are still finding an activity difficult as they do not understand what is being asked, you should move on to something different. You should also ensure that you do not spend a lot of time correcting pupils if their written or spoken target language contains errors — it is better to model the correct language or repeat back the correct word or phrase.

Some pupils may take a long time to become confident in a second language and it will be apparent that they understand much more than they are able to say. This is not unusual and staff must not push pupils into talking before they are ready. The most important thing to do is to encourage and praise pupils wherever possible, repeating the correct language structure or learning point back to them so that they develop a positive view of themselves.

It can take longer to detect a specific learning difficulty if a pupil is bilingual. This is because staff may feel that the pupil is finding school more difficult just because of their development of the target language. If you find that a particular child is not able to manage the tasks set as they are not making progress, you should always speak to the class teacher.

## Encourage learners to become increasingly independent in their learning

You will need to show that you are encouraging pupils to manage their learning as far as possible themselves as they make progress in the target language. As you should be supporting them both individually and in groups, there should be a natural progression as they become more competent in the target language, although they may continue to need some individual language-based support. You may need to use assessment for learning as they progress (see TDA 3.7) so that they can see for themselves how learning is assessed.

## Provide feedback to the teacher on the learner's participation and progress

When working with bilingual and multilingual pupils, you will need to provide frequent feedback to others on their progress in relation to:

- the learning activities
- language development
- subject knowledge, understanding and skills.

In a secondary school, the other professionals you will need to report to will be the form and subject teacher, and possibly the SENCO and EAL teachers who may visit the school. You should have opportunities to contribute to meetings and/or paperwork concerning the children with whom you are working, for example, IEPs (Individual Education Plans). It is important that there is a joined-up approach between all those who are working with bilingual pupils, so that their progress can be measured.

**CASE STUDY:** Dealing with the challenge of language demands

Madie is working with Haima, who is in Year 9. Although she speaks some English, Haima is very quiet and lacks confidence, particularly in a larger group. Today while they are working on a group geography activity, Madie directs a question at her which Haima is unable to answer. Madie repeats the question by rephrasing and then waits for a response.

- What should Madie do next in order to maintain Haima's confidence?
- What other strategies could she have used when seeking to find out if pupils understand the text?

## CASE STUDY: Providing feedback to the subject teachers

Jay is often asked to work with Leyla in Year 10, who has been at the school for a year and is a Turkish speaker. Although her English is good, there are some gaps in her understanding. Leyla does not have an IEP or any kind of learning plan, as the SENCO has said that she does not need one. Although Jay is asked to work with her, he does not have any specific areas to work on or guidance as to what to do with her. He feeds back to the subject teachers about Leyla informally at the end of each lesson when time permits.

- Is there anything else that Jay could do to monitor Leyla's progress more effectively?
- What should he do if the subject teacher is unwilling to help him plan specific activities to help Leyla?

## Getting ready for assessment

To gather evidence for this unit, you may wish to speak to your assessor about the pupil or pupils with whom you work and the kinds of strategies you have used to help support their listening, speaking, reading and writing in the target language, and how these relate to the teacher's plans. You can set up a professional discussion to do this, although be clear on the assessment criteria you are aiming to cover.

## Check your knowledge

1. Are the following true or false?
   a) A 'silent period' is normal when children are learning a new language.
   b) Pupils should be encouraged to talk in the target language as much as possible at every opportunity.
   c) You should stop any bilingual support once pupils are able to speak in the target language.
   d) We should correct pupils' mistakes when they are learning another language.
   e) Bilingual pupils should always be grouped together in classrooms.

2. What should you take into account when interacting with bilingual pupils?

3. How might a pupil's age affect their ability to learn a second language?

4. How can you ensure that you personalise language for individual learners when interacting with them?

5. Why is it important that you always remember to consider the self-esteem of the pupil when working on language activities, and how can you do this?

6. Give four examples of strategies you should use when working with bilingual learners.

7. Where would you go to find resources to support bilingual learners?

### Websites and references

The following websites are regularly updated with articles and information to support the inclusion of speakers of additional languages.

www.britishcouncil.org – the British Council is the UK's international culture relations body
www.education.gov.uk – the standards site has information under EAL learners
www.mantrapublishing.com – this company produces a range of books in different languages
www.naldic.org.uk – the National Association for Language Development in the Curriculum is an organisation which aims to raise attainment of EAL learners. The website contains a number of links and resources, as well as information on the latest research into bilingualism
www.teachernet.gov.uk – Teachernet – type in 'EAL' under 'search'

Bialystok, E. (2001) *Bilingualism in Development: Language, Literacy and Cognition*, Cambridge: Cambridge University Press

# TDA 3.18 Provide bilingual support for teaching & learning

This unit is for those who use the pupil's first language to support teaching and learning in schools. If you speak another language, you may be asked to use this knowledge to help assess pupils' educational abilities and support needs. You may also be involved in providing support and liaising with families in order to promote pupil participation.

## By the end of this unit you will:

1. be able to contribute to assessment of bilingual learners
2. be able to provide bilingual support for learners
3. be able to support communication with families of bilingual learners
4. be able to contribute to reviews of communication with families of bilingual learners.

# Be able to contribute to assessment of bilingual learners

## Carry out an initial assessment of bilingual learners using learners' preferred language

An initial assessment provides the necessary information for the careful planning of learning activities needed of newly arrived learners including:

● first language and ethnic background

● fluency in English

● previous educational experience and achievements

● wider needs such as a learner's home situation.

As a bilingual assistant, you may be called upon to carry out an initial assessment of pupils in school. This will be important as it is the quickest and most effective way of finding out information about the pupil. The school will need to work promptly in order to gather as much information as possible about the pupil's background and previous educational experience. This is so that they will be able to consider and devise the most effective way of supporting the pupil from the start. It is also very important for **bilingual learners** and their families that their home language and heritage is recognised in school.

Bilingual pupils may have always lived in this country or may have recently arrived; they may be reasonably confident in two languages or proficient in their home language but not in the target language. Whatever their background, children will need to know that their culture and status are valued, as this helps them to feel settled and secure, factors which contribute to their being able to develop skills in a new language. Children need to want to learn; if they feel isolated or anxious, they are more likely to find it difficult. Initial assessments should be carried out in a way which is not intimidating or daunting for them.

As well as seeking information from parents and other schools about pupil background and their home language, you will need to find out about the pupil's wider needs, such as their circumstances and whether there are any issues of which the school should be aware. You should receive guidance from teachers

about the kinds of assessment they would like you to carry out and how to go about it. You may also be asked to assess and observe their level of English and to monitor their progress.

The QCA also produced guidance, *A language in common: assessing English as an additional language* on how to assess pupils who are in the early stages of learning English. This is so that there is some standardisation in how bilingual pupils are assessed, although individual local authorities may have produced their own versions. It enables teachers to track pupil progress in speaking and listening, reading and writing. The guidance comprises detailed descriptors for features of English language use up to level 1 of the National Curriculum (ref QCA/00/584).

Following assessment, staff can build up a profile of each pupil. This can then be amended as more information is gathered and pupil levels in speaking and listening, reading and writing can be added.

| | |
|---|---|
| **Name:** | Gita Kowalski |
| **Date:** | 15/06/10 |
| **Boy/girl:** | Girl |
| **Date of birth:** | 15/07/1998 |
| **Year group:** | 8 |
| **Date arrived in UK:** | 20/05/2010 |
| **Date admitted to school:** | 07/06/2010 |
| **Languages spoken:** | Polish |
| **Languages pupil can read:** | Polish |
| **Languages pupil can write:** | Polish |
| **Previous school in UK:** | – |
| **Previous school elsewhere:** | Poland |
| **Community school:** | – |

*Example of a pupil profile – preliminary statement. Source: Secondary Induction for Teaching Assistants: Inclusion (TDA, 2006).*

## Over to you!

What kinds of assessments have you carried out on bilingual pupils who are new to your school? How have you worked with pupils and their families to gain information about their backgrounds, both in their home and target language?

## Work with relevant people to assess the experience, capabilities and learning style of bilingual learners

**Relevant people** in this context may include:

● family members

● teachers responsible for the learner

● ethnic minority achievement co-ordinator

● bilingual language support teacher

● bilingual teaching assistants

● EAL (English as an additional language) specialist teacher

● language co-ordinator

● English/Welsh/Gaeilge language teacher

● relevant local authority advisory or **peripatetic** staff.

## Key terms

**Relevant people** – those with a need and right to provide and receive information about bilingual learners as relevant to the setting

**Peripatetic** – working in a succession of places, each for a short time

## Functional skills

### Maths: Representing

Have you carried out any initial assessment of the pupils you work with? If so, then you could calculate what percentage of your class are above, below or average for the level they are working at. You could also calculate the ratio of support to children underachieving in the assessment process.

If you are working on initial assessments, you should have some additional guidance from teachers and others who are both internal and external to the school as to the work you are required to carry out. All of those who have been and will be involved with the pupil may need to contribute and support the assessment process.

● **Family members** should work closely with the school, in particular at the initial stages, in order to support them in assessing pupils' backgrounds and experiences.

● **Teachers responsible for the learner** will need to be closely involved as they will need to have a starting point for pupil learning. You should be guided by them as to the kinds of assessments you are required to carry out.

● The **ethnic minority achievement co-ordinator** may be based at the local authority and will co-ordinate the progress of pupils from ethnic minorities. They may not come to the school but will need to be sent information about whole-school achievement and particularly initial competence in the target language.

● You may have a **bilingual language support teacher** in your school who is able to advise you and the class teacher about how to work on assessments with bilingual pupils who are new to the school.

● There may be **bilingual teaching assistants** in the school with the same role as yourself and with whom you may need to co-ordinate the assessment process.

● The **EAL (English as an additional language) specialist teacher** may come from the local authority in order to support pupils in school who speak English as an additional language. It is likely that they will come on a regular basis and work with staff and pupils in order to help raise achievement. They may also help with initial assessments.

● Your school may have a **language co-ordinator** who will work with you on initial assessments and suggest additional support strategies.

- Although the **English/Welsh/Gaeilge language teacher** will work on the target language, they will be able to advise on initial assessments.

- The local authority may provide other **relevant local authority advisory or peripatetic staff** who are able to give you support when working with bilingual pupils in the initial stages.

## Functional skills

ICT: Developing, presenting and communicating information

You could produce an information chart showing all the professionals listed above and how they can be contacted if you require their input. Your chart could be done on the computer and then printed numerous times so you could share this resource with other members of the team you work in.

## Reflect

Which of the professionals above have you been involved with when assessing bilingual learners? How have they supported you in doing this?

## Why a specialist assessment may be required and procedures for arranging this

Most pupils, over a period of time, will be able to understand and communicate in an additional language. It is quite common for pupils to pick up English or Welsh as an additional language quickly when they start school, as they have another language to relate it to. They may need support in order to develop their spoken and written English/ Welsh language skills, but as these develop, the support should be required less.

However, in some cases, speaking English/Welsh as an additional language may hide additional language or other needs. As a bilingual teaching assistant, you will be able to tell if pupils are proficient in their own language or not; this can help to assess whether there is a language disorder or learning delay. In this situation, always speak to your class teacher and

SENCO (Special Educational Needs Co-ordinator), who will need to refer the pupil for **specialist assessment**, either to an educational psychologist or a speech and language therapist.

Pupils may also have health or care needs which may not be apparent to others but which you pick up as part of your initial assessment or shortly afterwards. If you have any concerns about these issues, you should speak to your class teacher and SENCO in order to ensure that any necessary referral is made.

## Key term

**Specialist assessment** – an assessment administered and interpreted by an appropriately qualified professional to explore specific needs, often in detail, for example, on proficiency in the first language, special educational needs, or a health or care assessment

**CASE STUDY:** Referring pupils for specialist assessment

Gabriele has been in school for one month and is in Year 7. You have been asked to assess her language needs. She has always spoken Lithuanian at home and you did not pick up any issues during your language assessment. However, on meeting her mother and discussing her home background, you feel that it would be appropriate to refer Gabriele and possibly her family for more specialist assessment as to her care needs. Her mother appears to be struggling to manage her situation as a single parent in this country and has asked you on several occasions whether you can go to her home to provide extra help with school work, even though you have explained to her that you are unable to do this. Gabriele often appears to be dirty and her clothes and hair are untidy.

- What should you do first?
- How can you best support Gabriele and her family?

## Provide feedback to learners and others on the outcome of the assessment and the implications

As a bilingual assistant, it is likely that you will be involved in providing feedback to pupils and their families as well as other professionals about pupil progress, whether this concerns their learning, language development or well-being. Pupils should be involved in the procedure as much as possible, unless it is inappropriate due to the nature of the discussion. The best way in which to do this is to set aside regular intervals with pupils to discuss their progress and to think about any additional support they might need.

The most commonly used method of tracking pupil progress is by target setting and monitoring. This will enable pupils, staff and parents to see the focus of the work that is being done in school and to assess how successfully it is being implemented. You may be invited to contribute to parents' evenings and other events in order to support teachers and other staff in passing on information to parents. If you are asked to speak to parents about pupil learning, you should have an opportunity to speak to teachers beforehand so that you know what information they need to have passed on and how they would like you to structure what you say.

## Provide information and support to relevant people

If you provide regular support to bilingual pupils, you need to give information and support to colleagues and other professionals, particularly if pupils speak very little English. Information about pupils' development in English and also their knowledge and use of their home language, which may reflect their confidence in using language generally, is very useful. A pupil who has a working knowledge of one language already understands the purpose of language and the process involved, and is more likely to be able to apply it to another language. The feedback you give to colleagues may be written or verbal depending on the school policy. You may also be required to attend meetings with others, with or without the pupil and family present, in order to pass on and exchange information and to ensure that everyone involved with the pupil is aware of any specific needs they may have.

---

**Language support plan:** Spring term 2011

**Name:** Ajay Sharma    **Year:** 7    **Date:** 12th January 2011

**Targets:**
1. Understands instructions and routines used in the classroom
2. Knows and uses subject specific vocabulary
3. Is able to join in with small group discussion
4. Can write basic sentences in English

**Support:** Support in English, history and geography lessons with Mrs Kaur (TA)

**Review:** End of Spring term 2011

**Signed:** _____    _____
　　　　　　　　(teacher)　　　　　　　　　　　　(parent)

*Example language support plan.*

**BEST PRACTICE CHECKLIST:** Providing information and support

- Pass on information to colleagues about pupils' development in English and also their knowledge and use of their home language, which may reflect their confidence in using language generally.

- Keep a record of the feedback you give to colleagues so that the information is available to others if required at a later date.

- If required, attend meetings in order to pass on and exchange knowledge so that everyone is well informed.

*How might other pupils who speak the target language be able to help?*

# Be able to provide bilingual support for learners

## Use learners' preferred language to introduce and settle them into the learning environment

When you first meet bilingual pupils who are new to the school, whatever their age, you will need to introduce them to the learning environment in the most accessible way. As you are working as a bilingual assistant, you should use their preferred language in order to do this, whether this is their first or target language. You will need to speak to them about the rules and routines of the school and show them around different areas of the learning environment so that they are able to settle in more quickly. If they would prefer to do this in the target language, or if you have other pupils in school who speak their target language, you may decide to take other pupils with you to help and to point out things which an adult might not!

## Work with relevant people to identify learning activities that promote personalised learning

When you have settled the pupil into school and have spoken to others about how best to support their learning needs, it is likely that there will be some

consensus from educational and other professionals about a focus for their language development. This may be documented in an individual plan in order to maintain a focus on their targets. Although **personalised learning** does not mean that the pupil will have one-to-one support separate from other pupils, it should ensure that their progress is monitored and has a focus.

You should have agreed with others the kinds of activities which will best promote the pupil's language development and which will help them in their

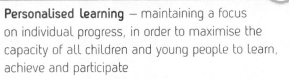

**Key term**

**Personalised learning** — maintaining a focus on individual progress, in order to maximise the capacity of all children and young people to learn, achieve and participate classroom activities. It is likely that you will also be working with other children and young people, as it will be important for bilingual pupils to be using their language in context. You may, for example, decide to focus on specific vocabulary which they will need in the subject area or project they are studying within the class, or work on language activities which will also support what they are doing.

## Use bilingual support strategies to meet individual learner needs

A key part of your role will be using bilingual support strategies in order to meet learner needs. This will be in different circumstances, whether these are individual, group or whole-class sessions. You will need to ensure that you use a range of these so that you maximise the opportunities for developing pupils' language skills and the development of the target language.

### Interpreting oral and written information

Pupils may need you to interpret information for them in their first language, in particular when they are new to the school and there is a lot of information for them to take in.

### Using shared language or appropriate target language to explain information or instructions

In a similar way, pupils may need you to explain information or instructions which are being given to the class or group by the teacher. You may need to discuss with them how they will go about a particular task, on their own or alongside other pupils.

### Supporting the use of learners' first languages

Bilingual pupils may sometimes need you to support the use of their first language. If their first language is not fully developed because of a special educational need or difficulty in communication, you may need to encourage its use in a learning context.

### Link

For more on this aspect see TDA 3.17, Support bilingual learners.

### Developing bilingual learning resources

As a bilingual assistant, you will be well placed to develop a bank of bilingual learning resources.

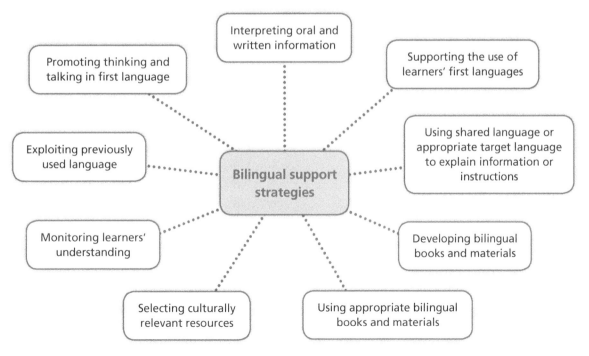

*Why is it important to use a range of strategies?*

If you are working in a school where these already exist, you should still be on the lookout for additional resources which will be of benefit to pupils, and store them so that they are accessible to others.

## Using appropriate bilingual books and materials

You may have resources such as bilingual books which are designed to show both the first and target language as the story or information is set out. These may be helpful to use in different contexts – for example, a bilingual pupil at the earlier stages will find it helpful to see the text in the target language, while a more competent linguist might try to guess how it has been translated.

## Selecting culturally relevant resources

In the same way that you have used bilingual learning resources, you should also select those which are culturally relevant to the child. In this way you will be able to motivate and involve them further in their learning, as they will be more able to identify with the context.

### Functional skills

ICT: Using ICT
English: Speaking, listening and communication
How many bilingual or culturally relevant resources do you have in your setting? You could photograph all the different resources you have and then use them in a discussion to show your peers how your setting supports bilingual and multicultural children.

## Monitoring learners' understanding

When checking that pupils have understood, make sure that you use both their target and home languages. In this way you will be able to monitor their understanding more closely.

## Exploiting previously used language

As you will be working with bilingual pupils regularly, you will be able to use prior knowledge of language they have used and remind them about the context and how it links to their experiences.

## Promoting thinking and talking in first language

Bilingual pupils who are in the earlier stages of learning a second language may need you to encourage them through talking about their learning in their first language. In this way they may be more likely to develop their thinking skills.

## Provide good role models of both the first and target language

While working with bilingual pupils, it is vital that you provide a good role model for both the first and **target language**. You should ensure that you always use the correct form of language, as pupils will be taking this in when they are working with you. You should not correct any mistakes which they or others make, but repeat back in the correct form, using the right word or grammatical construction so that they hear it.

### Key term

**Target language** – the additional or second language needed by bilingual learners, for example, English as an additional language (EAL), or Welsh or Gaeilge as a second language

## Use learners' first language to draw on previous knowledge and experience

Use of a pupil's first language will be important in the classroom context as through this you will be able to go back and revisit their previous learning or experience. They may be unable to explain or talk about what they have done in the target language, but their first language knowledge will enable you to talk to them about the extent of any prior knowledge. It can be frustrating for bilingual pupils who are unable to carry out an activity or join in with a discussion because of the constraints of their knowledge of the target language.

Karen is working with Andres, who has recently transferred to Year 8 in the school. He speaks Spanish as his first language. Karen is supporting him in geography where the topic is sources of energy. Andres is able to talk about this in Spanish but not in English.

- How could Karen support Andres in this activity?
- Why is it important that he is able to join in with the discussion?

## Maintain and develop learners' first language in learning contexts

Despite keeping a focus on the target language and on pupils' skills in this, you should also ensure that pupils' first language skills are continuing to be developed. Although they will use this language at home, they may not have done so in a learning context; this may mean that they have more difficulty in applying what they are learning in the target language to their first language. This may be particularly true in the case of mathematical language or vocabulary which has a tendency to be more abstract, as pupils may find it more difficult to understand how the two languages relate to one another. Similarly, if pupils are learning a new topic such as a historical period, they may not have learned the vocabulary in their first language and this would be a good opportunity to introduce it.

# Be able to support communication with families of bilingual learners

## Interact with families in a way that demonstrates a non-judgemental attitude, values diversity and promotes trust

When communicating with bilingual learners and their families, you will need to be sensitive not only to language but also to different cultural needs. You will need to show that you are there to support them and that the process is one of inclusion. As you communicate with families, you should show that you respect them and that you value the contribution that they and their child make to the school community. This should also be evident through the ethos of the school which should value diversity and cultural differences. As a bilingual speaker, you may already be aware of these issues, which may be around dress or diet, but may also be to do with religious or cultural customs with which you may not be familiar. The school's policies will welcome pupils and families from all cultures and you need to make sure that you follow these policies.

If your communication methods are not effective for whatever reason and you find that some families are unable or reluctant to liaise with the school, you may need to adapt the support provided. As in all school practice, you need to identify any issues, evaluate how effective your methods are and think

Obi is occasionally working in class with Asabi, who is in Year 9 and has been in the country for two years but speaks Yoruba at home. She is able to speak English competently although she occasionally has some difficulty with more specialised vocabulary. Obi occasionally takes Asabi out of class to focus on words which she may need as part of her topic.

- Is it important that Asabi should have a bilingual speaker to help her with this vocabulary?
- Do you think that Obi and Asabi should work together inside or outside the classroom?

about whether any amendments or improvements may be necessary. Examples of adapting what you do may be:

● through providing additional opportunities for parents to come into school. These may be through specific events and support networks for bilingual parents, particularly if they are reluctant or unsure about approaching the school. You may also invite parents into school to speak to pupils about cultural issues, such as different festivals

● being able to translate important letters that go home or provide alternative support so that families can access the information.

---

### Functional skills

**ICT: Developing, presenting and communicating information**
You could design a poster to be displayed in your setting that shows all the cultural festivals during the academic year. Your poster would need to be bright, with illustrations and text. Think carefully about who will be looking at your poster so that you can make sure that it is suitable for its audience.

---

## Provide accessible information to families as agreed by the setting

If you are a bilingual teaching assistant working in a school with a high percentage of bilingual learners, it is likely that you will be involved in providing support and information to families. You should have opportunities to liaise with the named governor or teacher in the school who is responsible for advising teachers about EAL (English as an additional language) learners. There should also be systems in place to enable you to pass information to parents and carers and for them to pass information to the school. Where school documents need to be available for parents and families whose first language is not that used in school, you may need to provide help to ensure that the information is communicated.

## Encourage families to share information about their child to support the setting

Parents or carers of bilingual children may sometimes speak very little, if any, English themselves. In this situation the school needs

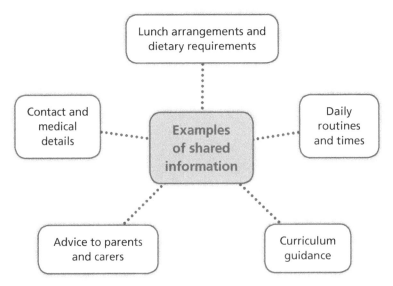

*What is shared information?*

to devise additional strategies to encourage their involvement and understanding (see also communicating with families on pages 254–55). It is important that parents and carers feel able to approach the school and share information in order to maximise the opportunities to communicate. This may start informally or, in schools with a high percentage of EAL pupils, may be approached in a more structured way. Families of bilingual pupils may have complex needs themselves as well as communication issues and the school may be one of the first points of contact for them to access additional support and become established in local communities. Through school events, community projects and extended schools programmes, parents should be encouraged to be included in a variety of ways. However, remember that if you are passing information between school and families, this is all you should be doing. Be careful not to include your own opinions or ideas about what should be happening on either side without consulting with other staff first.

You may be communicating with pupils and families who are refugees or have come from situations where they have experienced difficult circumstances. In this case, seek outside support from your local authority to ensure that you are offering as much help, support and advice as possible. As a bilingual speaker, you will be well placed to offer the information. Pupils who have had unsettled backgrounds may take longer to settle into school, and communication and language development may be affected.

### Portfolio activity

Write a reflective account to show how you encourage and support the exchange of information with families. How have you personally been involved in this?

### Functional skills

**English: Writing**
When writing this account, it is important that you consider your punctuation, spelling and grammar. Try to plan your account first to make sure that you include all the relevant information.

## Accurately record and pass on any information provided by families

You should make sure that any information which you gather from families is appropriately recorded and passed on to the relevant people as soon as possible. It will help you in this situation either to make notes or to record what is being said using a voice recorder, as it will be difficult for you to remember all aspects of the conversation, even if you have prepared specific questions in advance. Make sure you write minutes of the meeting which are clear and set out according to school policy. You will also need to ensure that you observe confidentiality when passing on information to others, particularly if you are given sensitive information.

### Knowledge into action

Keep any records which you have gathered yourself and use them for your portfolio, either by showing them to your assessor or removing names for confidentiality and copying the paperwork.

### Functional skills

**ICT: Using ICT**
It is important to remember that if you are sending confidential information electronically or storing it electronically, then it should be password protected. A secure password is one that contains a variety of uppercase and lowercase letters, and numbers.

# Be able to contribute to reviews of communication with families of bilingual learners

## Consult relevant people about the effectiveness of communication with families of bilingual learners

Forms of communication may be:

● verbal or non-verbal

● informal or formal.

As the ability to communicate with families of bilingual learners is an important part of the overall process of pupil learning, it is likely that you will need to consult others regularly about how effective this is and whether you need to make any changes to your approach as a team. You should consider all aspects of communication and whether it is successful at different stages, for example:

● when the pupil first enters school

● when targets are being set

● the way in which targets are reviewed

● the day-to-day communication between school and families

● how much parents and families are involved with the school

● how easy it is to pass information to parents and vice versa.

At the same time as thinking about the different stages, you will also need to look at the following.

### Verbal and non-verbal methods of communication

It may be easier to tell if verbal methods of communication are effective, but you should also think about the effectiveness of non-verbal methods such as letters, emails and other ways in which information is passed between families and those professionals who are working with the pupil.

### Formal and informal methods of communication

Again, because parents should be involved in meetings and reviews, it will be easier to assess whether formal methods of communication are effective. However, you should also consider informal methods such as social events or after-school activities when you may be talking to parents.

### Skills builder

Look at the list of stages above and go through it, thinking about formal/informal and verbal/non-verbal methods which are used at each stage. How can you consult others about these? Why will this be useful when reviewing communication methods?

## Use knowledge of communication with families to contribute to reviews of communication methods

When reviewing communication methods with others, you will need to think about how effective your communication with families has been. As a bilingual speaker you will be well placed to consider the difference that your contribution makes to the overall process. You should think about the information you have been able to gather and how you think that this has supported the pupil and the difference that it has made. You will also be able to ask others how this has made a difference to their work and whether it has been effective.

## Identify any communication difficulties or issues due to differences

Communication differences between individuals may create barriers to effective communication between them, and can relate to:

● language

● sensory impairment

- speech, language or communication impairment
- cognitive abilities
- emotional state
- culture.

## Work with relevant people to resolve any communication difficulties or issues

There may be a number of difficulties which arise when communicating with pupils and their families which are a barrier to effective working, due to differences in communication methods. You may need to intervene and clarify any misunderstandings or difficulties as they arise – alternatively you may be asked to speak to parents if problems have arisen between families and other professionals during the course of their work with pupils.

### Language

Although you speak the pupil's first language, there may still be issues around their communication with other professionals. You may be asked to clarify or explain any points or issues which arise.

### Sensory impairment

Individuals with whom you are working may have a sensory impairment such as a visual or hearing impairment. You may need to adapt your communication methods or involve others to support your communication with them.

### Speech, language or communication impairment

If, over a period of time, parents or pupils find communication difficult, this may indicate that they have a speech, language or communication impairment. If it is clear that communication is being hindered, think about ways of changing your approach to meet the needs of pupils and their families, or find out whether they can be referred for specialist support.

### Cognitive abilities

You may find that parents are having difficulty in understanding the process despite your speaking their first language. It is possible that there are issues with their cognitive abilities and you may need to seek additional support for them.

### Emotional state

Communication methods may also be hindered due to the emotional state of parents or families. They may have had a difficult transition while moving to this country or have faced issues which make the situation very difficult for them. There may also be a reluctance on the part of the family to become involved in school life. This may be due to anxiety about what it involves and how the system differs from their previous experience.

### Cultural differences

Although you may speak the language, there may be cultural differences about which you are not aware but which mean that communication is hindered. You may need to work with your support or advisory teachers in order to ensure that any misunderstandings are dealt with as soon as possible.

## Getting ready for assessment

Write a reflective account to show the kinds of events and opportunities your school has to encourage communication with families of bilingual and multilingual pupils. Have there been measureable benefits? Why do you think these are important? If you have had to adapt the ways in which you communicate with families, outline how you have done this.

As with TDA 3.17, Support bilingual learners, rather than writing this down as a reflective account, you may wish to have a professional discussion with your assessor to show how you provide bilingual support for teaching and learning. Plan this so that you can decide which of the assessment criteria you want to cover. Your assessor may also wish to speak to the parents, teachers or other professionals with whom you work to support bilingual learners.

## Functional skills

**English: Speaking, listening and communication**
When holding your discussion, plan some of the points you wish to cover before you sit down with your assessor and then listen carefully so that you can respond in an appropriate way.

## Check your knowledge

1. Why should the initial assessment of a bilingual pupil be in their first language rather than in English?

2. What other professionals may be involved in assessments and decisions about the pupil?

3. What kinds of strategies might be effective when working with bilingual pupils in their first language?

4. Why is it important to maintain pupils' first language skills?

5. What should you do in order to be a good role model for language?

6. How can families be encouraged to share information with schools? Why is this important?

7. What kinds of communication issues might there be when working with parents and families?

### Websites
(See also those listed at the end of TDA 3.17 Support bilingual learners.)

www.continyou.org.uk – this is an organisation that supports inclusion and lifelong learning

www.naldic.org.uk – the National Association for Language Development in the Curriculum has a large amount of material, articles and suggestions on issues surrounding bilingual pupils

www.teachernet.gov.uk – visit this site for further ideas for supporting EAL pupils

# TDA 3.19 Support disabled children & young people & those with special educational needs

To work with children or young people who have special educational needs or disabilities you will need to be able to relate well to a variety of different people, including parents, carers and other professionals. You may have a high level of responsibility and need to work in partnership both with the pupil and with those who support them, both at home and to provide educational provision.

## By the end of this unit you will:

1. understand the rights of disabled children and young people and those with special educational needs

2. understand the disabilities and/or special educational needs of children and young people in your care

3. be able to support the inclusion of disabled children and young people and those with special educational needs

4. be able to support disabled children and young people and those with special educational needs to participate in the full range of activities and experiences

5. be able to support others to respond to the needs of disabled children and young people and those with special educational needs.

# Understand the rights of disabled children and young people and those with special educational needs

## The legal entitlements of disabled children and young people and those with special educational needs

As a teaching assistant working at this level it is likely that you will be supporting intervention groups, individuals and groups of pupils who have **special educational needs** on a regular basis. You will need to know about the entitlements which these children and young people have and the laws which affect the provision which your school makes for them. There have been a number of changes to legislation in the UK in recent years which have affected this and a gradual increase in the rights which these pupils have. A brief list is outlined in Table 1 in date order.

### Key terms

**Disabled** – the Disability Discrimination Act (DDA) defines a disabled person as someone who has a physical or mental impairment that has a substantial and long-term adverse effect on their ability to carry out normal day-to-day activities

**Special educational needs** – children or young people who learn differently from most children or young people of the same age, and who may need extra or different help from that given to others

| Legislation | Details |
| --- | --- |
| Education Act (1981) | Based on the findings of the Warnock Report (1978) which highlighted the needs of children with special educational needs and set out ways that children should be supported. The Act gave additional legal responsibilities to local authorities as well as power to parents. |
| Education Reform Act (1988) | Introduced the National Curriculum into all schools in England and Wales. Allowed schools to change or modify what was taught for SEN pupils if the basic curriculum was not appropriate for them. |
| Children Act (1989) | Stated that the welfare of the child must at all times be considered and their rights and wishes should be taken into consideration. |
| Education Act (1993) | Required that a Code of Practice be introduced for guidance on identification and provision of special educational needs. Introduced the role of the Special Educational Needs Co-ordinator (SENCO) and parents were able to challenge local authorities about providing for pupils with SEN. |
| Disability Discrimination Act (1995) | Made it illegal for services such as shops and employers to discriminate against **disabled** people. Required better access to buildings and facilities for disabled people. |
| Special Educational Needs and Disability Act (SENDA) 2001 | Strengthens the rights of parents and children who have special educational needs to a mainstream education. The Disability Rights Commission (DRC) Code of Practice (2002) provides guidance for schools to support pupils with a disability and meet their duties set out in this Act. |

| Legislation | Details |
|---|---|
| Children Act 2004 | The purpose of this Act was to improve the outcomes for children through integrated planning and delivery of services. The Green Paper Every Child Matters (2003) was produced as a framework for the Act. This sets out the five outcomes – stay safe, be healthy, enjoy and achieve, make a positive contribution and achieve economic well-being – which all organisations and agencies involved with children must work towards. |
| Disability Discrimination Act (2005) | Extended the 1995 Act to include all public bodies including schools. Schools must produce a Disability Equality Scheme which sets out how they will fulfil their duties under the Act. |
| Equality Act 2010 | Brings together nine equality laws. It sets out the legal responsibilities for public sectors to ensure equality of opportunity. It provides greater protection for disabled children and their families. |

*Table 1: Legislation relating to disabled children and young people and those with SEN.*

## Over to you!

Investigate some of the laws which are interconnected, for example, Education Acts, Children Acts, Every Child Matters. Why is it important to know about these? How much do they affect your practice on a day-to-day basis?

## Functional skills

**ICT: Developing, presenting and communicating information**
**English: Reading**
You could create a timeline of legislation that includes information from the chapter and further research. Your timeline will help you to see visually how legislation has changed and influenced the way we work today.

## The assessment and intervention frameworks

### SEN Code of Practice 2001

The Code of Practice 2001, changed the way in which assessment and intervention for children and young people was carried out in schools. Most importantly, the following came into effect.

- A child with SEN should have their needs identified which will normally be met in mainstream schools or early education settings.
- Those responsible for SEN provision must take into account the views and wishes of the child.
- Professionals and parents should work in partnership.
- Provision and progress should be monitored and reviewed regularly.
- Local Education Authorities (LEAs) should make assessments in accordance with prescribed time limits.

The Code of Practice also outlines the way in which assessments should be carried out in early years, primary and secondary settings, and gives a clear structure to the way in which assessments are carried out.

### School Action

At this stage, the school will put additional strategies in place if the pupil is finding it hard to keep up with their peers. This will usually take the form of additional targets on an Individual Education Plan (IEP).

### School Action Plus

If the pupil has been on School Action for some time and has not made sufficient progress, they may be moved on to School Action Plus. This means that the school will consult outside agencies for further assessments, advice or strategies for supporting the pupil's needs.

## Statement of Special Educational Need

This means that the pupil will be assessed as to whether they need a statement of SEN and additional support in school. The school will need to gather all the paperwork from professionals who have worked with the pupil, in addition to providing evidence of the strategies they have used. If the pupil has SEN or a disability, it is likely that they will have been assessed before transferring to the secondary school and may already have a statement.

## The Common Assessment Framework (CAF)

This was introduced on a national scale in 2006 and is designed to be used across all children's services. Its purpose is to identify additional needs at an early stage through a holistic approach to children's needs and to encourage the working together of different agencies. It is not designed purely for those who have special educational needs and may be used where pupils are at risk from harm or you are concerned about an aspect of their behaviour. If you have concerns about a child, you should always speak to your school's SENCO.

## The importance of early recognition and intervention

The Special Educational Needs Code of Practice in 2001 introduced the identification and early intervention for young children before they start full-time primary education. The reason for this was that the sooner intervention can be put in place for pupils with these needs, the greater the benefits for their learning. Many early years workers had been able to identify children who would need extra support but there was no mechanism for starting to put provision in place before the child started school. This meant that the process was delayed when provision could have been put in place. Following the introduction of the Code of Practice, more children have entered school with a statement of special educational need

or on Early Years Action or Early Years Action Plus. The benefits of this are:

● maximum information will be available to all professionals

● pupils will start to receive support sooner

● professionals in school are prepared for the arrival of children with specific needs and are able to put in provision sooner

● any adaptations can be made to the environment before the child starts to attend school.

**CASE STUDY:** The importance of early recognition

Ethan has a disability and has always used a wheelchair. He is about to transfer to his local secondary school. Although his mother has filled in all the forms for the school and they have been notified, there has been no dialogue between them about preparing both Ethan and the school for his arrival.

● How else can the school ensure that they find out in advance about pupils who have additional needs?
● What benefits would there have been for both sides if there had been more communication at these initial stages?

## The purpose of individual plans

Pupils who have special educational needs may need to have individual education plans to ensure that they have access to the curriculum. Although lesson plans should always include differentiated activities for pupils who have additional educational needs, these may need to be personalised further and individual education plans (IEPs) will give pupils specific targets to work on. If you plan alongside the teacher, you may be able to make suggestions at this stage for the pupils you support. You may also have had input from other professionals as to the kinds of strategies or equipment which you are able to use. Any additional training you have had around

# INDIVIDUAL EDUCATION PLAN

Name of pupil: Sara Chambers

Date of birth: 22nd Oct 1996

| Refer to Diagnostic summary sheet for background and assessment data |
| --- |

This IEP current from: Sept 2010          to Dec 2010

Review date: Jan 10th 2011

| | |
| --- | --- |
| Summary of current level of performance | Sara demonstrates a good attitude towards her work and shows good concentration during activities. However she is quite withdrawn and is reluctant to participate in a group activity.<br><br>Her reading and comprehension is significantly below the level of the majority of her peers. Although she is reasonably fluent when reading texts and will attempt new vocabulary at times she is unable to discuss what she has read. This is having a detrimental affect on research work in other areas of the curriculum.<br><br>Sara's punctuation has shown improvement but her grammar still lacks consistency. She finds it difficult to organise her own ideas and does not always take the purpose and audience for her writing into account. |
| Present educational needs | Sara requires:<br><br>Encouragement to become involved as she lacks confidence in giving own views relating to written materials during group and class work.<br><br>Opportunities to plan and revise writing, understanding that the structure of writing needs to take account of its purpose and audience.<br><br>Encouragement to read through her own writing so that she is aware of any inconsistencies |

| Long-term goals | Reading/speaking | Writing | Writing – grammar |
| --- | --- | --- | --- |
| | Extract and explain main points in the text when working within a small group of peers | Structure writing to suit the purpose of the task | Use subject/verb agreement and tense consistently in writing |

*Part of an individual education plan.*

the needs of the individual may also give you ideas about the kinds of activities and resources which will be beneficial.

You may still need to adapt work, however, if the pupil is finding it challenging. You will need to monitor pupil participation and intervene if necessary so that they are able to achieve the learning intention.

### Portfolio activity

If you are working with an individual pupil as a learning support assistant, you should have a copy of their individual education plan. Remove the name of the pupil and highlight and annotate the plan to show how you support the pupil towards achieving their targets.

## The principles of working inclusively

Inclusion does not just refer to pupils with special educational needs (SEN), but all pupils through the benefits of equal opportunities in schools. However, inclusion has come to be associated more closely with special educational needs as the term has been used widely since the introduction of the SEN Code of Practice in 2001. The theory is that with the right training, strategies and support, nearly all pupils with SEN can be successfully included in mainstream education. The benefits of inclusion should be clear – that all pupils are entitled to be educated together and are able to access the same education without any form of discrimination or barriers to participation.

When you are working with SEN pupils, you will find that many professionals and parents speak about the danger of 'labelling' children and young people. This is because it is important that we look at the needs of the individual first, rather than focusing on the pupil's disability or impairment. In the past, the medical model of disability has been used more frequently than the social model (see Table 2) and this kind of language has promoted the attitude that people with disabilities are individuals who in some way need to be corrected or brought into line with everybody else. This has sometimes led to unhelpful labelling of individuals in terms of their disabilities rather than their potential. You should be realistic about the expectations you have of the pupils you support and consider their learning needs. For some, although not all, the curriculum will need to be modified and pupils may need additional support. However, you should not assume that all SEN pupils will always need additional support and you should encourage them to be as independent as possible.

| Medical model | Social model |
| --- | --- |
| Pupil is faulty | Pupil is valued |
| Diagnosis | Strengths and needs defined by self and others |
| Labelling | Identify barriers/develop solutions |
| Impairment is focus of attention | Outcome-based programme designed |
| Segregation or alternative services | Training for parents and professionals |
| Ordinary needs put on hold | Relationships nurtured |
| Re-entry if 'normal' or permanent exclusion | Diversity is welcomed and pupil is included |
| Society remains unchanged | Society evolves |

Table 2: Medical and social models of disability, from Disability Discrimination in Education Course Book: Training for Inclusion and Disability Equality.

**BEST PRACTICE CHECKLIST:** Working inclusively with children with disabilities or SEN

- Have high expectations of all pupils.

- Celebrate and value diversity, rather than fear it.

- Be aware that all pupils have more in common than is different.

- Encourage the participation of all pupils in the curriculum and social life of the school.

- Work to include pupils in the main activities of the class wherever possible.

- Develop 'can do' attitudes in pupils through appropriate degrees of challenge and support.

# Understand the disabilities and/or special educational needs of children and young people in your care

## The relationship between disability and special educational needs

Pupils with special educational needs are defined on page 6 of the 2001 Code of Practice as having a learning difficulty if they have 'a significantly greater difficulty in learning than the majority of children of the same age' or 'a disability which prevents or hinders them from making use of educational facilities of a kind generally provided for children of the same age'. Disability is therefore considered a special educational need only if it hinders the pupil from participating in the day-to-day activities which are enjoyed by others. Having a disability may mean that a pupil has additional needs and therefore needs support. However, not all pupils who have a disability will have a statement of special educational needs, as many are independent and able to participate without support.

**CASE STUDY:** Disability and special educational needs

Fiona is in Year 9 and has a disability which means that her mobility is affected and she is unable to walk very far or use stairs. She is able to move around the classroom with her frame if needed and her wheelchair is only used when she needs to leave the classroom. She is unable to participate in some PE activities with other pupils, although she has strength in her upper body and is able to participate in most lessons.

- Do you think that Fiona requires a statement of special educational needs and support from an assistant?

## Particular disabilities and/or SEN of children with whom you work and special provision required

For these assessment criteria you will need to identify specifically the details of particular disabilities or special educational needs of pupils with whom you work and discuss how you have managed them with the support that is available to you. You will need to show how you have worked with others in the school and local authority to provide a high-quality service to these pupils. For example, you should have information from within your school through teachers and the SENCO about the pupil's needs. You may also work with professionals such as occupational therapists or physiotherapists who may advise you on the kind of **special provision** and additional equipment or specialist aids which should be provided by the school and give suggestions as to how you can best support pupils.

### Key term

**Special provision** — provision which is additional to, or otherwise different from, the provision made generally for children of their age in mainstream schools in the area

## Over to you!

Talk to your assessor or write a reflective account to provide details of the pupil or pupils with whom you work and how you support them. Always remember to change names.

## Functional skills

### English: Writing
When writing your reflective account, it is important that you plan your work through before you start. You need to make sure that your writing is clear and uses a range of sentence structures with good spelling, punctuation and grammar.

## The expected pattern of development

You will need to show how the pupil or pupils you are supporting differ from their peers in their expected pattern of development. If you work with pupils of a particular age range, it will be easier for you to identify whether they are fitting the normal pattern of development for their age, as you will be very familiar with what the rest of the class is able to do.

## Link

For all stages of physical, cognitive, communication and social/emotional development, see CYP 3.1, Understand child and young person development.

## Knowledge into action

Consider the needs of a pupil you support alongside the expected pattern of development for their age in the corresponding area (for example, physical, cognitive, social/emotional). You may wish to use the stages in CYP 3.1. Alongside the expected pattern, record the stage which the pupil has reached and how this has an impact on the pupil and their level of involvement in school activities.

## Functional skills

### ICT: Using ICT
You could type up a report that shows the level the pupil has reached alongside the expected pattern and include some examples of work to support what you are saying. You could scan their work in, remove any names and then insert them into your report as evidence.

# Be able to support the inclusion of disabled children and young people and those with special educational needs

## Obtain information about the needs, capabilities and interests of the children with whom you work

You will be able to obtain information from:

- children and young people themselves
- family members
- colleagues within the setting
- external support agencies
- individual plans.

It is important that you get to know pupils and find out about their capabilities and interests as soon as you can, to best support them both through the curriculum and in additional ways. Before they start at the school you may be able to visit them at their previous school or at home to speak to them and also parents about their needs and any specific information which is required. It is also likely that the SENCO will want to set up a meeting so that the school can discuss with parents or carers and the child themselves how they plan to work together. Many parents who have children with disabilities or special educational needs will have become experts on the need or condition. They will also be in a good position to offer support to others as they will be sympathetic to their situation and will have experienced the same kinds of difficulties.

Partnerships with parents and families are crucial to the process of working with pupils who have special educational needs. Schools will need to ensure that they are as supportive as possible through clear communication and discussion with parents.

Schools may wish to meet or talk to any other agencies or professionals who have worked with the pupil in the past. If these professionals are not available, they will be invited to send reports and recommendations in order to assist the school in making provision. If the pupil is not new to the school, you should have the opportunity of meeting with colleagues to discuss their progress alongside the pupil where possible and to look at previous paperwork. On a more informal level, it is very important that you get to know that pupil's interests so that you can support them through a greater awareness of their personality.

### CASE STUDY: Obtaining information about pupils' needs and interests

Naadir has been working part-time at his local secondary school for the last term as an individual support assistant. The school has recently asked if he can increase his hours, as there is a new pupil arriving at the school the following week who has Down's syndrome. He has been given some records by the SENCO about the pupil's needs and a meeting has been arranged with the parents to which he has also been invited before the pupil starts at the school.

- What else could Naadir do to obtain more information about the pupil?
- Why is this so important?

## Barriers to participation for disabled children and young people and those with special educational needs

All pupils, whatever their needs and abilities, have an equal right to education and learning, without

barriers to participation. Equal opportunities should include not only access to provision but also to facilities within and outside the school setting. Schools and other organisations which offer educational provision must by law ensure that all pupils have access to a broad and balanced curriculum.

### Key term

**Barriers to participation** — anything that prevents the child or young person participating fully in activities and experiences offered by the setting or service

### Physical barriers

Since the Special Educational Needs and Disability Act 2001 called for the amendment of the Disability Discrimination Act 1995, there should be no reason that a child or young person who has a disability or special educational need should not be able to gain access to an educational institution or to its facilities. If you are supporting a pupil who has additional needs, make sure that all staff are aware of the provision which needs to be made to ensure that they are able to participate. This may mean adaptations to the environment or the purchase of additional resources or equipment.

### Organisational barriers

Your school should have an up-to-date equal opportunities or inclusion policy which sets out its priorities for developing inclusion. It should also ensure that all staff who are working with pupils who have additional needs are fully trained and able to do so with the full support of the school.

### Barriers in the attitudes of the school community – staff, parents and other pupils

This barrier can be one of the more challenging to overcome, as it may be hard to change opinions and attitudes of others. You should always remember that the needs of the child or young person come first and to stand up for the rights of the pupils you support.

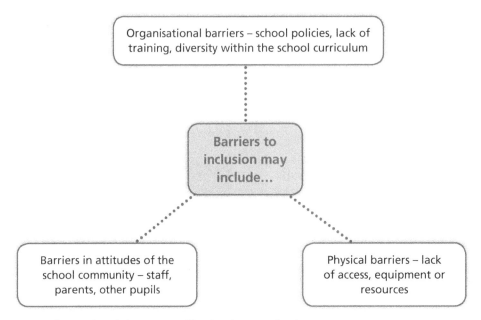

*Think of examples of these types of barriers in your school.*

## How to remove barriers to participation

Provision in schools may be affected by any of the barriers described, if the school does not take active steps to ensure that they do not occur.

You will need to be able to show that in your work with children and young people, you actively remove any barriers to participation which exist as they arise. These may be straightforward, such as improved training opportunities or meetings set up to ensure that all staff are aware of the needs of the pupil. The most important aspect of this is continued communication between the school, home and outside agencies on a regular basis to ensure that the pupil's needs are being met in the most effective way. However, barriers may also be to do with attitudes of others which may be more difficult to challenge. While you should always remain professional, you may find it appropriate to refer those who hold particular views to your SENCO or Head Teacher.

**CASE STUDY:** Removing barriers to participation

Paula has been told that she is going to be working with Philip, a pupil who is on the autistic spectrum. Philip is in Year 8 but is not new to the school. Paula is an experienced assistant but has not supported an autistic pupil before.

- Why might Paula be a barrier to Philip's participation in teaching and learning activities?
- What can she do to ensure that this does not happen?

### Functional skills

**ICT: Finding and selecting information**
You could use search engines to search the Internet for any courses in your local area that you could attend to help develop your knowledge in particular areas. You may not need to attend the course at the moment, but you could bookmark the page so you know where to look in the future, in case you are ever in a similar situation to Paula.

# How to involve and consult children, young people and others at each stage to support participation and equality of access

You should ensure when working with pupils that they are involved at each stage in discussing and identifying steps or targets which need to be taken, to encourage their **participation**. Pupils should be able to work with you to talk about what they will be doing in each subject, why they need to have additional support, and how success will be measured. At these different stages a range of **others** may be present, but the constants should be their support assistant, their parents, the class teacher and the SENCO. At review meetings there may also be representatives from the local authority or other professionals who come into school to work with the pupil.

## Reflect

How often do you attend meetings where the pupil is being discussed but is not present? If they are not included, have you been told why? Why is it important that pupils should be part of the process?

# Ways of supporting inclusion and inclusive practices in your work

It is important to remember that the child or young person should be at the very heart of your practice, and that your role is to empower them to be able to achieve to the best of their ability. This will involve getting to know them, finding out about their strengths, dreams and needs, so that you can ensure that they are valued and given as much support as they need.

As well as your support for individuals, you can also show that you support whole-school **inclusion** and inclusive practices in a number of ways. You will need to speak to your assessor about your school's inclusion or equal opportunities policy and identify the way in which pupils who have special educational

needs and disabilities are included in all school activities. You should also be able to identify the measures which are taken in your school to promote inclusion and the kinds of attitudes and expectations which staff and parents may have towards pupils who have special educational needs. You should as part of your practice always ensure that you include all children and young people both in curricular activities and through the wider work of the school — for example, in school councils, sports activities or school productions.

## Key terms

**Participation** — asking children and young people what works, what does not work and what could work better, and involving them in the design, delivery and evaluation of services, on an ongoing basis

**Others** — according to own role, these may be family members, colleagues within the setting or professionals external to the setting

**Inclusion** — a process of identifying, understanding and breaking down barriers to participation and belonging

## Skills builder

Consider the different ways in which your school supports inclusion and inclusive practices. How have you worked with others to ensure that pupils who have special educational needs are given a school experience which supports their wider learning?

## Functional skills

**English: Speaking, listening and communication** You could complete this Skills builder activity in the form of a discussion with your study group. You should listen carefully to what others say so that you can respond in an appropriate way and move the discussion forward. This is a good way of sharing practice.

# Be able to support disabled children and young people and those with special educational needs to participate in the full range of activities and experiences

## Identify and implement adaptations that can be made to support the participation of all pupils

When working with other staff to support pupil participation, you will need to consider the different adaptations you may have to make in relation to different aspects of what you are doing.

Adaptations can be made to support participation of disabled children and young people and those with special educational needs in relation to:

● **the learning environment** – for example, specialist equipment, a separate seating area, or where pupils sit in the classroom (such as a pupil with a hearing impairment who needs to sit near the front)

● **activities** – if tasks are too difficult or unsuitable, pupils may become frustrated or anxious, which will in turn make them reluctant to attempt further activities. You could find out exactly what pupils are able to do by asking others who work with them or have supported them in the past

● **working practice** – for example, the pupil you support may require adult supervision during break time, which will mean that you will need to have your break at a different time from other staff

● **resources** – to make activities more accessible for the pupils you are supporting. Be on the look-out for additional resources which may benefit them in class.

*Have you had to make adaptations to your learning environment for pupils?*

### Portfolio activity

Consider the kinds of adaptations you have needed to implement in order to support disabled pupils or those with special educational needs. How have these enabled them to participate more fully in the activities carried out by other children?

## Supporting pupils to use specialist aids and equipment as necessary

If you work with specialist equipment, you will need to be able show this to your assessor and explain how it is used. For example, you may work with a pupil who needs to use mobility equipment such as a walking frame in order to access the curriculum fully. In this instance you should talk through its use and your role in setting it up and using it safely for the pupil. The increased use of technology in schools has meant that pupils will often have aids which require you to have specific training. If you are unable to show your assessor, you will need to have a professional discussion or write about what is involved.

## Ways of supporting participation and equality of access

As a teaching assistant, you should be working regularly with a wide range of people to support **equality of access** to teaching and learning of those with disabilities and special educational needs. Although you may be working with pupils as individuals and in groups during school activities, there will also be a support system to guide you and ensure that you are given access to additional information. You should also talk to pupils on an ongoing basis about their own individual preferences and interests so that you can ensure that their wishes and needs are taken into account. Speaking to parents regularly is also important, as they may be able to pass on information which is helpful to you on a day-to-day basis.

Other professionals are also likely to come into school to speak to parents, the pupil and to the class teacher and SENCO about pupil progress and participation. They will provide advice and support, and may set targets for the pupil.

### Key term

**Equality of access** – ensuring that discriminatory barriers to access are removed and allowing for children and young people's individual needs

### Link

See also page 267 – How to involve and consult children, young people and others at each stage to support participation and equality of access.

# Be able to support others to respond to the needs of disabled children and young people and those with special educational needs

## Supporting others to observe the needs, capabilities and interests of pupils and to participate in activities with them

Although you may be the individual who knows the most about the pupil and is able to support them effectively, you will not be with them at all times. Your role may be shared or they may only have support for a few hours each week. Others in school should also know about the needs, capabilities and interests of the pupil so that they are able to respond to their needs if you are not present. If the school is small, it may be that all staff are aware of the needs of all pupils in the school. However, in a larger institution you may need to discuss pupils' needs both formally at staff meetings and informally to ensure that all information is passed between staff.

### Over to you!

How is this kind of information passed around in your school? Why is it important that as many staff as possible are aware of the needs of some pupils?

### Functional skills

ICT: Developing, presenting and communicating information
You could set up an email group where you send an email to a group of people that needs the relevant information. If you are going to send confidential information electronically, then the file that you send should be password protected so that it is not accessible to all.

**CASE STUDY:** Supporting others to participate in activities with pupils

Michael is in Year 7 and has a stutter and a communication disorder. Although this means that he does have some difficulties, he is a very enthusiastic and able child. When involved in a project which interests him, he can become overexcited and very frustrated. Today his year group is going on an educational visit to the Natural History Museum. You usually support Michael's group but because you are required to support pupils in a different class, he will be assigned to a group supported by another teaching assistant, Claire. She has not met Michael before.

- What might be the issues in this situation?
- Why should you ensure that Claire knows something about Michael's needs?

## Work with others to review and improve activities and experiences provided

You should ensure that you work in a cycle in order to identify and improve the kinds of activities which are provided for pupils who have special educational needs and disabilities. As you should be doing this for all pupils, and those with disabilities and special educational needs are included in this, the review should take place as a matter of course. You will need to review:

- the curriculum you are using with pupils
- use of the learning environment
- the resources available
- the kinds of activities which have been successful and why, and those which have been less successful and why.

As well as discussing the provision, you should also ensure that you include the pupils in the same way or by giving them evaluative questions to consider. This can then feed into the provision the following year.

# Evaluation form for pupils

| What have you found most enjoyable this year and why? |
| --- |
| What have you found least enjoyable and why? |
| Are there any subjects which you find particularly easy or challenging? |
| Have you found any resources or equipment particularly helpful? |
| What do you think the most successful part of the school year has been? |
| If you had the opportunity to change anything, what would it be? |

*How can you use the information a form such as this asks for?*

## Getting ready for assessment

The most useful way of gathering evidence for this unit is to have a professional discussion with your assessor. You should decide beforehand what you would like to cover so that you are ready to answer, but should be able to talk about the particular needs of the pupil or pupils you support and your role in relation to this. An example of a plan for discussion might be:

- look through and talk about the pupil's IEP and discuss their needs

- describe the relationship between the school and the pupil's parents, and specific support which is needed

- explain how you plan to support the pupil's individual needs and the use of any specialist terminology or equipment.

### References and websites
There are a number of magazines and periodicals which are available for school staff who support pupils with special educational needs. You should also keep up to date by reading the *Times Educational Supplement* and checking websites such as those listed here.

- *Special Children*
- *Special Magazine*
- SEN Code of Practice (2001) – DFES publications. Ref: DfES 581/2001

Support for families

**www.bbc.co.uk/health**– this website has advice for a range of conditions and illnesses
**www.cafamily.org.uk** – this is a national charity for families of disabled children
**www.direct.gov.uk** – go to 'Disabled people' for advice and support
**www.parentpartnership.org.uk** – National Parent Partnership Network, a national organisation supporting parents and children
**www.specialfamilies.org** – this is a national charity for families of disabled children

CAF (Common Assessment Framework) – for more information go to **www.education.gov.uk**; you can also download the publication at **http://publications. education.gov.uk** – ref: 0337-2006BKT-EN

## Check your knowledge

1. What is the main piece of recent legislation which has affected the teaching and learning of children and young people with disabilities and special educational needs?

2. Why is it important for a pupil's needs to be recognised as early as possible?

3. Name four ways in which you can get to know the pupil you are supporting. Why is this so important?

4. What kinds of barriers to participation might exist when working with pupils?

5. Where might adaptations need to be made when working with pupils who have disabilities or special educational needs?

6. Should all pupils with disabilities or special educational needs have an IEP? If not, should they have anything else to support their learning?

7. How can you effectively review the kinds of activities and experiences which are provided in your school for pupils with disabilities and special educational needs?

# TDA 3.20 Support children & young people with behaviour, emotional & social development needs

This unit is for teaching assistants who support children and young people who have behaviour, emotional or social development needs. You will explore these needs and their influence on development. You must demonstrate how you work with others to support behaviour management strategies and to support children and young people to build relationships and become confident and independent learners.

## By the end of this unit you will:

1. understand the influences impacting on the behaviour, emotional and social development of children and young people

2. understand the special educational needs of children and young people with behaviour, emotional and social development needs

3. be able to support the behaviour management of children and young people with behaviour, emotional and social development needs

4. be able to support children and young people with behaviour, emotional and social development needs to develop relationships with others

5. be able to support children and young people with behaviour, emotional and social development needs to develop self-reliance and self-esteem.

# Understand the influences impacting on the behaviour, emotional and social development of children and young people

Behaviour, emotional and social development can be affected by a range of internal and external factors.

## How upbringing, home circumstances, and physical and emotional health could affect ability to relate to others

### Home circumstances and upbringing

For children to progress in all areas of their development they must experience consistency in care, a loving and supportive home, and the opportunity to interact with others. For some children their upbringing and home circumstances can fall short of these basic needs and this will impact on their development. From birth children develop their behaviour and social skills from what they see and experience within the home. Children who experience lack of interest, lack of attention or even domestic violence or abuse are likely to develop behaviour, emotional and social difficulties.

Families will have different views on the expectations of children's behaviour although this will not necessarily have a negative impact. Problems arise where there are mixed messages. Children need to know boundaries and may become confused if these are applied inconsistently. Children also need attention from others but may learn that the only way to attract this is through unacceptable behaviour.

### Physical and emotional health

Children's physical and emotional health will have a direct bearing on their ability to interact with others. Those with serious ill health or disability will face particular difficulties in building new friendships. Children with a physical disability, for example, cannot join in as easily with play activities as their friends. This difficulty is exacerbated when children also have sensory impairment and/or communication difficulties.

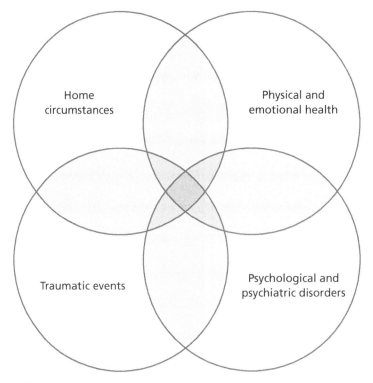

*Influences on children's ability to relate to others.*

When children have a delay in their emotional health they have less resilience to **transitions**. This will affect their ability to deal with difficult situations and to build friendships. Emotional health is critical to all other areas of a child's development.

Parents of teenagers are well aware of the difficulties young people experience during puberty. Emotionally it is a difficult period for young children, starting at around 11 years for some girls and 13 years for boys. Hormonal changes cause mood swings and a lack of confidence, which affects the way in which young people relate to others. It is a critical time for young people as they are developing their sense of self-worth and sexual awareness.

### Key term

**Transitions** – processes of change or events when children change from one stage or state to another

## The impact of negative or traumatic home experiences

Children may experience negative or traumatic events at some stage in their life. While some children appear to be able to bounce back from these difficult events, others will be seriously affected and unable to cope. Children who are refugees or asylum seekers may have experienced significant trauma in their lives. Even where children do not experience events such as terrorist attacks, natural disasters or accidents, first hand, these may still have a significant impact on them.

## How psychological and psychiatric disorders may impact on relating to others

Behaviour, emotional and social difficulty (BESD) describes children with a range of behavioural problems which may delay learning and other areas of development. Where these difficulties impact on children's ability to function effectively in school, it will result in an assessment of a child's needs. This will enable the necessary support to be put into place. It is not always possible to identify the reasons for BESD. In recent years there has been more research in relation to disorders experienced by children and young people. There is also a greater understanding of mental health disorders and ways they may be triggered by traumatic events. Research suggests that at least one in ten children between 5 years and 16 have some form of mental disorder (source: Office for National Statistics).

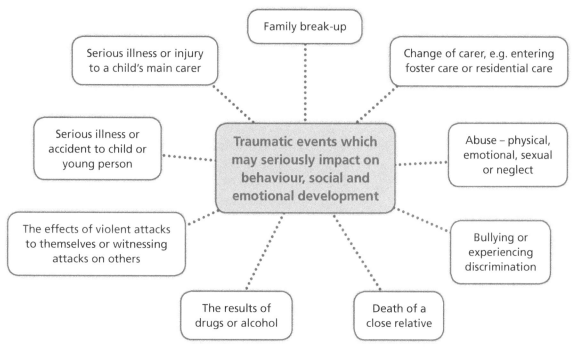

*Traumatic events which may seriously impact on behaviour, social and emotional development.*

| Disorder | Impact on behaviour, emotional and social development |
|---|---|
| Hyperkinetic disorders | Sometimes referred to as Attention Deficit Hyperactivity Disorder (ADHD) or Attention Deficit Disorder (ADD). Young children are often fidgety and like to be on the move, but children with hyperkinetic disorder are overactive and have problems in concentration compared to other children. This disorder is more common in boys. Children are distracted very easily, act without thinking and have difficulty in taking turns. This can lead to difficulties in making friends. Children often settle down in their mid-teens. |
| Emotional disorders | Includes disorders such as depression, eating disorders and post-traumatic stress disorders. These may be short term or reoccur at different times in a child's life. These disorders affect all aspects of their life as children often lose interest in their school work and outside interests. Their self-esteem is also affected. Children struggle to maintain friendships and make new friends. |
| Conduct disorders | Children with conduct disorder (CD) find difficulty in functioning in a school setting, as they deliberately display aggression towards others. Oppositional Defiant Disorder (ODD) causes children to have extreme tantrums and be rude, defiant and unco-operative. Conduct disorders seriously affect their ability to form relationships, as children find it difficult to understand the feelings of others. |
| Tourette's syndrome | Tourette's syndrome is a neurological disorder. It often appears between the ages of 7 and 10 years, but is more severe in early teens, improving as young people reach their 20s. Children display involuntary movements or sounds. It is sometimes associated with inattention and impulsive behaviour. It affects children's emotional and social development. Children may be teased or bullied and find difficulty in forming friendships. |
| Schizophrenia and bipolar disorder | These mental illnesses are rare in children and young people, and unlikely to be present until children reach their mid-teens. These are serious illnesses which cause young people to become confused in their thinking and experience hallucinations. These illnesses will affect the way young people feel about themselves and their relationships with others. |

Table 1: Disorders and their impacts on development.

## How medication may impact on abilities, behaviour and emotional responsiveness

Medication may be used for behaviour disorders. These treatments can have a positive effect and help children to function more positively. There is continued controversy around the success of medication. Children with ADHD, for example, may be treated with stimulant medication. This medication is not a cure but provides a calming effect and makes children less impulsive. Children with ADHD who take this medication may be inconsistent in their responses to learning activities.

They may work well in the morning, but then become less focused as the medication wears off. Medication can have side effects such as reducing appetite or causing sleep problems, which will also impact on the child's physical development and self-esteem. Antidepressants are sometimes used by children with extreme anxiety disorders and depression. These may help to alleviate the worst symptoms, but the side effects may cause children to become agitated or withdraw.

Medication for behaviour disorders will affect children differently, so if you know a child is receiving medication, it is essential that their responses in school are monitored and any concerns reported.

# Understand the special educational needs of children and young people with behaviour, emotional and social development needs

## Particular behaviour, emotional and social development needs of children and young people

Every school will have a behaviour policy which outlines how the behaviour, social and emotional needs of all children and young people will be supported. When children display particular behaviour, emotional and social development needs they will require additional support. You may be aware of children who:

● experience emotional and social difficulties

● are withdrawn or isolated or display school phobic reactions

● are disruptive, hyperactive and lack concentration

● have immature social skills or personality disorders

● present challenging behaviours arising from complex needs.

## Individual support plans of children and young people with behaviour, emotional and social development needs

Behaviour, emotional and social needs will be supported through **School Action** or **School Action Plus**. Where there is lack of progress at this stage, or complex needs are identified, children may undergo statutory assessment and a **statement of special educational need** will be drawn up. Whatever level of support is required, an individual learning plan (ILP) or individual behaviour plan (IBP) will be put into place. Children with behaviour, emotional and social needs are found across all ability levels, including those with additional learning needs and those who are gifted and talented. Whatever the need, early intervention is critical to prevent the child falling behind with work and to reduce the need for exclusion.

Plans may be in relation to the child's:

- behaviour
- difficulty in building relationships with other children and/or adults
- lack of self-reliance and self-esteem.

Your role will be to work alongside teachers and other professionals to provide the additional support which is identified within the plan. Children may have low-level needs where support can be provided within the school. Where there are more complex needs, specialist support may be provided by outside agencies such as psychology services.

In Scotland there is a different process. Instead of statements, children's additional support for learning (ASL) needs are analysed and where necessary a co-ordinated support plan (CSP) is set up.

Individual behaviour plans will include goals, which support the needs of each child and are additional to the outcomes for other children of the same age. The plans should include:

- information about the child's previous achievement
- the long-term goals for the child's progress
- specific targets for the child to work toward
- what help will be given and how (the strategy, by whom and when)
- specific resource requirements
- how and when success will be measured.

When using information about children for your portfolio evidence, remember to remove all names and information which would allow the child to be recognised, to ensure confidentiality.

## Functional skills

### English
Completing this Portfolio activity is great way of developing all three areas of your functional skills in English, as you will be required to read, write and possibly hold discussions with others to obtain all the relevant information.

# Be able to support the behaviour management of children and young people with behaviour, emotional and social development needs

## Identify and set behaviour goals and boundaries for children and young people with behaviour, emotional and social needs

Your role in setting goals and boundaries may be in a situation where a child has recently been identified as having behaviour, emotional and social development needs, and a new plan is being agreed. Alternatively you may take part in reviewing a pupil's progress and agreeing a new set of goals.

A number of people will be involved in setting goals, including the form teacher and other adults in the school who support the child. The child or young person and their family should be central in this process. For children with complex needs, professionals such as an educational psychologist may also support and advise on appropriate goals and strategies.

Behaviour goals can only be effective where children are involved in setting them, rather than having goals imposed upon them. It is important that children see the reason for each goal and how it relates to them. Goals and boundaries should be clearly focused and appropriate for the individual child. Expecting a young person with conduct disorder to work co-operatively in a group over an extended period may be unachievable. This young person is being set up to fail to meet their goal.

Goals should also be positive. Rather than 'you must not talk in class when the teacher or teaching assistant is explaining what to do', an alternative could be to 'listen when the teacher or teaching assistant is explaining what you must do'.

---

**BEST PRACTICE CHECKLIST:** Setting behaviour goals

- Start with the child's previous achievements — what they can do.
- Involve the child at all stages.
- Set a small number of goals. This will depend upon the child's stage of development and difficulty, but set no more than three or four.
- Use SMART targets — specific, measurable, achievable, realistic and time-bound.
- Ensure that the learner understands what the goals mean (using age-appropriate language) and what they need to do to achieve these.
- Use positive language.

---

**CASE STUDY:** Setting goals for a child with ADHD

Clive supports Jamal in Year 9, who has ADHD. He contributes to developing behaviour goals and boundaries. A new outcome is to work without distracting others in the class. Three new goals have been planned. Jamal will:

- not shout out in class when the teacher is speaking
- remember to bring his pen, pencil, ruler and calculator to each maths class
- be less disruptive.

Clive suggests that one of the goals is negative and could be reworded and that one of the goals is not SMART.

- Which goal did Clive identify as not being SMART?
- Rewrite the goal to make it SMART.
- Identify the goal which is negative and rewrite to make it a positive goal.

## How goals and boundaries support children and young people to develop and consolidate social and emotional skills

For children and young people who lack understanding of accepted social behaviour, goals and boundaries provide a supportive framework. Children must want to change their behaviour. Goals and boundaries provide direction to enable children to make the right choices, supporting the development of their social and emotional skills. By being involved in setting goals, the children also take on some responsibility for their actions. Goals and boundaries must be relevant and children must be able to see what is in it for them.

---

**Functional skills**

**ICT: Developing, presenting and communicating information**
You could use the computer to design a poster suitable for the age of the pupils you work with that shows the goals and boundaries for their classroom. Your poster will give you the opportunity to try different layouts and editing techniques including text, colour and images.

---

## Support children, young people and others to understand and apply goals and boundaries

Supporting children with behaviour, emotional and social difficulties can be a challenging role, but also rewarding when you see children beginning to apply goals and boundaries. As you become more experienced and knowledgeable, you may find that others in the school look to you for support and advice. In your role you may also be required to liaise with parents to discuss how well strategies are working and any difficulties they are experiencing in applying the goals and boundaries within the home environment.

Children with BESD require a great deal of support from you in the form of positive reinforcement and encouragement. A smile, thumbs-up or a 'well done' can make the difference and provide a reminder of what they are working towards. You must also be aware that with older pupils overt praise, given in front of their peers, can have the opposite effect. It is helpful for some learners to have a regular time — perhaps just before lunch or at the end of each session, when you can review each small step they have taken toward the goal. This will give pupils the opportunity to discuss concerns and any barriers they perceive to achieving their goals and boundaries.

When a pupil is experiencing difficulty in meeting a goal, you could think of ways to help them work towards it. For example, a goal for a Year 7 pupil was to raise her hand when she wanted to speak to the teacher, rather than calling out. The girl was finding it difficult to wait for her name if she knew an answer or had an idea. The teacher and teaching assistant agreed that the TA would draw the teacher's attention as soon as the child raised her hand, to reduce the risk of her becoming frustrated by waiting. Gradually the pupil was able to wait for a longer period.

*Do children discuss their concerns about achieving goals with you?*

### Knowledge into action

What strategies might you use with the following children and young people to support them to meet their goals?

1. Rafiq is in Year 11. His goal is to arrive at the class on time with everything needed for the lesson.

2. Caitlin is in Year 9. Her goal is to listen and respond appropriately to others when working in a small group.

3. Philip is in Year 7. He finds maths difficult and is continuously distracting his peers. His goals are to keep on task during the lesson and to ask for support when he does not understand.

## Work collaboratively with others to manage disaffection and challenging behaviour

Each school will have a behaviour policy in place which identifies the expectations of behaviour of all children and young people, and the rewards and sanctions which are in place which help to support the policy. Head teachers and governors must also develop a policy which supports children's holistic development and underpins the Every Child Matters framework. All staff must be aware of relevant policies so that there is a common approach to supporting behaviour and planning a curriculum which promotes behaviour, social and emotional development.

## Link

You can find more information on the Every Child Matters framework in TDA 3.6, Promote equality, diversity and inclusion in work with children and young people.

When children and young people are disaffected and/or display more challenging behaviour, there need to be personalised approaches to their behaviour management. It is important that all staff are aware of these and apply the agreed approaches in all aspects of the child's school life. Progress would be impeded if agreed approaches to behaviour management were used in some lessons but not others, or not supported at lunch or break times. The child and their family are central to this process. You may be invited to planning and review meetings which involve the child and their family to discuss and agree their role in implementing the agreed approaches.

## Contribute to the provision of safe and supportive opportunities to establish community-based rules and develop social interaction

### Establishing rules

Pupils with BESD have often experienced a disruptive home life and inconsistent expectations of their behaviour. They will frequently test out boundaries to see how far they can push them, so it is important that these are both clear and upheld consistently by staff.

Where there are too many rules for behaviour, it will be increasingly difficult for children to adhere to these, so fewer targets which are attainable are preferable. It is important that rules and boundaries for behaviour are agreed by all those working in the school and by the children themselves. In some schools, learners contribute to this process through school councils. It is beneficial if all pupils are involved in discussion to agree the rules for their own class and for group work.

### CASE STUDY: Supporting pupils with reading and writing difficulties

Angie has just begun her role in the secondary school. As part of her role she has been asked to provide additional support for a group of pupils from Year 11, in maths. Two of the pupils are making progress, but it is felt that because of lack of concentration they are not meeting their full potential. Two of the pupils have individual behaviour plans. One finds difficulty in expressing emotions and sometimes loses his temper when he finds work difficult. Another pupil displays anxiety during maths and has been missing lessons or walking out. On the first session Angie took time to get to know the pupils, and during the second session she suggested that they agree some rules for working together.

- Why is it important for Angie to involve the pupils?
- Why are rules important?
- What should Angie take into consideration when writing the rules?

### Developing social interaction

Social interaction can be particularly difficult for pupils with BESD. It is important that opportunities for social interaction are integrated within all areas of the curriculum, such as working together in pairs or small groups on class projects. Groupings should be flexible so that pupils are not always working with the same person, although this should be carefully managed so as to avoid clashes of personality. Even where children are working individually, you might look for opportunities to encourage positive interaction between children. For example, one teaching assistant observed that a pupil who had particular problems in relating to others had an interest and skills in ICT. She drew on this knowledge, asking the pupil to show another child how to copy and paste an illustration for his work. This strategy also helps to promote a positive image of pupils with BESD to their peers.

Whole-school approaches such as Social and Emotional Aspects of Learning (SEAL) help to establish community rules and support children to develop their social interactions. It is also helpful if children are involved in lunch time or after-school activities, where they can socialise in a supportive and controlled environment. By getting to know children's personal interests, you will be able to guide them towards suitable activities.

## Promoting positive behaviour and managing inappropriate behaviour

Part of your role is to manage inappropriate behaviour. This happens when behaviour conflicts with the accepted values and beliefs of the setting or society. This can be difficult so you may need to refer to other professionals from time to time. Children with BESD often have trouble controlling their emotions and this may spill over into aggressive acts. Inappropriate behaviour may be displayed through:

- verbal abuse, for example, rudeness, swearing, racist or sexist remarks
- writing
- non-verbal behaviour
- physical abuse.

### Promoting positive behaviour

Although it is important to understand strategies to manage inappropriate behaviour, the focus should be on ways to promote wanted behaviour.

### Managing inappropriate behaviour

When inappropriate behaviour is displayed, it should be recognised and actions taken. You should help the child to understand that it is the behaviour of which you disapprove and not themselves. For low-level and attention-seeking behaviour, the appropriate action may be to ignore what has happened and give attention to others who are working effectively. For other behaviours, it is important that you know the sanctions that are available and how to apply these fairly and consistently.

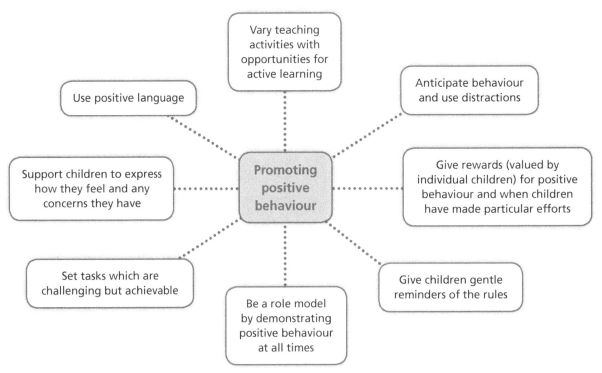

*Which methods do you consider most successful for promoting positive behaviour?*

There will be a structure of sanctions that can be applied depending on level of behaviour — for example:

- use of orange/red cards or detention
- losing part of break time
- withdrawal of privileges
- **restorative justice**
- referral to senior member of staff.

### Key term

**Restorative justice** — programme in which pupils are encouraged to consider the impact of their actions or words by making amends directly to the victim or community that has been harmed

In extreme situations, a child may be excluded or expelled. This will be used as a last resort and for children with special educational needs (SEN) or disability, not before all other approaches have been explored.

The use of sanctions should be used with care. Some sanctions may make children's difficulties worse. Missing break time for a child with hyperkinetic disorder will make them even more fidgety during the next lesson. Restorative justice is often more effective and appropriate for children with BESD. For example, if a child or young person has intentionally spoiled the work of another pupil they should help them to redo it.

### Bullying

Children with BESD may be the victims of bullying or become bullies themselves. Bullying can take the same forms as listed for inappropriate behaviour. There has also been an increase in cyber-bullying via the Internet and mobile phones. Whatever form it takes, bullying must always be taken seriously. The school must have a policy which supports and protects children from bullying.

### Over to you!

Check the sanctions which are available for you to use and for details of when to refer inappropriate behaviour to others.

# Be able to support children and young people with behaviour, emotional and social development needs to develop relationships with others

## Providing opportunities for children with behaviour, emotional and social development needs to establish social contacts

Schools must provide a wide range of opportunities for all children to establish social contacts in all aspects of school life. This could be through learning programmes such as Social and Emotional Aspects of Learning (SEAL). Opportunities for social contact should be integrated in all lessons. Extracurricular activities also provide excellent opportunities for children to establish social contacts.

The environment and organisation of the curriculum can influence the extent to which children establish social contacts as follows:

- the classroom — setting up learning areas will encourage children to sit and work in small groups
- teaching and learning through group activities
- vary groupings so that children have the opportunity to work with different children and in different groups
- lunch or after-school clubs which reflect children's interests.

## Encouraging co-operation between children and young people

Even where the organisation of the school facilitates social contact, you may need to provide additional encouragement for children with BESD. It is important to take into consideration the age of children and their stage of development, and have realistic expectations. You will also need to take into account children's language skills. Children with well-developed language skills find it easier to form relationships. If children have communication difficulties, you should help them to develop their skills to enable them to overcome barriers.

As children enter secondary education, they are beginning to search for their own identity and understand how they fit into social groups. Transition from primary school to Year 7 can be particularly traumatic for children who have difficulty in forming friendships. They need to feel accepted and valued. As they approach adolescence, children with BESD are likely to face additional difficulties in building relationships.

Although support is required to help children and young people to form social contacts, this should be handled with care so that children do not appear to be 'singled out'. Strategies may include:

- whole-group activities, such as drama or role play, which give children and young people the opportunities to practise social rules
- buddy systems — pairing a child with one who has similar interests
- modelling social skills — taking part in a group, taking turns in conversation, asking questions
- encouraging children to take part in after-school clubs and lunchtime activities
- drawing attention to children's strengths and abilities in group situations.

## Interacting with others to provide a positive and consistent example of effective interpersonal relationships

You should be aware of your own behaviour at all times, not only in class but around the school. Children will also notice your interactions with colleagues, so your behaviour should be professional and appropriate. Children will take their lead from your own actions and the way you speak to others. Speak with respect to pupils at all times, even when they may be displaying challenging behaviour and answering back. You should never use sarcasm.

## Responding to conflict and inappropriate behaviour with due consideration for own and others' safety

Your role is likely to involve dealing with extremes of behaviour. It is important that you remain calm so that the situation is not inflamed and you do not to get into arguments. If you anticipate children becoming frustrated, you might defuse conflict by using humour. If conflict is unavoidable, it is helpful to give children time out to allow them to calm down before speaking to them about their actions. When the behaviour involves others in the class, you should separate children and speak to them individually.

If you feel uncomfortable when dealing with conflict or incidents are becoming more frequent, it is important to seek help. Information, advice and support will be available within the school from the SENCO or a teacher who has experience with the child. The school will also have contact with outside agencies such as behaviour units or psychological services.

In situations where you or other adults or children are put at risk, it is essential that you send for help. Physical restraint may be used when others are at risk from harm. It is essential that you are aware of the guidelines for dealing with violent pupils and the use of restraint within your own school. If you work with children who are likely to have violent outbursts, you may well receive training on ways to restrain children safely.

## Strategies for helping rebuild damaged emotional relationships

Whatever support strategies have been put into place, inevitably there are times when there is a breakdown in relationships between a child or young person and their peer(s) or between a child or young person and an adult. This may include yourself or another member of staff.

Initially it will be necessary to talk to each party to try to understand the underlying problem. This will also give you the opportunity to help children to recognise and come to terms with their own feelings. Wherever possible, encourage and support the child to resolve any conflict to rebuild a relationship. The way you approach this will depend upon a child's stage of development. Where the breakdown is more serious, it may be necessary to involve a senior teacher or outside agency.

## Supporting children to review their social and emotional skills and the impact of these on others

Children should be at the centre of the process of planning, support and review of progress. It is important that you identify a regular time to sit with the child to discuss how they feel about their skills, any difficulties they are experiencing and how they think that other children might view their actions. These discussions will help children to take responsibility for their actions and to understand that there are alternative actions they could take. Support should involve:

- encouraging children and young people to think about the consequences of their actions
- supporting children and young people to think about the way others feel about their actions
- providing opportunities for children and young people to consider other choices available to them.

# Be able to support children and young people with behaviour, emotional and social development needs to develop self-reliance and self-esteem

## Encouraging and supporting children and young people to communicate their feelings, needs and ideas, make decisions and accept responsibility

All children and young people need the opportunity to be self-reliant. This is particularly important for children with BESD who may lack self-esteem and confidence in their own ability. If your role is to support a pupil with BESD, you must ensure that you are not overprotective. Look for ways that you can support independence and not do things which children and young people can do for themselves. You need to allow children to make mistakes in a controlled environment for them to be able to develop and grow.

Children's self-esteem directly relates to their behaviour, social and emotional development. Supporting children to develop a good self-image and self-reliance is essential to enable them to reach their full potential. Your own reactions to children will affect how they feel about themselves and their willingness to become independent learners, so it is important that you show children how you value their contribution.

### Encouraging and supporting children to communicate feelings, needs and ideas

Developing a good relationship with children is key to building sufficient trust so that children feel able to share their feelings, needs and ideas with you. You may agree a regular meeting time to talk through their needs. You can also support children within planned group activities such as role play or case studies. Opportunities to express feelings through art work, music or drama can be particularly effective for children who find communicating their feelings difficult.

As you get to know individuals, you will become more aware of when they need to talk or are worried. You can then encourage discussion – for example, 'I've noticed that you look a bit worried about your work today.' Your conversations should not always centre around problems. Find out about children's outside interests and school activities where they are making good progress to open a conversation – for example, 'I saw you playing football for the school last night. I was impressed with your passing skills.'

### Reflect ?

Be aware that children may disclose sensitive information about themselves such as bullying or abuse. Do you understand how to respond and the procedures you should take?

### Skills builder

Plan and implement a small group activity which will support children to communicate feelings, needs or ideas. Reflect on the activity in relation to the response of children or young people.

## Encouraging and supporting children to make their own decisions

You cannot make children behave in a particular way. Children must make their own decisions on how they will behave. It is important therefore that children are given opportunities to make the right choices. This can be achieved by explaining the consequences of different actions. For example: 'Sanjay, if you get back

to your task you will still have time to complete it by lunch, but if you continue to chatter you may have to stay behind to finish – it's your choice.'

## Encouraging and supporting children to accept responsibility for their actions

As well as rewarding achievement and effort, you should also observe when children have accepted responsibility for inappropriate actions. Show children you have recognised that, although the action was unacceptable, the way they have dealt with it is pleasing. For example, 'Walking out of the class wasn't the best choice when you felt frustrated, but I was pleased to hear you apologised to Mrs Williams when you had calmed down.'

Restorative justice can be particularly effective to support children to accept responsibility for their actions. If the sanction is proportionate to the action, it will be viewed as fair – not only by the child who has behaved inappropriately but also their peers. This form of justice helps children to see the link between their behaviour and the consequences.

## Supporting children to refocus when self-control has been lost

The progress which children make towards their goals is not always smooth. They may make great strides or appear not to progress for a while. Children may even take a step backwards and display inappropriate behaviour. When they lose control, children may also lose sight of their goals and agreed strategies. It is important that you support children and young people to understand the reasons for their outburst. This may be because events in the child's life are making their behaviour, social and emotional difficulties worse. You should remind children that everyone feels angry at some stage and that life sometimes appears unfair, but that they must remember how to deal with feelings in a positive way. You must give children time to reflect on and discuss events. You can then support children to refocus by:

- recognising that this is a 'blip' and that they are still working towards their targets

- recognising why in this situation they were unable to use strategies to deal with their feelings

- reflecting on what happened and the alternative choices which were available to them

- reassuring children that learning to control anger is a skill and they need to practise it.

## Opportunities for children and young people to develop self-management skills

Supporting children involves providing a safe and secure environment which gives opportunities for them to develop self-management skills. The following skills reduce children's reliance on others and help them to feel more positive about their own abilities:

- problem-solving skills

- decision making

- exercising choice

- self-expression

- general life skills.

## Strategies for recognising and rewarding achievement and effort

You should give children regular feedback on their progress. This could be a word or a smile to show that you are approving and that they are making the right choices. You will also have rewards that you can use such as stickers, house points or certificates. Some schools use raffle tickets which are entered for a prize draw at the end of term. What works with some children and young people may be totally inappropriate for others. As you get to know individuals, you will begin to find which they prefer.

Rewards should only be used when there is real achievement or effort. Rather than saying, 'Well done, I'm pleased with the way you worked in class today,' be specific about their achievement — 'I noticed that you started work on those maths problems really quickly today.' Rewards should also be given when children make small steps towards targets and not only when these are achieved.

### Functional skills

**English: Writing**
You could develop your writing skills by writing a letter to a parent/guardian of one of the children that you support, provided you have permission from the class teacher or Head Teacher. Your letter could include information on how they are doing in class and how they are developing their skills. Your letter would need to be formal and use a suitable layout. Take care with your punctuation, spelling and grammar in your letter, and make sure that you use appropriate language.

## Getting ready for assessment

For learning outcomes 1 and 2, you will have gathered evidence of your knowledge and understanding. As you move on to outcomes 3, 4 and 5 you will need to collect evidence of your own skills to provide support for children with behaviour, emotional and social needs. Share the learning criteria for the unit with the teacher and Special Educational Needs Co-ordinator (SENCO) and discuss the opportunities you will have to demonstrate your skills. You can then discuss your plans with your assessor.

### Websites

**www.angermanage.co.uk** – British Association of Anger Management
**www.nasen.org.uk** – aims to promote the education, training, advancement and development of all those with special and additional support needs
**www.rcpsych.ac.uk** – Royal College of Psychiatrists
**www.teachernet.gov.uk/teachingandlearning/socialandpastoral/seal_learning** – Teachernet, Social and Emotional Aspects of Learning (SEAL)

## Check your knowledge

1. Identify three traumatic events which may affect children and young people's behaviour, emotional and social development.

2. In what ways do kinetic disorders affect children and young people's behaviour and how might this influence their emotional and social development?

3. Why are there concerns about medication to control behaviour disorders?

4. Why might children and young people undergo a statutory assessment?

5. What is SEAL?

6. Identify five ways that you can promote positive behaviour.

7. What is meant by restorative justice?

8. Identify three ways to reward children's efforts or achievements.

# CYPOP 44 Facilitate the learning & development of children & young people through mentoring

Learning mentors are involved in helping to remove barriers to learning and raise pupil achievement in school. Working alongside the teacher, you will need to demonstrate how you mentor pupils in a formal or informal capacity, demonstrating how you take pupils' needs into account.

## By the end of this unit you will:

1. understand how to facilitate the learning and development needs of children and young people through mentoring

2. be able to support children and young people to address their individual learning and development needs

3. be able to promote the well-being, resilience and achievement of individual children and young people through mentoring

4. be able to review the effectiveness of the mentoring process.

# Understand how to facilitate the learning and development needs of children and young people through mentoring

## The interpersonal and communication skills required to facilitate learning and development needs

In order to work with children and young people as a mentor it is essential for you to have effective interpersonal and communication skills. It is important to be able to work with pupils to identify their learning and development needs, as well as offer pastoral support.

### Link

See also TDA 3.1, Communication and professional relationships with children, young people and adults, for strategies for effective communication.

Interpersonal and communication skills include:

- effective listening skills
- open questioning techniques
- use of appropriate body language
- giving constructive feedback
- empathising with children and young people while maintaining professional boundaries
- encouraging children and young people to participate and communicate effectively in the mentoring process.

### Effective listening skills

These are important communication skills and you should take the time to make sure that you are actively listening to pupils. Listening to what they tell you is vital as it values what they are saying, reinforces self-esteem and is a crucial part of building relationships.

### Reflect

How do you show that you are actively listening to pupils? For example, do you make eye contact? How do you react to what they are saying?

### Link

For more on active listening, see TDA 3.3, Support learning activities.

### Open questioning techniques

These will enable you to encourage pupils to speak about issues which concern them without trying to 'lead' their answers. For example, when asking them questions, you should not give them questions which will lead to a yes or no answer, but which will encourage them to talk in more depth, by using questioning words such as what, when, why or how.

### Use of appropriate body language

Make sure that you show your interest by the way in which you act when speaking to pupils — for example, sitting alongside the child or young person so that you are not 'talking down' to them. You should also ensure that your body language is a positive reaction to what they are saying and that you are encouraging them to communicate with you.

### Giving constructive feedback

Constructive feedback is about how you offer verbal support to pupils when they are working. You should always ensure that the feedback you give them is shared in a way that is helpful rather than critical. The pupil should be left feeling that what they have said or done is worthwhile, even if they may still need to do more work on it.

### Empathising with children and young people while maintaining professional boundaries

The way in which you interact with pupils should always remain professional — you will need to ensure that you set boundaries with them and adhere to these. You should always maintain the relationship of professional carer to child. However, when mentoring, you will also need to show consideration and empathy with pupils. This should be possible in an environment in which you and the pupil are clear on ground rules.

## Encouraging children and young people to participate and communicate effectively in the mentoring process

Children and young people will need to be able to participate and communicate effectively with you and to engage in the mentoring process for it to work. You will need to develop trust and positive relationships with them and find out all about them so that effective communication is a natural progression. You should also use all of the strategies above to ensure that they are encouraged by the way in which you communicate with them.

### Skills builder

Ask a colleague to observe you working with your mentee for 15 minutes. Request that they note which of the interpersonal and communication skills listed here you have used when working with pupils.

### Functional skills

ICT: Developing, presenting and communicating information
You could transfer this list into a table on the computer and then add columns titled 'How I am going to maintain this' and 'How I am going to improve this'. This table will be a good way of identifying any targets for your professional development. You could share your completed table with your assessor.

## How different learning styles and methods impact on learning and development

Different learning styles and methods include those in the following diagram.

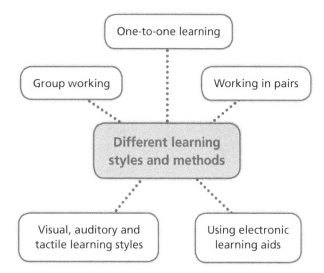

*Which of these methods are you most familiar with?*

The way in which work is presented and how they go about learning will affect how pupils learn, as they may all approach learning in a slightly different way.

Ideally all pupils should have a wide range of learning experiences and methods so that they can find out about the way in which they learn best.

### One-to-one learning

In situations where pupils are learning one to one, they will have the full attention of an adult and will be able to ask questions whenever needed. Often pupils with special educational needs will have one-to-one support to enable them to have full access to the curriculum. However, pupils who are learning in this way may also be restricted in their learning as they may find it easier to seek assistance than to try ideas out for themselves. This is why individual support assistants will often support a whole group which includes their named pupil, so that they are there to support the individual if needed.

### Working in pairs

Working in pairs gives pupils the opportunity to talk to another person during the learning process. This is useful both for sharing ideas and also for supporting pupils who may need additional confidence in order to speak out. Teachers will often ask pupils to discuss ideas with a talk partner, or work together, so that they are working together rather than through another adult.

## Group working

In a similar way, working in groups will enable pupils to share ideas, as well as giving them experience in listening to others and allocating responsibilities.

---

**CASE STUDY:** Working in groups

Leanne is working with a Year 7 class which has been asked to work in groups to design and make board games for young children. She notices that one of the groups seems to be taking a long time to make a decision on their design and there is some arguing. Leanne goes over to find that one very able member of the group is taking over and telling the group what to do; this is annoying the others as he is not listening to their ideas.

- What do you think is happening here?
- How could Leanne support the group?
- Why is this learning process important for all pupils but particularly for the one who is taking over with his ideas?

---

## Using electronic learning aids

Electronic learning aids are a form of learning which is constantly changing due to the rapidly moving world of technology. An electronic aid can be any kind of electrical assistance or support for learning, so it may be computer based or through hand-held devices such as PDA's (personal digital assistants) which may be connected to a central workstation. Electronic learning aids may also be used by pupils with special educational needs to support their access to the curriculum and enhance their learning.

---

**Functional skills**

Maths: Representing
ICT: Developing, presenting and communicating information
How many electronic learning aids have you got in your setting? How often are they used? What percentage of the child's week is spent using electronic resources to support their learning? You could log all the electronic resources you have in a database for everyone to access. This would be a good way of auditing the equipment you have in school.

---

## Visual, auditory and tactile learning styles

Visual, auditory and tactile learning styles were first developed by psychologists in the 1920s, who believed that most individuals have a dominant way of learning, or learning style. For example, visual learners may find it easier to learn by looking and reading, while tactile or kinaesthetic learners may prefer a more practical, hands-on approach. This method has been adopted in recent years by educationalists along with Howard Gardner's Multiple Intelligences, which refers to seven learning styles. Broadly speaking, pupils should have the opportunity to learn in different ways, and teaching and learning activities should be presented so that all pupils have equal opportunities whatever their learning style.

| Learning style | Description |
| --- | --- |
| Visual | Seeing and reading |
| Auditory | Listening and speaking |
| Tactile or kinaesthetic | Touching and doing |

*Table 1: Learning styles.*

---

**Over to you!**

What is your learning style? Take a learning styles test at www.businessballs.com/vaklearningstylestest.htm

---

# Be able to support children and young people to address their individual learning and development needs

## Support children or young people to express their goals and aspirations

A key part of your work as a learning mentor will be to encourage and develop children's communication skills and self-esteem so that they are able to speak out and express themselves. This is because those learners who need this kind of pastoral support are often those who are the most vulnerable and disadvantaged, and who need additional time with adults and other children. As well as communication skills, the level of children's self-esteem and how they feel about themselves and school will form a key part of their ability to learn and make the most of the school environment. You may need to encourage pupils who are reluctant to come to school or who have had limited social experiences to take part in a wider range of activities, so that they broaden their horizons. You will also need to give the child or children with whom you are working your time and positive attention through the activities you offer them on a regular basis.

Opportunities to support pupils may be varied but could include:

- giving pupils positions of responsibility such as group leaders, captains, school council members

- encouraging them to take part in a variety of extracurricular activities, particularly if they have low self-esteem as a learner and have other skills or abilities they want to develop

- spending additional time with them both on a one-to-one level and with other pupils so that they have the input of both an adult and their peers

- being approachable and available to them if they need to speak to you at any time.

## Link

You can find additional information on ways to support young people to make informed choices about their future learning and career aspirations in CYPOP 9, Provide information and advice to children and young people.

## Knowledge into action

The table below gives further examples of the kinds of skills you will need to have in your role as a learning mentor. Which of these do you use as part of your role? Can you think of any others which are not listed but which you do with pupils? Which of these do you think continue to develop their confidence and support them in developing goals and aspirations?

| A learning mentor should... | A learning mentor should not... |
|---|---|
| • act as a role model<br>• be an active listener<br>• challenge the assumptions that others have of pupils and that they have of themselves<br>• observe pupils to assess their needs and devise supportive strategies<br>• be involved in running after-school activities<br>• work one to one with pupils<br>• identify early signs of disengagement<br>• form professional friendships with pupils<br>• give guidance<br>• negotiate targets<br>• be a reliable, approachable, non-judgemental and realistic supporter of pupils, families and staff<br>• run pupil drop-in sessions<br>• work with small groups on anger management, self-esteem and emotional literacy etc.<br>• support families<br>• develop pupils' self-esteem<br>• develop strategies to improve attendance and punctuality<br>• support KS2/3 transfer and key transitions in learning<br>• liaise with outside agencies to gain additional support for pupils and the school<br>• support mentees in class as part of a structured programme of mentoring support. | • be involved in *counselling* (involving properly qualified professionals, formal referrals and parental consent) sessions with pupils<br>• be a teaching assistant<br>• be the person to whom a pupil is sent when naughty and/or sent out of class<br>• be expected to support teachers in delivering Literacy and Numeracy lessons<br>• co-ordinate and administer whole-school attendance monitoring<br>• be child protection co-ordinator<br>• *teach* gifted and talented pupils. |

*Table 2: Clarification of the learning mentor role, based on DfES Learning Mentor guidance (Source: Haringey Council's Learning Mentor Guidance document).*

# Support children or young people to identify ways of removing barriers to achievement

Pupils you are mentoring on a regular basis may feel disempowered or unable to achieve due to a number of barriers. It is likely that they will need you to support them in identifying and removing these. Barriers may take a number of different forms and may come both from the learner themselves or from others.

Barriers to achievement may include:

● low levels of literacy/numeracy or communication skills

● bias and stereotyping in the learning process

● low learner motivation

● parental and/or peer influence.

## Low levels of literacy/numeracy or communication skills

Pupils may have low levels of literacy and/or numeracy or find it difficult to express themselves well. This may make it difficult for them to see ways of moving on with their learning. They may need to spend time talking with you about how they can overcome this, whether it is through additional learning support or through taking more time to plan their work with you or others.

## Bias and stereotyping in the learning process

You may find that you experience degrees of stereotyping from others when you are working with children. This could come from either pupils or adults, and you will need to handle it sensitively. Stereotyping means expecting particular characteristics of certain groups of people. For example, people might say that particular groups such as women, black people or gay people have particular characteristics. If you are working with a group of pupils, you may find that others in the group hold antisocial opinions or ideas. You should challenge biased opinions immediately so that children do not think that they are acceptable. The school environment should be one which welcomes all individuals equally and celebrates diversity.

## Low learner motivation

Low motivation is likely to come from a lack of interest in the activity but may also come from feelings of inadequacy or because pupils feel they are unable to participate in learning activities due to a lack of self-esteem. Pupils may need you to encourage them and give them plenty of praise. Children also need to be given plenty of opportunities to be in control of situations and to make decisions in a safe environment. As adults we can support this by making sure that activities give children opportunities to make choices in their learning and develop an awareness of risk.

## Parental and/or peer influence

Children will be influenced in a positive or negative way by the interactions and messages which they receive from adults and from their peers. If a child is continually told that they are no good or is given very little attention, or no positive attention, they will not develop a good self-image. This in turn can lead to a lack of confidence and reluctance to participate in learning activities. Your role will be to motivate pupils by giving them support and encouragement through the development of positive relationships, so that they feel confident enough to be able to work effectively.

---

**CASE STUDY:** Removing barriers to achievement

Brett is in Year 8 and has been working with Gary, his learning mentor, for two terms. He finds learning difficult and has low self-esteem, and his mother does not have time to work with him at home. She says that it is up to the school to manage his learning. Gary has been speaking to Brett and his teacher about different ways in which he can try to support Brett. They have worked with him to devise an action plan to support his learning (see below for more on these). However, Gary feels that it is also important to try to work alongside Brett's mother and to try to raise his self-esteem.

• What could the team at school do and how could they involve Brett?

• How might they work with Brett's mother to support him?

# Action plan to address individual learning and development needs of children or young people

An action plan for learning:

- sets clear targets and outcomes appropriate for the individual learner
- sets clear timescales for achievement
- agrees the support that will be provided to help achievement of targets
- agrees clear review and revision processes and procedures.

When developing action plans to address individual development needs, you should make sure that you follow any agreed formats which are used by the school. In order to make them SMART you will need to be careful that you look closely at the targets you are formulating. You should work through these with the pupil and discuss them as they are being set, and ensure that they understand what the targets mean.

- **Specific** – you must make sure that the target states clearly what is required.
- **Measurable** – you should ensure that you will be able to measure whether the target has been achieved and what level of confidentiality is required.
- **Achievable** – the target should not be inaccessible or too difficult for the pupil.
- **Realistic** – you should ensure that the pupil will be able to attain what is being set in the time available and that any others involved have been consulted.
- **Time-bound** – there should be a time limit set to achieve the target. This gives an opportunity to look again at the action plan and discuss the pupil's progress.

It is not advisable to set more than three or four targets as they may then seem less achievable to the pupil. There should also be regular contact with the families or carers of the children receiving support, to encourage positive family involvement in the pupil's learning. Work with pupils should generally be regular, short and focused, and aimed at giving

them the opportunity to discuss issues and to work on targets in their action plan.

You may wish to identify stages towards the goals being set. These will be helpful to the pupil as they will be able to see progress even within a short space of time. However, the targets themselves should not be too ambitious. Depending on the needs of your pupils, you should be able to set realistic timescales. If you are unsure about whether a pupil will be able to meet targets, perhaps because you do not know them well, it is advisable to start with less challenging targets or to work closely with the teacher.

## Portfolio activity

For your portfolio, include an annotated copy of an action plan which you have worked on with a pupil. Highlight each target and show how they relate to the pupil's prior learning and experiences. Show how you have made decisions about the rate of progress and the timescales selected.

## Functional skills

### English: Writing
Setting SMART targets is important in the child's learning. You could design a sheet to help the child to understand what a SMART target is, so that they can be more involved in the setting of targets. Think about how you are going to transfer the information into language suitable for the child who you work with.

## CASE STUDY: Developing an action plan to address individual needs

Jenny is an experienced learning mentor who has just started to work with Aaron, who is in Year 10 and has some anger management issues. She has had an initial meeting with the SENCO to find out about what has been happening and what she needs to work on with Aaron. However, when Jenny asks about an action plan, she is told not to worry, just to make sure she takes this term to get to know him.

- Should Jenny say anything else?
- Can she do anything in this situation?

## BROOK MEADOW COMMUNITY SCHOOL

**Learning mentor support plan Date:** 14th Jan 2011

**Pupil:** Natalie Jones     **Mentor:** Rachel Davis

**DOB:** 7th May 1999     **Form Teacher:** Tim Richardson

**Reason for referral:**
attendance / punctuality [✓]   social / emotional [ ]   under achievement [ ]
transition / new to school [ ]   bullying behaviour [ ]   abusive behaviour [✓]
poor concentration [ ]   physical aggression [ ]   trauma / personal [ ]
other [ ]   (please state)

**IEP:** YES / (NO) (please circle)

**Other agencies involved:** (give details) None

| Concern | Target | Action | Monitoring |
|---|---|---|---|
| Reports about angry outbursts / verbal abuse towards teachers or peers on average 3X each week | Reduce the number of reports to one per week | 1:1 sessions with mentor 2X weekly. Mentoring group session 1X each week (dealing with feelings / anger) | Form teacher to monitor reduction in number of referral forms |
| Truancy on average 3 days each month | Reduce the number of missed school days by 50% | Report to mentor on arrival for brief discussion. Parents to be contacted if absent when register is taken am and pm | Mentor to check registers each week |

**Date for review:** 4th March 2011

**Signatures:**

R Davis _____ (Mentor)    Natalie Jones _____ (Pupil)

T Richardson _____ (Form tutor)    A Jones _____ (Parent)

*An example of an action plan.*

# Be able to promote the well-being, resilience and achievement of individual children and young people through mentoring

## The importance of promoting the well-being, resilience and achievement through mentoring

When mentoring individual pupils, you will need to be able to work with them to promote their **well-being**, **resilience** and achievement. In order to do this, you should get to know the pupils well so that you can find out their areas of strength and greater confidence as well as those of vulnerability. You should value their views and opinions, and show them that you are

### Key terms

**Well-being** — being in physical and mental good health, resulting in a positive outlook and feelings of happiness

**Resilience** — the ability to withstand normal everyday disappointments, hurts and assaults to one's confidence without it affecting self-esteem

interested in what they have to say. In this way you will have a better starting point for the mentoring process.

Pupils who are more vulnerable will need to develop their confidence so that they are able to feel better about themselves and the learning process.

It is likely that you will be doing this anyway through mentoring although you may not have given a 'title' to what you are doing — for example, by:

- being upbeat and positive with pupils
- sharing jokes
- being able to remember details of things which are important to them.

You will need to nurture an atmosphere of positive acceptance when working with pupils. Children and young people who feel more confident and positive about themselves generally are more likely to achieve well in school and feel happy — you will need to promote this in your demeanour and the way in which you interact with pupils. Pupils must also learn to be resilient — that is, to be able to cope with upset and disappointments which will come their way. It may be that as a mentor you are more likely to be able to talk to them about these kinds of issues. We need to emphasise to pupils that these kinds of disappointments are part of life and that they will happen to everyone at different times.

## Over to you!

Think of the different ways in which you promote well-being, resilience and achievement of pupils you mentor. In particular, how can you promote physical and mental good health through the kinds of activities you carry out in school?

## Functional skills

**ICT: Developing, presenting and communicating information**
You could complete this short activity in the form of a short presentation. You could share your presentation with your peers as a good way of sharing good practice.

## Mentoring strategies and activities that support well-being and resilience

Feelings of well-being and resilience will develop naturally in children and young people in different ways both through their experiences and their relationships with others. However, with the pupils you support, extra help may be needed for them to continue to develop sufficiently in these areas. They will need to be exposed to a broad range of different situations in order to give them greater confidence.

### Working with others

Pupils' emotional well-being and resilience is directly related to their ability to relate to others. They may not be confident when working in a group and may need support in order to give input and express their ideas. You may need to question them in a way which is non-threatening in order to bring out their ideas, or encourage them to support one another — for example, by discussing with a partner first to build up their confidence.

### Looking at different scenarios/role plays and thinking about and discussing how the child or young person is feeling

These kinds of discussions can be very helpful to pupils who are unsure when talking about their particular situation or emotions. They may not realise that others will be empathetic or that it is normal to behave or think in a particular way when faced with a particular scenario. In this way they will be talking about the individual in the situation rather than themselves, which they may find less threatening.

### Using problem-solving techniques

Pupils need to learn to be able to develop problem-solving skills so that they have experiences in managing these kinds of situations for themselves. They will need to be able to approach tasks and problems in a structured way which enables them to develop logical thought. Some find it useful to draw thought diagrams and flow charts so that they can look at a problem in a more visual way, while others may prefer to talk things through. If you can support pupils in identifying their preferred learning style and way of working, they can find ways of approaching a problem which suit them.

## Using decision making

Where pupils are asked to make decisions about their learning or be responsible for decision making, their ability to do this will relate to their own experiences and ages. Decisions such as selecting a topic for research or the method of presenting information will help children and young people to feel more confident. If pupils are always told what to do without any explanation or involvement, they are more likely to challenge adults, which can cause a range of problems. However, by encouraging them to make choices, you will be supporting their confidence and emotional well-being. Children and young people who have been encouraged to make decisions and choices about matters which affect them will be more willing to accept boundaries.

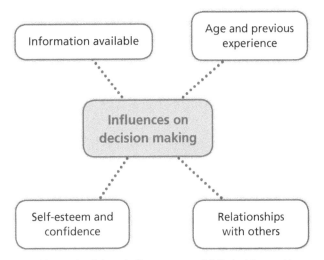

Consider each of these influences on a child's decision making.

---

**CASE STUDY:** Supporting well-being and resilience

Ross works in Year 9 as a learning mentor for two pupils. He arrives one morning to find that one of the girls he works with has been upset by an incident on the way to school. She has become very quiet and is not focused on the activity which he had planned to do with her.

- What should Ross do?
- Why is it important that they talk about what has happened to her?

---

---

**BEST PRACTICE CHECKLIST:** Supporting well-being and resilience

- Provide pupils with choices during activities and tasks, for example, giving more open-ended activities.
- Give them a variety of activities individually, in pairs and in groups.
- Recognise children's individual strengths and reflect on these when encouraging and praising.
- Give pupils relevant information to enable them to make informed choices.
- Discuss the effects of their decisions on others in the group if it is a shared activity.
- Use books and other resources to provoke discussion about different situations.
- Be positive and non-judgemental — comment on the behaviour or view rather than on the individual.

---

# Be able to review the effectiveness of the mentoring process

## Progress of individual children or young people against their action plans

At the end of the mentoring cycle, you will need to work with children and young people to consider how successful they have been at meeting the targets on their action plans. As their mentor, you will need to sit with pupils and their parents or carers to discuss their progress. When reviewing plans, you will need to make sure that pupils are able to think about the progress they have made so far and discuss any difficulties they have faced, so that they can apply this to setting future goals and suggest improvements. Similarly, where they have been successful, they should be able to look at factors that have influenced this.

Pupils should review their plans regularly with you to keep them motivated and also to check their progress. However, you should also remember that the plan is a working document and if circumstances change or it becomes apparent that the target is too ambitious, you should be able to amend it before the review date. Make sure that you note down any changes as soon as they happen and date them for information.

### Portfolio activity

Using an action plan which you have reviewed, annotate it to show how you have worked together to suggest changes at different times and have filled in the review column.

## Effectiveness of the mentoring process in facilitating learning and development

The mentoring programme in your school should be regularly evaluated to ensure that it is having an effective impact on the learning and development of pupils, and you may be involved in doing this. It may also be a requirement of your local education authority as it is essential that there are systems in place to monitor and evaluate the quality and impact of the learning mentor programme. The kinds of data and information which are useful might include:

● careful planning of work and mentoring sessions

● reviews of work with individual pupils

● pupil, teacher and parent evaluations

● review of targets and priorities in the action plan

● monitoring of cohorts (by ethnicity, gender, EAL (English as an additional language) and so on)

● monitoring of attendance, punctuality and exclusions

● performance appraisal for learning mentors

● line manager observations of learning mentor work.

It may be difficult for you to assess your own competence when mentoring pupils, as the process can be a slow one and any progress you make may well take considerable time. However, there should be opportunities for you to have an appraisal as part of your own professional development and this will enable you to consider, alongside your line manager, the effectiveness of your mentoring work with pupils.

The Every Child Matters initiative also highlights the importance of involving learners in the evaluation of work undertaken with them. This may take place through interviews or questionnaires, or through discussion following the process so that pupils have the chance to say what they think and mentors to act upon it.

*How can you help a pupil to get the most out of a review of their progress?*

## Getting ready for assessment

To gather evidence for this unit, it would be useful for your assessor to observe you carrying out a mentoring session with an individual or group of pupils. You should talk through the process from the beginning, discussing how you have formulated action plans bearing in mind the needs of pupils, how you have reviewed them and who was involved, and in particular how they have been evaluated.

### Websites and references

**www.cwdcouncil.org.uk/learning-mentors** – Children's Workforce Development Council offers information on learning mentors
**www.teachers.tv** – Teachers TV: enter 'Learning mentors' in the search for video and other links

DfES (2000) *Good Practice Guidelines for Learning Mentors* (ISBN 1841856169) – available from the DfE website, search for it in 'Publications': an excellent and very helpful document containing a number of references, case studies and websites for further reference.

George, Stephanie (2010) *The Learning Mentor Manual*, Sage Publications

## Check your knowledge

1. Give examples of four interpersonal and communication skills which you might need to facilitate the learning and development needs of children and young people.

2. How might the way in which a pupil learns impact on their learning and development?

3. Which of the following might you do to encourage a pupil to express their goals and aspirations? Why is it important that they should be able to do this?
   a) Spend time getting to know them.
   b) Ask them lots of questions.
   c) Give them opportunities to try a range of activities.
   d) Be approachable.

4. What barriers to achievement have you come up against when mentoring pupils? How have they been overcome?

5. How can you promote pupil resilience through the use of different strategies?

6. What kinds of systems might your school have in place for monitoring the effectiveness of the mentoring process?

7. How can you personally think about your own professional development as part of this?

# CYPOP 9 Provide information & advice to children & young people

This unit is for practitioners who have a responsibility to provide impartial advice and guidance to young people. It will support you to develop your own knowledge and skills to engage with young people to establish their individual needs. You must demonstrate ways to provide young people with relevant information and advice and ways that you support them to make informed choices.

## By the end of this unit you will:

1. understand the role of practitioners in providing information and advice to children and young people

2. be able to establish and address the information and advice needs of children and young people

3. be able to provide children and young people with appropriate information and advice to enable them to make informed choices.

# Understand the role of practitioners in providing information and advice to children and young people

Following the introduction of the Education and Skills Act 2008, there is a statutory requirement for all state-maintained schools, including academies, special schools and referral units to provide impartial information, advice and guidance (IAG) for children and young people from Year 7 to Year 11. In practice, advice is often provided beyond these age groups, starting in primary school. Pupils at post-16 also require continuing support and advice as they progress to higher education, training or work. These reforms were introduced in response to concerns that a growing number of young people were leaving school without clear direction, often described as NEETs (not in education, employment or training).

## The importance of providing accurate and up-to-date information and advice

The purpose of information, advice and guidance (IAG) is to enable young people to become independent and have the confidence to make their own decisions about their learning and career development. There has never been more choice regarding learning and career opportunities. While this can increase young people's interest and motivation, it can also cause confusion and uncertainty. It is critical, therefore, that accurate and up-to-date information is given from the time that young people transfer to their secondary school.

Accurate, impartial and up-to-date advice and guidance is key to implementing the six principles (shown below) which are set out in the document, *Statutory Guidance: Impartial Careers Education*.

### Comprehensive information and guidance

At Key Stage 3, young people are beginning to make choices about the range of pathways and subjects they will follow at Key Stage 4. Then young people must make decisions about post-16 education, training and work. Young people must be informed about the range of opportunities available, not only offered within their own setting but also, for instance, in local sixth form centres, colleges and work-based providers. The information must include:

- the different routes available

- the implications of their choices for post-16 education, training and work

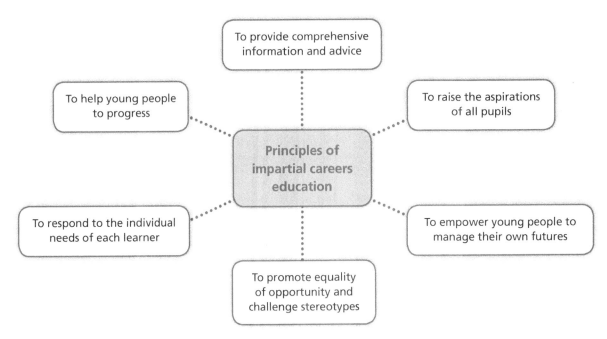

*How does your school implement the six principles?*

*What will this choice mean for you?*

- the range of career options including pay rates, benefits and advancement

- progression opportunities to further and higher education

- opportunities for work with training.

Young people must also be informed about the support which is available for them to continue into study or training at 16, particularly those young people who are from families with restricted finances. As children approach 16 they must be provided with information about:

- the guarantee for further learning at 16–19

- financial support for training or further or higher education, for example, eligibility for educational maintenance allowance (EMA) or grants.

## Raising aspirations

Helping young people to focus on their own achievements and setting realistic challenges will help young people to recognise possibilities for future learning and career development, encouraging them to reach their full potential. A regular review and updating information at Key Stage 4 will help to keep pupils engaged and motivated, supporting their progress toward their chosen pathway.

## Empowering young people

Young people not only need to be given information about the choices that are available to them but also the skills to investigate careers and educational opportunities for themselves. It is important that they recognise any barriers which may exist to their plans and know how to overcome these.

## Responding to individual needs

All advice and guidance must start with the individual young person. While it is important that practitioners encourage young people to aim high, the information and advice given must be relevant for the individual's aspirations, needs and abilities. They need accurate and current information on learning pathways which will help them to achieve their own career goals. Some young people may need to be directed toward specialist services to enable them to fulfil their ambitions.

### Functional skills

**English: Speaking, listening and communication**
You could do role-play guidance interviews with your study group peers to help you to develop your speaking, listening and communication skills. You will need to listen carefully so that you know how to respond.

## Helping young people to progress

Young people need an understanding of how the curriculum relates to them and its relevance for further progress in education and towards meeting their career aspirations. Accurate advice and information must be provided to enable young people to:

- apply for further or higher education

- take advantage of work-related opportunities such as work experience, taster courses or voluntary work

- apply for work, including how to prepare for the interview process.

## Promoting equality of opportunity

Learners must be provided with accurate information and advice on their rights to equal access to education, training and work. It is also important that the full range of options are explored and are not restricted to stereotypical areas of learning or work, for example, relating to gender or race.

## The role of practitioners in providing impartial information and advice

Although there will be a lead practitioner in school who has overall responsibility for information, advice and guidance, it is expected that all those supporting children and young people in school will have a role to play in implementing IAG as part of the 14–19 reforms. This includes providing impartial information, relating not only to careers, but also to a range of issues which affect young people's progress. Information, advice and guidance should be embedded in the curriculum. It may also be taught discretely as part of personal, social, health and economic education (PSHE), careers education, or work-related learning. Information and advice will be organised through group activities or on a one-to-one basis. There is also a requirement that schools work closely with the Connexions service to deliver and assess the effectiveness of this guidance.

### Functional skills

**ICT: Developing, presenting and communicating information**
You could create a leaflet on the computer that contains the names and contact details of information and advice groups that you use often in your role. You could email this leaflet to other members of the school team so that they could also use it for reference.

## Impartial advice and guidance

When providing written information such as leaflets or websites, this is likely to be factual data relating to courses of study and careers opportunities. However, when giving advice and guidance, there is a danger that the practitioner might influence the young person because of their own views, experiences and preferences. Practitioners should avoid making subjective comments, by informing young people of:

- the strengths and weaknesses of each route

- the impact that decisions at a particular stage will have on future decisions

- where to get additional information.

Impartial advice by its very nature should be objective. If you notice that a child excels in a subject or has particular skills, you may be tempted to guide young people in a particular direction. While it is important to review and discuss the young person's strengths, you must listen and take into account their personal interests and aspirations.

Danny has made excellent progress in school and has excellent achievement in a number of subjects. He is expected to gain an A–A* in science and mathematics. Danny is also interested in the media and would love to get into radio. He has just finished work experience at the local radio station. One day his science teacher reviewed his work and discussed his career ambitions. She told him that it was difficult to get into the media industry and suggested that he would be throwing away his achievements in science. She said that she would get information on careers in medical research.

- What is likely to be Danny's reaction?
- How could the teacher have remained impartial?
- What information should Danny be given?

Impartial advice must always be:

- in the best interest of the young person
- unbiased
- based upon the most up-to-date information from the local or national labour market.

## Supporting young people with special educational needs or disabilities

Children with special educational needs will need additional support and advice to ensure a smooth transition at this critical period of their life. At Year 9 practitioners must work with the young person, their family and other relevant adults (such as a Connexions advisor or health worker) to produce a transition plan. This outlines what young people need to live independently. It includes aspects such as education, employment, housing, health and transport. The local education department is then responsible for ensuring that services are put into place to support the young person to meet their goals. In Year 11 a further assessment under section 140 of the Learning and Skills Act (2000) is completed. Section 140 is similar to the transition plan as it reflects on progress and plans for the next stage of education, employment and/ or training.

### Every Child Matters

Impartial advice focuses on the individual needs of young people. It is underpinned by the outcomes set out in the Green Paper Every Child Matters:

- stay safe
- be healthy
- enjoy and achieve
- make a positive contribution
- achieve economic well-being.

# Be able to establish and address the information and advice needs of children and young people

## Encouraging participation and engagement to establish information and advice needs

From Years 7 to 11, schools have a statutory duty to provide careers education (CE). This should form a continuous cycle of review, information, advice and guidance. Many young people are unsure of their own needs and require support to reflect on their own skills and achievements and relate these to the opportunities available. This cycle is shown on the following page.

### Finding out the young person's academic and personal achievements

At the start of this cycle practitioners must start to build a picture of the young person through personal tutorials or group activities. A range of information should be discussed and recorded including:

- academic qualifications
- other qualifications for example, first aid, lifeguard
- school reports
- employer testimonials.

### Discussing interests, preferences and career aspirations

To be able to provide appropriate information, practitioners need to get to know what motivates the

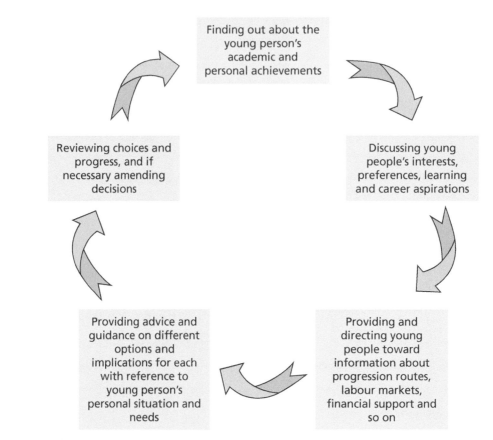

*Information, advice and guidance must be regularly reviewed.*

young person through giving them opportunities to discuss and explore their wider interests. These may be within or outside of school. Some young people may have particular skills in sport; they may be a member of a team or take part in swimming competitions, for example. Others may have interest in art or music or enjoy tinkering with engines. Finding out what makes young people tick will be the first step to finding out their preferences and needs.

Understanding the young person's background is also important. Their family and personal circumstances will also have a bearing on the advice which they require to support their smooth transition. This could be in relation to:

● the financial circumstance of the family

● level of support from parents or carers

● a special educational need or disability

● the health of other family members.

Each young person will have different aspirations, skills and interests, requiring information and advice to be adapted to meet their individual circumstances. It would not be effective to assume a 'one size fits all' approach. Discussing higher education courses with young people who are working at foundation level would be inappropriate, although they could be given information on the steps they could take towards higher level education.

## Engaging with young people

Young people may be reluctant to explore personal issues and personal aspirations. Building an effective relationship is essential to engaging with young people to establish their needs. You must consider how you will put young people at their ease by providing an environment which is conducive to this process. For example, you should consider the seating arrangements. A more informal setting with low-level seating may lead to a more relaxed and open discussion rather than a classroom.

Use active listening when trying to establish needs; it is essential to spend more time listening than speaking. Only by using active listening skills can you learn about the young person's preferences and needs. You must be particularly aware of your own body language by maintaining eye contact and having an open posture. Young people will easily pick up that you are not taking them seriously.

Young people may be reluctant to discuss their needs and perhaps guarded in the information they give about themselves. Thoughtful and open questioning can put young people at ease and help you to establish their thoughts and possibly fears. Rather than 'Did you enjoy the work experience?', you might ask, 'I noticed that your work experience report was really positive — what did you enjoy most about the work?'

## Personal, social, health and economic education (PSHE)

Personal, social, health and economic education is a non-statutory curriculum subject. There are two strands: personal well-being and economic well-being and financial capability.

Personal well-being introduces issues and develops skills which may not be covered in other subjects.

Although activities may appear not to have a direct relevance to establishing advice needs, young people will have opportunities to become engaged in discussion around a range of issues which are important to them. Group activities can help young people to recognise and identify their own potential and feel more positive about themselves. This will help pupils to extend their knowledge about life choices and reflect on their own interests and preferences. They will also be supported to develop essential skills for adulthood and the world of work such as:

- developing relationships
- learning how to deal with issues and conflict
- listening/speaking and presenting information
- organisational skills
- life—work balance
- work ethics.

Economic well-being and financial capability draws together aspects of careers education and enterprise.

*Why is positive body language important in a situation like this?*

Its purpose is to improve motivation and progression by supporting young people to manage their own finances and develop economic understanding by making links to their own career prospects. It will also help them to identify their own needs relating to financial issues.

**BEST PRACTICE CHECKLIST:** Establishing young people's needs

- Use active listening.
- Do not make assumptions.
- Start conversation with a positive reflection on the young person's interests or achievements.
- Be aware of and use strategies if necessary to overcome barriers to communication.
- Finish sessions by summarising what has been discussed.

## Selecting information from appropriate sources

You may provide paper-based sources of information or direct young people to web-based sources. It is useful to have paper-based information to refer to, to distribute and discuss in IAG sessions or display for pupils and parents. Information which is available on paper is almost always provided online too. This has the advantage of being more easily updated. Paper-based sources may include prospectuses, careers leaflets and 14–19 routes. Useful web-based sources include careers information from skills councils, local and national labour market data and **UCAS** information.

Young people should be informed of the different roles and responsibilities of individuals and the services available within the school or from external agencies.

### Key term

**UCAS** – Universities and Colleges Admissions Service, an organisation through which applications are processed for entry to higher education

## Connexions

Connexions is a local service which provides a wide range of information for practitioners and young people. This includes a careers database, job vacancies, course searches, financial and personal advice for young people, for example. Useful publications such as *Which Way Now* (for Year 9 pupils) and *It's Your Choice* (for Year 11 and 12 pupils) include activities where pupils can reflect on their own needs and choices. These are also available as interactive activities on the Connexions website given at the end of this unit. Information is available online, by telephone or through a one-to-one advisory service. Schools will work in partnership with Connexions services. They also provide support, advice and training relating to careers education and guidance to staff in schools.

### Over to you!

Find out about your local Connexions services and the name and contact details of who you can contact for advice.

## Verifying the accuracy and currency of information

Any information you provide for young people should always be checked for currency, and should contain accurate data and information. You should always:

- check the reliability and currency of data used about labour markets
- use recognised sources of information
- use materials that are appropriate for the age and stage of development of the young person
- keep abreast of changes in the local, regional and national labour markets
- seek information directly from organisations or specialists if you are unsure
- join support groups such as schools cluster groups
- seek feedback from young people, staff and others on the usefulness of information
- undertake regular training for IAG.

Young people will also need to develop their own research skills so that they can make their own decisions on the relevance, reliability and currency of materials. You should remind pupils that when searching for information on the Internet they should ensure that the information is from a reliable source such as a government or educational site. They should also ask the following questions.

- What is the purpose of the site – is it commercial, educational or a government site?

- Who is the author and what are their credentials?

- What is the date and when was it updated?

- Is it a UK site?

- Are their clear headings/subheadings and is it easy to navigate?

- Does it provide the necessary information and does it answer my questions?

### Functional skills

**ICT: Finding and selecting information**
These bullet points highlight some very important aspects to consider when using information from the Internet. Looking at the last site that you used for reference, could you answer the questions?

## Approaches to managing situations when children's choices differ from those of their carers

Parents and carers will inevitably have a direct influence on the choices made by young people. They should be kept fully informed at each stage of the support and guidance process. When parents are involved in the process of careers education there is a greater likelihood that they will be able to support their children to make informed choices. Young people will then cope more easily with transitions and feel more confident about their choices. Schools involve parents by providing information through careers evenings, inviting them to careers reviews, providing information on different career routes and the school prospectus.

Connexions provide information written specifically for parents and carers.

There may be instances, even where information has been provided, where parents and carers have different views from their children. It is important that when this occurs it is dealt with sensitively to prevent a negative impact on the young person's motivation and progress. This may happen where parents or carers:

- do not value education

- have set ideas about the career they wish their child to pursue

- overestimate or underestimate their child's educational abilities and skills

- lack knowledge and understanding about learning routes and qualifications

- have set views on pathways based on gender or culture.

You may become aware of these differences when discussing options with the young person, during a review or parents' evening, or if you work closely with the young person the parent may request a meeting. It is essential to talk through any differences. Initially these discussions will give you an understanding of why differences have occurred. These differences may be easily managed if they are because of lack of understanding about a new qualification and the value of this for the pupils' progression opportunities. Differences may also occur because of personal circumstances, preferences, views and traditions. When managing these situations, views should be fully explored with the parent or carer and the young person. Depending on the individual situation, you should:

- provide information on different pathways, subjects, qualifications and the structure and value of each

- give information on alternative routes which would lead to the same goal (the young person or the parent may not have considered an alternative and it could be a way to compromise)

- stress the young person's strengths and achievements, but be realistic about predicted grades and the implications for applications to higher-level study and career routes

- give information on financial support available (parents may not always disclose if they have difficulty)

- give information on the longer-term benefits of continuing in education such as career prospects and financial rewards

- give information on where to seek additional and/or specialist information.

Where a resolution and agreement cannot be found, it would be helpful if another adult such as a Connexions advisor could also be present.

## Reflect ?

How would you manage the following situations?

1. Viktor has told you that he is keen to study a Higher Diploma in engineering alongside mathematics, English and science GCSEs. Later he comes to you to say that his dad has said he must leave school and get a job.

2. Kerry is well motivated and has worked hard. She is studying four A levels and an AS. She is predicted to achieve grade Cs in her A levels. She said that she wants to apply for medicine as her mum wants her to follow in the family tradition. The prospectus for her chosen university shows that she will need to achieve at least three at A–A*.

3. Robert has done a lot of research on Apprenticeships; he has spoken to a local employer and has been offered a place. His dad says that Apprenticeships are a waste of time and he should stay on to do A levels as that is what employers really want.

## Functional skills 💬

**English: Speaking, listening and communication**
The situations in the Reflect could be used as good discussion starters. When holding a discussion, think carefully about the language that you use and try to keep the discussion moving.

# Be able to provide children and young people with appropriate information and advice to enable them to make informed choices

## The importance of providing opportunities to make informed choices

Once needs have been established, there must be opportunities for young people to explore all options to enable them to choose their preferred route. They must be aware that choices at each stage will have implications on their future progress. They will have many questions which will need to be answered to support their decisions. These opportunities will be available through targeted careers information sessions, and work-related learning.

### Work-related learning

Work-related learning supports young people to develop their knowledge, understanding and skills about issues related to work. It may involve:

- work experience

- enterprise activities

- careers education.

Participation in the range of work-related activities helps to raise young people's awareness of the options available to them.

### Work experience

Work experience is encouraged in many schools to engage young people. This will be organised in different ways depending on the school curriculum, timetable and the young person's needs. Some courses have a work experience element. Young people who choose the Apprenticeship route will study alongside work. It is important that the experience is used effectively to help young people to focus on their own skills and interests, and practitioners should give young people time

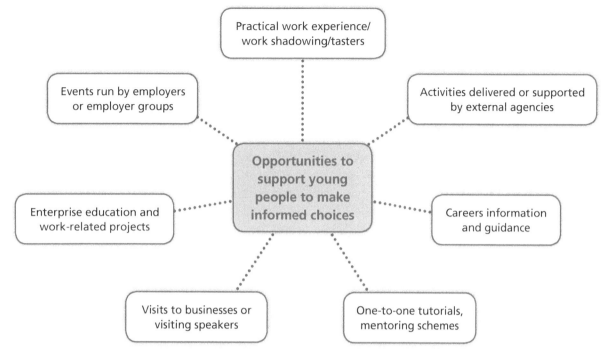

*How many of the opportunities above are available at your school?*

to reflect on the experience. Work experience may help learners to make decisions about their future by gaining an insight into different industries and roles.

## Enterprise education

Enterprise education is a statutory component of work-related learning at Key Stage 4. Enterprise activity takes place over the equivalence of five days. During enterprise, young people must undertake an activity which develops a 'can do' attitude and develops the necessary skills to progress in learning or employment. There are wide-ranging examples of enterprise activities. These may be carried out in a work placement, in partnership with a local business or linked to school activities. Being engaged in an activity will require pupils to:

- generate ideas and make decisions
- plan
- overcome problems
- monitor progress
- evaluate outcomes.

### CASE STUDY: Being enterprising

Ofsted describes the following enterprise project carried out in one school.

'Graphic design students were set the task of designing a more up-to-date and attractive logo for a local company. They worked with a graphic design consultant to produce a design which was eventually used by the company. The work also contributed to the students' portfolio of assessed coursework. The activity proved highly motivational and resulted in some very good-quality work.'

- What are the benefits of this type of participation?
- How will this activity help pupils to make informed choices?

## Careers education

Schools have a statutory duty to provide careers education in Key Stages 3 and 4, and beyond this stage for pupils with a statement of special educational needs or disability. The purpose of careers education is to present information, advice and guidance which will help young people to make informed decisions based upon impartial, accurate and up-to-date information. It should also support young people to manage transitions to higher education and employment. Participation should take place at regular intervals in the young person's time at school (see page 306 for information on the IAG cycle). Careers education may be delivered by a careers teacher within the school or by an external agency, or a combination of both. It should also be embedded into the school's curriculum to help young people to see the relationship between subjects and work opportunities.

## CASE STUDY: Challenging stereotypes

Alex is a teaching assistant. Last year he undertook training in IAG and now supports young people in making decisions about their learning and career options. Over the last two weeks, during small group discussions he has overheard the following.

1. Two Year 11 pupils have been researching different pathways and have been looking at Apprenticeships. One pupil who is keen on a career in engineering said that he was considering an Apprenticeship when he had completed his A levels. His friend told him that Apprenticeships were only for people who had poor results and he should apply to university.

2. A group of Year 9 pupils were researching materials about different careers. One of the boys sorted out the leaflets and gave information about traditionally female careers to one of the girls, saying, 'I think you will be more interested in these leaflets.'

- How should Alex respond in each situation?
- What activities could Alex introduce to challenge misunderstandings and stereotypes?

## Evaluating with the young people the choices available to them

It is essential that young people know the range of options open to them and the various routes which will enable them to achieve their career goals. The 14–19 reforms have widened choice through providing four main pathways: GCSEs, 14–19 Diplomas, Apprenticeships or Foundation Learning. The choice can seem quite daunting for young people. It is not only about selecting a subject which they enjoy but the level of qualification, the way they learn and the method of assessment.

### Functional skills

**ICT: Developing, presenting and communicating information**
You could use a software package on the computer like Microsoft® Word® to create a flow chart that shows the pupils the options available to them for their career progression once they have completed school.

### Link

For more information on each pathway, see TDA 3.14, Support delivery of the 14–19 curriculum.

### Knowledge into action

Research each of the four available pathways and availability of different subjects in your locality. Go on to find out about the structure of each, levels, method of learning, how young people will be assessed, any work requirements and so on.

### Choices in Key Stage 4

In Years 8 or 9, young people must begin to make decisions about what they will study in Years 10 and 11 (Key Stage 4). Pupils must understand the subjects that they must continue to study and understand the importance of these for their future learning and work opportunities. Some specialist schools may expect young people to include particular subjects.

*Which route will lead to my chosen career?*

In addition to these subjects, young people will also have an entitlement to work-related learning including enterprise. The statutory curriculum and options are explored more fully in TDA 3.14.

GCSEs are a more traditional route and are valued by schools and employers. However, many young people are now selecting an alternative pathway such as Apprenticeships or Diplomas. Choices can become complex as young people are not restricted to one pathway. Within each pathway there are further choices — there are increasing numbers of vocational GCSEs, Diplomas offer 14 lines of learning and there are almost 200 Apprenticeships. No single school can offer the whole range of subjects across the different pathways on offer so it is important that young people are informed of the opportunities available in their local area. This may be offered in partner schools or local colleges.

For some young people a work-based route may be more appropriate. Apprenticeships can be a good choice for children who prefer hands-on activity but should not be viewed as only for pupils who are not progressing or who are disengaged. Apprenticeships can lead to higher education such as Foundation degrees and are a good alternative to more traditional forms of study. You should also be aware of the widening choice at Foundation Stage. Some pupils may still not be ready to progress to advanced level studies but they still require challenge and a course of study which will motivate them.

At this stage young people will need to know about:

● the pathways and range of subject areas

● how each qualification is structured, its content and how each will be assessed

● where they will be able to study — whether it will mean attending another setting

● how their choice will help them to progress to further learning or work

● what support is available, including financial support.

## Functional skills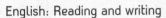

### English: Reading and writing

You could select a pathway that a young person may take — for example, an Apprenticeship or Diploma — and produce a leaflet that summarises the information you have gathered about that pathway. This would develop both your reading and writing skills. Think carefully about the age of the reader so that you can make sure that the language in your leaflet is suitable.

## Choices post-16

In Years 10 and 11 young people will have to consider their options post-16. Young people will require detailed advice and guidance about what is available and the implications for their progression into higher education or into work at 18. They must choose whether to:

- stay in education — many pupils may be still unsure about the career they want to pursue and may need advice on subjects and learning pathways which will allow them to keep their options open

- choose an Apprenticeship — these are for young people who have clear ideas on the career they wish to pursue

- go directly into work — pupils who choose this should be given advice on the implications of entering work directly and the advantages of seeking work with training.

Young people will need to know about:

- the different pathways and subjects offered locally

- grades required to secure a place on a higher level course or to apply for work

- skills required for higher level learning or work

- where they can study

- the local and national labour market

- opportunities for training alongside work

- opportunities for foundation learning if level 2 is not appropriate

- how to apply for further study or work.

## Portfolio activity

Consider the following examples and what type of information and advice may be required.

1. Paul is in Year 9 and struggling with academic subjects. He receives additional support in mathematics and English and he is predicted to achieve D–E in GCSEs in these subjects. He admits that he does not like school and has a high absence record. Paul never seems to sit still and lacks concentration. He spends much of his spare time watching or participating in sports.

2. Claire is in Year 11 and starting to think about her career options. Claire achieved an A grade in her higher Diploma in Environmental and Land-based Studies, and good grades in English, mathematics and science. She has now progressed to the Advanced Diploma in this line of learning. She undertook work experience at her local parks department. She really enjoyed the work but feels unsure if as a female she will have opportunities for advancement.

## How to check that the young person has understood the range of options available

Information about the range of options can be confusing so it is important that young people are given time to explore and ask questions so they are able to digest the information. Opportunities and time must be given to enable young people to explore materials and review learning. You will need to:

- check understanding

- summarise, particularly where information is complex or lengthy

- present information clearly and logically

- invite feedback, to find out if the information you are giving is appropriate for the pupils.

## CASE STUDY: Checking understanding

Gina is a teaching assistant who supports careers education in Year 11. Following a visit from a local employer to discuss Apprenticeships, Gina gave pupils Post-it® Notes™ and asked them to write down questions concerning any aspects of Apprenticeships about which they still felt unsure. Any questions which could not be answered following the talk were researched and answered at the next careers session.

- How might this strategy help Gina to establish if the pupils had a good understanding of Apprenticeships?
- What other strategy might she have used in this session?

## Skills builder

Carry out a mini research project into young people's understanding of the options available to them. You could produce a questionnaire with questions such as the work placement requirements of a Diploma or what subjects are compulsory. You could summarise the results and share with other staff to help you to understand young people's misconceptions.

## Recording the interaction following all organisational procedures and legal requirements

When supporting young people with IAG, it is essential that you understand the boundaries of your own role and responsibilities in obtaining and recording information.

A trusting relationship which encourages young people to be open and honest about their feelings, concerns and needs can only be developed if confidentiality is observed. Your school will have policies and procedures which you must adhere to when recording any interactions with children and/or their parents.

Policies regarding confidentiality are underpinned by the principles set out in the Data Protection Act 1998.

## Over to you!

Find out about ways that information is recorded (there may be school record forms available on an electronic system), where it is stored and who has access to information.

When discussing a young person's needs and providing advice, it is important that you explain that you will need to make notes to help you to support them and that any personal information discussed will be treated confidentially. You should also explain that this may mean that you need to pass on information to others who can help, with their consent. When recording information you must ensure that it is:

- relevant
- up-to-date
- objective
- stored securely.

If a young person tells you information which indicates that they are at risk of harm or abuse, you must advise them that you cannot keep the information confidential and that you have a duty to pass this on to your manager or the designated person responsible for safeguarding. For more information, refer to CYP 3.3 Understand how to safeguard the well-being of children and young people.

## Functional skills

**Maths: Interpreting**
You could speak to the Year 11 tutors and find out the destinations of last year's learners. From this you could do a mathematical study on what percentage of learners went on to FE, work, Apprenticeships and so on. You could display your results in a table or graph.

## Getting ready for assessment

At this stage you should begin to build a folder with IAG information. You could collect a range of current information such as:

- prospectuses from your own school and local sixth forms and colleges

- information on different pathways available such as Diplomas or Apprenticeships.

- leaflets on career pathways.

It will also be beneficial to obtain the advice and guidance booklets from Connexions – or even carry out the interactive activities online.

You should also begin to develop your skills so that you are able to demonstrate these to achieve learning outcomes 2 and 3. You could work alongside an experienced careers advisor for a number of sessions, taking time to discuss the outcomes. When you feel ready, you could provide support yourself and ask for feedback and use this to reflect on your own strengths and areas you need to improve.

## Functional skills

**English: Speaking, listening and communication**
By working alongside a careers advisor, you will be using all the skills that you have developed in speaking, listening and communication. It may be useful to write some notes as you observe what they do, so you have something to look back at to support you when you are working independently.

## Check your knowledge

1. Which piece of legislation sets out the statutory requirement for schools to provide information, advice and guidance to young people from Year 7 to Year 11?

2. Identify two curriculum subject areas which support the delivery of careers education.

3. Identify the four main pathways at Key Stage 4.

4. Identify a government agency which supports schools to deliver careers education.

5. What is Foundation Learning and why might it be appropriate for some young people?

6. Give three reasons why young people's choices might differ from those of their carers.

7. Suggest three ways that you can check if young people have understood the information you have provided.

8. Which legislation underpins a school's confidentiality policy?

## Websites

**www.apprenticeships.org.uk** – information about Apprenticeships

**www.cegnet.co.uk** – supporting careers education and training

**www.connexions-direct.com** – information and advice service for young people

**www.direct.gov.uk** – Diploma information

**www.hestem.ac.uk** – HE STEM programme (science, technology, engineering and maths)

**www.nationalcurriculum.co.uk** – National Curriculum

**www.ssatrust.org.uk** – Specialist Schools and Academies Trust (SSAT)

**www.teachernet.gov.uk** – TeacherNet

**www.ucas.ac.uk** – UCAS

**www.ukces.org.uk** – information on the Sector Skills Councils

For this unit you will need to understand the policies and procedures for conducting tests and examinations. You will also be required to demonstrate your own skills in preparing, implementing and ending tests and examinations. Your skills will need to be shown in relation to preparing and setting up examination rooms. You must demonstrate that you are not only able to follow the centre's procedures for tests and examinations, but are also able to respond appropriately to unexpected situations which may occur, including emergencies.

## By the end of this unit you will:

1. understand policy and procedures for the conduct of tests and examinations
2. be able to prepare for tests and examinations
3. be able to prepare candidates for tests and examinations
4. be able to implement invigilation requirements
5. be able to end tests and examinations.

# Understand policy and procedures for the conduct of tests and examinations

## Explain the centre's tests and examinations policy

Before exploring policy and procedures, it is useful to consider the role of the invigilator. This person has a critical role to ensure that all candidates have equal opportunity to demonstrate their knowledge, understanding or skills. The invigilator has the responsibility to:

● help to prepare the room

● conduct a test or examination

● uphold the integrity of tests and examinations

● ensure the security and confidentiality of papers before and after tests and examinations

● prevent **malpractice**

● ensure confidentiality and security of candidate scripts

● deal effectively with emergency situations.

> **Key term**
>
> **Malpractice** – improper conduct or negligence

All centres which administer tests and examinations must have clear policies and procedures in place. These must comply with regulations for conducting examinations.

Examinations and tests may be set internally by the centre or externally by an examination board. For external examinations, including general and vocational qualifications, the Joint Council for Qualifications (JCQ) has produced Instructions for Conducting Examinations. These instructions are sometimes referred to as ICE. Centre policies and procedures must comply with these instructions. They are updated each year so it is important that you familiarise yourself with the current instructions before each examination or test.

Procedure may differ according to the types of examination, for example:

● written examination

● practical examinations such as for science or art

● on-screen tests.

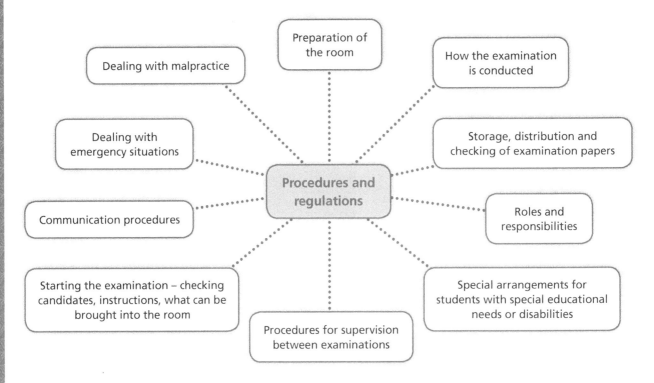

*Procedures and regulations.*

Obtain a copy of your centre's policy and procedures for administering examinations and procedures. Also obtain the current JCQ document *Instructions for Conducting Examinations*. You should be able to obtain a copy of these documents from the centre's examinations officer.

**English: Reading**
You could develop your reading skills by reading both documents and then writing a short summary of the policies and procedures that you follow.

## Procedures and regulations for the conduct of external examinations and any inspection procedures

The head of the centre has overall responsibility to ensure that external examinations are conducted in line with JCQ regulations. As an invigilator it is important that you understand policy and procedures, and are able to conduct the examination in line with awarding body regulations. The conduct of examinations may be inspected at any time by JCQ officials. An inspector may visit the examination room. They must carry an identity card or a letter of authority to do this. They will usually report to the examination officer from the centre, who will accompany them during the inspection.

## Access arrangements that may be required for candidates with additional needs

To ensure that candidates have equality of access to the assessment process, **reasonable adjustments** or **special considerations** may be required. As an invigilator you should be aware of the special arrangements for individual candidates. The Joint Council for Qualifications set out clear guidelines for centres on situations where there may be special arrangements.

**Reasonable adjustments** — arrangements agreed before examination to reduce the effects of 'substantial disadvantage' because of an additional need or disability. Reasonable adjustments must be made in line with the Disability Discrimination Act 1995

**Special considerations** — adjustments made to marks or grades, after the examination, because of a temporary situation which is likely to affect the candidate's performance

Reasonable adjustments may be applied for when a candidate is known to have:

- additional learning needs
- sensory needs
- physical needs
- behavioural or emotional needs.

Adjustments may include:

- additional support, for example, a scribe, signer, reader or practical assistant
- using different methods of recording knowledge and understanding, for example, use of a word processor or voice input system
- additional time (usually between 10 and 20 per cent) or supervised breaks
- modified papers, for example, enlarged text, coloured paper, Braille papers
- an alternative room or particular position in the examination room, for example, space for wheelchair access, close to a door if breaks are required.

The adjustments or access arrangements will be varied and depend upon the candidate's individual needs; however, they should not give the candidate an unfair advantage. For example, support staff using sign language must interpret the information accurately and not provide additional information. A practical assistant may not help a candidate with a task which is assessing the candidate's ability to perform.

## Special considerations

Special considerations will be given to candidates who experience physical or emotional difficulties immediately before or during an examination. In these situations, applications for consideration can be submitted to allow adjustments to be made during the marking process. The amount of consideration will depend upon the severity of the difficulty experienced by the candidate. This may vary from serious events such as the death of a close family member through to less serious events, such as the candidate suffering severe hay fever on the day of examination.

---

### CASE STUDY: Reasonable adjustments

Jamie is an A-level candidate. He has cerebral palsy which particularly affects his ability to use his left hand. Jamie will be sitting his A-level science examination in the summer term so the centre applies for an adjustment to be made. The reason given is that there is a practical element to the examination. Jamie would find it difficult to set up equipment to carry out an experiment as it would require the use of two hands.

Amina is a Society, Health and Development Diploma candidate. She has a good understanding of the units she has studied but has dyslexia, so finds it difficult to express her understanding clearly. Her handwriting often becomes illegible if she tries to write quickly or is under pressure.

- What adjustment is likely to be agreed for each of these candidates?
- How can the centre ensure that these adjustments do not give the candidates an unfair advantage?

---

## Procedures for responding to health, safety and security emergencies

The centre policy must include procedures to follow in the event of an emergency. Candidates must never be left unsupervised so there should be a way of communicating if it is necessary to call for help – for example, if a candidate is taken ill or is injured during an examination. This may be a two-way radio, mobile phone or a person situated outside the room to take messages. Procedures and paperwork will be in place for reporting any incidents which occur.

There must also be procedures if an evacuation is necessary in the event of fire, gas or bomb threat. The JCQ provide guidelines for emergency situations. The school's policy must adhere to this but may also include additional procedures relating to the particular circumstances in the school, such as the layout, staffing availability or communication systems that are in place. As with normal procedures during evacuation, candidates must leave their belongings, including examination papers, in the room. Once outside the building, the candidates must not communicate with each other or with other pupils or students at the centre, as examination regulations still apply. This rule, which will be explained later in the unit, must be stated at the start of the examination. It is important as an invigilator to take a register and room plan with you to ensure that the examination can be restarted efficiently. The procedures will include:

- stopping the examination
- how candidates should evacuate the room
- supervision of candidates when out of the room
- restarting the examination
- recording and reporting events.

## Why a candidate may need to be supervised between tests and examinations

In some situations, candidates may require supervision outside of the examination time.

During periods when there are a number of external tests and examinations, it is inevitable that there may be a clash in timetabling. When candidates have two or more examinations scheduled for the same session, one or more may need to be held earlier or later in the day. If the candidate sits an examination early, they must be supervised until at least an hour after the published start time for that examination.

In unusual circumstances candidates may have three or more examinations scheduled for the same day. Where the total examination time is more than six hours at level 3 or more than five and a half hours for level 1 or 2 qualifications, candidates may need to sit one of the examinations the following day. This will mean overnight supervision including travel to and from the centre. In these circumstances supervision can be carried out by a member of staff at the centre or the candidate's own parents or carer. The centre must be satisfied that there will be no infringements and complete a JCQ Timetable Variation and Confidentiality Declaration form.

The supervisor must follow the same regulations as the invigilator. This is to ensure that the examination is carried out fairly and the candidate does not have the opportunity to share information about the examination with other candidates.

# Be able to prepare for tests and examinations

## Correct procedures for setting up an examination room

Setting the room up in preparation for an examination is critical for the smooth running of the examination. It is important that you arrive early to ensure that everything is in place before candidates arrive. This includes checking the room layout and that sealed examination papers, stationery and ensuring that any specialist equipment is available and working. The room should be comfortable for candidates with adequate heating, lighting and ventilation. The room should be situated where noise levels can be kept at a minimum.

Your centre may have its own policy but this will need to comply with the requirements of the examination board.

### Written examinations
It is likely that the tables and chairs will be set up for you, but the invigilator must ensure that the layout complies with JCQ regulations and/or specific requirements of the particular examination. Normally the desks must all be front-facing, but for practical art examinations using easels, these may need to face inwards. Space between tables must be at least 1.25 metres. If classrooms are used, it may be necessary to remove work or information relating to the subject of the examination which would give an unfair advantage to candidates.

### Functional skills

**Maths: Representing**
You could do a scale drawing of the room that you work in. On your scale drawing you could add the maximum number of exam tables that would fit based on them being set 1.25 metres apart. How many exams could take place in your classroom? What percentage of the year group could sit their exam in your classroom?

*What effect do you think external noise has on candidates?*

## On-screen tests

You may be required to invigilate on-screen or ICT tests or examinations. Rooms for on-screen tests will require a layout which does not allow candidates to view the screens of others. The appropriate software should have been downloaded in preparation. If information is to be printed, it is important to check that printers are working and stocked with ink, toner and adequate paper. Technical support should be available.

## Information for students

Essential information for candidates must be clearly displayed. Regulations and warnings to candidates must be displayed both inside and outside the examination room to ensure that students entering the examination room know about the rules. These are provided by the JCQ and available as A3 posters. They can be obtained from the centre's examination department. It is important that you are familiar and understand these so that you are able to answer any questions that a candidate may have in relation to them. Posters will include:

- regulations for on-screen tests
- regulations for written examinations
- warnings to candidates — for example, about mobile phones.

Other information which must be clearly displayed is more specific to the centre and the particular test or examination(s) being conducted. This includes:

- notices in corridors and outside the room stating that an examination is in progress
- the seating plan
- a clock which is accurate and can be clearly viewed by all candidates
- the centre number (the centre's unique number which candidates must write on their answer paper).

As the test or examination commences, the invigilator must also display the start time and end time of the examination.

**SEATING PLAN**

| DATE | MAY 25TH 2010 | | TIME 9.30 | |
|------|--------------|---|-----------|---|
| EDEXCEL | GCSE | ENGLISH LITERATURE HIGHER | 12133H | 2 HRS 15 MINS |
| AQA | GCE | HUMAN BIOLOGY | HB101 | 1 HR 30 MINS |

FRONT OF HALL

| A | B | C | D | E |
|---|---|---|---|---|
| James Smith Candidate No 8002 12133H | Paul Foster Candidate No 8008 12133H | Salma Begum Candidate No 8014 12133H | Lauren Williamson Candidate 8020 12133H | Mandeep Sandhu Candidate No 4017 HB101 |
| Eleanor Whitehouse Candidate No 8003 12133H | Amit Choudhuri Candidate No 8009 12133H | Harry Baxter Candidate No 8015 12133H | Elizabeth Fielding Candidate No 8021 12133H | Kirstie Allen Candidate No4018 HB101 |
| Paul Adams Candidate No 8004 12133H | Zara Fisher Candidate No 8010 12133H | Melanie Price Candidate No 8016 12133H | Richard Blake Candidate No 8022 12133H | Sukhdeep Singh Candidate No 4019 HB101 |
| Grace Reynolds Candidate No 8005 12133H | Scott Davies Candidate No 8011 12133H | Amy Ward Candidate No 8017 12133H | Scott Davies Candidate No 4014 HB101 | Neil Peters Candidate No 4020 HB101 |
| Kirandeep Kaur Candidate No8006 12133H | Samit Patel Candidate No 8012 12133H | Sian Williams Candidate No 8018 12133H | Isabel Sanderson Candidate No 4015 HB101 | Leon Brown Candidate No 4021 HB101 |
| Amy Ward Candidate No 8007 12133H | Jade Summers Candidate No 8013 12133H | Kate Madeley Candidate No 8019 12133H | Michelle Cross Candidate No 4016 HB101 | |

*An example of a seating plan.*

## Supplies of authorised stationery and materials

As an invigilator, your responsibility is to ensure that you have the correct stationery, examination papers and any other materials. This will include the examination papers and sufficient supplies of authorised stationery – for example, additional answer sheets appropriate for the examination (such as lined or graph paper) and security tags to attach loose papers. If the examination is online, the software will be downloaded in preparation for the examination.

## Arrangements for the safe custody of question papers and other materials

The question papers will have arrived at the centre well before the examination takes place. There are strict regulations about the checking and storage of papers. There will be authorised persons – usually the examinations officer, head teacher or deputy head teacher – who will receive the papers. They must check that the correct papers have been sent and that they have not been tampered with. If there are concerns, these must be reported. There are also strict rules about where test and examination papers or electronic test materials should be kept. This must be a safe or secure cabinet which is bolted to a wall or floor. Keys or security codes must be held only by the authorised staff.

After the exam, the candidate examination scripts, question papers, registers and seating plans must be returned to the examination office immediately. The centre must keep all scripts confidential and secure. Scripts must be sent to the relevant awarding body on the same day as the exam wherever possible.

The invigilator is responsible for the examination papers once these are collected or delivered by the examinations officer. The invigilator must ensure that the examination papers are:

● kept secure until the start of the examination

● not removed during the examination – by candidates or centre staff

● returned at the end of the examination.

Find out where examination papers are stored in your own centre and who is responsible for checking and ensuring the security of these.

When collecting examination papers, it is important that you check they are correct, for example, the correct level of examination, subject and code, before opening the pack. This should be done before candidates enter the room. If there is any doubt, you must contact the examinations officer immediately. On some occasions where there is an error in an examination paper, an **erratum notice** will be provided. Examination papers must never be left unattended once they have been collected and are normally left in their packets until the start of the examination. Where there are timed assessments which require candidates to complete assessment over more than one session, papers must be collected and kept securely between sessions.

**Key term**

**Erratum notice** – a list of corrected errors in the examination paper

## Specific requirements for the test or examination and/or the candidates involved

There may be specific requirements for the test or examination so it is important that you take time to read through instructions carefully so that you can give unambiguous guidance to the candidates. Specific requirements describe any changes to the usual examination procedures. For instance, regulations may state that candidates must spend a specific length of time reading through a case study before they are allowed to start writing. For some examinations candidates are allowed to use set books or dictionaries.

As an invigilator you must also know any specific requirements for groups or individual candidates, such as those explained in the previous section of this unit. Requirements may be in relation to additional time, support or specialist equipment. Candidates who have specific requirements should be identified on the register and it is also good practice if these candidates are identified on the invigilator's seating plan. When preparing for the examination you should check with the examinations officer or a senior invigilator if the information about specific requirements, in relation to the examination or individual candidates, is unclear.

## Checking any emergency communication system if available

However well prepared they may be, it is essential that the invigilator is able to summon emergency help or advice from the examinations officer or authorised person via an efficient communication system. This may be a two-way radio or a mobile phone (which is set to silent). Some centres may have a person positioned outside the examination room who can take messages. Before the examination, it is important to test the communication system.

# Be able to prepare candidates for tests and examinations

## The importance of having the examination room ready at the scheduled time

Examinations are a stressful time for all candidates. Being well prepared is essential for the smooth running of examinations and will:

- create a calm atmosphere as candidates enter the room
- ensure that the examination begins on time
- reduce the risk of errors or malpractice.

## Correct procedures for admitting candidates into the room and performing necessary checks

You will need to perform checks for:

- verifying the identity of the candidates
- ensuring that no inadmissible equipment or materials are brought into the examination room

- confirming candidates are seated according to the seating plan
- ensuring that candidates have the correct papers and materials.

It is likely that, even where you may be the only invigilator, you will be supported by other staff at the start of the examination. A register of all candidates who are entered for the examination must be available so that you can check the identity of individuals as they enter the room. Where there are external candidates who are not known to the centre they must produce evidence of their identity. Candidates who have access to the seating plan before entering the room can then walk directly to their seat. It is important that candidates understand that examination conditions are in place the moment they enter the room.

Only authorised materials must be available for candidates. Any materials, coats and bags will ideally be left outside the examination room but where these are allowed to be taken into the room, they should be placed well away from the candidates. Candidates must not have access to electronic equipment such as mobile phones, mp3 players, reading pens or any other storage devices. Examination papers normally state where calculators may or may not be used. Unless there is advice on the examination paper to the contrary, calculators may be used. Dictionaries may not be used unless there are specific instructions. Pencil cases may be taken in to the room but must be transparent. If candidates bring other types of pencil cases, they must remove the contents.

Although there will be notices outside the room, it is important that candidates are reminded to remove any unauthorised materials before the examination begins. You must also remind them that any items found after the examination begins will be removed and treated as malpractice.

The centre will also have its own policy on food or drink that can be taken into the examination room. This may depend upon the length of the examination and individual needs of candidates. The policy must be in line with regulations. For example, if drinks and food are allowed all packaging and labels must be removed.

*What would you do if a student's mobile phone rang during the exam?*

## Before the examination

Once the candidates are seated, the invigilator must make final checks that they are prepared for starting the test or examination. A final check should be made that candidates are seated according to the plan. The invigilator must have a register of candidates and a copy of the plan. At this stage the invigilator must also check that there are no bags, coats or other inadmissible equipment or materials within reach of the candidates. A final check should also be made on the examination papers and any materials which are required.

## Procedures for candidates who are not on the list or who arrive late

There may be instances where there is a candidate listed who does not show or a candidate appears who is not on the list. If a candidate does not attend, they may have been officially withdrawn from the examination. The candidate's name and examination number should have been crossed out by the exams officer, but on rare occasions this may not have been done. If a candidate does not show, it is important to notify the examinations officer so that the candidate can be contacted immediately. If a candidate appears who is not on the list, their name should be added to the register and a report sent to the exams officer. It is important to check if there is a separate register

which may have been missed. Always check with the examinations officer if you have concerns or believe there is a discrepancy.

## Candidates who arrive late

Candidates who arrive late may be allowed to sit the test or examination, but this is at the discretion of individual centres. You must check your centre's policy on this before the exam begins. If the candidate is allowed into the examination room, it is important to keep the disruption to a minimum.

Candidates are classed as very late if they arrive one hour after the start of the examination, for examinations with a duration of more than one hour, or if they arrive 30 minutes after the start of an examination with a duration of under one hour. In this instance, even if the centre's policy allows the candidate to sit the examination, an official report form, provided by the JCQ, must be completed and sent to the awarding body. The invigilator must warn the candidate that the awarding body may not accept the script. This report must include the reasons for the late arrival. The invigilator must note the time of arrival for late or very late candidates. They can be allowed the full time of the examination.

### Reflect

Read through your centre's examination policy. Do you know:

- the rules for late candidates
- the procedures for candidates who do not show for an examination
- where inadmissible equipment and materials are stored during the examination
- whether food or drink are allowed?

### Functional skills

**English: Writing**
Once you have found out the information mentioned above, you could produce a leaflet for candidates containing all the information. Think carefully about your audience and make sure that the language that you use is suitable for the age of your readers.

# Be able to implement invigilation requirements

## Ensuring all rules and regulations are strictly applied and followed

The rules and regulations for examinations are very clear and agreed by the major awarding bodies. The invigilator must understand the rules and regulations. A checklist for invigilators is available within the JCQ ICE document. This should be readily available and referred to before each examination. If for any reason the regulations are not adhered to, it will constitute malpractice and the centre will be sanctioned. When rules and regulations are not followed, the result may be:

- a candidate or group of candidates being given an unfair advantage
- candidates not being able to demonstrate their knowledge, understanding and skills
- a candidate or group of candidates is not allowed reasonable adjustment which would give them equality of access
- the integrity of the qualification is compromised
- the reputation of the centre or the awarding body is damaged
- confidentiality is compromised.

## Giving clear and unambiguous instructions to candidates

When all the checks have been made and the candidates have the correct papers and any required materials, you must start the examination promptly. Candidates may be anxious at this stage and may find more difficulty in understanding instructions. The JCQ provides information on the instructions which must be given.

Instructions must be clear and unambiguous. For example, rather than, 'As there are different examinations happening today it's important that examination papers are checked,' you could say, 'Check that you have the correct paper for your subject and level.' The following information (see Table 1 below) must be given before the start of the examination.

### On-screen tests

When invigilating on-screen tests, additional information must be given. This must include:

- how to check that they are logged on correctly
- ways to navigate the screen
- how to call for technical help.

### Written tests and examinations

Candidates must also be given instructions on how they must or must not write information on answer

| Information for candidates | Reasons |
|---|---|
| The fact that examination regulations apply and they must not communicate with other candidates | Candidates must understand that examination rules apply until they leave the room and that any breach of the rules will result in disqualification. |
| How to attract the invigilator's attention | Candidates must raise a hand so they do not disturb other candidates. |
| Checking that they have the correct paper | Asking candidates to do this will ensure no errors have been made when distributing papers. There may be more than one examination taking place in the room or candidates with the same or similar names. |
| Instructions on the front of the paper | Reading these out to the candidates ensures that they take time to think about what they must do rather than beginning the paper immediately. |
| Any erratum notices | The awarding body may have sent notices about mistakes in the text or diagrams. Read these out to draw candidates' attention to this. |
| Emergency procedures | Candidates must be clear on what to do if they must evacuate the room and that examination regulations still apply. |

Table 1: Information required for candidates, and reasons why.

books. This information includes the importance of using black ink, including rough work on the stationery provided, crossing out rough work, not using correction pens, highlighters or pale gel pens within answers. Candidates must also understand the importance of entering their full name, reference number and any other personal details which may be required. It is important that, as an invigilator, you are aware of any particular information which must be given in relation to individual examinations – for example, art examinations or on-screen tests.

When instructions are given, you must very clearly state the duration of the exam and finally the instruction to start. The JCQ advises invigilators to use the simple statement, 'You may start now.' You should immediately write up the start and end time of the examination on a board which can be seen by all candidates.

### Knowledge into action

Read through the instructions for starting an exam and write your own script in clear and unambiguous language which you can use when starting an examination.

## Correct procedures for completing an attendance register

You will need to know the correct procedures for completing an attendance register including specific requirements for candidates who are:

● withdrawn from a test or examination

● not on the register

● late for a test or examination

● absent from a test or examination.

The register will be provided by the examination office. It must be completed before the end of the examination and handed in with the scripts. You must follow the centre and awarding body requirements for completing the register. The information will show candidates who are:

● present

● absent

● added as they are not listed on the register

● late.

*How does seeing this information benefit candidates?*

## The centre's procedures for dealing with issues during an examination

It is inevitable that you will need to deal with queries or other issues during an examination, so it is important that you are equipped to do this. It is essential that you know what **not** to do as well as the correct action to take.

Consider some of the issues which you may need to deal with as an invigilator (see diagram below).

The centre's policy will outline the procedures to take, but these must reflect the regulations set out by the JCQ and/or awarding body. You may need to take action immediately and record the action you have taken and report it at the end of the examination. For example, a mobile telephone must be removed from the candidate and turned off; a first-aider must be summoned immediately if a candidate is taken ill. Other issues may need to be recorded and reported later, such as concerns about a candidate who asks to leave the room on more than one occasion.

Candidates may cause a disturbance intentionally or unintentionally. Individuals who are nervous may tap their feet or a pen. A quiet word may be all that is needed. It is important that you consider other candidates when taking action and do not add to the disturbance. In some instances, however, such as a serious noise nuisance or a fire alarm, there will be a requirement to stop and start the examination again. Additional time should then be added. Accurate records must be kept on the time the examination was stopped and the reason why.

### Leaving the room

There may be occasions when candidates ask to leave the room during an examination. This may be:

● to use toilet facilities

● because they feel ill

● because they are unable to answer more questions

● because they have finished the examination.

When a candidate needs to leave the examination room temporarily, they must always be accompanied by a responsible person. This may be done by a second invigilator or by summoning another person. The candidate may be allowed to add the time they miss to the end of the examination, so the time they leave and restart must be logged. This will be at the discretion of the individual centre.

Candidates may want to leave the examination early because they feel unable to respond to the questions or they finish the test early. Regulations require candidates to remain in the examination room for at least 30 minutes for an examination with a duration of under one hour, and at least 60 minutes for an examination with a duration over one hour. Your centre must comply with these minimum times but may have additional rules and procedures. It is important to remind a candidate who requests to leave early that they may not return to the examination. There will also be a policy and procedure on the latest time a candidate can leave the examination room, as this can cause a disturbance for other candidates.

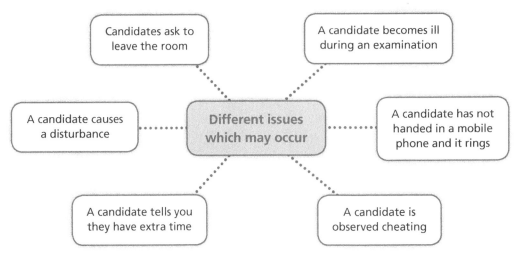

*You must know what to do if these issues occur.*

**BEST PRACTICE CHECKLIST:** Invigilating tests and examinations

**Always:**

- remain calm when dealing with new issues
- be vigilant and keep a record of any disturbance and the time it happened
- record details of any concerns of cheating and report them immediately
- change your position in the room regularly, ensuring all candidates remain in view
- keep evidence of any cheating
- respond quickly if a candidate raises their arm.

**Never:**

- leave candidates unattended or undertake other tasks
- take a decision about whether a candidate can continue with an examination
- stand over a candidate as they work
- talk to other invigilators unless it is essential
- allow a candidate back into the examination room if they leave early
- agree that there is an error in the paper unless this information was given by the awarding body.

When in doubt, you must call for advice.

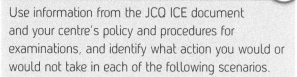

**Skills builder**

Use information from the JCQ ICE document and your centre's policy and procedures for examinations, and identify what action you would or would not take in each of the following scenarios.

1. A candidate raises their hand and asks advice on the meaning of a technical word within a science examination paper.

2. A candidate tells you that because they have dyslexia they are always allowed 25 per cent extra time in their examinations.

3. During the examination you notice that a candidate is wearing ear phones.

4. One candidate has not been writing and asks to leave the examination room after 15 minutes.

# Be able to end tests and examinations

## Demonstrate the correct procedures for ending tests and examinations

As when you start the examination, you must also give clear and unambiguous information at the end of the examination. You must stop the exam in line with the end time displayed and the examination clock. At this time you must clearly ask candidates to stop writing and put down all writing materials. You must also ask candidates to stay in their seats until all scripts have been collected. For online tests or ICT examinations, you must instruct candidates to save all work and to close down the software.

When candidates have stopped writing, you must remind them to check their information on their scripts and any supplementary papers and to fasten them together (usually with treasury tags). You should collect all papers from the examination that has ended before allowing candidates to leave the room.

The invigilator's role and responsibility does not stop at the end of the exam. The scripts must be placed in register order. You must then ensure that all scripts, the completed register, seating plan, examination papers, records, and other relevant information is returned to the examination officer. You must also draw attention to any reports and information about any issues or incidents which have occurred during the examination. Scripts are confidential; they must not be shown to others or left unattended. You are responsible for these until they are signed over to the examinations officer.

## Ending tests and examinations when all candidates are due to finish at the same time or different times

There may be two or even more examination end times for groups or individual candidates. This may happen because:

- there is more than one examination taking place in the same room
- individuals have additional time because of special arrangements.

When there is more than one examination, you must state clearly which examination is at an end. Candidates sitting examinations which end first must be positioned nearer the door to create the minimum disturbance.

## Getting ready for assessment

The majority of this unit will need to be assessed in the workplace and you should ensure that your assessor is able to observe you undertaking an invigilation. Make sure that you are able to show how you are prepared for the invigilation and have set up the examination room correctly and checked for specific requirements (such as further guidance or supervision of candidates between examinations). If there are candidates in the examination who have additional needs, for example, reading assistance, a scribe or a sign interpreter, you should also outline details of these to your assessor in advance. You will need to show you know how to start and end tests and examinations, and deal with specific situations such as access arrangements, emergencies and suspicion of malpractice if required.

## Check your knowledge

1. What does the acronym ICE stand for?

2. Give three reasons why reasonable adjustments may be made.

3. Give a reason why a candidate may have to be supervised between examinations.

4. Identify four types of information which must be displayed inside an examination room.

5. Define the term 'special consideration'.

6. What is an erratum notice?

7. How does the invigilator know if a calculator can be used in an examination?

8. At what stage are candidates deemed to be very late for an examination?

### Websites

**www.edexcel.com** – Edexcel
**www.jcq.org.uk** – Joint Council for Qualifications
**www.teachernet.gov.uk** – TeacherNet

# ASDAN TW3 Team working

Teams in primary schools comprise different groups of people who work together in order to achieve shared objectives for supporting individuals or groups of pupils, as well as the whole school team. You will need to be able to contribute to the effectiveness of the team and work alongside others for the benefit of pupils. You will need to show that you can recognise and respond to issues impacting on team effectiveness. You should also be able to contribute to the development of the team through providing support and advice.

## By the end of this unit you will:

1. plan collaborative work with others
2. seek to develop co-operative ways of working and check progress towards agreed objectives
3. review work with others and agree ways of improving collaborative work in the future.

# Plan collaborative work with others

## What makes groups or teams effective in the workplace

You may belong to a number of different **teams** within your school. Whether these are year group, subject, class or school based, you will need to understand your role within that team and how it fits in with that of others.

To understand what makes a team effective in the workplace, it is important to look at a number of factors.

- **Communicate regularly** — a team cannot be effective unless there are regular opportunities for discussion, whether these are formal or informal. It is vital for teams to get together to ensure that they have all the information they need and that all members are able to contribute their ideas.

### Functional skills

ICT: Developing, presenting and communicating information
You could set up email groups with your team members in order to create another opportunity for communicating. This is especially effective if not all members of your team work the same hours.

### Key term

**Team** — people with whom you work on a long-, medium-, or short-term basis, relating to the support provided for a specific pupil or group of pupils

- **Share roles** — the roles of different team members should complement one another so that there is a balance of responsibilities.

- **Have a sense of common purpose** — the key part of working in a team is that you will be working with others towards a common objective. This means that in order to be effective, you will all need to have a shared vision about what you want to achieve.

- **Have equal levels of commitment** — all members of the team should be well motivated and have equal levels of commitment. They should also be open to change and never become complacent about what they are doing.

- **Members work for the team rather than for themselves** — the needs of the group should be more important than the needs of each individual. They will also be accountable for the outcomes as a team rather than as individuals.

- **Members are open about facing and resolving issues** — it is important that the team is able to discuss and debate any issues which arise in the course of the work of the team, so that different ideas can be aired.

*Characteristics of an effective team.*

● **All members of the team are valued and respected** — the team should be able to consider the ideas and opinions of all members and not gossip or show disrespect in other ways.

---

**CASE STUDY:** Team communication

Jan is a teaching assistant who works with a team of seven other people in the art department; the team includes teachers, assistants and other support staff. The team works well and has been together for some years, including going through a successful Ofsted inspection. It has always met regularly to plan together and discuss any issues. The art co-ordinator has recently left and there is a new teacher leading the team who says that it is not necessary for them all to meet as there is not enough time in the school day, and it will be enough for the teachers to get together and then pass information on to others.

- What do you think about this arrangement?
- What might be a better idea?

---

**Reflect** ❓

Consider different teams you have worked with in the past and which have worked best. What have been the features which have made these teams stand out?

## Realistic objectives for working together and what needs to be done to achieve them

Although there will be different members of your team with various responsibilities, as a team member you should be invited to contribute to the overall group process and may do this in different ways. Your form teacher or line manager should be the person to whom you report in order to agree your responsibilities, and these should be part of your job description. It is important that this job description is up to date, so that you can be sure that you are fulfilling your role and be clear where you fit in as part of your team.

*Members of teams should have regular opportunities to meet together and agree realistic objectives.*

# Share relevant information to help agree roles and responsibilities

As a team member, you will get to know those with whom you work quite well. You should make sure that you are able to strike a balance between being professional and also being open and friendly with other members of your team. You may work with different groups or teams in school on a short-, medium- or long-term basis. Although your role may be the same within each, these different teams will be focusing on different areas within the school. These may be:

- **supporting a named child** – assistants who work with individual children may work alongside others such as the SENCO, or other professionals who come into the school to support a child who has special educational needs (see page 22 for the types of professionals who may come in to schools)

- **supporting a subject area** – assistants will work with subject teachers but there may also be other adults or assistants within the class who work together. You should plan and discuss learning activities alongside teachers or at least have access to plans so that you have a clear understanding of what you are expected to do within the class on a weekly and daily basis. Plans should show the roles of other adults as well as learning intentions and whether activities are whole class, group or individual (for more on planning with teachers, see TDA 3.10)

- **within a year group** – the school will have several classes within each year group. Year groups may work very closely together and support one another in planning and moderating children's work

- **within a key stage** – each key stage is a distinct phase within the school. Key stage co-ordinators will support teachers across different subject areas

- **within the school** – all members of staff within a school are part of a team and will support one another. For example, the ICT co-ordinator will be able to offer help and advice to any member of staff on integrating ICT skills within other subject areas.

Sometimes you may find that you are part of a team which is only together for a short time – for example, if you are on a working party to organise a Christmas production or a summer fair. In this situation it is also important for someone to take charge and ensure that different members of the team are able to work efficiently and cohesively together.

In each of these situations, members of the team will need to understand their role and how it fits in with the roles of other members of the team. The most important part of any role within a team is communicating effectively with others. There should be clear and consistent methods of communication so that all members of the team feel that their opinions are valued. As part of this process you should attend regular meetings that give you a clear idea of how what you are doing fits in to the school or team as a whole. If you have a team leader, they should identify action points in any meetings you attend and give a timescale in which they will need to be carried out.

## Portfolio activity

Consider the different teams to which you belong in school. Write a reflective account to outline your role and consider how you work with others as part of a team.

## Functional skills

**English: Writing**
When writing your reflective account, make sure that you consider a suitable layout and who your audience is going to be. Take care with your punctuation, spelling and grammar.

# Agree suitable working arrangements with other team members

Although you may be aware of one another's roles in your team and are able to work effectively together, it is also important to be flexible and able to support others in different ways. While you are in school you need to focus on your role, but there may be times when you need to come to an agreement about how your arrangements fit together as individuals in a broader context. This is because at any one time, members of the team may have issues of their own which may impact on their work. If you notice that a colleague is not their normal self, for example, it may be appropriate for you to offer them support in order to acknowledge this. Support staff may work in a range of school situations and you may not know what pressures they are under as part of their job. Many members of the team will have families and all will have another life outside school which at different times may have an impact on their ability to provide the same level of support for the school. You should be sensitive to any changes in behaviour or ability to juggle the demands of home and school, or to cope with what they have been asked to do at work.

## CASE STUDY: Supporting team members

One day each week, Alison supervises pupils in the study area at lunchtime. She and other teaching assistants share the role, each working for 30 minutes. One day last week, Rehana did not arrive to relieve her so Alison had to stay until another colleague arrived. This left her only 15 minutes to eat her lunch. At the end of the day, Alison went to complain to her line manager, the Special Educational Needs Co-ordinator, as this was the second time she had been let down by Rehana. Her manager told her that Rehana's daughter had had an accident and had injured her leg. She said that Rehana was preoccupied as she was very worried about her daughter, who might need an operation.

- What might have been an alternative approach?
- How could the situation be resolved if Rehana was unable to fulfil her duties for the time being?

# Seek to develop co-operative ways of working and check progress towards agreed objectives

## Organise and carry out tasks efficiently to meet own responsibilities

As a team member in school, there may be very little time for you to carry out tasks, so it is important for you to be able to organise your time efficiently in order to meet the demands of your role. Different individuals will organise their time in different ways, but lists and reminders can help you to keep track of your responsibilities, or you can diarise deadlines and dates which are important so that you can prioritise your time. It may be that you also have individual professional targets to meet as part of your performance management (see SfCD SHC 32), but these should be tied in with what you are doing on a daily basis, rather than 'extra' tasks. As part of your team, you should always be supportive to others and try to balance responsibilities so that individuals do not have more to do than their colleagues.

### Knowledge into action

Consider the different ways in which you organise your time in order to carry out tasks efficiently as part of your role. How do you balance tasks as part of your individual role and those you carry out as part of a team?

## Seek effective ways to work co-operatively, including ways to resolve conflict

In order for individuals to work co-operatively, it is important for members to have good interpersonal skills. These are sometimes the most difficult skills to have, as within any team there will be a number of personalities. Individuals will need to have the skills to relate to one another well and be sympathetic, supportive and helpful. Members of the team should be sensitive to the needs and feelings of others, and encourage those who they know are finding work challenging or difficult. This may be due to other issues which they have to deal with outside school.

There may be a combination of factors which makes it difficult for individuals to focus and tackle problems in the work environment. This may mean reading others' body language at times or realising that now may not be a good time to approach another member of the team with a problem. There may also be a member of the team who is much more of a speaker than a listener. This can be a problem if the person does not give others the chance to have their say.

## Valuing the expertise of team members

You should remember that all members of the team are equally important, and that your expertise and that of your colleagues is unique to each person's experience. If you are experienced or approachable, you may find that others come to you for help or advice. You should always think about your role and theirs within the team when doing this, while remaining supportive. Where you do not feel that it is appropriate for you to deal with a particular issue, you may need to refer to someone else within the team. You must remain non-judgemental about others and not allow your own opinions to intrude or cloud any decisions you may have to make. You may also find that you have an area of expertise which may be helpful to others, and in this situation you should offer it.

If you are working in a team, you should always respect the opinions and knowledge which others bring. In order to have a good working relationship with them you will need to show that you consider their opinions and experience. Bad feeling can quickly cause problems and unrest within teams.

*It is important to be sensitive to the needs and feelings of others in the team.*

You are part of a large secondary school which holds weekly or fortnightly meetings for all teaching assistants as required. This week, two of the teaching assistants who work in Year 7 are speaking to the group about some of the strategies they have been using with their classes to manage classroom behaviour following a course they have attended. Some of the teaching assistants are speaking over what the two are saying, and are clearly not listening.

- Why is it important that schools give all staff opportunities to feed back to colleagues following development opportunities?
- Give two reasons why all staff should be attentive in this situation.

## Resolving conflict

However well your team works together, it is likely that at some stage there will be an **issue** or problem within it. This will need to be resolved before the team can move on and continue to progress.

Examples of the type of issues that may arise when working with colleagues are:

- poor co-operation between members of the team
- interpersonal conflicts between members of the team.

There may be a number of reasons for this, among them:

- misinformation or incomplete information given to all team members

### Key term

**Issue** – situation or circumstance that hinders or prevents effective team performance

- resistance to change
- pressure to conform to a team decision which does not take account of individual preferences
- dominance of some team members, leading to inequality during decision making
- inability of individuals to accept feedback
- interpersonal conflict
- unproductive levels of competition.

As part of a team, you should remember that you will always get along with some personalities more than others, but this should not mean that you cannot relate in some way to all members of your team, as you will have a common purpose. Also in the course of your work you may find that work or home pressures may affect the way in which team members relate to one another. It is important to try to minimise conflict so that bad feeling and resentment do not build up over time. In order to do this, you should try to resolve any issues as soon as possible through the appropriate channels. Communication is the most important factor, as many conflicts arise due to either misunderstandings or lack of time to discuss what is happening. If you find that another member of your team appears to be making your work more difficult due to their attitude or opinions, you will need to either try to resolve the situation or refer the issue to a senior member of staff.

You should be familiar with your school's policy for dealing with difficulties in working relationships and practices. This is usually known as the grievance policy. The policy will give you information and details about how to approach any problems you may face when working with others. As an example, most policies will advise a set way of dealing with issues as they arise. There should be separate guidelines for individuals wishing to raise a grievance and for collective disputes.

# GRIEVANCE POLICY

## Informal procedure (recommended course of action)

1) Speak directly and confidentially to the person or persons with whom you have a grievance. If agreement is not reached the issue should be taken directly to the Head Teacher. If the grievance is with the Head Teacher take the issue to the Chair of Governors.

2) The Head Teacher or Chair of Governors will act as mediator and encourage both parties to resolve the issue as soon as possible and to avoid using the more formal procedure. Parties may be represented by a trade union representative or colleague if required. If the issue is not resolved within seven days of the grievance being raised, it should progress to the next level, i.e. the formal stage.

3) A record of the mediation meeting and any agreed actions by both or either party should be kept on file so that it can be referred to if required.

## Formal procedure

1) If the informal procedure does not resolve the issue or it has not been resolved to the satisfaction of both parties, a letter should be sent to the Clerk to the Governors outlining progress so far. This should then be addressed by the grievance sub-committee of the governing body.

2) A meeting will be called between all parties by the grievance sub-committee and each person given the opportunity to put forward their side. There will be opportunities for questioning and responses by all.

3) If there is still no resolution, the matter may be passed to the Director of Education of the local authority and/or the unions.

*A school's grievance policy.*

## BEST PRACTICE CHECKLIST: Working in teams

- Be considerate and respectful towards others within your team.

- Carry out your duties well and cheerfully.

- Do not gossip or talk about other people in your team.

- Make sure you discuss any problems as they arise.

- Speak to the appropriate team member if you need help.

- Prepare for and contribute to meetings.

- Acknowledge the support and ideas of other team members.

There will also be school policies relating to areas such as confidentiality and all members of teams should be aware of issues surrounding the exchange of information. You should be aware of whom you need to speak to on a professional level if you find that there are problems within your team or group which are affecting your work.

### Portfolio activity

Reflect on an issue or problem which you have encountered when working in a team. You may wish to have a professional discussion with your assessor about how you resolved the problem, so that they can record it for your portfolio. Alternatively you can write a reflective account to show how you have dealt with any issues which have arisen. If you write it up, be careful how you do this if your portfolio is likely to be seen by others in your team.

## Share accurate information on progress and agree changes to achieve objectives

As part of your role within your team, you will need to feed back in an accurate way on your progress to other team members. This may be done during a team meeting or more informally. You should be able to discuss progress frankly with other members

of your team so that any concerns can be addressed and so that all members of the team are up to date with what is happening. It will also be helpful to have others' input and ideas to support your role, as you may find that they are able to offer fresh ideas and insights. You may then need to amend your plans to integrate the ideas of other members of your team.

### CASE STUDY: Developing timetables

Anna works as a higher level teaching assistant (HLTA) and support staff team leader in a special school. As part of her continuing professional development, she has been working on finding new ways of developing the timetables for individual support assistants so that the children are supported more effectively. Although she has started to do this, the task has been made increasingly difficult due to the variations in start time of the support staff in the mornings.

- What could Anna do in this situation?
- How could other members of her team support her in what she is doing?

## Review work with others and agree ways of improving collaborative work in the future

### Provide a detailed account of what went well and less well from own point of view

When you are working in a team, it is important to have opportunities to share and discuss in detail various approaches which you have used and also to listen to the ideas of others. It is likely that you will have opportunities to do this with other members of your team, both formally and informally, on a regular basis. This may be because the outcome has not gone as well as the team had expected, but it also may be that things have gone particularly well and you need to identify why so that it can be repeated in the future. There will be benefits to members of the team who are less experienced and also to those who may have more fixed ideas about how they approach things.

## Formal approach

This will usually be directly through meetings, INSET (In-Service Education and Training) or other training, when you may be invited to discuss strategies and ideas. This will be useful as it will enable you to ensure that you are following school policy in your own practice and will give you the opportunity to raise any concerns. You may also be able to listen to those who may have used similar approaches, so that you can discuss what has worked or been less effective.

## Informal approach

If you have good communication skills, it is also likely that you will be talking to other members of your team about how you approach your role on an informal basis. This is valuable as it gives you the opportunity to share different aspects of your role and may give you another perspective on issues or concerns as soon as they arise. Others may also be able to suggest alternative sources of information or help.

You may have opportunities to share ideas with others who are not directly involved in your own team but have similar experiences and are able to share these, for example, other support staff in school **cluster groups** or **collaboratives**.

### Key term

**Cluster group/collaborative** — group of individuals from different schools who come together to share ideas and experiences

*It is useful to discuss approaches you have used with others.*

Mike has just spent his break talking to Anne, another assistant who works in Key Stage 4, about a pupil she is supporting. She has just had a difficult session with him and over coffee talks about the kinds of problems which are coming up. Mike knows the boy well as he worked in his class. During the course of the discussion, Mike is able to talk to Anne about the kinds of strategies which he used with him which she may find useful.

- In what ways will this informal chat be useful?
- How else might Mike help Anne in the long term?

## Identify factors influencing the outcome of working with others, including own role

When considering the outcome of working with others, you will need to think first about the kinds of factors which will affect their work within the team.

### How information is given to them

Everyone in your team will work slightly differently and it may take some time for you to become used to different styles and preferences held by other people. You should be aware that their learning styles may be such that they find it easiest to absorb information in a particular way – for example, if you tell them something verbally, they may find it hard to remember (see learning styles on page 292 for the different ways in which individuals may find it best to absorb and process information). Others may ask for informal reminders, and some may complete what they need to do straight away if they are able to or if they are more methodical.

### Personalities within the team

Different personality types may find working in teams difficult and take some time to adapt. This may be because they are used to working on their own. They may be quieter personalities and feel uncomfortable speaking out in a group, or be returning to the workplace after a break and feel less confident. Individuals in any team will have a range of interactive styles. This means that they will have different personalities and may approach things in their own ways, which will usually be a strength but may sometimes cause problems!

There are a number of personality types which are referred to in the work of Isabel Myers and based on the theories of Carl Jung. These form the basis of the Myers-Briggs Type Indicator® (MBTI®) identity test, which is often referred to and used in business training to encourage managers to think about how they relate to their teams. These 16 personality types will all have their own strengths and areas to focus on, and none of these are 'right' or 'wrong'.

### Over to you!

Have a look at www.personalitypathways.com/type_inventory.html and see whether you can find out your personality type using the test. Although you are not working in this context, it is interesting to consider how your own personality will affect the way in which you relate to others and the success or challenges within your team.

### Reflect

Consider the different teams you belong to, whether at work or to do with leisure activities, family, college and so on. How do the different personalities in each context affect team dynamics?

### Stage in team development

Research surrounding the effectiveness of teams shows that they will pass through certain stages before they can operate effectively. One of the most succinct definitions has been reached by Tuckman (1965) and others, who believed that all groups need to go through a process of maturing before they are able to function efficiently, due to the different personalities within them. The process has been divided into four stages: forming, storming, norming and performing.

- At the **forming** stage, members of the team are just starting to get together and a leader emerges. Members of the group will need to have a clear sense of identity and purpose.

- When **storming**, members will start to view themselves as more of a team and will have reached an understanding of what is expected of them. There may be a challenge to the leader during this stage. Individuals will need to have clear roles and opportunities for participation within the group.

- **Norming** defines the stage at which the team organises itself into work groups and starts to develop different areas of activity. At this stage, the group will need to establish a culture around shared norms and values that they all agree on.

- **Performing** is the ideal state to which all teams aspire. The group is comfortable with one another and works effectively together.

These four stages may not have clear boundaries and teams may sometimes become 'stuck' at a particular stage, or go backwards and not develop fully. John O'Sullivan (2003) in his *Manager's Handbook*, describes a fifth phase of development, the 'transforming' stage, where the team continues to develop and improve. However, Harpley and Roberts (2006) describe the 'dorming' phase, when the team may fall into a state of complacency about its achievements and does not continue to move forward. This is usually avoided through consistent communication and planning.

## Level of support from other members of the team

As you get to know them, you may find out that others in your team have strengths or weaknesses in a particular area, or work better if particular support is given to them or if they are able to support others. This may need to be accommodated in different ways within the team.

## Level of experience

Different members of the team may or may not have experience of various situations in school. This may influence the outcome of their work with others.

## Clear purpose to what they are doing

Members of the team will need to be clear on the purpose of what they are doing. If they are motivated and enthusiastic about their targets, they are more likely to carry out their roles effectively.

## Identify ways of improving own work with others

In education, we are always encouraged to reflect on our work and to consider ways in which we can improve. Even if things are going well, it is useful to think about ways in which we can improve our approach or our methods. We can do this by:

- **asking others for feedback on our work.** Your school may or may not have performance management or appraisals for support staff. However, it is still worthwhile for you to ask your line manager periodically or those with whom you work for some feedback on your progress, particularly if you have limited experience

- **making sure we regularly reflect on what we are doing.** If you find that you have been working with others but it has not been successful, it will be useful for you to reflect on what happened and to consider ways in which you might have handled it differently if you were to approach it again. You may find it helpful to discuss what happened with a more experienced member of staff so that they can put forward ideas and suggestions of their own

- **attending regular training and keeping up to date with current practice.** You should have regular opportunities to attend training and INSET to keep you up to date. This will also give you the chance to discuss how you approach different situations in school and to find ways to improve

- **respecting and valuing the contribution of others.** When working with others, you will need to make sure you listen to them and take on board what they are saying. This is important — often people do not really hear others' views because they are too busy thinking about their own or are too eager to put their ideas across. You should remember that all contributions are important and valid.

### Knowledge into action

Consider the different ways in which you seek to find ways of improving your work with others. How does this make a difference to your practice?

## Getting ready for assessment

In order to gather evidence for this unit, you need to show how you support other members of your team and also how you deal with any issues that have arisen. Your assessor may be able to observe you in a team meeting. You will also need to have a professional discussion or write a reflective account to show how you have dealt with any issues that have arisen within your team. If you write an account, be careful how you do this if your portfolio is likely to be seen by others in your team.

### Websites and references

**www.humanmetrics.com** – this site enables you to take a test to discover your personality type
**www.myersbriggs.org/my-mbti-personality-type/mbti-basics** – more about Myers-Briggs test
**www.personalitypathways.com/type_inventory.html** – another site that allows you to take a test to discover your Myers-Briggs personality types
**www.tda.gov.uk** – the Training and Development Agency provides information on roles and responsibilities and national occupation standards for teaching and support assistants

O'Sullivan J. (2003) *Manager's Handbook*, Leamington Spa: Scholastic
Harpley A. and Roberts A. (2006) *Helping Children to be Skillful Communicators*, David Fulton Publishers

## Check your knowledge

1. What different 'teams' might you belong to in a secondary school?

2. How does being in a team support your work in school?

3. Give three examples of problems which may exist within a team.

4. Why is it important to be receptive to the views and ideas of others within your team?

5. Where in your school would you find information on how to deal with any difficulties you may have within your team?

6. What are the stages of team development sometimes known as?

7. How might you go about seeking to improve your work within your team?

# School life

## My story: Martin

I work in Key Stage 4 as a learning mentor at a secondary school in a large city. I work mainly with boys who have become disillusioned with school work. Many have serious issues at home and some have been in trouble with the police. There is a high incidence of absence within the group and I was finding it increasingly difficult to keep these young people focused on their school work. As they were studying for their GCSEs, this was a critical time. I asked my line manager, who is the head of Key Stage 4, and the intervention teacher for a meeting so that we could discuss strategies to support these pupils. In my spare time I am a judo coach so I suggested starting a judo club at lunchtime. They agreed to this and after only six weeks there has definitely been a renewed enthusiasm and no absences on the days we hold the club. On other days a colleague started a music group. One spin-off from this is that the young people have developed their self-esteem. Several pupils have even formed a band and will be performing at the end-of-term concert. Some members of my judo group are asking if they can enter competitions. It has helped them to focus in school and they now feel that they are achieving.

## Ask the expert

**Q** Can I take the initiative if I have an idea?

**A** If you have an idea which you think will benefit the children and the school, you should definitely put it forward to your line manager or department head. It is likely that they will be keen to put your ideas into practice, particularly as you work closely with pupils and will know about their interests. Always make sure you ask before you start to arrange anything though, and remember that it may impact on other members of your team.

### VIEWPOINT

If there are no meetings for teaching assistants in your school, try suggesting to other members of your team that this might be a good idea. If it is not possible, this may be because there are very few times that everyone is available, as often support staff have so many different roles in school. Find out about other ways in which you could communicate – such as through email or through having access to staff meeting minutes – so that you are able to receive information which is important.

# TDA 3.8 Supervise whole-class learning activities

This unit is for support staff who supervise whole-class learning activities in the absence of a teacher. Cover supervisors are regularly used in secondary schools and you will need to know and understand your school's policy as well as the specific requirements of the lesson you are supervising.

## By the end of this unit you will:

1. be able to prepare for supervising whole-class learning activities

2. be able to supervise whole-class learning activities

3. be able to support learners in completing work set for them

4. be able to conclude whole-class learning activities.

# Be able to prepare for supervising whole-class learning activities

## The school policy and procedures for cover supervision

Before you begin work as a **cover supervisor**, you should be clear on the school's policy and what you are expected to do as part of your role. Cover supervisors should be used in the place of teachers where plans have been set out for the class and the cover supervisor is clear on what they have been asked to do. There should be guidelines about the extent of the cover and the use of cover supervisors in school. The role of a cover supervisor is not the same as that of a teacher and the tasks that pupils are asked to do should aim to give curriculum continuity rather than active teaching during staff absence. If teachers are to be absent for a long period, it is unlikely that a cover supervisor will be used long term, as specified work should only be carried out by a qualified teacher.

In addition, in 2003 the Workforce Agreement Monitoring Group (WAMG) was set up to monitor the remodelling of the school workforce after the introduction of the National Agreement. The WAMG comprises unions, employers and governments, and sets out guidelines for the use of cover supervisors after the introduction of PPA (planning, preparation and assessment) time for teachers. Since 2003 the WAMG has continued to develop workforce reform in schools and has also introduced the changes in roles and qualifications available to support staff.

The National Agreement included the following objectives:

● progressive reductions in teachers' overall hours

● changes to teachers' contracts, including a limit on the amount of cover for absent colleagues that teachers and head teachers were expected to employ

● new arrangements for deploying support staff.

*(Source:* www.tda.gov.uk*)*

The policy for cover supervision should include details of how this will be used in the school, its appropriate use, and roles and responsibilities of key staff. It should also outline how the process will be monitored and reviewed within the school.

### Key term

**Cover supervisor** — the person employed to carry out the process of administering cover, who will also provide lesson cover when necessary and revert back to teaching assistant duties when no cover administration is required

### Portfolio activity

Find a copy of your school's cover policy and outline the key points which are relevant to your role. Include your school's procedures for cover supervision and use this for your portfolio to cover this assessment criterion.

### Functional skills

**English: Reading**
By completing this Portfolio activity you will be summarising the key points and developing your reading skills. You could do this in groups of three from different settings so that you can compare the different policies.

## The work set for the class, details of the learning resources required and any specific instructions

Learning resources to support learning activities include:

● materials

● equipment (including ICT)

● software

● books and other written materials.

Specific instructions may relate to, for example:

● learners with special educational needs

- the seating plan
- behavioural issues
- extension activities
- homework.

## Work set for the class

Before you undertake the learning activity, you should make sure that you have been left with clear instructions as to what you are required to do. This means making sure that you have everything you need in order to carry out the lesson. You should have been given a lesson plan which should set out the introduction, main activity and differentiation for the class. You should also be able to identify the learning objective so that you are able to pass this on to pupils and they can measure their own progress towards achieving it.

## Learning resources

This may sound obvious, but it is worth making sure that you have had details of any learning resources you may need to carry out the activity. Read through the plan and check that you will not need to find additional resources or materials before the lesson, such as software for computers, or specific equipment for the lesson. You should not assume that there will be sufficient resources, even if you know the class well, as items may have been borrowed or used by other staff. Although you may have been given worksheets, books or other resources by the teacher you are covering for, ensure that you have enough and that pupils will have access to everything they need. For more on organising resources, see the next section.

## Specific instructions

These may not always be outlined on the lesson plan, but if possible you should speak to the teacher who has set the work in order to find out more about the class, and the way in which it is set out. This includes seating plans or information about pupils who may need particular attention. You should in particular ask about pupils who may have special educational needs (SEN), speak English as an additional language or have problems with their behaviour. You can then be prepared and can consider the kinds of strategies which you are able to use.

If there is a pupil in the class with a statement of special educational needs, you may also have additional staff in the classroom who will be there to support them in accessing the curriculum. If the staff are not familiar with the lesson plan, you should make sure that you speak to them about it beforehand so that they are able to consider the needs of the pupil they are supporting and whether resources will need to be adapted.

You should also check that the teacher has left an extension activity that you can give to pupils who complete the work, and whether there is any homework which you should set at the end of the lesson (for more on extension activities, see page 354). If the teacher is not available, try to talk to other staff who may have ideas, or who know the class, so that you are as prepared as possible.

---

**CASE STUDY:** Obtaining the work set for the class

Kate has been asked to cover a Year 7 geography lesson the following day. She usually works within the geography department and so is familiar with organisation and schemes of work. However, she does not know the Year 7 class as she has not met them before. The teacher is off sick for the week and has sent in a plan, but Kate does not have any further information about the class.

- What could Kate do in order to best support the class?
- How could she ensure that she has all the information she needs?

---

## Organising the resources required for the learning activities

Once you are clear about the resources you will need for the learning activity, you should ensure that you have checked through the plan so that the resources are ready for use when needed. As well as checking these and ensuring you have enough for the class, you may need to look at whether equipment, such as ICT resources, is in working order.

You will also need to check that you have:

- written materials, books, worksheets

- curriculum-specific equipment — for example, art resources or maths equipment — if needed; make sure that any equipment is in working order and that you know how to use it

- ICT equipment which may be used for any subject

- any software which you need for the lesson

- specific equipment or resources for any pupils who have special educational needs.

It can also be helpful to have a box of resources of your own so that you are able to provide pupils with additional equipment if needed. This can help if pupils have not brought their own or if there is a shortage of items within the class.

## Confirming the learning environment meets relevant requirements

As well as checking the learning environment for resources before the start of the lesson, you should ensure that it meets health and safety requirements. This is relevant whatever learning environment you are working in, which may not always be the classroom but

*Are you able to help pupils when using ICT equipment?*

other areas both within or outside the school. Although you will not have time to do an in-depth safety check, you should look around and make sure that:

- fire exits are clear and pupils are aware of what to do in an emergency

- pupils will be able to have safe access around the class, including those who have any special educational needs or specialist equipment

- the room is generally tidy and free from hazards

- pupils have access to any safety equipment which is needed for the activities which are to be carried out

- the environment meets relevant security requirements.

If you do notice any hazards or health and safety issues which you cannot deal with yourself, you should report them straight away in accordance with school policy.

### Knowledge into action

Next time you are covering a class, spend some time checking the environment for health and safety issues. How do you report issues if you are unable to deal with them yourself?

### Link

For more on this topic, see CYP 3.4, Support children and young people's health and safety.

# Be able to supervise whole-class learning activities

### Link

For more on this topic, see TDA 3.3, Support learning activities.

## Giving clear instructions to learners on the work to be completed

When you are giving pupils instructions on work they are about to do, you should go through it in stages and check that they are clear. You will need to confirm with them that they understand the requirements of the activity and the order in which they are to work through it.

## Responding to questions from learners about process and procedures

Your role as a supervisor should not entail active teaching activities, so the lesson plan should not be overly complicated to administer; however, there may be issues within the group if the task is not clear to them. At the beginning of the lesson, make sure that you give the class the opportunity to ask questions about the task and check that they all know what they need to do. This will save you answering individual queries later for those who have not understood the requirements of the task.

## Appropriate strategies for supervising completion of the work set

When pupils are working on the activity, you should monitor what they are doing to check that they are on task and focused. You can do this by:

● working through the task in phases and stopping the class at different times to check their progress and discuss what they are doing

● making sure they are in groups which will maximise their ability to work – in other words, ensure you have spoken to the teacher about seating plans

● giving pupils notification at different stages of how much time they have left

● speaking to the class as a group or in smaller groups about their progress throughout the task

● asking pupils to put up their hand if they have any queries.

It is likely that you will use a mixture of these strategies to ensure that pupils remain on task and complete their work; however, you may also need to support them further if they are finding any aspect of the activity challenging or need more clarification on what they have been asked to do.

# Ways of managing the behaviour of learners to ensure a constructive learning environment

As well as being clear on what pupils are expected to do during the session, you should consider how you will manage pupil behaviour prior to the start of the lesson. Effective behaviour management should be planned for rather than hoped for, and you will need to be clear with pupils about your expectations from the start. This is very important since poor behaviour will mean that learning is less likely to take place. The DfE induction training booklet for teaching assistants outlines the following core principles for behaviour management which are a helpful way of checking yourself when considering behaviour management strategies.

## Core principles of behaviour management

● Plan for good behaviour

● Work within the 4 Rs framework

● Separate the (inappropriate) behaviour from the child

● Use the language of choice

● Keep the focus on primary behaviours

● Actively build trust and rapport

● Model the behaviour you want to see

● Always follow up on issues that count

● Work to repair and restore relationships

*(Behaviour management module, induction training for teaching assistants in primary and secondary schools, DfES 2004.)*

### Link

For more on this topic, see TDA 3.4, Promote children and young people's positive behaviour.

## Plan for good behaviour

This means that you will need to be consistent with rewards and strategies that you use with pupils.

Ensure that you use praise and encouragement where you can, as well as correcting inappropriate behaviour. You should consider in advance the kind of behaviour that may take place which you may need to challenge and have clear strategies for dealing with it of which pupils are aware. In this way you will have a clear set of consequences for dealing with inappropriate behaviour as well as rewards for those who behaved well.

## Work within the 4 Rs framework

The 4 Rs show a balance between rights, responsibilities, rules and routines. They outline the importance of pupils taking responsibility for their actions and seeing the outcomes of the choices that they make. Within the framework, adults should work together to use language in a positive way while reducing opportunities for confrontation.

## Separate the (inappropriate) behaviour from the child

This is important as it means that you will be making the behaviour unacceptable rather than the pupil — for example, 'That wasn't a sensible thing to do' does not infer that the pupil's personality or identity is at fault, but that the choice they have made is wrong.

## Use the language of choice

By emphasising that the pupil has chosen their behaviour, you will be giving them more responsibility for the consequences.

## Keep the focus on primary behaviours

Often in situations where behaviour has become an issue, adults have been drawn into arguments with pupils. They will often respond to being corrected by the use of language such as 'but they did it to me first' or by transferring the blame in some other way so that they get the last word and feel better about being spoken to in front of their peers. If you remain focused on the primary behaviour, this is less likely to happen.

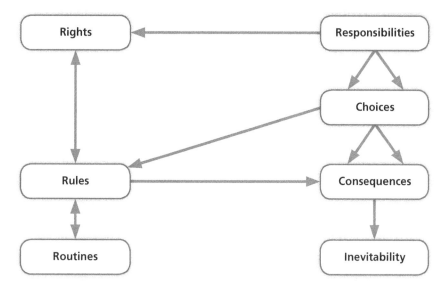

*The 4 Rs framework (source: Behaviour management module, induction training for teaching assistants in primary and secondary schools, DfES 2004).*

## CASE STUDY: Managing the behaviour of learners

Look at the following scenario and different ways of handling it.

Helen is covering a maths lesson for a colleague with a class of Year 8 pupils. She notices Leo flicking pencils at the back of the class and causing disruption within his group, so decides to speak to him.

### Scenario A

Helen: 'Leo, stop flicking pencils and get on with your work.'

Leo: 'Oh but miss, Delainey started it, she threw a rubber at me.'

Helen: 'I didn't see Delainey throw a rubber at you.'

Leo: 'Oh miss she did and it hurt, she always gets me in trouble.'

Helen: 'Delainey, did you throw a rubber at Leo?'

### Scenario B

Helen: 'Leo, stop flicking pencils and get on with your work.'

Leo: 'Oh but miss, Delainey started it, she threw a rubber at me.'

Helen: 'Leo, I saw you flicking pencils. You can choose to stop or you can choose to go on a warning.'

- In scenario A, how has Helen been ineffective in managing Leo's behaviour and why?
- Why is it important to curtail inappropriate behaviour as quickly as possible?

## Knowledge into action

Think about the way in which you manage behaviour and in particular how you keep focused on primary behaviours. Focus on repeating the instruction and outlining the consequences as in the example in the case study. Trial it with pupils and see whether it makes a difference.

## Actively build trust and rapport

This means that you should take time to develop positive relationships and build trust with pupils through your consistent responses to them.

## Model the behaviour that you want to see

We cannot expect pupils to behave appropriately if they see adults contradicting what we are asking them to do. Make sure you are consistent and calm when managing behaviour.

## Always follow up on issues that count

Take time to show pupils that you mean what you say when managing behaviour and be positive about future expectations.

## Work to repair and restore relationships

Following confrontations about behaviour, make sure that you notice positive attempts by the pupil to behave well, even if these are small, and praise them. In this way they will be more likely to repeat the positive behaviour, as they will receive attention for it.

## Ways of encouraging learners to take responsibility for their own learning

It is important that you are able to encourage learners as much as possible to take responsibility for their own learning. The purpose of this is twofold.

- Pupils should recognise that learning is not something which is done to them but is something in which they are actively involved and need to take responsibility for.

- Your role is that of an enabler rather than a doer — pupils should be working on activities themselves and trying to find their own solutions as much as possible, rather than seeking your input.

The most important way of encouraging learners to take responsibility is by giving them clear learning objectives and outcomes for the lesson. Pupils need to know what they are setting out to achieve in order to be able to achieve it. They will then be able to measure what they have learned against the objective.

During the lesson, you can encourage learners to take more responsibility through the ways in which you question and persuade them to think about their work. If learners are finding a task challenging and ask you for help, make sure you respond in a way which

encourages them to think further about what they are doing, rather than leading them to the answer. Another way of encouraging learners to take more responsibility is by pairing them with one of their peers so that they can support one another in assessing what they have achieved against the learning objective.

> ### Link
>
> For more on this topic, see TDA 3.7, Support assessment for learning.

> ### CASE STUDY: Encouraging learners to take responsibility
>
> Bronwen has been asked to cover a class of Year 10 learners who are working on an English literature activity to write a critical appreciation of a poem. She has outlined what they need to do and given them the learning objective. The class has carried out an activity like this before and it should be straightforward for them. However, several of the group are repeatedly asking questions and disrupting the work of others.
>
> - What could Bronwen say to the class in this situation?
> - How can she encourage them to take responsibility for their learning?

## Problems that might occur and how to deal with these

You may find that you are faced with a number of problems as you are supervising whole-class learning activities. Some of these may be avoided, for example, through planning for effective behaviour management or through giving pupils clear instructions. Problems could take different forms but may relate to any of the following factors.

### The learning activities

You may find that the learning activity which has been set is not at the right level — in other words, pupils either find it too difficult or are able to complete it quickly. In this situation you may be able to modify the work for them yourself, but if you are not confident about doing this or have been asked not to, you may

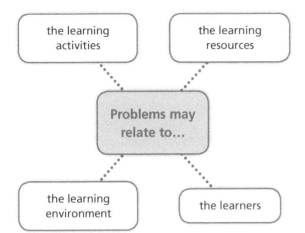

*Potential sources of problems.*

need to have extension or gap-filling activities prepared so that pupils have alternative work to do.

Pupils may not be clear on what they have been asked to do. Make sure instructions are always clear and that you have given plenty of time to going through lesson requirements and learning objectives before pupils start working.

## The learning resources
You may find that there are insufficient resources for the activity or that equipment is not in working order before you start the lesson. Always check in advance that you have everything you need, as mentioned earlier in this unit.

## The learning environment
There may be problems with the learning environment. These may be caused by a number of issues, such as:

● the environment is too hot/cold/noisy to carry out the work required (always make sure that you know how to adjust the temperature if the room is too hot or cold)

● there may not be sufficient space for all pupils to carry out the activity safely.

## The learners
You may not know the learners well or be familiar with their names. This can be an issue, particularly if there are behaviour problems within the group. Taking an attendance register at the start of the class can help with this, as it will give you an opportunity to speak to them and clarify names, and also to get

some idea of any difficult pronunciation if necessary. Behaviour is likely to be your most common problem with learners and planning for good behaviour should be part of your practice. Make sure that all pupils are clear on warnings and sanctions so that there are clear outcomes for any poor behaviour.

### Link
For more on this see TDA 3.4, Promote children and young people's positive behaviour.

### Over to you!
Write a reflective account detailing the kinds of problems you have faced when supervising whole-class learning activities. Include the kinds of strategies you have used and how you have overcome them, so that you can use this for your portfolio.

### Functional skills
**English: Writing**
When writing your reflective account, it is important to plan it out before you start so that you can organise your account into paragraphs. Use a variety of different sentences within your account and keep your spelling, punctuation and grammar accurate.

## Be able to support learners in completing work set for them
While you are supervising learning activities, you may need to be able to support learners in completing their work. As you will be supervising a large group or class, you may not be able to spend a great deal of time with individuals or groups, but should be able to monitor and keep pupils on task.

### Link
For more on this, see TDA 3.3, Support learning activities.

## Skills and techniques for monitoring learners' responses to learning activities

As outlined in TDA 3.7, when you are supervising learning activities you will need to be able to monitor pupils and assess their progress towards learning objectives. As well as the methods already discussed, it can be helpful to note down those pupils who are making particularly good or below average progress, by writing down things which they have said or recording how they have approached a particular activity if this is different from the way the majority has handled it.

## Assessing how well learners are participating and the progress they are making

You can assess pupils in different ways, through:

● questioning them to check their learning

● observation

● encouraging pupils to self-assess and then taking feedback

● testing.

It is not likely that you will be asked to administer tests as part of your support role, but you will need to be able to feed back to the teacher about pupil participation and progress following the session.

## Ways of supporting learners to stay on task and complete the work set

If you need to encourage learners to stay on task during the session, there may be several reasons for this.

● The task is not set at the correct level for the pupil and they either are unable to complete it independently or rush through it.

● The pupil is demonstrating inappropriate behaviour.

● The pupil is distracted by the behaviour of others around them.

● There are insufficient resources available for all pupils.

In each of these situations, you will need to refocus pupils as soon as possible so that they do not start to distract others. When there is a problem with the task, you should ensure that pupils have done all they can and go back and read through to ensure that there is no more that they can do. If pupils are distracted by others in the class or are misbehaving for whatever reason, you will need to address their behaviour straight away so that this does not continue. In the case of insufficient resources, adequate preparation and planning should mean that you have enough. If for any reason this is not the case, pupils may need to share or send for other resources during the session.

---

**CASE STUDY:** Supporting learners to stay on task

Adam is covering a physics session in which pupils have been asked to write up an experiment which they carried out on the previous day. Although the majority of the group is working well on the activity, within 20 minutes two pupils say that they have completed the task.

• What should Adam do first in this situation?
• How can he best support the learners?
• How can Adam ensure that all pupils complete the task to the best of their ability?

---

## Extension activities for learners who have completed assigned work before the end of the lesson

As a cover supervisor, you should be prepared in advance for pupils who have completed their work before the end of the lesson. The teacher should have given you extension activities or work for pupils to do if the main activity is completed; however, you may find it useful to have a bank of activities to give to pupils. These may or may not be subject related — if you always work in the music department, for example, and have just covered a music lesson, you may find it easier to think of activities relating to that subject. However, if you are not a specialist, you may prefer to have a bank of more general gap fillers — for example, reading or problem-solving activities.

Depending on how you work, it may be helpful to have extension activities available to pupils so that they can go straight on to them following the main task. However, you may prefer to monitor this by asking that pupils tell you when they have finished.

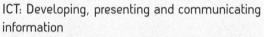

## Skills builder

Gather together a range of extension activities which you have used with pupils so that you are able to show your assessor when they observe you in class. Alternatively, be able to show them the extension activity you have prepared for the session on that day.

## Functional skills

**ICT: Developing, presenting and communicating information**
Using ICT and the computer can support the job of making worksheets. Worksheets need to be informative and appealing to their audience in order to be useful. You could apply a number of different layout techniques in producing these resources and build a file of worksheets that you could store and use in the future.

# Be able to conclude whole-class learning activities

## Applying school procedures

When concluding learning activities with the class you are covering, you will need to ensure that you follow the school's procedures at all times for:

- collecting any completed work and returning it to the appropriate teacher
- collecting in any learning resources
- informing learners of any follow-up work or homework set for them
- dismissing learners at the end of the lesson
- reporting back as appropriate on the behaviour and participation of learners during the lesson, and any issues arising.

## Collecting any completed work and returning it to the appropriate teacher

You should do this straight away or as soon as possible after the end of the lesson. If the class has been in a specific teacher's room or if the completed work is not portable, you may be able to leave the work in an appointed place; however, it is likely that you should take any written work with you. Make sure that you have agreed with the teacher where you are going to leave any work and that you follow school policy.

## Collecting in any learning resources

You will need to collect in and return any learning resources to the correct place or ask pupils to do this for you. Make sure that any equipment which needs to be signed in and locked away, such as laptops or cameras, has been correctly returned.

## Informing learners of any follow-up work or homework set for them

You should inform learners of any follow-up work or homework in good time before the end of the lesson, so that they have time to take down any notes and are clear about what they need to do. Depending on your school policy they may need to write this in their planner or home contact book.

## Dismissing learners at the end of the lesson

There may be a particular routine for doing this in the school, for example, asking the class to stand up and say 'Good afternoon' at the end of the session. Make sure that you dismiss learners on time so that they are able to get to their next lesson.

## Reporting back as appropriate on the behaviour and participation of learners during the lesson, and any issues arising

The quickest and easiest way of doing this may be through verbal contact with the teacher. However, if you are not able to do this straight away, you should record what has happened during the lesson so that you do not forget, and so that the teacher has a record. The school's policy may be that you record outcomes and learner participation on the lesson plan, in which case it may help you to jot things down during the lesson.

## Functional skills

### ICT: Developing, presenting and communicating information

When reporting back to a teacher who you have covered for, you may find email an appropriate method of communication. Not only will you have a written record of what you have said, but it is also a quick method of recording. It is important to consider confidentiality when using email and maybe use initials to describe a particular incident.

## Link

For more on this topic, see TDA 3.3, Support learning activities.

## BEST PRACTICE CHECKLIST: Supervising whole-class learning activities

- Ensure you are fully prepared and have as much information as you can about the class and the lesson.
- Check that you have enough resources and equipment for all learners.
- Check the environment and look out for health and safety issues.
- Be clear when giving instructions to pupils about what they need to do.
- Monitor pupils' progress and behaviour during the lesson.
- Encourage pupils to take responsibility for their own learning.
- Support learners as they work and keep them on task if necessary.
- Be clear when handing out any extension activities or homework.
- Ensure that you follow school policy at all times.

## Getting ready for assessment

The majority of this unit will need to be assessed in the workplace and you should ensure that your assessor is able to observe you covering a lesson. Make sure that you are able to show how you are prepared for the lesson in advance and have adequate resources and equipment. If there are pupils in the class who have special educational needs, or if there are any behavioural issues which you will need to address, you should also outline these to your assessor in advance. During the session you should ensure that you monitor pupil learning and behaviour effectively and work with pupils to keep them on task, giving out extension activities where appropriate. Finally, you will need to conclude the session effectively and set any homework or follow-up work.

## Check your knowledge

1. What is the main difference between cover supervision and the work of a supply teacher?

2. What kinds of details should you receive before you are asked to cover lessons?

3. What can you do to ensure that you have enough equipment and resources before the start of the lesson?

4. What specific aspects of health and safety should you check prior to carrying out the lesson?

5. Give two strategies you could use when supervising work to keep pupils on task.

6. How can you prepare for positive behaviour and ensure that the learning environment remains constructive throughout the session?

7. Name three ways in which you can ensure that you monitor and support pupils' learning as they work on learning activities.

8. Why is it important to conclude learning activities effectively and according to school procedures?

## Websites

**www.socialpartnership.org** – WAMG website
**www.tda.gov.uk** – additional information and links for cover supervisors

# Glossary

## A

**Active learning** — learners are involved and interact in the learning process

**Advocacy** — putting forward a person's views on their behalf and working for the outcome that the individual wishes to achieve

**Anti-discriminatory practice** — taking positive action to counter discrimination, which involves identifying and challenging discrimination, and being positive in your practice about differences and similarities between people

**Appraisal** — a regular meeting to discuss your development progress

**Assessment for learning** — using assessment as part of teaching and learning in ways which will raise learners' achievement

**Assessment of learning** — an evaluation of what learners know, understand and can do at a particular stage

**Assessment opportunities and strategies** — the occasions, approaches and techniques used for ongoing assessment during learning activities

**Attainment targets** — set out the knowledge, understanding and skills that children are expected to reach by the end of each key stage

**Autistic spectrum** — a spectrum of psychological conditions characterised by widespread abnormalities of social interactions and communication, as well as severely restricted interests and highly repetitive behaviour

**Autonomy** — doing things in a self-governed way

## B

**Balanced approach** — taking into account child's age, needs and abilities, avoiding excessive risk taking, not being risk averse and recognising the importance of risk and challenge to a child's development

**Barriers to participation** — anything that prevents the child or young person participating fully in activities and experiences offered by the setting or service

**Behaviour support plan** — plan setting out arrangements for the education of children and young people with behaviour difficulties

**Bilingual learners** — pupils who have been exposed to two or more languages, both those newly arrived and new to the language used to deliver the curriculum, and those more advanced bilingual learners who can communicate confidently but need further support in academic contexts

## C

**Challenging behaviour** — behaviour which may involve verbal or physical abuse, or behaviour which is illegal or destructive

**Cluster group/collaborative** — group of individuals from different schools who come together to share ideas and experiences

**Code of conduct** — an agreed set of rules by which all children are expected to behave

**Community cohesion** — the togetherness and bonding shown by members of a community, the 'glue' that holds a community together

**Concept map** — a diagram showing relationships between different ideas or concepts

**Confidential information** — information that should only be shared with people with a right to have it, for example, your teacher, your line manager or an external agency

**Cover supervisor** — the person employed to carry out the process of administering cover, who will also provide lesson cover when necessary and revert back to teaching assistant duties when no cover administration is required

**Curriculum** — all the learning which happens in the school which includes formal and informal learning

**Curriculum area** — all forms of organised learning experienced across the curriculum. For example, thematically structured work in the primary phase, single subjects, vocational subjects and cross-curricular work in the 14–19 phase

## D

**Disabled** — the Disability Discrimination Act (DDA) defines a disabled person as someone who has a physical or mental impairment that has a substantial and long-term adverse effect on their ability to carry out normal day-to-day activities

**Dyscalculia** — a learning disability or difficulty involving innate difficulty in learning or comprehending mathematics

**Dyspraxia** — a brain condition causing co-ordination problems, poor concentration and poor memory

## E

**Early years education** — education for children up to the age of 5 in Nursery and Reception classes

**Equality of access** — ensuring that discriminatory barriers to access are removed and allowing for children and young people's individual needs

**Erratum notice** — a list of corrected errors in the examination paper

**Evaluating** — assessing how well the teaching and learning activities achieved

**Extended school provision** — extra out-of-school activities, such as breakfast and after-school clubs

**Extrinsic** — outer or separate from

## F

**Facilitator** — someone who supports the process of learning

**Fine motor skills** — control of the smaller muscles, such as those in the fingers — for example, holding a pen

**Format** — the way in which results of observations are recorded and presented

**Formative assessment** — ongoing assessment of pupils' progress, such as understanding skills and participation. This does not provide any final grade

**Functional skills** — essential knowledge of English, Mathematics and ICT to prepare pupils for future learning and work

## G

**Global developmental delay** — a brain disorder where an individual may struggle with, for example, speech and fine/gross motor skills

**Gross motor skills** — control of the larger muscles, typically those in the arms legs — for example, kicking a ball

## H

**Hazard** — something that is likely to cause harm

**HLTAs** — higher level teaching assistants, who act as specialist assistants within a particular curriculum area

**Holistic** — emphasising the functional relation between parts and the whole

## I

**Inappropriate behaviour** — behaviour that conflicts with the accepted values and beliefs of the school and community

**Inclusion** — a process of identifying, understanding and breaking down barriers to participation and belonging and the right for all children to participate fully in the curriculum

**Incubation period** — the length of time between initial contact with an infectious disease and the development of the first symptoms

**Individual education plan (IEP)** — targets and planned implementation strategies for pupils with special educational needs

**Intrinsic** — something natural or belonging to

**Issue** — situation or circumstance that hinders or prevents effective team performance

## K

**Kinaesthetic learner** — someone who learns best through physical experience: touching, feeling and doing their objectives

## L

**Learning outcomes** — broad statements of what pupils will know, understand and be able to do at the end of a topic or period of study

**Learning objectives** — statements of intentions, what pupils are expected to do and achieve by the end of the activity

**Level** — the levels of qualification relate to National Qualification Framework and the Qualification and Credit Framework (for vocational and work-related qualifications). These frameworks group together qualifications which are of similar difficulty

**Level descriptions** — descriptions for each subject of what pupils characteristically achieve at that particular level. There are eight level descriptions with an additional level which describes exceptional performance

## M

**Malpractice** — improper conduct or negligence

**Materials** — written materials and consumables needed for the learning activity, including general classroom items, written materials and curriculum-specific materials

**Milestones** — measurable points in development; the term is usually used to describe stages in children's development where progress can be measured

**Mnemonics** — systems for improving and aiding the memory

**Multi-sensory approach** — activities which require children to use a range of senses — auditory, visual and kinesthetic (touch) to receive and express information

## O

**Others** — according to own role, these may be family members, colleagues within the setting or professionals external to the setting

## P

**Participation** — asking children and young people what works, what does not work and what could work better, and involving them in the design, delivery and evaluation of services, on an ongoing basis

**Partnership working** — working with the teacher to support teaching and learning towards shared goals, for example in whole-class plenary sessions

**Passive learning** — learners do not interact or engage in the learning process

**Pattern of development** — usual rate of development (usual time frame in which development takes place) and sequence of development (usual order in which development occurs)

**Peripatetic** — working in a succession of places, each for a short time

**Personal, learning and thinking skills** — essential skills for successful learning and personal development, set out in six areas: independent enquirers, team workers, effective participants, self-managers, reflective learners, creative thinkers

**Personalised learning** — maintaining a focus on individual progress, in order to maximise the capacity of all children and young people to learn, achieve and participate

**Personalised learning goals** — goals which reflect the learning objectives of activities and take account of the past achievements and current learning needs of individual learners

**Planning** — deciding with the teacher what you will do, when, how and with which pupils, to ensure that planned teaching and learning activities are implemented effectively

**Plenary** — a session, usually at the end of the lesson, when all pupils come together to discuss what they have learned and achieved

**Positive relationships** — relationships that benefit children and young people, and their ability to participate in and benefit from the setting

**Procedures** — steps your setting says you must follow

**Professional development** — ongoing training and professional updating

**Programme of study** — outlines the knowledge, understanding and skills that children and young people are expected to acquire for each National Curriculum subject

**PSHE** — personal, social, health and economic (PSHE) education

## R

**Reasonable adjustments** — arrangements agreed before examination to reduce the effects of 'substantial disadvantage' because of an additional need or disability. Reasonable adjustments must be made in line with the Disability Discrimination Act 1995

**Reflective practice** — the process of thinking about and critically analysing your actions with the goal of changing and improving occupational practice

**Regression** — going backwards in terms of development to an earlier stage

**Relevant people** — those with a need and right to provide and receive information about bilingual learners as relevant to the setting

**Resilience** — the ability to withstand normal everyday disappointments, hurts and assaults to one's confidence without it affecting self-esteem

**Resources** — furniture and equipment needed to support the learning activity, including classroom furniture and curriculum-specific equipment, such as computers for IT or apparatus for science

**Restorative justice** — programme in which pupils are encouraged to consider the impact of their actions or words by making amends directly to the victim or the community that has been harmed

**Review of behaviour management** — opportunities to discuss and make recommendations about behaviour, including bullying, and the effectiveness or rewards and sanctions, including class, year and school councils, class or group behaviour reviews, and whole-school policy reviews

**Risk** — the likelihood of a hazard's potential being realised

## S

**Sanctions** — penalties for disobeying rules

**School Action and School Action Plus (or Early Years Action for under 5s)** — a stepped approach which identifies the additional support requirements of the child or young person. School Action Plus is for when additional advice and guidance from outside services are required to meet children's needs

**School community** — all personnel contributing to the work of the school including pupils, teachers, support staff, volunteer helpers, parents and carers, and other professional agencies

**School improvement plan** — document which sets out priorities for the school over a four- or five-year period

**School policy** — the agreed principles and procedures for the school

**School self-evaluation** — document which looks at and evaluates the school's progress

**Sector Skills Councils** — independent, UK-wide, employer-led organisations which aim to drive improvements in knowledge and skills

**SEN Code of Practice** — document which sets out the requirements for the identification and monitoring of pupils with special educational needs

**Special considerations** — adjustments made to marks or grades, after the examination, because of a temporary situation which is likely to affect the candidate's performance

**Special educational needs** — children or young people who learn differently from most children or young people of the same age, and who may need extra or different help from that given to others

**Special provision** — provision which is additional to, or otherwise different from, the provision made generally for children of their age in mainstream schools in the area

**Specialist assessment** — an assessment administered and interpreted by an appropriately qualified professional to explore specific needs, often in detail, for example, on proficiency in the first language, special educational needs, or a health or care assessment

**Standards** — statements about how tasks should be carried out and the minimum acceptable quality of practice that should be delivered

**Statement of special educational need** — a statement which contains the details of a child's needs, following an assessment, and the provision which must be put into place to support those needs

## T

**Target language** — the additional or second language needed by bilingual learners, for example, English as an additional language (EAL), or Welsh or Gaeilge as a second language

**Team** — people with whom you work on a long-, medium-, or short-term basis, relating to the support provided for a specific pupil or group of pupils

**Transition plan** — a review carried out with the child, their family and relevant agencies to support young people with special educational needs to move to their adult stage of education, training or work

**Transitions** — processes of change or events when children change from one stage or state to another

## U

**UCAS** — Universities and Colleges Admission Service, an organisation through which applications are processed for entry to higher education

**UCAS points** — points or tariffs allocated to different qualifications. They help universities to differentiate between applicants when offering a place on an undergraduate course

## W

**Well-being** — being in physical and mental good health, resulting in a positive outlook and feelings of happiness

# Index

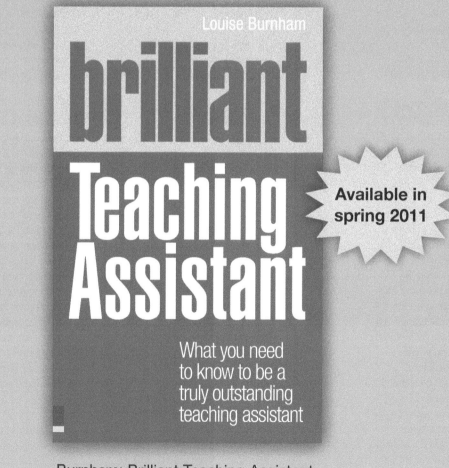